Junior Worldmark
Encyclopedia of the States

6th Edition

Junior Worldmark Encyclopedia of the States

6th Edition

VOLUME 4:

Tennessee to Wyoming, District of Columbia, Puerto Rico, US Caribbean and Pacific Dependencies, and US Overview

Drew Johnson and Cynthia Johnson, Editors

Kathleen J. Edgar, Project Editor

U·X·L

A part of Gale, Cengage Learning

GALE
CENGAGE Learning

Detroit • New York • San Francisco • New Haven, Conn • Waterville, Maine • London

GALE
CENGAGE Learning·

Junior Worldmark Encyclopedia of the States, 6th Edition

Drew Johnson and Cynthia Johnson, Editors

Project Editor: Kathleen J. Edgar

Contributing Editor: Elizabeth P. Manar

Managing Editor: Debra Kirby

Rights Acquisition and Management: Robyn V. Young

Imaging and Multimedia: John L. Watkins

Composition: Evi Abou-El-Seoud

Manufacturing: Wendy Blurton, Dorothy Maki

Product Manager: Douglas A. Dentino

Product Design: Kristine A. Julien

For product information and technology assistance, contact us at **Gale Customer Support, 1-800-877-4253.** For permission to use material from this text or product, submit all requests online at **www.cengage.com/permissions.** Further permissions questions can be emailed to **permissionrequest@cengage.com**

Cover photographs: © CAN BALCIOGLU/Shutterstock.com (Golden Gate Bridge); © Orhan Cam/Shutterstock.com (US Capitol); © Joseph Hardy/Shutterstock.com (Las Vegas); © Doug Lemke/Shutterstock.com (Portland Head Light); and © kaarsten/Shutterstock.com (map outline). End sheet map: © Dcarto/Dreamstime.com; state and US flags: © Philip Lange/Shutterstock.com; DC and Puerto Rico flags: © Globe Turner, LLC/Shutterstock.com.

LIBRARY OF CONGRESS CATALOGING-IN-PUBLICATION DATA

Junior worldmark encyclopedia of the states / Drew Johnson and Cynthia Johnson, editors; Kathleen J. Edgar, project editor. — 6th Edition.
  pages cm
  Includes bibliographical references and index.
  ISBN 978-1-4144-9859-1 (set : alk. paper) — ISBN 978-1-4144-9860-7 (vol. 1 : alk. paper) — ISBN 978-1-4144-9861-4 (vol. 2 : alk. paper) — ISBN 978-1-4144-9862-1 (vol. 3 : alk. paper) — ISBN 978-1-4144-9863-8 (vol. 4 : alk. paper) — ISBN 978-1-4144-9864-5 (ebook)
  1. United States—Encyclopedias, Juvenile. 2. U.S. states—Encyclopedias, Juvenile. I. Johnson, Drew, 1970- editor. II. Johnson, Cynthia, 1969- editor. III. Edgar, Kathleen J.
  E156.J86 2013
  973.03—dc23   2012050641

Gale
27500 Drake Rd.
Farmington Hills, MI 48331-3535

978-1-4144-9859-1 (set)   1-4144-9859-4 (set)
978-1-4144-9860-7 (vol. 1)   1-4144-9860-8 (vol. 1)
978-1-4144-9861-4 (vol. 2)   1-4144-9861-6 (vol. 2)
978-1-4144-9862-1 (vol. 3)   1-4144-9862-4 (vol. 3)
978-1-4144-9863-8 (vol. 4)   1-4144-9863-2 (vol. 4)

This title is also available as an e-book.
ISBN-13: 978-1-4144-9864-5   ISBN-10: 1-4144-9864-0
Contact your Gale, a part of Cengage Learning, sales representative for ordering information.

Printed in China
1 2 3 4 5 6 7 17 16 15 14 13

Table of Contents

Cumulative Table of Contents

Junior Worldmark Encyclopedia of the States, 6th Edition, presents profiles of the 50 states of the nation, the District of Columbia, Puerto Rico, the US dependencies, and an overview of the United States, arranged alphabetically in four volumes. Junior Worldmark is based on the reference work, *Worldmark Encyclopedia of the States.* The Worldmark design organizes facts and data about every state in a common structure. Every profile contains a map, showing the state and its location in the nation.

This sixth edition of *Junior Worldmark Encyclopedia of the States* is now in full color. The thoroughly updated edition describes various facets of the individual states, including historical, economic, social, and geographic information. In addition, the set features all new photographs, about 350 total, which richly illustrate many aspects of each state, including capitol buildings, tourist attractions, parks and forests, famous people born in the state, and the like. Each state's political history is documented in the updated table listing the governors who have served the state since its founding. The population

profiles and population by race graphics give users of Junior Worldmark access to the latest US decennial Census (2010) data for each state as well as 2011 population estimates for each state's largest cities.

Figures for each state's estimated 2011 population as well as the state's ranking among the 50 states can be found in the State Data Tables appendix—new for this edition. The appendix, which includes 10 tables, provides valuable statistical data that allow users to easily compare information between the states. Other topics covered in the appendix are educational attainment, violent crime, poverty status, unemployment (December 2012 figures along with historical highs and lows), language spoken, the death penalty, health insurance, household income, and race. Each volume also includes a greatly enhanced cumulative subject index to all four volumes.

Sources

Due to the broad scope of this encyclopedia, many sources were consulted in compiling the information and statistics presented in these volumes. Of primary importance were the publications of the US Census Bureau, including the American Community Survey; the US Department of Labor; the US Department of Agriculture; the US Fish and Wildlife Service; the US Forest Service; the US Geological Survey; the US Environmental Protection Agency; US Department of Transportation; US Department of Energy; US Department of Health and Human Services; US Department of Education; the Centers for Disease Control and Prevention; the Federal Bureau of Investigation (FBI); and the Pew Forum on Religion and Public Life, among others. Finally, many fact sheets, booklets, and state statistical abstracts were used to update data not collected by the federal government.

Profile Features

The structure of *Junior Worldmark Encyclopedia of the States*—40 numbered headings—allows student researchers to compare two or more states in a variety of ways. Each state profile begins by listing the origin of the state name, its nickname, the capital, the date it entered the union, the state song and motto, and a description of the state coat of arms. The profile also presents a textual description of the state seal and the state flag as well as a color image of the state flag. (Images of the state flags for the entries in each volume are also found on the end pages of that volume.) Next, a listing of the official state animal, bird, fish, flower, tree, gem, etc. is given.

The introductory information ends with the standard time given by time zone in relation to Greenwich mean time (GMT). The world is divided into 24 time zones, each one hour apart. The Greenwich meridian, which is 0 degrees, passes through Greenwich, England, a suburb of London. Greenwich is at the center of the initial time zone, known as Greenwich mean time

(GMT). All times given are converted from noon in this zone. The time reported for the state is the official time zone.

The body of each state's profile is arranged in 40 numbered headings as follows:

1 Location and Size. The state location is detailed. Statistics are given on area and boundary length. Size comparisons are made to the other 50 states of the United States.

2 Topography. Dominant geographic features including terrain and major rivers and lakes are described.

3 Climate. Temperature and rainfall are given for the various regions of the state in both English and metric units.

4 Plants and Animals. Described here are the plants and animals native to the state. Endangered or threatened species are also discussed.

5 Environmental Protection. Destruction of natural resources—forests, water supply, air—is described here. Information on major environmental concerns as well as hazardous waste sites is also included. Steps taken to address various environmental issues are also discussed.

6 Population. Census statistics are provided in graphics highlighting general population figures and population by race. Population density and major urban populations are summarized.

7 **Ethnic Groups.** The percentages of major ethnic groups in the state are provided. Where appropriate, some description of the influence or history of ethnicity is provided.

8 **Languages.** The regional dialects of the state are summarized as well as the number of people speaking languages other than English at home.

9 **Religions.** The population is broken down according to religion and/or denominations. A brief discussion of the state's religious history is provided where appropriate.

10 **Transportation.** Statistics on roads, railways, waterways, and air traffic are provided.

11 **History.** Includes a concise summary of the state's history from ancient times (where appropriate) to the present.

12 **State Government.** The form of government is described, and the process of governing is summarized. A table listing the state governors, updated to early 2013, accompanies each state entry.

13 **Political Parties.** This section describes the significant political parties through history, where appropriate, and the influential parties as of the early 2010s. Also included are 2012 federal election results, including the presidential winner in each state as well as information on the state's US senators and party affiliations of its US representatives.

14 **Local Government.** The system of local government structure is summarized.

15 **Judicial System.** The structure of the court system and the jurisdiction of courts in each category is provided. Crime rates as reported by the Federal Bureau of Investigation (FBI) are also included. Also summarized is the state's continued practice or abolition of capital punishment.

16 **Migration.** Population shifts in the early 21st century are summarized. Brief historical summaries are included where applicable.

17 **Economy.** This section presents the key elements of the economy. Major industries and gross state product (GSP) figures are also summarized.

18 **Income.** Personal income and the poverty level are given as is the state's ranking.

19 **Industry.** Key industries are listed as well as important aspects of industrial development.

20 **Labor.** Statistics are given on the civilian labor force, including numbers of workers, major areas of employment, and unemployment figures.

21 **Agriculture.** Statistics on key agricultural crops, market share, and total farm income are provided.

22 **Domesticated Animals.** Statistics on livestock—cattle, hogs, sheep, etc.—and the land area devoted to raising them are given.

23 **Fishing.** The relative significance of fishing to the state is provided, with statistics on fish and seafood products.

24 **Forestry.** Land area classified as forest is given, along with a listing of key forest products and a description of government policy toward forest land.

25 **Mining.** Description of mineral deposits and statistics on related mining activity are provided.

26 **Energy and Power.** Description of the state's power resources, including electricity produced and oil reserves and production, are provided.

27 **Commerce.** A summary of the amount of wholesale trade, retail trade, and receipts of service establishments is given.

28 **Public Finance.** Revenues, expenditures, and total and per capital (per person) debt are provided.

29 **Taxation.** The state's taxation system is explained.

30 **Health.** Statistics on and description of such public health factors as disease and suicide rates, principal causes of death, numbers of hospitals and medical facilities appear here. Information is also provided on the percentage of citizens without health insurance.

31 **Housing.** Statistics on numbers of dwellings and median home values are provided, as well as average monthly rent and mortgage amounts.

32 **Education.** Statistical data on educational achievement and primary and secondary schools is given. Per person state spending on primary and secondary education is also provided. Major universities are listed; government programs to foster education are described.

33 **Arts.** A summary of the state's major cultural institutions is provided, as well as significant cultural events.

34 **Libraries and Museums.** The number of libraries, their holdings, and their yearly circulation is provided. Major museums are listed.

35 **Communications.** The state of telecommunications (television, radio, and telephone) is summarized. Activity related to the Internet is reported where available.

36 **Press.** Major daily and Sunday newspapers are listed together with data on their circulations.

37 **Tourism, Travel, and Recreation.** Under this heading, the student will find a summary of the importance of tourism to the state as well as factors affecting the tourism industry. Key tourist attractions are listed.

38 **Sports.** The major sports teams in the state, both professional and collegiate, are summarized.

39 **Famous People.** In this section, some of the best-known citizens of the state are listed. When a person was not born in that state, the birthplace is given.

40 **Bibliography.** The bibliographic and web site listings at the end of each profile are provided as a guide for further reading.

Note

Because many terms used in this encyclopedia will be new to students, each volume includes a glossary and a list of abbreviations and acronyms. New to this edition is an appendix featuring 10 tables comparing state information, most containing data from 2011 or 2012 reports released just prior to publication of this set. A comprehensive cumulative subject index to all four volumes appears at the end of each volume.

Acknowledgments

The editors of *Junior Worldmark Encyclopedia of the States, 6th Edition,* would especially like to thank Lisa Magloff and Bryan Aubrey for their research, editing, and copyediting support. And sincere thanks go to Christine O'Bryan for the graphics work. Special acknowledgment goes to the government officials throughout the nation who have given their cooperation to this project over the years.

Comments and Suggestions

We welcome your comments on *Junior Worldmark Encyclopedia of the States, 6th Edition,* as well as your suggestions for features to be included in future editions. Please write to: Editors, *Junior Worldmark Encyclopedia of the States,* U•X•L, 27500 Drake Road, Farmington Hills, MI 48331-3535; call toll-free: 1-800-877-4253; or send e-mail via www.galegroup.com.

Guide to State Articles

All information contained within a state article is uniformly keyed by means of a number to the left of the subject headings. A heading such as "Population," for example, carries the same key numeral (6) in every article. To find information about the population of Alabama, consult the table of contents for the page number where the Alabama article begins and find section 6.

Introductory matter includes:
Origin of state name
Nickname
Capital
Date and order of statehood
Song
Motto
Flag
Official seal
Symbols (animal, tree, etc.)
Time zone

Sections listed numerically
1   Location and Size
2   Topography
3   Climate
4   Plants and Animals
5   Environmental Protection
6   Population
7   Ethnic Groups
8   Languages
9   Religions
10 Transportation
11 History
12 State Government
13 Political Parties
14 Local Government
15 Judicial System
16 Migration
17 Economy
18 Income
19 Industry
20 Labor
21 Agriculture
22 Domesticated Animals
23 Fishing

24 Forestry
25 Mining
26 Energy and Power
27 Commerce
28 Public Finance
29 Taxation
30 Health
31 Housing
32 Education
33 Arts
34 Libraries and Museums
35 Communications
36 Press
37 Tourism, Travel, and
        Recreation
38 Sports
39 Famous Persons
40 Bibliography

Alphabetical listing of sections:
Agriculture **21**
Arts **33**
Bibliography **40**
Climate **3**
Commerce **27**
Communications **35**
Domesticated Animals **22**
Economy **17**
Education **32**
Energy and Power **26**
Environmental Protection **5**
Ethnic Groups **7**
Famous Persons **39**
Fishing **23**
Forestry **24**
Health **30**

History **11**
Housing **31**
Income **18**
Industry **19**
Judicial System **15**
Labor **20**
Languages **8**
Libraries and Museums **34**
Local Government **14**
Location and Size **1**
Migration **16**
Mining **25**
Plants and Animals **4**
Political Parties **13**
Population **6**
Press **36**
Public Finance **28**
Religions **9**
Sports **38**
State Government **12**
Taxation **29**
Topography **2**
Tourism, Travel, and
    Recreation **37**
Transportation **10**

Explanation of symbols
A fiscal split year is indicated by a
    stroke (e.g. 2010/11).
Note that 1 billion = 1,000
    million = 10^9.
The use of a small dash (e.g.,
    2010–11) normally signifies the
    full period of calendar years
    covered (including the end year
    indicated).

Glossary

Aggregate: Rock and other basic matter used for construction purposes.

Alpine: Generally refers to the Alps or other mountains; can also refer to a mountainous zone above the timberline.

Ancestry: Based on how people refer to themselves; ancestry refers to the ethnic origin, descent, heritage, or place of birth of the person or the person's parents or ancestors before their arrival in the United States. The Census Bureau accepted "American" as a unique ethnicity if it was given alone, with an unclear response (such as "mixed" or "adopted"), or with names of particular states.

Antebellum: Before the US Civil War.

Aqueduct: A large pipe or channel that carries water over a distance, or a raised structure that supports such a channel or pipe.

Aquifer: An underground layer of porous rock, sand, or gravel that holds water.

Biomass: Organic materials that are constantly being created, such as plants.

Blue laws: Laws forbidding certain practices (e.g., conducting business, gaming, drinking liquor), especially on Sundays.

Broadband: A form of Internet access characterized by high relative upload and download speeds.

Broilers: A bird (especially a young chicken) that can be cooked by broiling.

BTU: The amount of heat required to raise one pound of water one degree Fahrenheit.

Capital budget: A financial plan for acquiring and improving buildings or land, paid for by the sale of bonds.

Capital punishment: Punishment by death.

Cerebrovascular disease: An illness related to the vessels that send blood to and from the brain.

Civilian labor force: All persons 16 years of age or older who are not in the armed forces and who are now holding a job, have been temporarily laid off, are waiting to be reassigned to a new position, or are unemployed but actively looking for work.

Class I railroad: A railroad with high gross annual revenues. The actual amount of revenue varies over time; in the early 2010s, the annual revenue needed to classify as a Class I railroad was approximately $400 million.

Climate change: Changes over time in the measurable properties of Earth's climate, such as changes in average global temperatures (getting hotter or colder), changes in the amount of precipitation (rain and snow), and changes in other features of the climate.

Commercial bank: A bank that offers businesses and individuals a variety of banking services, including the right of withdrawal by check.

Compact: A formal agreement, covenant, or understanding between two or more parties.

Consolidated budget: A financial plan that includes the general budget, federal funds, and all special funds.

Constant dollars: Monetary values calculated so as to eliminate the effect of inflation on prices and income.

Conterminous US: Refers to the "lower 48" states of the continental United States that are enclosed within a common boundary.

Continental climate: The climate typical of the US interior, having distinct seasons, a wide range of daily and annual temperatures, and dry, sunny summers.

Council-manager system: A system of local government under which a professional administrator is hired by an elected council to carry out its laws and policies.

Credit union: A cooperative body that raises funds from its members by the sale of shares and makes loans to its members at relatively low interest rates.

Current dollars: Monetary values that reflect prevailing prices, without excluding the effects of inflation.

Demand deposit: A bank deposit that can be withdrawn by the depositor with no advance notice to the bank.

Electoral votes: The votes that a state may cast for president, nearly always cast entirely on behalf of the candidate who won the most votes in that state on Election Day.

Endangered species: A type of plant or animal threatened with extinction in all or part of its natural range.

Federal poverty level: A level of monetary income below which a person or family qualifies for US government aid.

Fiscal year: A 12-month period for accounting purposes.

Food stamps: Coupons issued by the government to low-income persons for food purchases at local stores.

General budget: A financial plan based on a government's normal revenues and operating expenses, excluding special funds.

General coastline: A measurement of the general outline of the US coast.

Geothermal: Describing energy that is found in the hot spots under the earth; describing energy that is made from heat.

Geothermal energy: Energy obtained from Earth's internal heat, which is maintained by the breakdown of radioactive elements. Geothermal means, literally, Earth-heat. Geothermal energy may be used either directly as heat (e.g., to heat buildings or industrial processes) or to generate electricity.

Global warming: A phenomenon in which the average temperature of Earth rises, melting ice caps, raising sea levels, and causing other environmental problems.

Gross state product: The total value of goods and services produced in the state.

Growing season: The period between the last 32°F (0°C) temperature in spring and the first 32°F (0°C) temperature in autumn.

Hispanic: A person who originates from Spain or from Spanish-speaking countries of South and Central America, Mexico, Puerto Rico, and Cuba.

Home-rule charter: A document stating how and in what respects a city, town, or county may govern itself.

Hundredweight: A unit of weight that equals 100 pounds in the United States and 112 pounds in Great Britain.

Infrastructure: The framework that is necessary to the functioning of a structure; for example, roads and power lines form part of the infrastructure of a city.

Inpatient: A patient who is housed and fed—in addition to being treated—in a hospital.

Installed capacity: The maximum possible output of electric power at any given time.

Kilowatt-hour: A unit of energy; one kilowatt of electrical power consumed over a one-hour period.

Massif: A central mountain mass or the dominant part of a range of mountains.

Mayor-council system: A system of local government under which an elected council serves as a legislature and an elected mayor is the chief administrator.

Medicaid: A federal-state program that helps defray the hospital and medical costs of needy persons.

Medicare: A program of hospital and medical insurance for the elderly administered by the federal government.

Metric ton: A unit of weight that equals 1,000 kilograms (2,204.62 pounds).

Metropolitan area: In most cases, a city and its surrounding suburbs.

Montane: Refers to a zone in mountainous areas in which large coniferous trees, in a cool moist setting, are the main features.

Net domestic migration: The number of people who have moved into a state from another state, subtracted by the number of people who have moved out of that state to another state. If the net domestic migration value is a positive number, this means that more people moved into that state than left it for another state in a given period of time. If net domestic migration is a negative value, then more people left a state than moved to it from another state.

No-fault insurance: An automobile insurance plan that allows an accident victim to receive payment from an insurance company without having to prove who was responsible for the accident.

Nonfederal physician: A medical doctor who is not employed by the US government.

Northern, north midland: Major US dialect regions.

Nuclear reactors: Nuclear reactors are complex devices in which fissionable elements such as uranium, thorium, or plutonium are made to undergo a sustainable nuclear chain reaction. This chain reaction releases energy in the form of radiation that (a) sustains the chain reaction; (b) transmutes (i.e., alters the nuclear characteristics of) nearby atoms, including the nuclear fuel itself; and (c) may be harvested as heat.

Ombudsman: A public official empowered to hear and investigate complaints by private citizens about government agencies.

Per capita: Per person.

Personal income: Refers to the income an individual receives from employment, or to the total incomes that all individuals receive from their employment in a sector of business (such as personal incomes in the retail trade).

Piedmont: Refers to the base of mountains.

Pocket veto: A method by which a state governor (or the US president) may kill a bill by taking no action on it before the legislature adjourns.

Proved reserves: The quantity of a recoverable mineral resource (such as oil or natural gas) that is still in the ground.

Public debt: The amount owed by a government.

Religious adherents: The followers of a religious group, including (but not confined to) the full, confirmed, or communicant members of that group.

Renewable energy: Energy obtained from sources that are renewed at once, or fairly rapidly, by natural or managed processes that can be expected to continue indefinitely. Wind, sun, wood, crops, and waves can all be sources of renewable energy.

Renewable energy source: An energy resource that is naturally replenished, such as sunlight, wind, or geothermal heat.

Retail trade: The sale of goods directly to the consumer.

Revenue sharing: The distribution of federal tax receipts to state and local governments.

Right-to-work: A measure outlawing any attempt to require union membership as a condition of employment.

Savings and loan association: A bank that invests the savings of depositors primarily in home mortgage loans.

Secession: The act of withdrawal, such as a state that withdrew from the Union in the US Civil War.

Seismology: The study of movement within the earth, such as earthquakes and the eruption of volcanoes.

Service industries: Industries that provide services (e.g., health, legal, automotive repair) for individuals, businesses, and others.

Short ton: A unit of weight that equals 2,000 pounds.

Social Security: As commonly understood, the federal system of old age, survivors, and disability insurance.

Southern, south midland: Major US dialect regions.

Special district: An administrative area distinct from a city, county, or state government. Special districts are often formed for a specific purpose, such as administration of a regional airport.

Subalpine: Generally refers to high mountainous areas just beneath the timberline; can also more specifically refer to the lower slopes of the Alps mountains.

Sunbelt: The southernmost states of the United States, extending from Florida to California.

Supplemental security income: A federally administered program of aid to the aged, blind, and disabled.

Tidal shoreline: A detailed measurement of the US seacoast that includes sounds, bays, other outlets, and offshore islands.

Time deposit: A bank deposit that may be withdrawn only at the end of a specified time period or upon advance notice to the bank.

Value added by manufacture: The difference, measured in dollars, between the value of finished goods and the cost of the materials needed to produce them.

Wholesale trade: The sale of goods, usually in large quantities, for ultimate resale to consumers.

Wind farm: A group of wind turbines that provides electricity for commercial uses.

Tennessee

State of Tennessee

ORIGIN OF STATE NAME: Probably derived from the Indian name *Tenase,* which was the principal village of the Cherokee.

NICKNAME: The Volunteer State.

CAPITAL: Nashville.

ENTERED UNION: 1 June 1796 (16th).

OFFICIAL SEAL: The upper half consists of the word "Agriculture," a plow, a sheaf of wheat, a cotton stalk, and the roman numeral XVI, signifying the order of entry into the Union. The lower half comprises the word "Commerce" and a riverboat. The words "The Great Seal of the State of Tennessee 1796" surround the whole. The date commemorates the passage of the state constitution.

FLAG: On a crimson field separated by a white border from a blue bar at the fly, three white stars on a blue circle edged in white represent the state's three main general divisions—East, Middle, and West Tennessee.

MOTTO: Agriculture and Commerce.

SONG: "When It's Iris Time in Tennessee"; "The Tennessee Waltz"; "My Homeland, Tennessee"; "Rocky Top"; "My Tennessee"; "Tennessee"; The Pride of Tennessee."

FLOWER: Iris (cultivated); Passion flower (wild flower).

TREE: Tulip poplar.

ANIMAL: Raccoon (wild animal); Tennessee cave salamander (amphibian).

BIRD: Mockingbird; bobwhite quail.

INSECT: Ladybug; firefly; honeybee.

REPTILE: Easter box turtle.

GEM: Freshwater pearl (from Tennessee River mussels).

ROCK OR STONE: Limestone; agate.

LEGAL HOLIDAYS: New Year's Day, 1 January; birthday of Martin Luther King Jr., 3rd Monday in January; Presidents' Day, 3rd Monday in February; Good Friday, Friday before Easter, March or April; Memorial Day, last Monday in May; Independence Day, 4 July; Labor Day, 1st Monday in September; Columbus Day, 2nd Monday in October (sometimes observed the day after Thanksgiving at the governor's discretion); Veterans' Day, 11 November; Thanksgiving Day, 4th Thursday in November; Christmas Day, 25 December.

TIME: 7 a.m. EST = noon GMT; 6 a.m. CST = noon GMT.

1 Location and Size

Situated in the eastern south-central United States, Tennessee ranks 34th in size among the 50 states. The total area of the state is 42,144

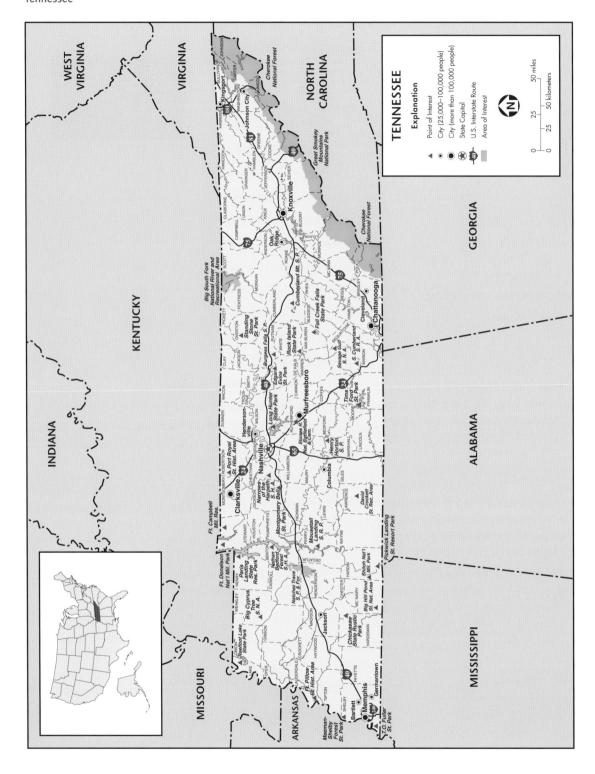

square miles (109,152 square kilometers), of which land occupies 41,235 square miles (106,789 square kilometers) and water 909 square miles (2,354 square kilometers). Tennessee extends about 430 miles (690 kilometers) from east to west and 110 miles (180 kilometers) from north to south. The boundary length of Tennessee totals 1,306 miles (2,102 kilometers).

2 Topography

Tennessee is divided topographically into six major physical regions: the Unaka Mountains, the Great Valley of East Tennessee, the Cumberland Plateau, the Highland Rim, the Central Basin, and the Gulf Coastal Plain. In addition, there are two minor physical regions: the Western Valley of the Tennessee River and the Mississippi Flood Plains.

Unaka Mountains in the east are part of the Appalachian chain and include the Great Smoky Mountains. The tallest peak is Clingmans Dome in the Great Smokies, which rises to 6,643 feet (2,026 meters).

The Great Valley to the west of the Unaka consists of long, narrow ridges with broad valleys between them. Since the coming of the Tennessee Valley Authority (TVA) in 1933, the area has been dotted with artificial lakes and dams, which supply electric power and aid in flood control.

The Cumberland Plateau is a region of contrasts, including both the Cumberland Mountains, which rise to a height of 3,500 feet (1,100 meters), and the Sequatchie Valley, the floor of which lies about 1,000 feet (300 meters) below the surface of the adjoining plateau.

The Highland Rim, in Middle Tennessee, is the state's largest natural region and encircles the Central Basin, an oval depression with a gently rolling surface.

The westernmost of the major regions is the Gulf Coastal Plain that embraces practically all of West Tennessee. In the northwest corner is Reelfoot Lake, the only natural lake of significance in the state, formed by a series of earthquakes in 1811 and 1812. The state's lowest point, 178 feet (54 meters) above sea level, is on the banks of the Mississippi in the southwest.

Waters from the two longest rivers—the Tennessee, with a total length of 652 miles (1,049 kilometers), and the Cumberland, which runs 687 miles (1,106 kilometers)—flow into the Ohio River in Kentucky. Tributaries of the Tennessee are the Clinch, Duck, Elk, Hiwassee, and Sequatchie rivers. Tributaries of the Cumberland River are the Harpeth, Red, Obey, Caney Fork, and Stones rivers and Yellow Creek. In the western part of the state, the Forked Deer and Wolf rivers are among those flowing into the Mississippi, which forms the western border with Missouri and Arkansas.

3 Climate

Generally, Tennessee has a temperate climate with warm summers and mild winters. The warmest parts of the state are the Gulf Coastal Plain, the Central Basin, and the Sequatchie Valley. Annual mean temperatures are around 60°F (16°C) in most parts of the state. The record high temperature for the state is 113°F (45°C), set at Perryville on 9 August 1930. The record low, -32°F (-36°C), was registered at Mountain City on 30 December 1917.

Average annual precipitation is 54.7 inches (138.9 centimeters) in Memphis and 48 inches (122 centimeters) in Nashville. Severe storms occur frequently. Snowfall varies and is more prevalent in East Tennessee than in the western section. Nashville gets about 10 inches (25.4 centimeters) of snow a year while Memphis only receives 5 inches (12.7 centimeters) annually.

4 Plants and Animals

With its varied terrain and soils, Tennessee has an abundance of native plants. Tree species include tulip poplar (the state tree) and shortleaf pine in the eastern part of the state; oak, hickory, and ash in the Highland Rim; gum maple, black walnut, and sycamore in the west; and cypress in the Reelfoot Lake area. In East Tennessee, rhododendron, mountain laurel, and wild azalea blossoms create a blaze of color in the mountains. More than 300 native Tennessee plants, including digitalis and ginseng have been used for medicinal purposes. In 2011, a total of 18 plant species occurring in Tennessee were listed as threatened or endangered by the US Fish and Wildlife Service, including the Blue Ridge goldenrod, Cumberland rosemary and sandwort, Roan Mountain bluet, and Virginia spiraea.

Tennessee mammals include the raccoon (the state animal), white-tailed deer, black bear, and bobcat. More than 250 bird species reside in Tennessee. Bobwhite quail, ruffed grouse, mourning dove, and mallard duck are the most common game birds. The state's 56 amphibian species include numerous frogs, salamanders, and newts. There are 58 reptile species, including three types of rattlesnake. Of the 186 fish species in Tennessee's lakes and streams, catfish, bream, and largemouth bass are some of the leading game fish.

Tennessee's Wildlife Resources Agency conducts an endangered and threatened species protection program. The state has an extensive list of 66 animal species that were listed as endangered or threatened in 2011, including seven species of darter (the snail darter is Tennessee's most famous threatened species), gray and Indiana bats, pallid sturgeon, Carolina northern flying squirrel, and numerous species of pearlymussel and mussel.

5 Environmental Protection

The Great Smoky Mountains in East Tennessee are sensitive to changes in air quality. In 1997, the state forged an agreement with the US National Park Service and the US Forest Service to ensure that the process for issuing permits for new industries in the area take into account both business and environmental concerns.

The streams of West Tennessee were extensively channelized for flood control beginning in the late 1800s, with a negative impact on both habitat and cropland. In the early 2000s the state worked with local citizens and the US Army Corps of Engineers to reverse this process by restoring the natural meandering flow to the tributaries of the Mississippi.

The Department of Environment and Conservation is responsible for air, land, and water protection in Tennessee. The department also manages the state park system and state natural areas. The Division of Pollution Prevention Assistance was established in 1993 to provide information and support to industries attempting to reduce their pollution and waste. In 2012, Tennessee had 15 sites on the US Environmental Agency's National Priorities List. These included contaminated groundwater at Alamo as well as the Oak Ridge Nuclear Reservation.

6 Population

Tennessee's population has increased since 2005, but its ranking among the 50 states has fallen from 16th to 17th, with a population of 6,403,353 residents in 2011. In that same year, the median age was 38.3. Those aged 65 or older accounted for 13.7% of all residents, while 23.3% were under the age of 18. The state's population density was 153.9 persons per square mile (59.4 persons per square kilometer) in 2010. The population is expected to reach 7,073,125 in 2025.

Memphis is the state's largest city, ranking 20th in the nation, with an estimated population in 2011 of 652,050 (metro area, 1,325,605). Nashville-Davidson had 609,644 residents, followed by Knoxville, with 180,761, and Chattanooga, with 170,136. In 2010, 75% of all residents lived in metropolitan areas.

7 Ethnic Groups

The largest groups of European immigrants in Tennessee are of English and German descent. According to the US Census Bureau, 16.7% of Tennessee's population in 2010 was African American, making it the largest racial minority in the state. Another 4.6% of the population was Hispanic or Latino, while 1.4% was Asian. For the period 2006–10, foreign-born residents in Tennessee averaged 4.4% of the total population, compared to the national average of 12.7%.

8 Languages

Tennessee English represents a mixture of North Midland and South Midland features as well as Southern features. Common are such

**Tennessee
Population Profile**

Total population per Census 2010:	6,346,105
Population change, 2006–10:	5.1%
Hispanic or Latino†:	4.6%
Population by race	
One race:	98.3%
White:	77.6%
Black or African American:	16.7%
American Indian/Alaska Native:	0.3%
Asian:	1.4%
Native Hawaiian/Pacific Islander:	0.1%
Some other race:	2.2%
Two or more races:	1.7%

Population by Age Group, Census 2010

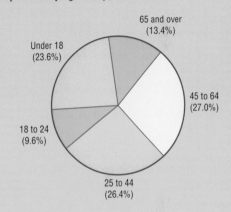

65 and over (13.4%)

Under 18 (23.6%)

45 to 64 (27.0%)

18 to 24 (9.6%)

25 to 44 (26.4%)

Major Cities by Population, 2011 Estimates

City	Population	% change 2005–11
Memphis	652,050	-3.0
Nashville-Davidson	609,644	11.0
Knoxville	180,761	0.4
Chattanooga	170,136	9.9
Clarksville	136,231	20.7
Murfreesboro	111,327	28.3
Jackson	65,187	5.0
Franklin	64,317	20.6
Johnson	63,815	8.7
Bartlett	55,055	17.3

Notes: †A person of Hispanic or Latino origin may be of any race. NA indicates that data are not available. Percentages may not equal 100 due to rounding.

SOURCE: U.S. Census Bureau. Census 2010 and Population Estimates. www.census.gov/ (accessed July 2012).

Tennessee Population by Race
CENSUS 2010

This table shows the number of people who are of one, two, or three or more races. For those claiming two races, the number of people belonging to the various categories is listed. The U.S. government conducts a census of the population every 10 years.

	Number	Percent
Total population	6,346,105	100.0
One race	6,236,096	98.3
Two races	103,173	1.6
White *and* Black or African American.	36,370	0.6
White *and* American Indian/Alaska Native	25,649	0.4
White *and* Asian.	15,145	0.2
White *and* Native Hawaiian/Pacific Islander.	1,476	—
White *and* some other race	12,638	0.2
Black or African American *and* American Indian/Alaska Native	3,492	0.1
Black or African American *and* Asian	1,971	—
Black or African American *and* Native Hawaiian/Pacific Islander.	528	—
Black or African American *and* some other race	2,381	—
American Indian/Alaska Native *and* Asian	384	—
American Indian/Alaska Native *and* Native Hawaiian/Pacific Islander	73	—
American Indian/Alaska Native *and* some other race	657	—
Asian *and* Native Hawaiian/Pacific Islander	533	—
Asian *and* some other race	1,482	—
Native Hawaiian/Pacific Islander *and* some other race.	394	—
Three or more races	6,836	0.1

SOURCE: U.S. Census Bureau. Census 2010. www.census/gov/ (accessed July 2012). A dash (—) indicates that the percent is less than 0.1.

non-Northern terms as *wait on* (wait for), *pullybone* (wishbone), and *light bread* (white bread). In eastern Tennessee are found *goobers* (peanuts), *tote* (carry), and *fireboard* (mantel). Appearing in western Tennessee are *loaf bread* and *cold drink* (soft drink). In Memphis, a large, long sandwich is a *poorboy.*

In 2011, some 93.1% of state residents five years and older spoke only English at home. Some 4.1% spoke Spanish, 1.3% spoke another Indo-European language, and 1% spoke an Asian or Pacific Islander language.

9 Religions

Two Protestant groups who originated on the Tennessee frontier in the first half of the 19th century were the Disciples of Christ and the Church of Christ. The Church of God (Cleveland, Tennessee) was established in the state in 1886 as a result of the greater Pentecostal movement.

According to the Pew Forum on Religion & Public Life, as of 2008, Evangelical Protestants still accounted for a majority of the population in Tennessee, with 51%. The largest single religious group in the state was the Southern Baptist Convention. Other Evangelical groups were the Churches of Christ, the Church of God (Cleveland, Tennessee), Independent Non-Charismatic Churches, and Assemblies of God. Mainline Protestant faiths represented 18% of the population. Only 7% of the state's population were Roman Catholic and 1% were Mormon. No other faith represented more than 1% of the population. Approximately 12% of

Tennessee's population was not affiliated with any religious organization, which was less than the national average of 16%.

10 Transportation

Memphis, Nashville, Knoxville, and Chattanooga are the focal points for rail, highway, water, and air transportation. All are located on important rivers and interstate highways, and all have airports served by the major airlines.

In 2009, Tennessee had 2,976 miles (4,789 kilometers) of freight railroad track. Amtrak provides north–south passenger service through Memphis on its route between Chicago and New Orleans. There were 25 freight railroads in the state in 2009, including six Class I railroads.

In 2009, Tennessee had 93,252 miles (150,074 kilometers) of roads. The major interstate highway is I-40, crossing east–west from Knoxville to Nashville and Memphis. In 2009, there were about 5.1 million motor vehicles registered in the state, including more than 2.8 million passenger cars, 151,000 motorcycles, and 2.18 million trucks. More than 4.4 million Tennesseans were licensed drivers that year.

The principal means of transportation during Tennessee's early history was water, and all the early settlements were built on or near streams. The introduction of steamboats on the Cumberland River in the early 19th century helped make Nashville the state's largest city and its foremost trading center. However by mid-century, that distinction would go to Memphis, located on the Mississippi River.

In 2009, Tennessee had 950 miles (1,529 kilometers) of navigable inland waterways. The completion in 1985 of the 234-mile (377-kilometer) Tennessee-Tombigbee

Waterway gave Tennessee shippers a direct north–south route for all vessels between the Tennessee River and the Gulf of Mexico via the Black Warrior River in Alabama. Although none of the waterway runs through Tennessee, the northern terminus is on the Tennessee River near the common borders of Tennessee, Alabama, and Mississippi. Freight ports are located at Memphis and Nashville.

In 2012, Tennessee had approximately 209 public and private airports and 111 heliports. Memphis International Airport is among the world's busiest cargo handling facilities, and it was also the state's major air terminal, with 5,047,362 passenger enplanements in 2009, making it the nation's 33rd-busiest airport that year.

11 History

When the first Spanish explorers arrived in the early 16th century, the Creek tribe was living in what is now East Tennessee, along with the Yuchi. About 200 years later, the powerful Cherokee drove them out of the area and established themselves as the dominant tribe. The Cherokee retained their tribal dominance until they were forced out by the federal government in the 1830s. Other tribes were the Chickasaw in West Tennessee and the Shawnee. The latter group occupied the Cumberland Valley in Middle Tennessee.

Explorers and traders from continental Europe and the British Isles were in Tennessee for well over 100 years before permanent settlements were established in the 1760s. By the mid-1700s, hundreds—perhaps thousands—of English adventurers had crossed the Appalachian barrier and explored the country beyond, claimed first by the colony of Virginia and later assigned to North Carolina. Perhaps the best known was Daniel Boone, who by 1760 had found his way into present-day Washington County, Tennessee.

With the conclusion of the French and Indian War in 1763, many people from North Carolina and Virginia began to cross the Alleghenies. Elisha Walden was among those who first led groups of "long hunters" into the wilderness. Two major areas of settlement developed. The larger one, in the northeast, was organized as the Watauga Association in the 1770s. The second major area was in the Cumberland Basin, where James Robertson established a settlement he called Nashborough (now Nashville) in 1779.

Statehood The Revolutionary War did not reach as far west as Tennessee, but many of the early settlers there fought in the Carolinas and Virginia. The Revolution was hardly over when Tennesseans began to think about statehood for themselves. In 1790, North Carolina ceded its western lands to the United States. Tennessee became known as the Southwest Territory. The population doubled to more than 70,000 in 1795, and steps were taken to obtain statehood for the territory. On 1 June 1796, President George Washington signed a bill admitting Tennessee as the 16th state. Andrew Jackson became the state's first US representative.

By 1809, Nashville, Knoxville, and other early settlements became thriving frontier towns. Churches and schools were established, industry and agriculture developed, and Tennessee became a leading iron producer.

Andrew Jackson's rise to prominence came as a result of his successful leadership at the Battle of New Orleans, fought at the conclusion of the War of 1812. He returned to Nashville a hero and was elected to the US Senate in 1823. Although Jackson received the most votes, the 1824 presidential election was decided by the House of Representatives, which chose John Quincy Adams as president. Jackson ran again in 1828 and won, serving then as president of the United States for eight years.

Early 19th Century Social reform and cultural growth characterized the first half of the 19th century. A prison was built, and the penal code was reformed. Temperance newspapers were published and laws passed to limit the consumption of alcoholic beverages. In 1834 a few women, embracing the feminist cause, were influential in giving the courts, rather than the legislature, the right to grant divorces.

More than most other Southern states, Tennessee was divided over the issue of slavery. Slaveholders predominated in the West, where cotton was grown profitably, as well as in Middle Tennessee. But in East Tennessee, where blacks made up less than 10% of the population, antislavery sentiment thrived. Supporters of emancipation urged that it be accomplished peacefully, gradually, and with compensation to the slave owners. At the constitutional convention of 1834, hundreds of petitions were presented asking that the legislature be empowered to free the slaves, while at the same time the convention sought to take the right to vote away from free blacks.

Considerable economic growth took place during this period. West Tennessee became a major cotton growing area. The counties of the Highland Rim produced tobacco in such abundance that, by 1840, Tennessee ranked just behind Kentucky and Virginia in total production. East Tennessee farmers grew fruits and vegetables for market.

Civil War Tennessee became a major battleground during the Civil War (1861–65), as armies from both North and South crossed the state. Many Tennesseans favored secession, but the eastern counties remained staunchly Unionist, and many East Tennesseans crossed over into Kentucky to enlist in the Union Army. In February 1862, Fort Donelson and Fort Henry were taken by General Ulysses S. Grant and naval Captain Andrew H. Foote, thereby opening the state to Union armies. Within two weeks Nashville was under Union army control; both sides suffered tremendous losses at the Battle of Shiloh, two months later.

President Abraham Lincoln established a military government for the conquered state and appointed Andrew Johnson to head it. Johnson, who had been elected to the US Senate in 1858, remained there in 1861, the only Southern senator to do so, refusing to follow his state into the Confederacy. In 1864, he was elected vice president under Lincoln.

Confederate forces launched two major campaigns—both unsuccessful—to retake the state, threatening Nashville in December 1862 and attacking Union forces at Franklin and Nashville two years later. In between, the Battle of Chickamauga (northern Georgia), in which the Confederates drove Union troops back to Chattanooga in September 1863, was one of the bloodiest engagements of the war.

After the Civil War Returning to the Union in 1866, Tennessee was the only former Confederate state not to have a military government during Reconstruction. Economic readjustment

was not as difficult as elsewhere in the South, and within a few years agricultural production recovered, but it did not exceed prewar levels until 1900. By the early 1880s, flour, wool, and paper mills were established in all the urban areas. By the late 1890s, Memphis was a leading cotton market and the nation's foremost producer of cottonseed oil.

As the 20th century dawned, the major issue in Tennessee was the crusade against alcohol, a movement with deep roots in the 19th century. In 1909, after the shooting of a prominent prohibitionist, "dry" forces enacted legislation that, in effect, imposed prohibition on the entire state. The prohibition movement helped promote the cause of women's suffrage, and in 1919, women were granted the right to vote in municipal elections. One year later, Tennessee became the 36th state to ratify the 19th Amendment to the US Constitution, thereby granting women the right to vote nationwide.

1920s to 1940s The 1920s brought a resurgence of religious fundamentalism. Nationwide attention was brought to the state with the trial and conviction of a high school teacher named John T. Scopes, who challenged a 1925 law that prohibited teaching of the theory of evolution in the public schools.

The 1930s brought the Great Depression, but they also brought the Tennessee Valley Authority (TVA), established a few weeks after Franklin Delano Roosevelt's presidential inauguration in 1933. By the late 1930s, power lines were being strung into remote areas bringing electricity to practically everyone. Inexpensive power became a magnet for industry, and industrial employment in the region nearly doubled in two decades. The building of an atomic weapons plant at Oak Ridge in 1942 was due in large measure to the availability of TVA power.

The Depression hurt many manufacturers, and farm prices declined drastically. The state was still was in the grip of financial depression when World War II (1939–45) began. Tennessee firms received defense contracts amounting to $1.25 billion and employed more than 200,000 people during the war, and industrial growth continued during the postwar period, while agriculture recovered and diversified. The chemical industry, spurred by high demand during and after World War II, became a leading sector, along with textiles, apparel, and food processing.

1950s to 1990s Considerable progress was made toward ending racial discrimination during the postwar years, although the desegregation of public schools was accomplished only after outbursts of violence at Clinton, Nashville, and Memphis. The killing of civil rights leader Martin Luther King Jr. in Memphis in 1968 resulted in rioting by blacks in that city. The most notable political development during the 1970s was the resurgence of the Republican Party.

The early 1980s saw the exposure of corruption in high places: former governor Ray Blanton and several aides were convicted for conspiracy to sell liquor licenses, and banker and former gubernatorial candidate Jacob F. "Jake" Butcher was convicted of fraud following the collapse of his banking empire. On the brighter side, there was a successful World's Fair in 1982, as well as the Knoxville International Energy Exposition.

The state economy was also bolstered by the arrival of both Nissan and General Motors plants. The state gained nearly 45,000 manufacturing

A view of downtown Nashville, one of the state's largest cities.
© KENNSTILGER47/SHUTTERSTOCK.COM.

jobs between 1982 and 1992, many of them in the automotive and other transport-related industries. Tennessee's unemployment rate fell to a 16-year low of 4.7% in 1994.

In 1992 school reform laws were passed by the state legislature, and in 1993, TennCare was created to replace Medicaid coverage for 1.5 million uninsured residents of the state.

21st Century In 2002, Democrat Phil Bredesen was elected governor. Under his leadership, Tennessee led the nation in attempting to collect mail-order and Internet sales taxes. By 2005, the governor had issued executive orders that established strict ethics rules for the executive branch. His administration also sought to guide the state through a fiscal crisis without raising taxes. Tennessee also demonstrated its commitment to improving education by raising pay for teachers.

The recession that began in 2008 had a severe impact on the state, as tens of thousands of manufacturing jobs were lost. However, by 2012 the state was recovering, led by increased government employment and new industry.

12 State Government

Tennessee's first constitution was adopted in 1796, just prior to the state's admission to the Union. The basic structure in that document remains basically intact, although the constitution has been amended approximately 40 times.

Executive authority is vested in a governor, elected to four year terms, who can approve or veto bills adopted by the legislature, and also has line-item veto power. Legislative power is placed in the Tennessee General Assembly, consisting of a 99-member house, who serve two-year terms, and a 33-member senate, who serve terms of four years. The governor is limited to two consecutive terms, but is reeligible after four years out of office.

The governor appoints a cabinet of 21 members. The speaker of the state senate

Tennessee Governors: 1796–2013

1796–1801	John Sevier	Dem-Rep	1897–1899	Robert Love Taylor	Democrat
1801–1803	Archibald Roane	Dem-Rep	1899–1903	Benton McMillin	Democrat
1803–1809	John Sevier	Dem-Rep	1903–1905	James Beriah Frazier	Democrat
1809–1815	Willie Blount	Dem-Rep	1905–1907	John Isaac Cox	Democrat
1815–1821	Joseph McMinn	Dem-Rep	1907–1911	Malcolm Rice Patterson	Democrat
1821–1827	William Carroll	Dem-Rep	1911–1915	Ben Walker Hooper	Republican
1827–1829	Samuel Houston	Democrat	1915–1919	Thomas Clark Rye	Democrat
1829	William Hall	Dem-Rep	1919–1921	Albert Houston Roberts	Democrat
1829–1835	William Carroll	Democrat	1921–1923	Alfred Alexander Taylor	Republican
1835–1839	Newton Cannon	Whig	1923–1927	Austin Peay III	Democrat
1839–1841	James Knox Polke	Democrat	1927–1933	Henry Hollis Horton	Democrat
1841–1845	James Chamberlain Jones	Whig	1933–1937	Harry Hill McAlister	Democrat
1845–1847	Aaron Venable Brown	Democrat	1937–1939	Gordon Weaver Browning	Democrat
1847–1849	Neill Smith Brown	Whig	1939–1945	William Prentice Cooper	Democrat
1849–1851	William Trousdale	Democrat	1945–1949	James Nance McCord	Democrat
1851–1853	William Bowen Campbell	Whig	1949–1953	Gordon Weaver Browning	Democrat
1853–1857	Andrew Johnson	Democrat	1953–1959	Frank Goad Clement	Democrat
1857–1862	Isham Green Harris	Democrat	1959–1963	Earl Buford Ellington	Democrat
1862–1865	Andrew Johnson	Republican	1963–1967	Frank Goad Clement	Democrat
1865	Edward Hazzard East	Prohibitionist	1967–1971	Earl Buford Ellington	Democrat
1865–1869	William Gannaway Brownlow	Whig-Rep	1971–1975	Bryant Winfield Dunn	Republican
1869–1871	DeWitt Clinton Senter	Conserv-Rep	1975–1979	Leonard Ray Blanton	Democrat
1871–1875	John Calvin Brown	Democrat	1979–1987	Lamar Alexander	Republican
1875–1879	James Davis Porter, Jr.	Democrat	1987–1995	Ned Ray McWherter	Democrat
1879–1881	Albert Smith Marks	Democrat	1995–2003	Don Sundquist	Republican
1881–1883	Alvin Hawkins	Republican	2003–2011	Phil Bredesen	Democrat
1883–1887	William Brimage Bate	Democrat	2011–	Bill Haslam	Republican
1887–1891	Robert Love Taylor	Democrat			
1891–1893	John Price Buchanan	Democrat	Conservative Democrat – Conserv-Rep		
1893–1897	Peter Turney	Democrat	Democratic Republican – Dem-Rep		

automatically becomes lieutenant governor. The secretary of state, treasurer, and comptroller of the treasury are chosen by the legislature.

Legislation is enacted after bills are read and approved three times in each house and signed by the governor. If the governor vetoes a measure, the legislature may override the veto by majority vote of both houses. Once every six years the legislature may offer voters the chance to call a convention for the purpose of amending the constitution.

The legislative salary in 2010 was $19,009, and the governor's salary of $170,340 was the eighth highest in the nation.

13 Political Parties

After the Civil War and Reconstruction, Tennessee primarily elected Democratic candidates for nearly a century, although East Tennessee remained a Republican stronghold. Although the 1920s saw a tendency away from one-party domination, Franklin D. Roosevelt and the government programs of the New Deal persuaded voters to elect more Democrats. Tennesseans voted overwhelmingly Democratic in the four elections won by Roosevelt (1932–44).

After World War II, the one-party dominance in Tennessee was tested again. Between 1948 and 1976, the only Democratic nominees to carry the state came from the South (Lyndon Johnson and Jimmy Carter), or from a border state (Harry Truman). In state elections, the Republicans made deep inroads into Democratic power during the 1960s and 1970s.

Tennessee voters, who gave Republican George H. W. Bush 57.4% of the vote in 1988, chose Bill Clinton in 1992 and 1996 with his Tennessee running mate, Al Gore. In the 2000

election, Republican George W. Bush received 51% of the vote to Democrat Al Gore's 48%. In 2004, President Bush won Tennessee by a margin of 56.8% to to Democrat John Kerry's 42.5%. Voter preference stayed Republican in 2008, with John McCain receiving nearly 57% of the vote to Democrat Barack Obama's 41.8%. In 2012, voters again chose the Republican challenger (Mitt Romney) over President Obama. As of June 2010, there were 3,547,745 registered voters in the state.

In 1994, Dr. Bill Frist, a heart surgeon, was elected a US senator on the Republican ticket, defeating Democrat James Sasser. He was reelected in 2000, and in December 2002, was elected the Senate Majority Leader. Frist did not run for reelection in 2006. Republican and mayor of Chattanooga Bob Corker Jr. won his open seat that year and was reelected in 2012. Former governor Lamar Alexander (Republican)

Tennessee Presidential Vote by Major Political Parties, 1948–2012

Year	Tennessee Winner	Democrat	Republican
1948	*Truman (D)	270,402	202,914
1952	*Eisenhower (R)	443,710	446,147
1956	*Eisenhower (R)	456,507	462,288
1960	Nixon (R)	481,453	556,577
1964	*Johnson (D)	635,047	508,965
1968	*Nixon (R)	351,233	472,592
1972	*Nixon (R)	357,293	813,147
1976	*Carter (D)	825,897	633,969
1980	*Reagan (R)	783,051	787,761
1984	*Reagan (R)	711,714	990,212
1988	*Bush (R)	679,794	947,233
1992	*Clinton (D)	933,521	841,300
1996	*Clinton (D)	909,146	863,530
2000	*Bush, G. W. (R)	981,720	1,061,949
2004	*Bush, G. W. (R)	1,036,477	1,384,375
2008	McCain (R)	1,087,437	1,479,178
2012	Romney (R)	960,709	1,462,330

*Won US presidential election.

Independent candidate Ross Perot received 199,968 votes in 1992 and 105,918 votes in 1996.

was elected US senator in 2002 and reelected in 2008. Republicans also dominate Tennessee's representation in the US House, with seven of the state's nine seats.

Democrat Phil Bredesen was elected governor in 2002 and reelected in 2006. However, he could not run again in 2010 due to term limits. Knoxville mayor Bill Haslam, a Republican, won in 2010. Following that election, the Republicans held 20 seats, or 60%, in the 33-member state senate, and 65% of the seats in the state house. That year there were 17 women serving in the state house and 7 women serving in the state senate.

14 Local Government

In 2010, Tennessee had 95 counties. The constitution specifies that county officials must include at least a registrar, trustee (the custodian of county funds), sheriff, and county clerk. Other officials have been added by legislative enactment. The state's incorporated places included 182 cities and 162 towns. In 2007, there were 475 special districts in the state.

There are three forms of municipal government: mayor-council (or mayor-alderman), council-manager, and commission. The mayor-council system is the oldest and by far the most widely employed. Tennessee has 16 elementary school districts, 16 secondary districts, and 120 unified school districts. In 2011, there were 303,316 full-time and 67,342 part-time state and local government workers in Tennessee.

15 Judicial System

The five-member Tennessee Supreme Court is the highest court in the state. The court has appeals jurisdiction only, holding sessions in Nashville, Knoxville, and Jackson.

Immediately below the supreme court are two appeals courts established by the legislature to relieve the crowded high court schedule. Circuit courts hear both civil and criminal cases. Tennessee also has chancery courts, which settle disputes regarding property ownership, hear divorce cases, and rule on a variety of other matters. At the bottom of the judicial structure are general sessions courts.

In 2010, Tennessee had a violent crime rate of 613.3 reported incidents per 100,000 people. The murder and nonnegligent manslaughter rate was 5.6 incidents per 100,000 inhabitants; forcible rape, 33.7; aggravated assault, 442.2; and property crime, 3,657.9. Tennessee's federal and state prisons in 2010 housed 51,684 inmates.

Tennessee has the death penalty, of which lethal injection is the sole method of execution for those sentenced after 1 January 1999. Those sentenced prior to the date can select electrocution. Six prisoners have been put to death in Tennessee since 1976. The most recent execution, as of September 2012, was in 2009. There were 88 prisoners on death row, as of 2012, including one woman.

16 Migration

The first white settlers in Tennessee, who came across the mountains from North Carolina and Virginia, were almost entirely of English extraction. They were followed by an influx of Scotch-Irish, mainly from Pennsylvania. About 3,800 German and Irish migrants arrived during the 1830s and 1840s. In the next century, Tennessee's population remained relatively stable, except for an influx of blacks immediately following the Civil War. There was a steady out-migration of blacks to industrial centers in the North during the 20th century.

Between 2009 and 2010, the total population (ages one and older) of Tennessee increased by 38,720, due to the net domestic in-migration of natives (16,629), the net domestic in-migration of immigrants (14), and the arrival from abroad of natives (14,175) and immigrants (7,902). Of the total foreign-born population in Tennessee in 2010, 9.5% were from Africa, 26.8% were from Asia, 11.3% were from Europe, and 49.4% were from Latin America. The top three countries of birth of the foreign born in Tennessee that year were Mexico (31.3%), India (4.3%), and China (3.7%). In comparison, the top three countries of birth in 1990 were Germany (10.6%), the United Kingdom (7.5%), and Canada (7%).

17 Economy

With the construction in the 1980s of a Nissan automobile and truck plant and a General Motors automobile facility, Tennessee has become an important producer of transportation equipment. The economy in Tennessee and the nation shrank when a global recession began in 2008. The state's gross state product (GSP) declined from nearly $231 billion in 2008 to $250.3 billion in 2010, ranking the state 21st in the nation. Tennessee's durable goods industry had the most growth, followed by nondurable goods and retail trade. Per capita GSP in 2010 was $39,730, ranking the state 41st. In 2008, there were 131,582 private nonfarm establishments and 465,545 nonemployer establishments in the state.

18 Income

In 2011, Tennessee ranked 36th among the 50 states, with a per capita personal income (including nonmonetary income) of $36,533, compared to the national average of $41,663. During the period 2008–10, the state's median annual household income of $40,026 also remained below the national average of $50,022. In 2011, 18.3% of Tennessee's residents were living below the federal poverty level, compared to the national rate of 15.9%.

19 Industry

On the eve of the Civil War, only 1% of Tennessee's population was employed in manufacturing. But by 1981, rapid industrial growth in the 20th century transformed the state, making Tennessee third among the southeastern states and 15th in the United States in the shipment value of its manufactured products. These shipments totaled $140.5 billion in 2007, as compared to $125.5 billion in 2004. Of that total, transportation equipment manufacturing accounted for the largest share, followed by computer and electronic equipment manufacturing and food manufacturing. Tennessee's four major metropolitan areas—Memphis, Nashville, Knoxville, and Chattanooga—account for the largest portion of the state's industrial workers.

20 Labor

In 2006, Tennessee's unemployment rate was 5.4%, as compared to the national average of 4.7%. Following the recession of 2008 and 2009, the state's unemployment rate rose to 9.4%, while the national average jumped to 9.6%. During this time, Tennessee had a civilian labor force of more than 3 million workers.

In August 2012, the civilian labor force in Tennessee numbered 3,109,800. That month, 264,100 people were unemployed, for an unemployment rate of 8.5%, compared to the national average of 8.1%. Those employed in nonfarm wage and salaried jobs that same month included: 117,500 in mining, logging, and construction; 313,500 in manufacturing; 553,700 in trade, transportation, and utilities; 132,200 in financial activities; 326,800 in business and professional services; 267,900 in leisure and hospitality; and 433,400 in government.

In 2011, 139,000 of Tennessee's employed wage and salary workers were members of unions, representing 5.6% of those so employed. The national average was 13%.

21 Agriculture

From the pre-Civil War period into the 1950s, cotton, followed by corn and tobacco, were the main crops grown in the state. However, by the early 1960s, soybeans became the leading source of farm income.

According to the US Department of Agriculture, there were approximately 10.9 million acres (4.4 million hectares) of land distributed among 78,300 Tennessee farms in 2010. The average farm size was 139 acres (56 hectares). Final agricultural output in 2011 was $4.467 billion, of which $2.15 billion was crop output. Soybeans were a primary crop, bringing in $461.3 million in farm receipts that year, followed by corn for grain

at $456 million and cotton at $401 million. Wheat, hay, and tobacco were also important agricultural commodities. The main types of tobacco are burley, a fine leaf used primarily for cigarettes; and eastern and western dark-fired, which are used primarily for cigars, pipe tobacco, and snuff.

Top export crops in 2011 included soybeans and soy products ($290 million in exports), cotton and linters ($174.6 million), wheat ($96.4 million), and feed grains ($65.5 million). Top agricultural counties in the state are Bedford, Warren, Bradley, Obion, and Robertson.

22 Domesticated Animals

Livestock products are as important as crops in Tennessee, with cattle being the highest income source. Cattle are raised throughout the state, but principally in Middle and East Tennessee. In 1930, fewer than a million cattle and calves were raised on Tennessee farms. By the end of 2010, that number had doubled. The state's livestock inventory that year also included 170,000 hogs and pigs as well as 35,000 sheep. Tennessee ranks sixth in the nation for number of horses and ponies.

In 2011, output from the domesticated animals industry was $1.3 billion. That year, sales of cattle and calves in Tennessee exceeded $586.3 million. With more than 41 million broilers and 1.7 million layers, poultry and eggs were the state's second most valuable livestock commodity, with farm receipts of $461.1 million in 2011. Tennessee is not a major dairy state, but dairy farmers produced 1 billion pounds (453,592 million kilograms) of milk from some 54,000 milk cows in 2007. Sales of dairy products that year exceeded $180 million.

23 Fishing

Fishing is a major attraction for sport but plays a relatively small role in the economic life of Tennessee. There are 17 TVA lakes and 7 other lakes, all maintained by the Army Corps of Engineers, and there are thousands of miles of creeks and mountain streams, all of which attract anglers. The state has 14 trout farms and about 2 million fish are supplied annually by two national fish hatcheries in the state (Dale Hollow and Erwin).

24 Forestry

In 2009, forests covered 14 million acres (5.7 million hectares), or more than 50% of Tennessee's total land area. Of the state's more than 13.5 million acres of commercial timberlands, nearly 10 million acres were oak. Loblolly-shortleaf pine is a common softwood, primarily growing in the eastern portion of the state. In 2011, output from forestry and forest services was $921 million.

The counties of the Cumberland Plateau and Highland Rim are the major sources of timber products, and in Lewis, Perry, Polk, Scott, Sequatchie, Unicoi, and Wayne counties, more than 75% of the total area is commercial forest. Approximately 80% of the state's forested areas are privately owned, 5% are federally owned national forests, and 7% are owned by other government agencies. Tennessee's two National Forests are Cherokee National Forest and Land Between the Lakes National Recreation Area.

25 Mining

The 2011, the estimated value of nonfuel mineral production in Tennessee was $848 million, representing 1.15% of the national output, and ranking Tennessee 25th in the nation. Production had increased from $737 million a decade prior. In 2010, 40.7 million metric tons of crushed stone were mined in the state, valued at $429 million; along with 5.5 million metric tons of sand and gravel, valued at $43.4 million; and 46.2 million metric tons of aggregate, valued at $472 million.

26 Energy and Power

The Tennessee Valley Authority (TVA) is the principal supplier of power in the state, producing 90% of electricity. Tennessee is also a leading producer of hydroelectricity east of the Rocky Mountains. The Sequoyah plant near Chattanooga and the Watts Bar facility between Chattanooga and Knoxville are operated by the TVA. Watts Bar 2 is scheduled to be the next US hydroelectric facility to come online in 2015.

Tennessee produced 23,000 barrels of crude oil (2012 figure); 5.1 billion cubic feet of marketed natural gas (2010 figure); and 1.8 million short tons of coal (2010 figure). As of June 2012, total net electricity generation was 6,953,000 megawatt hours (MWh). This included 14,000 MWh generated by petroleum-fired plants; 858,000 MWh by natural-gas fired plants; 3,106,000 from coal-fired plants; 2,434,000 MWh by nuclear power plants; 450,000 MWh from hydroelectric plants; and 89,000 MWh from other renewable sources.

27 Commerce

Tennessee's wholesale trade sector had sales of about $80 billion in 2007, as compared to

The hydroelectric Norris Dam was among the first such structures built by the Tennessee Valley Authority (TVA). © BRYAN BUSOVICKI/SHUTTERSTOCK.COM.

$98 billion five years prior. The state's retail trade sector had sales of $77.5 billion, or $12,563 per capita (per person). Motor vehicle and motor vehicle dealers accounted for the largest share of retail sales. In 2008, there were 7,291 wholesale trade establishments and 23,568 retail trade establishments.

In 2011, Tennessee's foreign exports totaled nearly $30 billion. Canada received more than $8 billion in exports from Tennessee, followed by Mexico, China, Japan, and Belgium. Top exports that year included medical devices and cotton.

28 Public Finance

The state budget is prepared annually by the Budget Division of the Tennessee Department of Finance and Administration and submitted by the governor to the legislature every January. The fiscal year lasts from 1 July to 30 June.

According to the 2010 Annual Survey of State Government Finances, Tennessee's total revenues were $29.72 billion, while total expenditures were slightly lower at $29.68 billion. The largest general expenditures were for public welfare ($10.0 billion), education ($9.0 billion), and highways ($1.6 billion). The state's outstanding debt totaled $5.8 billion, as compared to $3.6 billion in 2004.

29 Taxation

Sales taxes in 2009 accounted for most of Tennessee's tax revenues, of which the general rate was 7%, with local add-ons allowed up to 2.75%. Food purchased for consumption off premises (such as at home) is taxed but at a lower rate. Other state taxes include excise taxes on gasoline and cigarettes, a flat 6.5% corporate income tax, and a personal state income tax on dividend and interest income only. There is no state property tax; instead property taxes, which averaged $748 per capita (per person) in 2009, are collected on a local basis.

In 2011, Tennessee collected $10.86 billion in taxes, of which $8.2 billion came from sales tax and gross receipts; $1 billion from license taxes; and $1.26 billion from state income tax. The state tax burden was $1,696 per capita. Tennessee ranked 44th among the states in terms of tax burden.

30 Health

In 2011, Tennessee's infant mortality rate was 8.2 deaths per 1,000 live births. The overall death rate in 2009 was 8.67 deaths per 1,000 persons. In 2010, 20.1% of Tennessee adults smoked, compared to the US rate of 17.2%. That year, 67.8% of adults were overweight or obese, and 11.3% had been diagnosed with diabetes. The death rate from diabetes was 25.8 per 100,000 residents in 2009. Death rates from other diseases that year included cancers at 195.9 per 100,000; heart disease at 210.9 per 100,000; and cerebrovascular disease at 47.2 per 100,000.

In 2008, there were 14,751 people in Tennessee living with HIV/AIDS, 1.7% of the US total.

Tennessee's 121 community hospitals had about 21,000 beds in 2009. That year, there were 266 physicians and 984 registered nurses per 100,000 population. There were 50 dentists per 100,000 population in 2007 figure. The average expense for community hospital care was $1,464 per day. Approximately 15.4% of Tennessee's residents were uninsured, including 6.6% of children.

Tennessee has four medical schools: two in Nashville (Vanderbilt University and Meharry Medical School), one at Johnson City (East Tennessee State University), and one at Memphis (University of Tennessee).

31 Housing

In 2011, there were an estimated 2,829,125 housing units in Tennessee, of which 2,467,428 (87.2%) were occupied and 1,660,076 (67.3%) were owner-occupied. About 68.3% of all units (1,931,708) were single-family, detached homes, and 10.1% (285,188) were mobile homes. Utility gas and electricity were the most common energy sources for heating. It was estimated that 12,495 (0.5%) lacked complete plumbing facilities and 21,494 (0.9%) lacked complete kitchen facilities. The average household size was 2.5 people.

In 2011, the median home value in 2011 was $138,300. The median monthly cost for mortgage owners was $1,172, while renters paid a median of $715 per month.

32 Education

According to national statistics compiled by the US National Center for Education, for

One of the principal campuses of the University of Tennessee is located in Knoxville. © STEVEN FRAME/SHUTTERSTOCK.COM.

the 2009/10 school year Tennessee had 1,791 public schools and 972,549 students. Expenditures for the state's public education were $8.5 billion. The US Census Bureau estimated that during the period 2006–10, 82.5% of the state's population 25 years and older had completed four years of high school, a percentage that lagged behind the national average of 85%, and 22.7% had obtained a bachelor's degree or higher.

In 2008, there were 308,000 students enrolled in college or graduate school including 222,000 full-time students at the state's 106 degree-granting institutions. The University of Tennessee system has principal campuses at Knoxville, Memphis, Martin, and Chattanooga. Components of the State University and Community College System of Tennessee include Memphis State University (the largest), Tennessee Technological University, East Tennessee State University, Austin Peay State University, Tennessee State University at Nashville, and Middle Tennessee State University, along with 14 two-year community colleges located throughout the state. Well-known private colleges are Vanderbilt University in Nashville, Sewanee–The University of the South, and Rhodes College in Memphis.

33 Arts

Each of Tennessee's major cities has a symphony orchestra. The best known are the Memphis Symphony and the Nashville Symphony, the latter of which makes its home in the Tennessee Performing Arts Center, which includes three performing arts theaters and the state museum. The major operatic troupes are Opera Memphis, Nashville Opera, and Knoxville Opera. Nashville is known as "Music City, USA." The Grand Ole Opry, Country Music Hall of Fame, Ryman Auditorium, and numerous recording studios are located in the city.

Among the leading art galleries are the Memphis Brooks Museum of Art, the Dixon Gallery in Memphis, the Cheekwood Museum of Art in Nashville, the Knoxville Museum of Art, and the Hunter Museum of American Art in Chattanooga.

There are several state and local festivals reflecting the music and arts of the state. Elvis Week, in August, is celebrated each year in Memphis. Graceland is the site of the annual Elvis Presley Birthday Celebration (January) and Christmas at Graceland. The Dollywood theme park in Pigeon Forge, created by singer Dolly Parton, presents several festivals and musical events each year. The Tennessee Association of Craft Artists presents annual spring and fall fairs. The Memphis in May International Festival includes the following programs: the Beale Street Music Festival, International Week, the World Championship Barbecue Cooking Contest, and Sunset Symphony (featuring the Memphis Symphony).

The Tennessee Arts Commission (est. 1967) offers grant opportunities for such programs as the Individual Artist Fellowship, Arts Build Communities, and Arts Education programs. Humanities Tennessee sponsors a number of annual programs, including the Southern Festival of Books, the Tennessee Young Writers' Workshop, and the Letters About Literature contest.

34 Libraries and Museums

As 2009, there were 186 libraries in Tennessee, offering 3.2 million borrowers a total circulation of nearly 25 million. The largest libraries are the Vanderbilt University Library at Nashville, Memphis-Shelby County Library, Memphis State University Libraries, University of Tennessee at Knoxville Library, Knoxville-Knox County Library, and the Chattanooga–Hamilton County Library.

Tennessee has more than 127 museums and historic sites. The Tennessee State Museum in Nashville displays exhibits on pioneer life, military traditions, evangelical religion, and presidential lore. The Museum of Appalachia, near Norris, attempts an authentic replica of early Appalachian life, with more than 20,000 pioneer relics on display in several log cabins. Displays of solar, nuclear, and other energy technologies are featured at the American Museum of Science and Energy at Oak Ridge. There are floral collections at the Goldsmith Civic Garden Center in Memphis and at the Tennessee Botanical Gardens and Fine Arts Center in Nashville.

35 Communications

In 2010, 63% of all households in Tennessee had Internet access, with 59% having broadband access. As of 2012, the state had 406 broadcasting radio stations and 36 broadcasting television stations.

36 Press

According to the Audit Bureau of Circulations, Tennessee had 12 newspapers as of March 2012. Leading Tennessee newspapers, with their approximate daily circulations, were the Nashville *Tennessean* (119,796 daily, 216,434 Sundays), Memphis *Commercial Appeal* (118,978 daily, 155,864 Sundays), the *Knoxville News-Sentinel* (88,781 daily, 115,586 Sundays), and the *Chattanooga Times Free Press* (78,108 daily, 103,186 Sundays).

37 Tourism, Travel, and Recreation

The natural beauty of Tennessee, combined with the activity of the Department of Tourist Development, has made tourism a large industry in the state. According to US Travel's 2010 Economic Impact Report, Tennessee tourism increased 6.3% over the prior year. Visitor spending contributed $14.1 billion to the state's economy and supported nearly 175,000 jobs.

The Tennessee State Museum in Nashville is one of the largest state museums in the nation, with more than 60,000 square feet (5,574 square meters) of permanent exhibits and 10,000 square feet (929 square meters) available for temporary exhibits. The state has three presidential homes: Andrew Johnson's at Greeneville; Andrew Jackson's Hermitage near Nashville; and James K. Polk's at Columbia. Pinson Mounds, near Jackson, offers outstanding archaeological

A view of the Blue Ridge Mountains from Roan Mountains State Park in Tennessee. © DAVE ALLEN PHOTOGRAPHY/SHUTTERSTOCK.COM.

treasures and the remains of a Native American city. Other historical attractions include the Beale Street Historic District in Memphis, home of W. C. Handy, the "father of the blues;" and Graceland, the Memphis estate of singer Elvis Presley.

In addition to Opryland USA and the Grand Ole Opry at Nashville, top attractions include Dollywood, the Tennessee Aquarium, Bristol Motor Sports, Ober Gatlinburg, and Casey Jones Village.

There are 33 state parks, almost all of which have camping facilities. Extending into North Carolina, the Great Smoky Mountains National Park covers 241,207 acres (97,613 hectares) in Tennessee. Reservoirs and lakes attract thousands of anglers and water sports enthusiasts.

The Tennessee State Fair is held every September in Nashville. Other top annual events include the Dogwood Arts Festival, Bonnaroo Music & Arts Festival, Elvis Week, the National Storytelling Festival, and the Jack Daniel's World Championship Invitational Barbecue.

38 Sports

Tennessee has three professional major league sports teams. These are the National Football League's Titans, who relocated to Nashville from Houston before the 1997 season; the National Hockey League's Nashville Predators, who began playing in 1999; and the National basketball Association's Memphis Grizzlies, who relocated from Vancouver, British Columbia, in 2001. Minor league baseball teams play throughout the state including in Chattanooga, Memphis, Elizabethton, Johnson City, Jackson, Kingsport, Lynchburg, and Nashville.

Tennessee's colleges and universities provide the major fall and winter sports. The University of Tennessee Volunteers and Vanderbilt University Commodores, in the Southeastern Conference, compete nationally in football, basketball, and baseball. Austin Peay, Tennessee State, and Tennessee Technological universities belong to the Ohio Valley Conference. The University of Tennessee frequently competes in bowl games, with the most recent victory in the 2008 Outback Bowl. The University of Tennessee's women's basketball team, the Lady Vols, won National Collegiate Athletic Association (NCAA) titles eight times. They have won more games than any other women's NCAA basketball team in the country.

Other annual sporting events include the Iroquois Steeplechase in Nashville in May and two NASCAR races at the Bristol Motor Speedway, one in March and one in August.

39 Famous Tennesseans

Andrew Jackson (b. South Carolina, 1767–1845), the seventh president, moved to Tennessee as a young man. He won renown in the War of 1812 and became the first Democratic president in 1828. Jackson's close friend and associate, James Knox Polk (b. North Carolina, 1795–1849), was elected the nation's 11th president in 1844 and served one term. Andrew Johnson (b. North Carolina, 1808–1875), also a Democrat, remained loyal to the Union during the Civil War and was elected vice president with Abraham Lincoln in 1864. He became president upon Lincoln's assassination in 1865 and served out his predecessor's second term. Impeached because of a dispute over Reconstruction policies and presidential

White water rafting is a popular pursuit in Tennessee. Here, a group battles some rapids on the Ocoee River. © KENNSTILGER47/ SHUTTERSTOCK.COM.

power, Johnson escaped conviction by one vote in 1868.

Albert Arnold Gore Jr. (b. Washington, D.C., 1948–) was a senator from Tennessee before being elected to the vice presidency in 1992. Supreme Court justices from Tennessee include James C. McReynolds (b. Kentucky, 1862–1946) and Edward T. Sanford (1865–1930). Tennesseans who became cabinet officials include Secretary of State Cordell Hull (1871–1955) and Secretary of War John Eaton (1790–1856). Other nationally prominent political figures from Tennessee are Cary Estes Kefauver (1903–1963), two-term US senator who ran unsuccessfully for vice president

in 1956 on the Democratic ticket; Al Gore, Sr. (1907–1998), three-term member of the US Senate; and Howard Baker (1925–), who in 1966 became the first popularly elected Republican senator in Tennessee history. Nancy Ward (1738–1822) was an outstanding Cherokee leader, and Sue Shelton White (1887–1943) played a major role in the campaign for women's suffrage.

Tennessee history features several military leaders and combat heroes. John Sevier (b. Virginia, 1745–1815), the first governor of the state, defeated British troops at Kings Mountain during the Revolution. David "Davy" Crockett (1786–1836) was a frontiersman who

Singer Elvis Presley is still one of the most beloved entertainers today, many years after his death. © KEYSTONE PICTURES USA / ALAMY

literacy. Famous Tennessee writers include influential poet and critic John Crowe Ransom (1888–1974); author and critic James Agee (1909–1955), posthumously awarded a Pulitzer Prize for his novel *A Death in the Family*; poet Randall Jarrell (1914–1965), winner of two National Book Awards; and Wilma Dykeman (1920-2006), novelist and historian. Sportswriter Grantland Rice (1880–1954) was born in Murfreesboro. Basketball Hall of Fame member Oscar Robertson (1938–) and track and field legend Wilma Rudolph (1940–1994) were both born and raised in Tennessee.

Tennessee has long been a center of popular music, particularly in Nashville and Memphis. Musician and songwriter William C. Handy (1873–1958) wrote "St. Louis Blues" and "Memphis Blues," among other classics. Bessie Smith (1898?–1937) was a leading blues singer. Elvis Presley (b. Mississippi, 1935–1977) fused rhythm-and-blues with country-and-western styles to become one of the most popular entertainers ever. Tennessee-born singers include Tina Turner (1938–), Aretha Franklin (1942–), Dolly Parton (1946–), and Justin Timberlake (1981–). Actors Morgan Freeman (1937–) and Kathy Bates (1948–) were born in Memphis, and actress/singer Miley Cyrus (1992–) was born in Nashville.

fought the British with Jackson in the War of 1812 and later became a congressman. Nathan Bedford Forrest (1821–1877) and Sam Davis (1842–1863) were heroes of the Civil War.

Cordell Hull was awarded the Nobel Peace Prize in 1945 for his work on behalf of the United Nations. In 1971, Earl W. Sutherland Jr. (b. Kansas, 1915–1975), a biomedical scientist at Vanderbilt University, won a Nobel Prize for his discoveries concerning the mechanisms of hormones. Stanley Cohen (b. New York, 1922–) of Vanderbilt University won the Nobel Prize in medicine in 1986.

Sequoya (1770–1843) created an alphabet for the Cherokee language and promoted

40 Bibliography

BOOKS

Bristow, M. J. *State Songs of America*. Westport, CT: Greenwood Press, 2000.

Fenney, Kathy. *Tennessee Facts and Symbols*. Rev. ed. Mankato, MN: Capstone Press, 2003.

Finch, Jackie Sheckler. *Tennessee, Off the Beaten Path*, 9th ed. Guilford, CT: GPP Travel, 2009.

Lantier, Patricia. *Tennessee.* Milwaukee, WI: Gareth Stevens, 2006.

Sawyer, Susan. *It Happened in Tennessee: Remarkable Events that Shaped History.* 2nd ed. Guilford, CT: Globe Pequot Press, 2012.

Somervill, Barbara A. *Tennessee.* New York: Children's Press, 2009.

Temple, Oliver P. *East Tennessee and the Civil War.* Cincinnati, OH: R. Clarke Co., 1899. Reprint, Charleston, SC: Forgotten Books, 2012.

WEB SITES

"Economy at a Glance: Tennessee." *US Bureau of Labor Statistics.* http://www.bls.gov/eag/eag. tn.htm (accessed on November 16, 2012).

"Endangered Species Program." *US Fish & Wildlife Service.* http://www.fws.gov/endangered/ (accessed on November 16, 2012).

"State & County QuickFacts: Tennessee." *US Bureau of the Census.* http://quickfacts.census.gov/qfd/ states/47000.html (accessed on November 16, 2012).

Tennessee Department of Tourist Development. http:// www.state.tn.us/tourdev/ (accessed on November 16, 2012).

Tennessee Historical Society. http://www.tennesseehistory. org/ (accessed on November 16, 2012).

Tennessee Valley Authority. http://www.tva.gov/ (accessed on November 16, 2012).

TN.gov: Tennessee Government. http://www.tn.gov/ (accessed on November 16, 2012).

Texas

State of Texas

ORIGIN OF STATE NAME: Derived from *Tejas,* the Spanish pronunciation of the Caddo word *tayshas,* meaning "allies" or "friends."

NICKNAME: The Lone Star State.

CAPITAL: Austin.

ENTERED UNION: 29 December 1845 (28th).

OFFICIAL SEAL: A five-pointed star is encircled by olive and live oak branches, surrounded with the words "The State of Texas."

FLAG: At the hoist is a vertical bar of blue with a single white five-pointed star; a white horizontal bar above a red horizontal bar cover the remainder of the flag.

MOTTO: Friendship.

SONG: "Texas, Our Texas."

FLOWER: Bluebonnet; prickly pear cactus (plant).

TREE: Pecan.

BIRD: Mockingbird.

FISH: Guadalupe bass.

GEM: Texas blue topaz.

ROCK OR STONE: Petrified palmwood.

GRASS: Sideoats grama.

SHELL: Lightning whelk.

SPORT: Rodeo.

LEGAL HOLIDAYS: New Year's Day, 1 January; Confederate Heroes Day, 19 January; birthday of Martin Luther King Jr. Day, 3rd Monday in January; Presidents' Day, 3rd Monday in February; Texas Independence Day, 2 March; Cesar Chavez Day, 31 March (optional); Good Friday, Friday before Easter, March or April (optional); San Jacinto Day, 21 April; Memorial Day, last Monday in May; Emancipation Day in Texas, 19 June; Independence Day, 4 July; Lyndon Baines Johnson Day, 27 August; Labor Day, 1st Monday in September; Rosh Hashanah and Yom Kippur, September or October (optional); Veterans' Day, 11 November; Thanksgiving Day, 4th Thursday in November and the day following; Christmas, 24, 25, and 26 December.

TIME: 6 a.m. CST = noon GMT.

1 Location and Size

Located in the west south-central United States, Texas is the largest of the 48 conterminous states. The total area of Texas is 268,596 square miles (695,661 square kilometers), of which land comprises 261,231 square miles (676,586 square kilometers) and water covers 7,364 square miles (19,074 square kilometers).

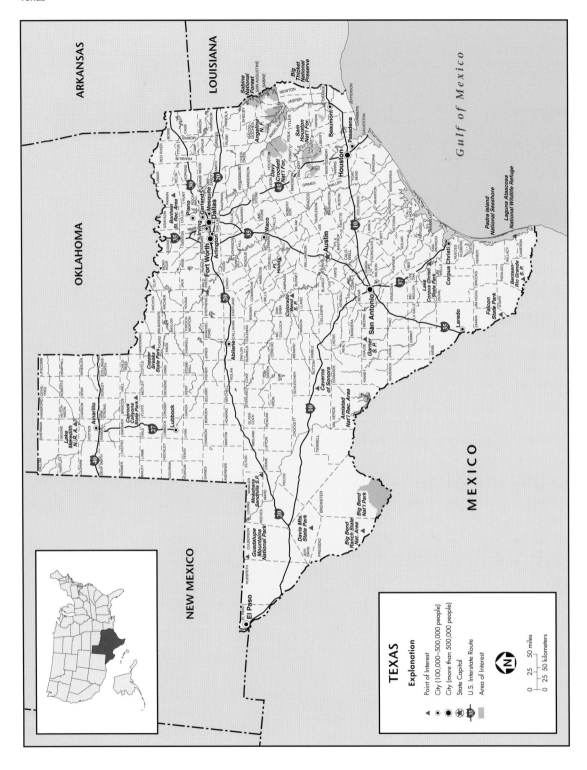

The state's maximum east–west extension is 801 miles (1,289 kilometers). Its extreme north–south distance is 773 miles (1,244 kilometers). The boundary length of the state totals 2,842 miles (7,360 kilometers), including a general Gulf of Mexico coastline of 367 miles (591 kilometers). Large islands in the Gulf of Mexico belonging to Texas are Galveston, Matagorda, and Padre.

2 Topography

Major regions in Texas are the Gulf Coastal Plain in the east and southeast; the North Central Plains, covering most of central Texas; the Great Plains, extending from west-central Texas up into the panhandle; and the mountainous trans-Pecos area in the extreme west. The Balcones Escarpment, a geological fault line running across central Texas, separates the Gulf Coastal and Rio Grande plains from the North Central Plains and south-central Hill Country. This fault line divides East Texas from West Texas, or watered Texas from dry Texas.

Much of the North Central Plains is rolling prairie, but the dude ranches of the Hill Country and the mineral-rich Burnet-Llano Basin are also found there. West of the Cap Rock Escarpment are the Great Plains, which stretch north–south from the Panhandle Plains to the Edwards Plateau, and which are just north of the Balcones Escarpment. The trans-Pecos region, between the Pecos River and the Rio Grande, contains the highest point in the state: Guadalupe Peak, with an altitude of 8,749 feet (2,668 meters).

Texas has few natural lakes, the largest being Caddo Lake, which lies in both Texas and Louisiana. Two artificial reservoirs are the Amistad (shared with Mexico) and Toledo Bend (shared with Louisiana). All together, the state contains nearly 200 major reservoirs (with a capacity of 5,000 acre-feet or larger) and more than 6,700 reservoirs total.

One reason Texas has so many reservoirs is that it has a number of major river systems, although none is navigable for more than 50 miles (80 kilometers) inland. Starting from the west, the Rio Grande, a majestic stream in some places but a trickling trough in others, imparts life to the Texas desert and serves as the international boundary with Mexico. Its total length of 1,896 miles (3,051 kilometers), including segments in Colorado and New Mexico, makes the Rio Grande one of the nation's longest rivers. It is exceeded only by the Missouri-Mississippi river system.

The Colorado River in Texas, which is not the same as the Colorado River that runs through the Southwest, is the longest river wholly within the state, extending about 865 miles (1,392 kilometers) on its journey across central and southeastern Texas to the Gulf of Mexico. The 12 other major rivers are the Pecos, the Nueces, the San Antonio, the Guadalupe, the Lavaca, the Brazos, the Trinity, the San Jacinto, the Neches, the Sabine, the Red, and the Canadian. Texas has more than 11,000 identifiable streams, many of which dry up in the summer and flood during periods of rainfall.

Underground limestone exists where a shallow sea covered central Texas about 100 million years ago. Caves formed where faults allowed rainwater to penetrate and dissolve the rock layers. The Caverns of Sonora, Inner Space Caverns, and Natural Bridge Caverns are among the seven show caverns equipped with trails and lighting. Eleven other "wild" caves offer guided tours to the public.

③ Climate

Generally, a maritime climate prevails along the Gulf Coast, with continental conditions inland. The Balcones Escarpment is the main dividing line between the two zones. Texas has two basic seasons: a hot summer that can last from April through October and a winter that starts in November and usually lasts until March. When summer ends, the state is too dry for autumn foliage, except in East Texas.

Temperatures in El Paso, in the southwest, range from an average January minimum of 31°F (0°C) to an average July maximum of 95°F (35°C). At Amarillo, in the panhandle, temperatures range from 22°F (-5°C) in January to 91°F (32°C) in July. At Galveston, on the Gulf, the range is from 48°F (9°C) in January to 88°F (31°C) in August. The record low temperature is -23°F (-31°C), recorded at Seminole on 8 February 1933. The record high is 120°F (49°C), recorded at Seymour, in north-central Texas, on 12 August 1936. That record was matched on 28 June 1994 in Monahans. Another startling contrast is in relative humidity, averaging 59% in the morning in El Paso, 73% in Amarillo, and 83% in Galveston.

Near the Louisiana border, rainfall exceeds 56 inches (142 centimeters) annually, while in parts of extreme West Texas, rainfall averages less than 8 inches (20 centimeters). Brownsville, at the mouth of the Rio Grande, has had no measurable snowfall during all the years that records have been kept. Vega, in the panhandle, averages 23 inches (58 centimeters) of snowfall a year.

In 2011, Texas had the warmest summer on record for any state. With an average summer temperature of 86.8°F (30.4°C), Texas just beat out Oklahoma's average of 86.5°F (30.3°C) that same summer. Both these averages surpassed the previous record of 85.2°F (29.6°C), which had been held by Oklahoma since 1934. With only 2.44 inches (6.2 centimeters) of rain, Texas also experienced its driest summer on record.

Texas is ranked second for the most hurricanes, with 63 tropical storms, including 19 major ones, making landfall since 1851. (Florida has had twice as many hurricanes.) The Galveston Hurricane of 1900, which claimed more than 6,000 lives, remains the deadliest. The highest sustained wind velocity in Texas history, 145 miles per hour (233 kilometers/hour), occurred when Hurricane Carla hit Matagorda and Port Lavaca along the Gulf Coast on 11 September 1961. On 28 August 2005, Hurricane Katrina flooded approximately 80 percent of New Orleans and caused damage to Texas-operated oil production sites in the Gulf of Mexico. This Category 3 hurricane claimed more than 1,800 lives.

Although hurricanes usually strike the Gulf Coast about once every decade, the next month, Hurricane Rita made landfall just east of Sabine Pass, Texas. Damages from the storm were estimated at $8 billion and the death toll was over 100 people. Just three years later, Hurricane Ike swept through Galveston Island on 13 September 2008. A 13-foot (4-meter) wall of water swept away nearly all vegetation, including lawns. The wind speeds were just below the 110 miles per hour (177 kilometers per hour) needed for a Category 3 ranking. Hundreds of miles of the Texas Gulf Coast were affected by the storm surge.

Besides droughts and hurricanes taking their toll in Texas, the state also lies in the path of "Tornado Alley," stretching across the Great Plains to Canada. On 11 May 1953, one of the state's deadliest tornadoes in the last century swept across Waco, killing 14 people and injuring approximately 600 others. The tornado destroyed about 600 homes and buildings and damaged another 1,000 buildings and 2,000 vehicles. Another strong tornado in Texas hit Jarrell on 27 May 1997, killing 27 people and removing 40 homes from their foundations.

4 Plants and Animals

Grassy pastureland covers about two-thirds of the state. Bermuda grass is a favorite ground cover. The prickly pear cactus saps moisture from the soil and inhibits grass growth, but it does retain moisture in periods of drought and will survive the worst dry spells, so (with the spines burned off) it can be of great value to ranchers as cattle feed in difficult times. The bean of the mesquite also provides food for horses and cattle when they have little else to eat and its wood is a favorite in barbecues and fireplaces.

Texas has more than 20 native trees, of which several, including the catclaw, flowering mimosa, and weeping juniper, are common only in Texas. Cottonwood grows along streams in almost every part of the state, while cypress inhabits the swamps. The flowering dogwood in East Texas draws tourists to that region every spring. Probably the most popular shade tree is the American (white) elm. The magnolia is treasured for its grace and beauty. The pecan is the state tree. Pines grow in East Texas and the trans-Pecos region. Gonzales County, in south-central Texas, is the home of palmettos, orchids, and other semitropical plants not found anywhere else in the state.

In 2012, there were 29 plant species occurring in Texas that were listed on the US Fish and Wildlife Service's list of threatened or endangered species, including the ashy dogweed, black lace cactus, large-fruited sand-verbena, South Texas ambrosia, Terlingua Creek cats-eye, Texas snowbells, Texas trailing phlox, and Texas wild-rice.

The nine-banded armadillo, the state animal, has gradually spread northward and eastward, crossing the Red and Mississippi rivers into the Deep South by sucking in air until it becomes buoyant and then swimming across the water. The armadillo is also notable for always having its young in litters of identical quadruplets. The chief predatory mammals are the coyote, bobcat, and mountain lion.

Texas attracts more than 825 different kinds of birds, with bird life most abundant in the lower Rio Grande Valley and coastal plains. Characteristic birds include the scissor-tailed flycatcher; Attwater's greater prairie chicken; the mockingbird, which is the state bird; and the roadrunner. The Gulf Coast is the winter nesting ground for the whooping crane. The golden eagle became federally protected in 1963 after Texas ranchers killed 20,000 of the species that allegedly preyed on lambs and other young livestock. Texas has its fair share of reptiles, including more than 100 species of snakes, 16 of them poisonous, notably the deadly Texas coral snake. There are 10 kinds of rattlesnake, and some parts of West Texas hold annual rattlesnake roundups.

In 2012, the US Fish and Wildlife Service listed 56 animal species occurring in Texas as threatened or endangered, including the Mexican long-nosed bat, ocelot, Texas blind salamander, Houston toad, black-capped vireo, two species of whale, and three species of turtle. Among the state's 18 National Wildlife Refuges, Caddo Lake is a Ramsar Wetland of International Importance.

5 Environmental Protection

The scarcity of water is the major environmental crisis in the state. Much of Texas has absorbent soil, a high evaporation rate, vast areas without trees to hold moisture, and a rolling terrain susceptible to rapid runoff. The Texas Water Commission and Water Development Board direct the state's water supply and conservation programs. The Lower Colorado River Authority was created in 1934 by the Texas legislature to "control, store, preserve, and distribute" the waters of the Colorado River and its feeder streams. The authority exercises control over a 10-county area stretching from above Austin to the Gulf Coast, overseeing flood control, municipal and industrial water supplies, irrigation, hydroelectric power generation, soil conservation, and recreation.

Since the Railroad Commission of Texas (RRC) regulates the oil, gas, and mining industries in the state, it is involved with oil spills and other situations in which the operations of these industries negatively impact the environment. Originally established in 1891 to regulate railroads, the commission extended its power to regulate oil and natural gas by virtue of its jurisdiction over the transportation of those products by rail and pipeline. The RRC's power continued to expand into gas utilities in 1920, buses and trucks in 1931, liquefied petroleum gas in 1939, and mining in 1976. After the federal government took over the regulation of transportation in 1984, the RCC continued to focus on regulation of the oil and gas industry in Texas. As of 2011, the RCC's four divisions included oil and gas, gas services (gas utilities), pipeline safety, and surface mining and reclamation.

As in other states, hazardous waste has become an environmental concern in Texas. The

**Texas
Population Profile**

Total population per Census 2010:	25,145,561
Population change, 2006–10:	7.0%
Hispanic or Latino†:	37.6%
Population by race	
One race:	97.3%
White:	70.4%
Black or African American:	11.8%
American Indian/Alaska Native:	0.7%
Asian:	3.8%
Native Hawaiian/Pacific Islander:	0.1%
Some other race:	10.5%
Two or more races:	2.7%

Population by Age Group, Census 2010

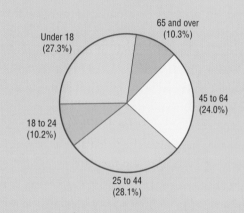

Major Cities by Population, 2011 Estimates

City	Population	% change 2005–11
Houston	2,145,146	6.4
San Antonio	1,359,758	8.2
Dallas	1,223,229	0.8
Austin	820,611	18.9
Fort Worth	758,738	21.6
El Paso	665,568	11.2
Arlington	373,698	3.0
Corpus Christi	307,953	8.6
Plano	269,776	7.9
Laredo	241,935	12.3

Notes: †A person of Hispanic or Latino origin may be of any race. NA indicates that data are not available. Percentages may not equal 100 due to rounding.

SOURCE: U.S. Census Bureau. Census 2010 and Population Estimates. www.census.gov/ (accessed July 2012).

Texas Population by Race
CENSUS 2010

This table shows the number of people who are of one, two, or three or more races. For those claiming two races, the number of people belonging to the various categories is listed. The U.S. government conducts a census of the population every 10 years.

	Number	Percent
Total population	25,145,561	100.0
One race	24,466,560	97.3
Two races	642,522	2.6
White *and* Black or African American	109,713	0.4
White *and* American Indian/Alaska Native	92,305	0.4
White *and* Asian	91,963	0.4
White *and* Native Hawaiian/Pacific Islander	6,898	—
White *and* some other race	240,679	1.0
Black or African American *and* American Indian/Alaska Native	13,834	0.1
Black or African American *and* Asian	11,132	—
Black or African American *and* Native Hawaiian/Pacific Islander	2,368	—
Black or African American *and* some other race	28,414	0.1
American Indian/Alaska Native *and* Asian	3,690	—
American Indian/Alaska Native *and* Native Hawaiian/Pacific Islander	468	—
American Indian/Alaska Native *and* some other race	13,156	0.1
Asian *and* Native Hawaiian/Pacific Islander	4,945	—
Asian *and* some other race	18,536	0.1
Native Hawaiian/Pacific Islander *and* some other race	4,421	—
Three or more races	36,479	0.1

SOURCE: U.S. Census Bureau. Census 2010. www.census/gov/ (accessed July 2012). A dash (—) indicates that the percent is less than 0.1.

agency that oversees compliance with hazardous waste statutes is the Hazardous and Solid Waste Division of the Texas Water Commission. In 2012, there were 50 hazardous waste sites listed on the US Environmental Protection Agency's National Priorities List. These include numerous disposal pits and groundwater plumes, as well as two army ammunition plants.

The three agencies that define wetlands provide different figures for the total wetlands in the state, with estimates ranging from about 6 million acres (2.4 million hectares) to 8 million acres (3.2 million hectares).

6 Population

In 2011, Texas ranked second among the 50 states in population, with an estimated total of 25,674,681. Texas has a relatively young population, with a median age of 33.7. Approximately 27.1% of the state's population was under 18 years of age, while 10.5% were 65 or older. The state's population is expected to reach 30,865,134 in 2025. The population density in 2010 was 105 persons per square mile (40.5 persons per square kilometer).

Houston was the largest city in the state and the fourth-largest city in the country with an estimated population of 2,145,146 (metro area, 6,086,538) in 2011. Other big cities in Texas were San Antonio, 1,359,758 (seventh in the United States); Dallas, 1,223,229 (ninth in the United States); Austin, 820,611; Fort Worth, 758,738; and El Paso, 665,568. In 2010, 89% of the state's population lived in metropolitan areas.

7 Ethnic Groups

Certain areas of central Texas are heavily Germanic and Czech. The first permanent Polish colony in the United States was established at Panna Maria, near San Antonio, in 1854. Texas has one of the largest colonies of Wends in the world, principally at Serbin in central Texas. Significant numbers of Danes, Swedes, and Norwegians have also settled in the state.

According to the 2010 Census, Hispanics and Latinos, mostly of Mexican ancestry, were the largest minority in Texas, with about 9,460,921 people, representing about 37.6% of the population. The 2,979,598 black Americans represented 11.8% of the population. Texas had the third-largest Asian population (behind California and New York) with 964,596 residents, or 3.8% of the state's population. There were also 170,972 Native Americans and Alaska Natives (0.7%) as well as 21,656 Native Hawaiians and Pacific Islanders (0.1%) living in Texas. In the period 2006–10, foreign-born residents in Texas averaged about 16% of the total population, as compared to the national average of 12.7%.

8 Languages

Most of the regional features in Texas English derive from the influx of South Midland and Southern speakers. There is a noticeable Spanish flavor from older as well as more recent word-borrowing. Texas pronunciation is largely South Midland.

Spanish has been the major foreign language influence. In areas like Laredo and Brownsville, along the Rio Grande, as many as 90% of the people may be bilingual. In northeast Texas, however, Spanish is as foreign as French. In the days of the early Spanish ranchers, standard English adopted *hacienda, ranch, burro, canyon,* and *lariat.* The presence of the large Spanish-speaking population was a major factor in the passage of the state's bilingual education law, which requires that numerous school programs be offered in both English and Spanish.

In 2011, some 65.3% of state residents five years old or older spoke only English at home. Some 29.5% spoke Spanish, 2% spoke another Indo-European language, and 2.5% spoke an Asian or Pacific Islander language.

9 Religions

When Texas was under the Mexican Republic, the Catholic Church was the sole recognized religious body; however, many Baptists, Methodists, and Presbyterians drifted in from the east. Today, Texas tends to be heavily Protestant in the north and east, and Catholic in the south and southwest. According to the Pew Forum on Religion & Public Life, in 2008, 57% of Texas's population was Protestant, while Roman Catholics represented 24%. Approximately 12% was not affiliated with any religious organization. Mormons, Jehovah's Witnesses, Buddhists, Hindus, and those in the Jewish tradition were each about 1% of the population.

10 Transportation

Transportation has been a severe problem for Texas because of the state's extraordinary size and sometimes difficult terrain. One of the more unusual experiments in US transport history was the use of camels in southwestern Texas during the mid-1800s.

Railroad travel became important for many years and total rail mileage in Texas still ranks higher than any other state, with more than 14,000 rail miles (22,500 kilometers) in 2009. The only rail passenger service in Texas is provided by Amtrak, which runs two routes: the Sunset Limited (New Orleans–Los Angeles) from Beaumont through Houston and San Antonio to El Paso, and the Texas Eagle (Chicago–San Antonio). There were 45 railroads in the state in 2009, including three Class I freight railroads.

In 2009, Texas had about 311,000 miles (500,506 kilometers) of public roadway, as compared to 303,000 miles (487,000 kilometers) five years prior. The leading interstates are I-10 and I-20, respectively linking Houston and the Dallas–Fort Worth areas with El Paso in the west, and I-35 and I-45, connecting Dallas–Fort Worth with, respectively, San Antonio (via Austin) and Galveston (via Houston). In 2009, the state had more than 15.3 million licensed drivers and more than 18 million licensed motor vehicles, including 8.7 million registered automobiles, 435,000 motorcycles, and 9 million trucks. Texas ranks second, behind California, in both number of drivers and vehicles. According to the US Department of Transportation, there were 3,071 highway fatalities in Texas in 2009, of which 1,235 involved alcohol.

River transport did not become commercially successful until the end of the 19th century, when the Houston Ship Channel was dredged along the San Jacinto River and Buffalo Bayou and another channel was dredged down the Neches River to make a seaport out of Beaumont. With 13 major seaports and many shallow-water ports, Texas has been a major factor in waterborne commerce since the early 1950s. The Port of Houston is the nation's second most active harbor. The Gulf Intracoastal Waterway begins in Brownsville at the mouth of the Rio Grande and extends across Texas to Florida where it connects with a similar waterway on the Atlantic. Up to 90 million tons (81.6 million tonnes) of cargo cross the 423-mile (680-kilometer) stretch across Texas each year.

After American entry into World War I, Texas began to build airfields for training grounds. When the war ended, many US fliers returned to Texas and became civilian commercial pilots, carrying air mail (from 1926), dusting crops, and mapping potential oil fields. In 2009, the state had 1,441 airports, including more than 300 public-use airports, 15 commercial airports, and 538 heliports. Dallas/Fort Worth International Airport ranked 10th worldwide and 4th nationally with 26,606,411 passenger enplanements in 2009. George Bush Intercontinental Airport in Houston was the seventh-busiest airport in the nation that year, with 19,285,930 passenger enplanements.

11 History

When the first Europeans arrived in the 16th century, the Native Americans in present-day Texas were still largely hunter-gatherers. Along the Gulf Coast and overlapping into northeastern Mexico were the Coahuiltecan and Karankawa peoples. In central Texas lived the Tonkawa, who hunted buffalo and used dogs for hauling. They proved extremely susceptible to European diseases and evidently died out, whereas the Karankawa migrated to northern Mexico.

About two dozen tribes of Caddo in eastern and northeastern Texas were, at the time of

European penetration, the most technologically advanced Native Americans living within the state's present borders. Having developed agriculture, the Caddo were relatively sedentary and village-oriented. Those belonging to the Hasinai Confederation called each other *tayshas,* a term that translates as "allies" or "friends." When the Hasinai told Spanish explorers that they were *tayshas,* the Spaniards wrote the word as *Tejas,* which in time became *Texas.*

In trans-Pecos Texas to the west, a fourth tribal group, the Jumano, lived. They were probably descendants of the Pueblo cultures. Some of the Jumano were nomadic hunters in the Davis and Chisos mountains, while others became farmers along the Rio Grande and the lower Rio Conchos.

Spanish Settlement The first European to enter Texas was Spanish explorer Alonso Alvarez de Piñeda, who sailed into the mouth of the Rio Grande in 1519. For more than 150 years, the Spanish had little interest in Texas, regarding it as too remote for successful settlement. Their attitude toward the colonization of Texas was changed, however, by fear of competition from the French with the establishment of Fort St. Louis by René-Robert Cavelier, Sieur de la Salle (1643–1687) on the Gulf Coast in 1685. Four years later, Captain Alonso de León, governor of Coahuila, sent out an expedition to expel the French and establish both a fort and a mission.

During the next several decades, a string of mission-forts were built across Texas. After fear of the French presence eased, Spain tended to neglect these establishments. But when the French entered Louisiana in force during the early 18th century, Spanish fears of French expansion were reignited. In 1718, the Spanish established a presence at the site of the present city of San Antonio. As a halfway post between Mexico and the Louisiana border, San Antonio grew to be the region's most important city during the Spanish period.

Mexican State Until the 19th century, the United States showed little interest in Texas. But the purchase of Louisiana Territory from the French by the US government in 1803 made Texas a next-door neighbor. "Filibusters" (military adventurers) began to filter across the border into Spanish territory. In 1810–11, the Mexicans launched their revolution against Spain, and though only an outpost, Texas as a Spanish-Mexican colony was naturally involved, becoming a Mexican state in 1813.

The Spanish finally gave up on Mexico in 1821, leaving Texas as a Mexican province with a European population of about 7,000. A year earlier, Moses Austin of Missouri had received permission from Spanish authorities to introduce Anglo-American colonists into Texas, presumably as a barrier against aggression by the United States. When Spanish rule ended, his son, Stephen F. Austin, secured permission from the new Mexican government to settle 300 families in the area between the lower Colorado and Brazos rivers. Other colonizers made similar arrangements to settle Anglo-Americans in the region. Texas thus began a pattern of growth through migration that has continued to the present day.

Most new settlers were non-Hispanics who often distrusted Mexico. They disliked Mexican culture and government; the Protestants among them disliked the dominance of the Roman Catholic Church. The incompetence of the Mexican government made the situation even worse. Troubled by a rising spirit of rebellion, the Mexican Congress enacted the Law of 1830, which forbade most immigration and imposed duties on all imports.

The Texas Revolution In the early 1830s, skirmishes began between Anglo-Texans and Mexicans. When Mexican president Antonio López de Santa Anna tried to enforce customs collections, colonists at Anahuac drove Mexican officials out of town. Santa Anna's answer was to place Texas under military jurisdiction. On 2 October 1835, Anglo-Texan civilians at Gonzalez defeated the forces of Colonel Domingo de Ugartechea in a battle that is generally considered to mark the start of the Texas Revolution.

Texas sent three envoys to Washington, D.C., to request aid from the United States. Sam Houston, who six years earlier had resigned the governorship of Tennessee, was named commander in chief of the upstart Texas army. In February 1836, Santa Anna led an army across the Rio Grande. The Mexicans concentrated outside San Antonio near a mission-fort called the Alamo. There, 187 or so Texans, commanded by Colonel William Barret Travis, had taken shelter. The Mexicans besieged the Alamo until 6 March, when Santa Anna's forces, now numbering more than 4,000, stormed the fortress. When the battle ended, all the Alamo's defenders, including several native Mexicans, were dead. Among those killed were Travis and two Americans who became legends—James Bowie and Davy Crockett.

On 27 March 1836, three weeks after the Alamo fell, the Mexicans killed 342 Texans after they had surrendered at Goliad, thinking they would be treated as prisoners of war. Coming on the heels of the Alamo tragedy, the "Goliad

The Alamo in San Antonio is considered sacred ground in Texas. © ROB WILSON/SHUTTERSTOCK.COM.

massacre" impelled Texans to seek total victory over Mexico. On 21 April, the Texans surprised the Mexicans during their siesta period at San Jacinto. Mexican losses were 630 killed, 280 wounded, and 730 taken prisoner, while the Texans had only 9 killed and 30 wounded. This decisive battle—fought to the cry of "Remember the Alamo, remember Goliad!"—freed Texas from Mexico once and for all.

The Republic of Texas and US Statehood For 10 years, Texas existed as an independent republic, recognized by the United States and several European nations. Sam Houston, the victorious commander at San Jacinto, became the republic's first nationally elected president. Strife-torn and short of cash, Texas joined the Union on 29 December 1845. The US annexation of Texas was largely responsible for the Mexican War, which was ended on 2 February 1848 by the Treaty of Guadalupe Hidalgo, under which Mexico dropped its claim to the territory between the Rio Grande and the Nueces River.

With the coming of the Civil War (1861–65), Texas followed its pro-slavery Southern neighbors out of the Union into the Confederacy. The state, which saw little fighting, suffered from the war far less than most of the South. During Reconstruction, Texas was governed briefly by a military occupation force and then by a Republican regime.

While most of the South was economically devastated, the Texas economy flourished because of the rapid development of the cattle industry. The widespread use of barbed wire to fence cattle ranches in the 1880s ended the open range and encouraged scientific cattle breeding. By 1900, Texas began to transform its predominantly agricultural economy into an industrial one.

Oil and Politics The process from agricultural to industrial was hastened by the discovery of the Spindletop oil field—the state's first gusher—near Beaumont in 1901, and by the subsequent development of the petroleum and petrochemical industries. World War I (1914–18) saw the emergence of Texas as a military training center. The rapid growth of the aircraft industry and other high-technology fields contributed to the continuing industrialization of the state during and after World War II (1939–45).

Texas politics remained solidly Democratic during most of the modern era, and the significant political conflict in the state was between the liberal and conservative wings of the Democratic Party. During the 1960s and 1970s, the Republican Party gathered strength in the state, electing John G. Tower as US senator in 1961 and William P. Clements Jr. as governor in 1978—the first Republicans to hold those offices since Reconstruction. Since then, the Republican Party has remained dominant.

On the national level, Texans have been influential since the 1930s, notably through such congressional leaders as US House Speaker Sam Rayburn and Senate Majority Leader Lyndon B. Johnson. Elected vice president under John F. Kennedy, Johnson was riding in the motorcade when Kennedy was assassinated in Dallas on 22 November 1963. Johnson, a Democrat, served out the remainder of Kennedy's term, then was himself elected to the presidency by a landslide in 1964. Johnson retired to his LBJ ranch in 1969.

The most prominent Texans on the national scene since Johnson are Republicans George H. W. Bush (who served as vice president for eight years under Ronald Reagan before being elected to the presidency in 1988) and his son George W. Bush (who won the presidency in 2000 and was reelected in 2004). George H. W. Bush was defeated by Bill Clinton in his 1992 bid for reelection.

Oil and Economics Texas benefited from a booming oil industry in the 1970s, but the boom collapsed in the early 1980s as overproduction caused world oil prices to drop. The government estimated that it lost $100 million in revenues for every one dollar decline in the price of a barrel of oil. To replace this lost revenue, the government in 1985 imposed or raised fees on everything from vanity license plates to day care centers. The state also took steps to encourage economic diversification by soliciting service, electronics, and high-technology companies to come to Texas.

In the late 1980s, a number of the state's financial institutions collapsed, brought down by the slump in the oil industry and unsound real estate loans. However, after 1986, oil prices increased and the state reaped the benefits of diversification efforts spurred by the oil price collapse. Although the petroleum industry was still the state's leading economic sector in the mid-1990s, high-technology and service sector jobs had played a major role in rebuilding the Texas economy.

In the early 2000s, Texas had the second-largest population of any state, behind California. The high rate of migration into Texas, which accompanied the oil boom, had a profound effect on the state's population distribution and political profile. Newcomers to the state have tended to share the fiscally conservative values of native Texans but are more liberal on other social issues such as civil rights.

In November 2000, George W. Bush was elected the 43rd president of the United States. He was raised in Midland, Texas, where he was active in the oil business before becoming governor of the state in 1994.

In early 2003, a redistricting plan brought before the state house of representatives caused controversy among Texas politicians. The redistricting plan initially favored the Republicans already in office. In efforts to stop the plan from becoming law, several of the Democratic representatives left Texas to prevent the quorum necessary to place a vote on the measure. After they used this same tactic later in the year, Governor Rick Perry called a special legislative session to consider the redistricting measures. Absent senators filed a lawsuit against this move, but eventually lost to a Supreme Court judgment in 2004.

An explosion on a BP-operated oil rig in the Gulf of Mexico on 15 July 2010, which killed 11 men and injured 17 others, resulted in the largest marine oil spill in US history. Before the wellhead was successfully capped three months later, nearly 5 million barrels of crude oil was released. According to the National Wildlife Federation, more than 8,000 birds, sea turtles, and marine mammals were injured or killed by the spreading oil. Recreational fishing was shut down for four months and commercial fishing faced long-term consequences from reduced marine populations. With currents carrying the oil toward Florida, Texas beaches were not closed over the summer, although tar balls did come ashore in July on several beaches.

In 2011, a severe drought fueled more than 30,400 wildfires that swept throughout the state. Approximately 4 million acres (1.6 million hectares) were destroyed, nearly doubling the previous record of 2.1 million acres (0.8 million hectares) burned in 2006. Nearly 3,000 homes were destroyed along with more than 2,700 other structures.

12 State Government

Texas has been governed by five constitutions since statehood, the last of which was ratified in 1876. Since that time, the Texas legislature has proposed more than 600 amendments, of which 474 were approved as of March 2012.

The state legislature consists of a senate of 31 members elected to four-year terms, and a house of representatives of 150 members elected to two-year terms. The state's chief executives are the governor and lieutenant governor, separately elected to four-year terms. Other elected executives include the attorney general, comptroller, and treasurer. There are no gubernatorial term limits.

To become law, a bill must be approved by a majority of members present and voting in each house, with a quorum of two-thirds of the membership present. The bill must then be signed by the governor or left unsigned for 10 days while the legislature is in session or 20 days after it has adjourned. A governor's veto may be overridden by a two-thirds vote of members present in the house of the bill's origin, followed by either a vote of two-thirds of members present in the house of representatives or two-thirds of the entire membership of the senate.

As of 2010, legislators received a salary of $7,200 per year; the governor's salary was $150,000 in 2012.

Texas Governors: 1846–2013

Years	Governor	Party	Years	Governor	Party
1846–1847	James Pinckney Henderson	Democrat	1915–1917	James Edward Ferguson	Democrat
1847–1849	George Thomas Wood	Democrat	1917–1921	William Pettus Hobby	Democrat
1849–1853	Peter Hasbrough Bell	Democrat	1921–1925	Patrick Morris Neff	Democrat
1853	James Wilson Henderson	Democrat	1925–1927	Miriam Amanda Ferguson	Democrat
1853–1857	Elisha Marshall Pease	Democrat	1927–1931	Daniel J. Moody	Democrat
1857–1859	Hardin Richard Runnels	Democrat	1931–1933	Ross Shaw Sterling	Democrat
1859–1861	Samuel Houston	Democrat	1933–1935	Miriam Amanda Ferguson	Democrat
1861	Edward Clark	Democrat	1935–1939	James V. Allred	Democrat
1861–1863	Francis Richard Lubbock	Democrat	1939–1941	Wilbert Lee O'Daniel	Democrat
1863–1865	Pendleton Murrah	Democrat	1941–1947	Coke Robert Stevenson	Democrat
1865	Fletcher S. Stockdale	Democrat	1947–1949	Beauford Halbert Jester	Democrat
1865–1866	Andrew Jackson Hamilton	Indep-Dem	1949–1957	Allan Shivers	Democrat
1866–1867	James Webb Throckmorton	Conservative	1957–1963	Price Marion Daniel	Democrat
1867–1869	Elisha Marshall Pease	Democrat	1963–1969	John Bowden Connally	Democrat
1870–1874	Edmund Jackson Davis	Rep-Prov	1969–1973	Preston Earnest Smith	Democrat
1874–1876	Richard Coke	Democrat	1973–1979	Dolph Briscoe, Jr.	Democrat
1876–1879	Richard Bennett Hubbard	Democrat	1979–1983	William Perry Clements, Jr.	Republican
1879–1883	Oran Milo Roberts	Democrat	1983–1987	Mark White	Democrat
1883–1887	John Ireland	Democrat	1987–1991	William Perry Clements, Jr.	Republican
1887–1891	Lawrence Sullivan Ross	Democrat	1991–1995	Ann Richards	Democrat
1891–1895	James Stephen Hogg	Democrat	1995–2000	George W. Bush	Republican
1895–1899	Charles Allen Culberson	Democrat	2000–	Rick Perry	Republican
1899–1903	Joseph Draper Sayers	Democrat			
1903–1907	Samuel Willis Tucker Lanham	Democrat			
1907–1911	Thomas Mitchell Campbell	Democrat	Independent Democrat – Indep-Dem		
1911–1915	Oscar Branch Colquitt	Democrat	Republican Provisional – Rep-Prov		

13 Political Parties

Until the last few decades, the Democratic Party had dominated politics in Texas. William P. Clements Jr., elected governor in 1978, was the first Republican since Reconstruction to hold that office. No Republican carried Texas in a presidential election until 1928, when Herbert Hoover defeated Democrat Al Smith, a Roman Catholic who was at a severe disadvantage in a largely Protestant state. Another Roman Catholic, Democratic presidential candidate John F. Kennedy, carried the state in 1960 largely because he had a Texan, Lyndon B. Johnson, on his ticket.

Republican and native son George H. W. Bush captured 56% of the vote in the 1988 presidential election and 41% in the 1992 election. In 2000, Texans gave another native son, Republican George W. Bush, 59% of the vote. Democratic candidate Al Gore received 38%. In the 2004 presidential election, Bush won 61.2% of the vote while Democrat John Kerry received 38%. The Republicans continued to dominate in Texas with John McCain receiving 55% of the vote in 2008, although he lost the presidential election to Democratic candidate Barack Obama. In 2012, Texas voters again favored the Republican candidate, Mitt Romney, over President Obama. The state has had 34 electoral votes in the presidential election since 2001.

In the November 1994 gubernatorial elections, George W. Bush upset Ann Richards to become governor. Bush won a resounding re-election in 1998 before leaving to run for president. Lt. Governor Rick Perry took over for Bush in 2000 and was elected to a full term in 2002. Perry was reelected in 2006 and 2010. He entered the 2012 presidential candidate race but dropped out in January of that year.

In 1993, Republican Kay Bailey Hutchison was elected to the US Senate to fill the seat vacated by Democratic senator Lloyd Bentsen, who resigned to become secretary of the Treasury in the Clinton administration. Hutchinson resigned in 2012 and was replaced by Republican Ted Cruz. Republican John Cornyn was elected to the US Senate in 2002 and reelected in 2008. Following the November 2012 elections, Texas Republicans held 24 seats in the US House of Representatives and the Democrats held 12 seats. In 2010, the Republicans controlled the state senate and house by a two-thirds margin. The senate was composed of 19 Republications and 12 Democrats, while 101 of the 150 seats in the house were held by Republicans. In 2012, there were 31 women serving in the state house, and six women serving in the state senate.

**Texas Presidential Vote
by Major Political Parties, 1948–2012**

Year	Texas Winner	Democrat	Republican
1948	*Truman (D)	750,700	282,240
1952	*Eisenhower (R)	969,227	1,102,818
1956	*Eisenhower (R)	859,958	1,080,619
1960	*Kennedy (D)	1,167,935	1,121,693
1964	*Johnson (D)	1,663,185	958,566
1968	Humphrey (D)	1,266,804	1,227,844
1972	*Nixon (R)	1,154,289	2,298,896
1976	*Carter (D)	2,082,319	1,953,300
1980	*Reagan (R)	1,881,147	2,510,705
1984	*Reagan (R)	1,949,276	3,433,428
1988	*Bush (R)	2,352,748	3,036,829
1992	Bush (R)	2,281,815	2,496,071
1996	Dole (R)	2,549,683	2,736,167
2000	*Bush, G. W. (R)	2,433,746	3,799,639
2004	*Bush, G. W. (R)	2,832,704	4,526,917
2008	McCain (R)	3,528,633	4,479,328
2012	Romney (R)	3,308,124	4,569,843

*Won US presidential election.

Independent candidate Ross Perot received 1,354,781 votes in 1992 and 378,537 votes in 1996.

Third parties have generally played a minor role in Texas politics. In 1968, George Wallace of the American Independent Party won 19% of the Texas popular vote and in 1992, native son Ross Perot ran independently and picked up 22% of the vote. As of May 2012, there were 13,065,425 registered voters in the state.

14 Local Government

The Texas constitution grants considerable autonomy to local governments. As of 2010, Texas has 254 counties, a number that has remained constant since 1931. The state also has 956 cities, 234 towns, 24 villages, and 1,036 public school districts. There were 2,291 special districts in the state in 2007. Each county is governed by a commissioner's court. Other elected officials generally include a county clerk, attorney, and treasurer. Texas has three federally recognized American Indian reservations. In 2011, there were 1,345,401 full-time and 278,765 part-time state and local government workers in Texas.

15 Judicial System

The Texas judiciary comprises the supreme court, the state court of criminal appeals, 14 courts of appeals, and more than 380 district courts. The highest court is the supreme court, consisting of a chief justice and eight associate justices. The court of criminal appeals, which has final jurisdiction in most criminal cases, consists of a presiding judge and eight associate judges. Justices of the courts of appeals sit in 14 judicial districts; each court has a chief justice and at least 2 associate justices. County, justice of the peace, and municipal courts handle local matters.

In 2010, Texas had a violent crime rate of 450.3 reported incidents per 100,000 people. The murder and nonnegligent manslaughter rate was 5.0 incidents per 100,000 inhabitants; forcible rape, 30.3; aggravated assault, 284.4; and property crime, 3,783.0. The population of Texas federal and state prisons in 2010 was 231,186 inmates. Texas has the death penalty and leads the nation in the number of executions, with 484 executions since 1976. The state carried out 17 executions in 2010, 13 in 2011, and 5 in the first half of 2012. Some 308 people were on death row in Texas, including 10 women, in 2012.

16 Migration

Estimates of the number of Native Americans living in Texas when the first Europeans arrived range from 30,000 to 130,000. Eventually, most were killed, fled southward or westward, or were removed to reservations. The first great wave of white settlers, beginning in 1821, came from nearby southern states, particularly Tennessee, Alabama, Arkansas, and Mississippi. Some of these newcomers brought their black slaves to work in the cotton fields. During the 1840s, a second wave of immigrants arrived directly from Germany, France, and eastern Europe.

Interstate migration during the second half of the 19th century was accelerated by the Homestead Act of 1862 and the westward march of the railroads. When the onset of World War II led to a shortage of laborers, the federal government formed the Emergency Farm Labor Program in 1942. Consequently, a significant proportion of post-World War II immigrants were seasonal laborers from Mexico, remaining in the United States either legally or illegally.

The US Department of Homeland Security reported approximately 863,500 foreign-born persons obtained legal permanent residence in Texas during the first decade of the 21st century. Of the more than one million foreign-born persons who obtained legal permanent residence in the United States during 2011, about 94,500 resided in Texas.

Between 2009 and 2010, the total population (ages one and older) of Texas increased by 246,934, due to the net domestic in-migration of natives (53,555), the net domestic in-migration of immigrants (21,362), and the arrival from abroad of natives (63,074) and immigrants (108,943). Of the total foreign-born population in Texas in 2010, 3.3% were from Africa, 18.6% were from Asia, 4.2% were from Europe, and 72.8% were from Latin America. The top three countries of birth of the foreign born in Texas that year were Mexico (60%), El Salvador (4.1%), and India (4%). In comparison, the top three countries of birth in 1990 were Mexico (59.4%), Vietnam (3.6%), and El Salvador (3.1%).

17 Economy

Traditionally, the Texas economy has been dependent on the production of cotton, cattle, timber, and petroleum. But in the 1970s, as a result of rising world petroleum prices, oil and natural gas emerged as the state's most important resource. The decades since World War II have also witnessed a boom in the electronics, computer, transport equipment, aerospace, and communications industries, which has placed Texas second only to California in manufacturing among all the states of the Sunbelt region.

In 1982, however, Texas began to be affected by worldwide recession. In addition, lower energy demand, worldwide overproduction of oil, and the resulting fall in prices caused a steep decline in the state's petroleum industry. The rise and fall in the oil industry's fortunes affected other industries as well. By the late 1980s, many banks that had speculated in real estate earlier in the decade had too much debt and were declared insolvent.

In the wake of the oil-centered recession, Texas began to diversify, successfully attracting high-technology industries. Electronics, telecommunications, food processing, services, and retail trade saw substantial growth in the late 1980s and helped Texas through the national recession of 1990.

The state suffered job losses during the national recession of 2001 and was faced with a large budget deficit. Higher oil prices following a Venezuelan oil strike and the US-led invasion of Iraq, however, benefited the Texan economy. In 2004, an estimated 54,098 new businesses were established while 55,792 businesses closed.

The economy in Texas and the nation shrank again when a global recession hit in 2008–2009. However, gross state product (GSP) in Texas increased from $1 trillion in 2009 to $1.1 trillion in 2010, ranking the state second in the United States, according to the US Bureau of Economic Analysis. Texas GSP grew by another 3.3% in 2011, as compared with 1.6% growth for the nation. Per capita GSP was $45,940 in 2010, ranking the state 24th. Durable goods manufacturing accounted for the greatest growth in Texas, followed by mining and wholesale trade. In 2010, there were 522,146 private nonfarm establishments and 1.9 million nonemployer establishments in the state.

18 Income

Per capita personal income (including non-monetary income) was $39,593 in 2011, ranking the state 26th. During the period 2008–10, the median annual household income in Texas of $47,601 was below the national average of $50,022. In 2011, 18.5% of the population lived below the federal poverty level, compared to the national rate of 15.9%.

19 Industry

The value of all shipments by manufacturers in 2007 was $593.5 billion, as compared to $385 billion in 2004. Three of the state's leading industrial products—refined petroleum, industrial organic chemicals, and oil field machinery—all stem directly from the petrochemical sector. Major oil refineries are located in Houston and other Gulf ports.

20 Labor

The global recession caused the unemployment rate in Texas to increase from 6.3% to 8.2% during 2009. This mirrored the impact nationwide, as the average rate rose from 7.8% to 9.9%. The unemployment rate in Texas remained at or above 8% until it began to decline in September 2011. As of May 2012, the rate had dropped to 6.9%, signaling an ongoing economic recovery. At this time, Texas had a civilian labor force of more than 12 million workers, of which 3.2 million were located in the Dallas–Fort Worth metropolitan area, 2.9 million in the Houston–Sugarland–Baytown metropolitan area, and nearly a million in San Antonio–New Braunfels as well as Austin–Round Rock.

In August 2012, the civilian labor force in Texas numbered 12,628,600. That month, 901,600 people were unemployed, for an unemployment rate of 7.1%, compared to the national average of 8.1%. Those employed in nonfarm wage and salaried jobs that same month included: 596,400 in construction; 853,600 in manufacturing; 2,158,200 in trade, transportation, and utilities; 651,300 in financial activities; 1,390,300 in business and professional occupations; 1,467,900 in education and health services; 1,094,200 in leisure and hospitality; and 1,798,600 in government.

Organized labor has never been able to establish a strong base in Texas. The earliest national union, the Knights of Labor, declined in Texas after failing to win a strike against the railroads in 1886 when the Texas Rangers served as strike breakers. That same year, the American Federation of Labor (AFL) began to organize workers along craft lines. The Congress of Industrial Organizations (CIO) succeeded in organizing oil field and maritime workers during the 1930s.

In 2011, 643,000 of Texas's employed wage and salary workers were members of unions, representing 6.3% of those so employed. The national average was 13%.

21 Agriculture

According to the US Department of Agriculture, there were approximately 130 million acres (52.6 million hectares) of land distributed among 247,500 Texas farms in 2010. Farmland covers more than three-fourths of the vast state, which has more farms than any other state—245,000 as of 2011. The average farm size was 527 acres (213 hectares). Texas ranks

Texas farmers had more than 13 million cattle and calves in 2010. © DOUGLAS KNIGHT/SHUTTERSTOCK.COM.

second among the 50 states in agricultural production, with one-third of production value attributed to crops.

Since 1880, Texas has been the leading producer of cotton (producing both Upland and American-Pima). After 1900, Texas farmers developed bumper crops of wheat, corn, and other grains by irrigating dry land and transforming the "great Sahara" of West Texas into one of the nation's foremost grain-growing regions. Texans also grow practically every vegetable suited to a temperate or semi-tropical climate.

Productive farmland is located throughout the state. Grains are grown mainly in the temperate north and west, and vegetables and citrus fruits in the subtropical south. Cotton has been grown in all sections, but in recent years, it has been extensively cultivated in the High Plains of the west and the upper Rio Grande Valley. Grain sorghum, wheat, corn, hay, and other forage crops are raised in the north-central and western plains regions. Rice is cultivated along the Gulf Coast and soybeans are raised mainly in the High Plains and Red River Valley.

Total agricultural output was $26.1 billion in 2011, of which crops accounted for $5.55 billion. Leading crops that year were cotton ($2.33 billion in farm receipts) and greenhouse/nursery products ($1.2 billion). Leading export crops in 2011 were cotton and linters ($2 billion in farm receipts), feeds and fodders ($588 million), feed grains and products ($507 million), and wheat and products ($466.6 million).

22 Domesticated Animals

About two-thirds of cattle fattened for market are kept in feedlots located in the Texas panhandle and northwestern plains. With sales of cattle and calves valued at $10.5 billion and sheep valued at $107 million in 2007, Texas ranked first in both of these commodities. In 2010, Texas farmers had 13.3 million cattle and calves, an inventory of 800,000 sheep, and 660,000 hogs and pigs.

In 2010, the state's 413,000 cows produced 8.8 billion pounds (4 million kilograms) of milk. In 2011, total domesticated animals output was $14.5 billion. Cattle and calves accounted for $11.15 billion, with farm receipts for dairy products amounting to almost $2 billion, and farm receipts for broilers of $1.67 billion.

Breeding of Palominos, Arabians, Appaloosas, thoroughbreds, and quarter horses is a major industry in Texas. The animals are most abundant in the heavily populated areas, and it is not unusual for residential subdivisions of metropolitan areas to include facilities for keeping and riding horses.

23 Fishing

In 2010, the commercial catch in Texas was nearly 90 million pounds (40 million kilograms), valued at $204 million. The most important catch was shrimp, followed by oysters and blue crabs. Black drum and snapper are also mainstays of the state's commercial fishing industry. Catfish farming is a common practice in ponds throughout Texas, ranking the state fourth in catfish production behind Mississippi, Alabama, and Arkansas. These four states accounted for 95% of the nation's catfish sales in 2011.

There are three national fish hatcheries in the state (Uvalde, Inks Dam, and San Marcos). Texas Parks & Wildlife Department operates five inland fish hatcheries in Athens, Brookeland, Electra, Graford, and San Marcos as well as three coastal fish hatcheries in Corpus Christi, Lake Jackson, and Palacios. Among the most sought-after native freshwater fish are largemouth and white bass, crappie, sunfish, and catfish.

24 Forestry

According to the US Department of Agriculture, Texas forestland covered more than 62 million acres (25 million hectares) in 2010. Commercial timberland comprised more than 14 million acres (5.6 million hectares). In 2011, a record number of wildfires had a devastating effect on the timber industry, wiping out an estimated $97 million worth of trees. Output from forestry and farm services amounted to $6 billion in 2011.

Private landowners control the majority of the state's forestland. In east Texas, 52% of forestland is privately owned and 22% is controlled by corporations. In central and west Texas, 73% is privately owned. National forestlands cover 9 million acres (3.6 million hectares), of which the US Forest Service managed 675,000 acres (273,162 hectares). This land is located in four National Forests in east Texas (Angelina, Davy Crockett, Sabine, and Sam Houston) and the Caddo-Lyndon B. Johnson National Grasslands in northeast Texas. The state also has five state forests: the E. O. Siecke, W. Goodrich Jones, I. D. Fairchild, John

Henry Kirby, and Paul N. Masterson Memorial State Forests.

The first large lumber mill was built in Texas in 1877, with a daily capacity of up to 100,000 board feet. Nearly all of the 12 million acres (4.9 million hectares) of forestland located in east Texas is timberland. In 2009, Texas timberlands yielded 1.4 billion board feet of lumber, 2 billion square feet of structural panels, and 2 million tons of pulp and paper products. Texas wood-treating plants process utility poles, crossties, lumber, and fence posts. Other value-added products include wood kitchen cabinets, prefabricated wood buildings, and wood furniture.

The Texas Forest Service provides professional forestry assistance to private landowners, manages several state and federal reforestation and forest stewardship incentives programs, coordinates pest control activities, and assists in protecting against wildfires statewide. In addition, the state agency has an urban and community forestry program, forest products laboratory, two tree nurseries, and a genetics laboratory.

25 Mining

The US Geological Survey's estimated value of nonfuel mineral commodities produced in Texas was nearly $2.87 billion in 2011, representing 3.8% of the national output. As of 2011, Texas was the nation's leading producer of both cement and crushed stone, and the state ranked second in construction sand and gravel (behind California), dimension stone (behind Georgia), and gypsum (behind Oklahoma). Lime, salt, industrial sand and gravel, and masonry cement were other nonfuel mineral commodities mined in the state.

In 2010, 118 million metric tons of crushed stone were mined in the state, valued at $822 million; along with 76.3 million metric tons of sand and gravel, valued at $564 million; and 195 million metric tons of aggregate, valued at $1.4 billion.

26 Energy and Power

Texas is the leader in energy production, with approximately 12% of the nation's total. The energy-rich state's vast deposits of petroleum and natural gas account for nearly 30% of US proved liquid hydrocarbon reserves, making it the largest producer and exporter of oil and natural gas to other states. Texas also produces more wind power than any other state.

The state's first oil well was drilled in 1866 at Melrose in East Texas. Texas crude oil reserves represent nearly one-fourth of the nation's total.

Texas produces more wind power than any other state. © W. SCOTT/SHUTTERSTOCK.COM.

Petroleum output in 2010 was 1,232 million barrels, representing more than 17% of the nation's total. Of this, motor gasoline accounted for 294 million barrels, or 9% of the nation's output. The state's 27 petroleum refineries can process more than 4.7 million barrels of crude oil per day.

In 2010, Texas had estimated crude oil reserves of 5.7 billion barrels, 24.4% of the US total; reserves of 89 trillion cubic feet of natural gas; 4 billion barrels of natural gas plant liquids; and 738 million short tons of recoverable coal.

Electric power industry net summer capacity was 108,257,500 megawatts in 2010. As of June 2012, total net electricity generation was 41,393,000 megawatt hours (MWh). This included 15,000 MWh generated by petroleum-fired plants; 21,521,000 MWh by natural-gas fired plants; 12,950,000 MWh by coal-fired plants; 3,654,000 MWh by nuclear power plants; 61,000 MWh from hydroelectric plants; and 2,778,000 MWh from other renewable sources. The state has four nuclear reactors in operation, two at the Comanche Peak plant and two at the South Texas plant.

27 Commerce

Wholesale sales exceeded $424 billion in 2007, compared to $397 billion in 2002; retail sales exceeded $311 billion, or $13,061 per capita (per person), compared to $228 billion five years prior. In 2008 Texas had 31,815 wholesale trade establishments and 77,669 retail trade establishments. According to the US Department of Commerce, Texas led the nation in exports for the 10th consecutive year, with $251 billion in exports in 2011, compared to $207 billion in 2010 and $129 billion in 2005. The majority of the state's exports went to Mexico, Canada, China, Brazil, and the Netherlands. Top exports were oil and machine parts.

28 Public Finance

The Texas budget operates on a "pay as you go" basis in that expenditures cannot exceed revenue during the budget cycle. The state's budget period runs on a biennial basis from September 1 of each odd-numbered year to August 31 of the following odd-numbered year. The state legislature meets from approximately January to May every odd-numbered year and writes a budget for the next two years. The governor's Office of Budget and Planning also prepares a budget for the legislature's consideration.

According to the 2010 Annual Survey of State Government Finances, total revenues in Texas were $120.3 billion and expenditures were $119.6 billion. The largest general expenditures were for education ($46.7 billion) and public welfare ($29 billion). Other major expenditures were $5.8 billion on highways, $4 billion on hospitals, and $3.7 billion on corrections. The state's outstanding debt at the end of the year exceeded $42 billion.

The gross state product (GSP) in Texas declined only a marginal 1.8% to $1,141.3 billion during the global recession of 2009, while most other states had two consecutive years of decline. At that time, manufacturing accounted for $23.7 billion (17.4% of GSP), followed by finance and insurance, at $18.4 billion (13.5% of GSP). Government represented $16.2 billion (11.9% of GSP) and real estate was $13.7 billion (10.1% of GSP). Wholesale trade, retail trade, information, professional and technical services, and health care and social assistance each contributed less than $10 billion.

29 Taxation

As Texas does not have individual or corporate income tax, the principal source of state tax revenue is the 6.25% sales and use tax. Local sale taxes range from 0 to 2% add-ons. The state also imposes selective sales (excise) taxes on motor fuels, tobacco products, and other selected items.

In 2011, Texas collected $43.2 billion in taxes, including $33.8 billion in sales tax and gross receipts; $6.7 billion in license taxes and fees; and $2.7 billion in income taxes. Property taxes, which are collected at the local level, averaged $1,475 per capita (per person) in 2009. The state tax burden was $1,682 per capita, ranking Texas as the state with the 45th-lowest tax burden.

30 Health

In 2011, the infant mortality rate in Texas was 6.2 deaths per 1,000 live births, nearly half of the state's rate in 1980. The overall death rate in 2010 was 7.53 deaths per 1,000 persons. Some 15.8% of Texas adults were smokers, compared to the US rate of 17.2%. That same year, 66.5% of adults were overweight or obese, and 9.7% had been diagnosed with diabetes. The death rate from diabetes was 22.5 per 100,000 residents in 2009. Death rates from other diseases that year included cancers at 163.8 per 100,000; heart disease at 178.6 per 100,000; and cerebrovascular disease at 43.6 per 100,000. In 2008, there were 63,018 people living with HIV/AIDS, 7.2% of the US total.

Texas's 428 community hospitals had 62,100 beds in 2009. That year, there were 216 physicians, 46 dentists, and 678 registered nurses per 100,000 residents. The average expense for hospital care was $1,923 per inpatient day, as compared to $1,055 in 2000. An estimated 26% of the state's residents were uninsured in 2010, including 16% of children, representing the highest percentage of uninsured residents in the nation.

The seven medical schools in Texas are Baylor College of Medicine, Texas Tech University School of Medicine, Texas A&M College of Medicine, University of Texas Medical School at San Antonio, University of Texas Southwestern Medical School at Dallas, University of Texas Medical Branch Galveston, and University of Texas Houston Medical School. The University of Texas Cancer Center at Houston is one of the nation's major facilities for cancer research. Houston is also noted as a center for cardiovascular surgery. On 3 May 1968, Houston surgeon Denton Cooley performed the first human heart transplant in the United States.

31 Housing

The variety of Texas architectural styles reflects the diversity of the state's topography and climate. In the early settlement period, Spanish-style adobe houses were built in southern Texas. During the 1840s, Anglo-American settlers in the east erected primitive log cabins. These were later replaced by "dog-run" houses, consisting of two rooms linked by an open passageway covered by a gabled roof, so called because pet dogs slept in the open, roofed shelter, as did occasional overnight guests. During the late 19th century, Southern-style mansions were built in

East Texas, and the familiar ranch house, constructed of stone and usually stuccoed or white-washed, with a shingle roof and a long porch, proliferated throughout the state; the modern ranch house in southwestern Texas shows a distinct Mexican-Spanish influence.

The US census estimated there were 10,099,242 housing units in Texas in 2011, of which 8,850,370 (87.6%) were occupied and 5,568,300 (62.9%) were owner-occupied. Around 65.1% of all units (6,573,800) were single-family, detached homes, and 7.6% (771,274) were mobile homes. Average household size was 2.87 people.

Most homes were heated using electricity or utility gas. In 2011, there were 71,499 units (0.8%) lacking complete plumbing facilities and 94,209 units (1.1%) lacking complete kitchen facilities. The median home value in 2011 was $127,700. Median monthly costs for units with a mortgage was $1,398. Median monthly rent was $813.

32 Education

According to national statistics compiled by the US National Center for Education for the 2009/10 school year, Texas had 9,232 public schools and 4,850,210 students. Expenditures for the state's public education were $49.8 billion. For the period 2006–10, the US Census Bureau estimated 80% of the state's population 25 years and older had completed four years of high school, a percentage that was lower than the national average of 85%; and nearly 26% had obtained a bachelor's degree or higher.

In 2008, there were 1,327,000 students enrolled in college or graduate school, including 724,000 full-time students at the state's 240 degree-granting institutions. The leading public universities are the University of Texas (UT) and Texas A&M University. UT's enrollment of 211,213 students in 2011 included 161,275 undergraduates, while Texas A&M had more than 50,000 students. Other state-supported institutions include the University of Houston and Texas Tech University.

The UT System comprises nine universities and six health institutions. The main campuses are located in Austin, Arlington, Brownsville, Dallas, El Paso, San Antonio, and Tyler. UT of the Permian Basin, located in Odessa, began as an upper-level university and added four-year degrees in 1991. UT–Pan American is a Hispanic-serving institution in Edinburg, near the Mexican border.

The first private college in Texas was Rutersville, established by a Methodist minister in Fayette County in 1840. The oldest private institution still active in the state is Baylor University, established in 1845 at Waco. Other major private institutions include Hardin-Simmons University, Rice University, Southern Methodist University (SMU), Texas Christian University (TCU), and Trinity University. Well known black-oriented institutions of higher learning include Texas Southern University in Houston and Prairie View A&M University.

33 Arts

The state's first theater was active in Houston as early as 1838. Stark Young founded the Curtain Club acting group at the University of Texas in Austin in 1909 and the little theater movement began in that city in 1921. The performing arts now flourish at Houston's Theater Center, Jones

Hall of Performing Arts, and Alley Theater, as well as at the Theater Center, National Children's Theater, and Theater Three at Dallas. The Margo Jones repertory company in Dallas has a national reputation and there are major repertory groups in Houston and San Antonio.

During the late 1970s, Texas also emerged as a center for motion picture production. The city of Austin has since become the host for the annual Austin Film Festival in October. In 1994, film and interactive media were added as elements of the annual South by Southwest Music Conference and Festival (SXSW), which was first held in 1987. Over the course of 25 years, SXSW has grown into a leading music, film, and interactive conference that showcases 2,000 musical acts from all over the globe and draws more than 30,000 participants.

Texas has five major symphony orchestras: the Dallas Symphony (performing in the Meyerson Symphony Center since 1989), Houston Symphony, San Antonio Symphony, Austin Symphony, and Fort Worth Symphony. The Houston Grand Opera performs at Jones Hall. Several cities have resident dance companies, and the ballet groups in Fort Worth, Houston, Austin, and Corpus Christi are notable.

Popular music in Texas stems from early Spanish and Mexican folk songs, black American spirituals, cowboy ballads, and German-language songfests. Texans pioneered a kind of country and western music that is more outspoken and direct than Nashville's commercial product and a colony of country-rock songwriters and musicians were active in the Austin area during the 1970s. Texans of Mexican ancestry have also fashioned a Latin-flavored music ("Tejano") that is as distinctly "Tex-Mex" as the state's famous chili.

There are a number of groups for writers and storytellers, including the Writers' League of Texas and the Texas Storytelling Association. In 2000, the National Center for Children's Illustrated Literature (chartered in 1997) opened in Abilene. Besides sponsoring its own museum of illustrated works, the center provides educational programs and exhibits for teachers and other display venues.

34 Libraries and Museums

In 2011, Texas had 561 public libraries and 202 academic libraries. The state's public library system had approximately 12 million registered borrowers and a total circulation of 166 million. The largest municipal libraries in Texas include the Houston Public Library and the Dallas Public Library. The University of Texas at Austin is noted for outstanding collections in the humanities and in Latin American studies. The Lyndon B. Johnson Presidential Library is located in Austin, as is the Lorenzo de Zavala State Archives and Library Building. Other notable academic libraries include those of Texas A&M University, the University of Houston, Rice University, Southern Methodist University, and Texas Tech University, all with collections of over one million volumes.

Among the state's more than 280 museums are the Texas Memorial Museum, the Dallas Museum of Fine Arts, the Dallas Museum of Art, the Amon Carter Museum of Western Art, the Modern Art Museum of Fort Worth, and the Kimbell Art Museum. Houston has the Museum of Fine Arts, Contemporary Arts Museum, and at least 30 galleries. Both Dallas–Fort Worth and Houston have become major centers of art sales. Other museums include the

Dallas is home to several art museums as well as one of the state's largest municipal library systems. © MANAMANA/SHUTTERSTOCK.COM.

Holocaust Museum in Houston, the National Museum of the Pacific War in Fredericksburg, and the National WASP World War II Museum in Sweetwater. (WASP is short for Women Air-force Service Pilots—a group of women who flew planes to help the US Army Air Corps during the war.)

National historic sites in Texas are Fort Davis (Jeff Davis County), President Lyndon Johnson's boyhood home and Texas White House (Blanco and Gillespie counties), and the San Jose Mission (San Antonio). Other historic places include the Alamo at San Antonio, the Presidio la Bahia in Goliad, Dwight D. Eisenhower's birthplace at Denison, the Sam Rayburn home in Bonham, and the John F. Kennedy memorials in Dallas.

A noteworthy prehistoric Native American site is the Alibates Flint Quarries National Monument, located in Potter County and accessible by guided tour.

35 Communications

In 2010, about 69.5% of all households had Internet access, with 66.8% having broadband access.

According to the Federal Communications Commission, Texas had more than 1,000 licensed radio stations in 2011, including 720 full-service FM stations and 300 daytime AM stations. The state also had 110 television broadcasting stations.

52

36 Press

The first newspaper in Texas was a revolutionary Spanish-language sheet published in May 1813 at Nacogdoches. The first modern newspaper was the *Galveston News* (1842), a forerunner of the *Dallas Morning News* (1885). In 2011, Texas had 73 newspapers, including 53 dailies, according to the Audit Bureau of Circulations.

The newspapers with the largest circulations in 2011 estimates were the *Houston Chronicle* (357,700 daily and 916,900 Sundays), the *Dallas Morning News* (255,500 daily and 702,800 Sundays), the *Fort Worth Star-Telegram* (275,300 daily and 228,200 Sundays), and the *San Antonio Express News* (143,600 daily and 353,500 Sundays). Leading magazines include the *Texas Monthly* and *Texas Observer,* both published in Austin.

37 Tourism, Travel, and Recreation

Travel spending, which had been on a steady rise, declined during the economic recession in 2009. It resumed growth in 2010, increasing by approximately 10%, and grew again in 2011. Direct travel spending at Texas destinations exceeded $52 billion in 2011, supporting about 545,000 jobs.

Numerous amusement parks in Texas are open in the warmer months. In addition to SeaWorld in San Antonio, there are Six Flags amusement parks located there and in Arlington. In West Texas, Wonderland Amusement Park is located in Amarillo and Joyland Amusement Park is located in Lubbock. Schlitterbahn Waterpark has three locations—north of San Antonio in New Braunfels, Galveston Island,

The San Antonio Riverwalk is very popular with tourists who enjoy visiting the shops, eating at the restaurants, and taking a boat ride down the waterway. © BRANDON SEIDEL/SHUTTERSTOCK.COM.

The Big Bend Ranch State Park is mostly situated in the Chihuahuan Desert. Part of the Rio Grande River is located in the park.
© MARY TERRIBERRY/SHUTTERSTOCK.COM.

and South Padre Island. There are more than 70 guest and working ranches throughout the state.

Outstanding attractions are found throughout the state. East Texas has one of the state's oldest cities, Nacogdoches, with the nation's oldest public thoroughfare and a reconstruction of the Old Stone Fort, a Spanish trading post dating from 1779. Tyler, which bills itself as the "rose capital of the world," features a 28-acre (11-hectare) municipal rose garden. The Gulf Coast region of southeastern Texas offers deep sea fishing and more than 600 miles of beaches, plus the Lyndon B. Johnson Space Center. Also, Spindletop Park in Beaumont commemorates the state's first great oil gusher.

The Hill Country of south-central Texas encompasses many tourist sites, including the state capital in Austin and the Lyndon B. Johnson National Historic Site. South Texas has the state's most famous historic site—the Alamo, in San Antonio. The Great Plains region of the Texas panhandle offers Palo Duro Canyon—the state's largest state park, covering 16,402 acres (6,638 hectares).

In addition to Palo Duro Canyon, notable state parks include Big Creek, Brazos Island, Caddo Lake, and Dinosaur Valley. State historical parks include San Jacinto Battleground. Texas is also home to Big Bend National Park and state park. Hunting and fishing are extremely popular in Texas.

The state fair is held in Dallas each October. Other top annual events include the Houston Livestock Show and Rodeo and the Terlingua International Chili Championship.

38 Sports

Texas has many major league professional sports teams. Football team the Dallas Cowboys are by far the most consistently successful state team, having advanced to eight Super Bowls and scoring five wins. The Houston Oilers also joined the National Football League in 1960, but moved to Tennessee and were renamed the Titans in 1997. They were replaced by an expansion team, the Texans, who played their inaugural season in 2002 at Reliant Stadium.

Professional basketball teams in Texas include the Houston Rockets, San Antonio Spurs, and Dallas Mavericks of the National Basketball Association as well as the Houston Comets and San Antonio Silver Stars of the Women's National Basketball Association. Major League Baseball teams include the Houston Astros and the Texas Rangers: The Rangers made it to the World Series in 2010 and 2011, but lost both times. Other Dallas teams include the Dallas Stars of the National Hockey League and the Dallas Burn and Houston Dynamo of Major League Soccer.

Parimutuel betting on horse races was legalized in Texas in the early 1990s and thoroughbred tracks are open near Houston and Dallas. Quarter horse racing is also popular and rodeo is a leading spectator sport. The Texas Motor Speedway in Fort Worth offers NASCAR and IndyCar racing. Participant sports popular with Texans include hunting, fishing, horseback riding, boating, swimming, tennis, and golf. State professional and amateur golf tournaments are held annually, as are numerous rodeos. The Texas Sports Hall of Fame was organized in 1951. New members are selected each year by a special committee of the Texas Sports Writers Association.

There are several colleges and universities in Texas with many elite teams in football, basketball, and baseball. The University of Texas Longhorns are traditionally strong in football, with over 40 bowl game appearances, and in baseball. Texas A&M University in College Station also has an elite football program. Texas Tech's women's basketball team has been consistently ranked as a top team in the national polls. Baylor and Rice universities both field outstanding baseball teams. The Rice University Owls won the 2003 College World Series.

39 Famous Texans

Two native sons of Texas have served as president of the United States. Dwight D. Eisenhower (1890–1969), the 34th president, was born in Denison. Lyndon Baines Johnson (1908–1973), the 36th president, was the only lifelong resident of the state to serve in that office, serving first as vice president under John F. Kennedy. Another native vice president was John Nance Garner (1868–1967), former Speaker of the US House of Representatives. George H. W. Bush (b. Massachusetts, 1924–) was elected president in 1988 on the Republican ticket and his son, George W. Bush (b. Connecticut, 1946–), was elected president in 2000.

Tom C. Clark (1899–1977) served as an associate justice on the US Supreme Court from 1949 to 1967. Texas native Sandra Day O'Connor (1930–) became the first female associate justice on the US Supreme Court.

President Lyndon B. Johnson (seated) is shown signing the Civil Rights Bill in 1968. COURTESY OF THE LIBRARY OF CONGRESS.

The state's most famous legislative leader was Sam Rayburn (1882–1961), who served the longest tenure in the nation's history as Speaker of the US House of Representatives. Barbara C. Jordan (1936–1996) was a forceful member of the House Judiciary Committee during its impeachment deliberations in 1974.

Famous figures in early Texas history include Moses Austin (b. Connecticut, 1761–1821) and his son, Stephen F. Austin (b. Virginia, 1793–1836), often called the "father of Texas." Samuel "Sam" Houston (b. Virginia, 1793–1863), adopted as a youth by the Cherokee, won enduring fame as commander in chief of the Texas revolutionary army and president of the Texas Republic.

Texas military heroes include Audie Murphy (1924–1971), the most decorated soldier of World War II (and later a film actor), and Admiral of the Fleet Chester W. Nimitz (1885–1966). Figures of history and legend include

James Bowie (b. Kentucky, 1796–1836), popularly credited with the invention of the bowie knife, and frontiersman David "Davy" Crockett (b. Tennessee, 1786–1836), both of whom lost their lives at the Alamo.

Howard Hughes (1905–1976), an industrialist, aviation pioneer, film producer, and casino owner, became a fabulously wealthy recluse in his later years. H. Ross Perot (1930–) became a billionaire as a computer software developer and was an independent presidential candidate in 1992 and 1996. Dan Rather (1931–) is known nationwide as a television reporter and anchorman.

Among Texas-born musicians, Scott Joplin (1868–1917) and Blind Lemon Jefferson (1897–1930) were famous ragtime and blues musicians, respectively. Buddy Holly (Charles Holley, 1936–1959) was an early rock and roll singer. Musicians Trini Lopez (1937–) and Johnny Rodriguez (1951–) have earned popular followings based on their Mexican-American backgrounds. Prominent country musicians include Willie Nelson (1933–), Waylon Jennings (1937–2002), Kenny Rogers (1938–), Nick Jonas (1992–), Selena Quintanilla-Pérez (1971–1995), and first *American Idol* winner Kelly Clarkson (1982–). R&B singers include Beyoncé Knowles (1981–) and Usher Raymond (1978–).

Texans who have distinguished themselves in the performing arts include Academy Award winners Reneé Zellweger (1969–) and Sissy Spacek (1949–). Other notable actors born in Texas include Tommy Lee Jones (1946–), Patrick Swayze (1952–2009), Owen Wilson (1968–), Forest Whitaker (1961–), Jennifer Love Hewitt (1979–), Jamie Foxx (1967–), Dennis Quaid (1954–), and Matthew McConaughey (1969–). Comedians Carol Burnett (1933–) and Steve Martin (1945–) were also born in Texas.

The imposing list of Texas athletes is headed by Mildred "Babe" Didrikson Zaharias (1913–1956), who gained fame as an All-American basketball player in 1930, won two gold medals in track and field in the 1932 Olympics, and was the leading woman golfer during the 1940s and early 1950s. Another Texan, John Arthur "Jack" Johnson (1878–1946), was boxing's first black heavyweight champion.

Baseball Hall of Famers from Texas include Tris Speaker (1888–1958), Rogers Hornsby (1896–1963), Ernie Banks (1931–), and Joe Morgan (1943–). Nolan Ryan (1947–), pitching legend for the New York Mets, California Angels, Houston Astros, and Texas Rangers, was born in Refugio.

Among other Texas sports greats are golfers Ben Hogan (1912–97), Byron Nelson (1912–2006), and Lee Trevino (1939–); race driver A(nthony) J(oseph) Foyt Jr. (1935–); and jockey William Lee "Willie" Shoemaker (1931–2003).

Notorious Texans include Clyde Barrow (1909–1934) and Bonnie Parker (1910–1934) of the infamous bank-robbing duo "Bonnie & Clyde." They were gunned down in a law enforcement ambush in Louisiana. Lee Harvey Oswald (1939–1963) was accused of the assassination of President John F. Kennedy and shot to death by Jack Ruby while in police custody.

40 Bibliography

BOOKS

Bristow, M. J. *State Songs of America.* Westport, CT: Greenwood Press, 2000.

Crutchfield, James A. *It Happened in Texas.* 2nd ed. Guilford, CT: TwoDot, 2008.

Heinrichs, Ann. *Texas.* Minneapolis, MN: Compass Point Books, 2003.

McAuliffe, Emily. *Texas Facts and Symbols.* Rev. ed. Mankato, MN: Capstone Press, 2003.

McDonald, Archie P. *Texas: A Compact History.* Buffalo Gap, TX: State House Press, 2007.

Murray, Julie. *Texas.* Edina, MN: Abdo Publishing, 2006.

Naylor, June. *Texas, Off the Beaten Path,* 9th ed. Guilford, CT: GPP Travel, 2011.

Somervill, Barbara A. *Texas.* New York: Children's Press, 2011.

WEB SITES

"Economy at a Glance: Texas." *US Bureau of Labor Statistics.* http://www.bls.gov/eag/eag.tx.htm (accessed on November 16, 2012).

"Endangered Species Program." *US Fish & Wildlife Service.* http://www.fws.gov/endangered/ (accessed on November 16, 2012).

"State & County QuickFacts: Texas." *US Bureau of the Census.* http://quickfacts.census.gov/qfd/states/48000.html (accessed on November 16, 2012).

"Texas Almanac." *Texas State Historical Association.* http://www.texasalmanac.com/ (accessed on November 16, 2012).

Texas State Historical Association: http://www. tshaonline.org/ (accessed on November 16, 2012).

Texas State Travel Guide. http://www.traveltex.com/ (accessed on November 16, 2012).

Texas.gov: The Official Website of the State of Texas. http://www.texas.gov (accessed on November 16, 2011).

Utah
State of Utah

ORIGIN OF STATE NAME: From the Ute Native American tribe, meaning "people of the mountains."

NICKNAME: The Beehive State.

CAPITAL: Salt Lake City.

ENTERED UNION: 4 January 1896 (45th).

OFFICIAL SEAL: The coat of arms with the words "The Great Seal of the State of Utah 1896" surrounding it.

FLAG: Inside a thin gold circle, the coat of arms and the year of statehood are centered on a blue field, fringed with gold.

COAT OF ARMS: In the center, a shield flanked by American flags shows a beehive with the state motto and six arrows above, sego lilies on either side, and the numerals "1847" (the year the Mormons settled in Utah) below. Perched atop the shield is an American eagle.

MOTTO: Industry.

SONG: "Utah, We Love Thee"; "Utah, This Is the Place."

FLOWER: Sego lily.

TREE: Blue spruce.

ANIMAL: Rocky Mountain elk.

BIRD: California sea gull.

FISH: Bonneville cutthroat trout.

INSECT: Honeybee.

GEM: Topaz.

EMBLEM: Beehive.

LEGAL HOLIDAYS: New Year's Day, 1 January; birthday of Martin Luther King Jr., 3rd Monday in January; Washington and Lincoln's birthdays, 3rd Monday in February; Memorial Day, last Monday in May; Independence Day, 4 July; Pioneer Day, 24 July; Labor Day, 1st Monday in September; Columbus Day, 2nd Monday in October; Veterans' Day, 11 November; Thanksgiving Day, 4th Thursday in November; Christmas Day, 25 December.

TIME: 5 a.m. MST = noon GMT.

Location and Size

Located in the Rocky Mountain region of the western United States, Utah ranks 11th in size among the 50 states. The state's area totals 84,897 square miles (219,883 square kilometers), of which land comprises 82,191 square miles (212,875 square kilometers) and inland water 2,706 square miles (7,009 square kilometers). Utah extends 275 miles (443 kilometers)

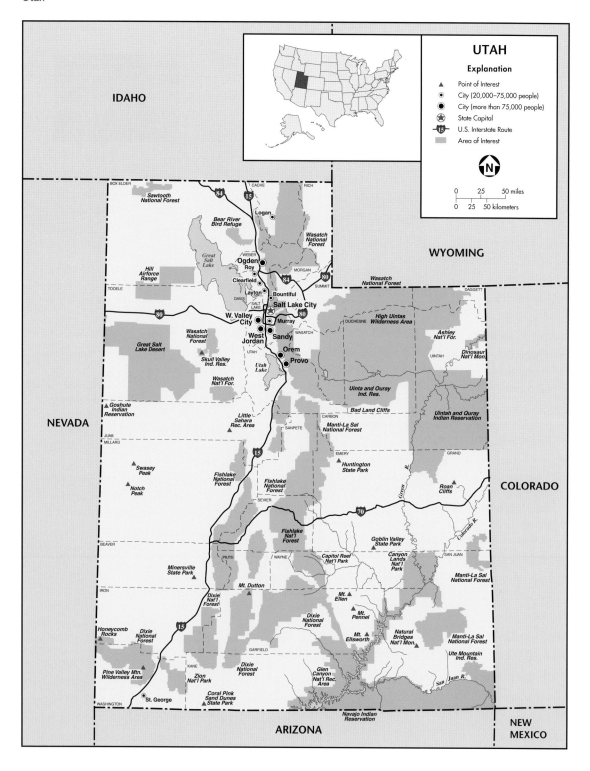

from east to west and 345 miles (555 kilometers) from north to south. The total boundary length is 1,226 miles (1,973 kilometers).

2 Topography

The eastern and southern two-thirds of Utah belong to the Colorado Plateau, a region characterized by deep river canyons. The Rocky Mountains are represented by the Bear River, Wasatch, and Uinta ranges in the north and northeast. The highest point in Utah, Kings Peak, is in the Uintas at an altitude of 13,528 feet (4,126 meters).

The arid, sparsely populated Great Basin dominates the western third of the state. To the north are the Great Salt Lake, a body of hypersaline water, and the Great Salt Lake Desert (containing the Bonneville Salt Flats). The lowest point in Utah, 2,000 feet (610 meters) above sea level, occurs at Beaverdam Creek in Washington County, in the southwest corner of the state.

The western edge of the Wasatch Range, or Wasatch Front, holds most of Utah's major cities. Two regions rich in fossil fuels are the Kaiparowits Plateau, in southern Utah, and the Overthrust Belt, a geologic structural zone underlying the north-central part of the state.

The largest lake is the Great Salt Lake, which covers about 2,250 square miles (5,827 square kilometers). Other major bodies of water are Utah Lake, Bear Lake (shared with Idaho), and Lake Powell, formed by the Glen Canyon Dam on the Colorado River. Other important rivers include the Green, flowing into the Colorado; the Sevier, which drains central and southern Utah; and the Bear, which flows into the Great Salt Lake.

3 Climate

The climate of Utah is generally semiarid to arid. At Salt Lake City, the temperature ranges from 28°F (-2°C) in January to 78°F (26°C) in July. The record high temperature, 117°F (47°C), was set at St. George on 5 July 1985. The record low temperature, -69°F (-56°C), was set at Peter's Sink on 1 February 1985.

The average annual precipitation varies from less than 5 inches (12.7 centimeters) in the west to over 40 inches (102 centimeters) in the mountains. The annual snowfall is about 59 inches (150 centimeters) and remains on the higher mountains until late summer. Salt Lake City averages 16.5 inches (41.9 centimeters) of snowfall annually.

4 Plants and Animals

Botanists have recognized more than 4,000 floral species in Utah's six major life zones. Common trees and shrubs include four species of pine and three of juniper, as well as the Utah oak, Joshua tree, and blue spruce (the state tree). The sego lily is the state flower. In 2012, 24 Utah plant species were classified by the US Fish and Wildlife Service as threatened or endangered, including five species of cactus, the dwarf bear-poppy, four species of milk-vetch, and the autumn buttercup.

Mule deer are the most common of Utah's large mammals. Other mammals include pronghorn antelope, lynx, Rocky Mountain bighorn sheep, and grizzly and black bears. Among native bird species are the great horned owl and plain titmouse. The pygmy rattler is found in southwest Utah and the Mormon cricket is unique to the state.

In April 2012, 17 Utah animal species were listed by the US Fish and Wildlife Service as threatened or endangered, including the Utah prairie dog, three species of chub, two species of sucker, southwestern willow flycatcher, and woundfin. Many birds and fish have been killed or endangered by the inundation of freshwater marshes with salt water from the flooding Great Salt Lake.

5 Environmental Protection

The Department of Natural Resources oversees water and mineral resources, parks and recreation, state lands and forests, and wildlife. The Department of Agriculture is concerned with soil conservation and pesticide control. The Department of Environmental Quality has separate divisions dealing with air quality, drinking water systems, water quality, and the regulation of water pollution, radioactive, hazardous, and solid wastes.

Air pollution is a serious problem along the Wasatch Front where over 70% of the state's population resided in 2010. Automobiles are a major contributor to the high levels of ozone and carbon monoxide impacting the communities in Salt Lake, Weber, and Utah counties. Also of considerable concern is the quality of drinking water.

Other environmental issues of concern in the state are chemical warfare agent storage and disposal and interstate transportation of hazardous waste for disposal. Another environmental problem is the pollution of Great Salt Lake by industrial waste. In 1996, the lake and its surrounding wetlands were designated a Hemispheric Reserve in the Western Hemisphere Shorebird Reserve Network. The move was

---

Utah Population Profile

Total population per Census 2010:	2,763,885
Population change, 2006–10:	8.4%
Hispanic or Latino†:	13.0%
Population by race	
One race:	97.3%
White:	86.1%
Black or African American:	1.1%
American Indian/Alaska Native:	1.2%
Asian:	2.0%
Native Hawaiian/Pacific Islander:	0.9%
Some other race:	6.0%
Two or more races:	2.7%

Population by Age Group, Census 2010

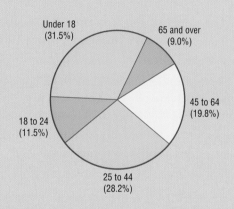

Under 18 (31.5%)
65 and over (9.0%)
45 to 64 (19.8%)
25 to 44 (28.2%)
18 to 24 (11.5%)

Major Cities by Population, 2011 Estimates

City	Population	% change 2005–11
Salt Lake City	189,899	6.6
West Valley	131,942	16.5
Provo	115,321	1.6
West Jordan	105,675	15.6
Orem	90,727	1.1
Sandy	89,200	-0.5
Ogden	83,949	7.2
St. George	74,770	16.5
Layton	68,495	10.9
Taylorsville	59,767	3.0

Notes: †A person of Hispanic or Latino origin may be of any race. NA indicates that data are not available. Percentages may not equal 100 due to rounding.

SOURCE: U.S. Census Bureau. Census 2010 and Population Estimates. www.census.gov/ (accessed July 2012).

Utah Population by Race
CENSUS 2010

This table shows the number of people who are of one, two, or three or more races. For those claiming two races, the number of people belonging to the various categories is listed. The U.S. government conducts a census of the population every 10 years.

	Number	Percent
Total population	2,763,885	100.0
One race	2,688,367	97.3
Two races	70,121	2.5
White *and* Black or African American	9,598	0.3
White *and* American Indian/Alaska Native	12,638	0.5
White *and* Asian	15,902	0.6
White *and* Native Hawaiian/Pacific Islander	6,885	0.2
White *and* some other race	17,835	0.6
Black or African American *and* American Indian/Alaska Native	608	—
Black or African American *and* Asian	466	—
Black or African American *and* Native Hawaiian/Pacific Islander	323	—
Black or African American *and* some other race	975	—
American Indian/Alaska Native *and* Asian	290	—
American Indian/Alaska Native *and* Native Hawaiian/Pacific Islander	292	—
American Indian/Alaska Native *and* some other race	1,194	—
Asian *and* Native Hawaiian/Pacific Islander	1,402	0.1
Asian *and* some other race	1,082	—
Native Hawaiian/Pacific Islander *and* some other race	631	—
Three or more races	5,397	0.2

SOURCE: U.S. Census Bureau. Census 2010. www.census/gov/ (accessed July 2012). A dash (—) indicates that the percent is less than 0.1.

taken in recognition of the area's importance to migratory waterfowl and shorebirds.

As of 2012, Utah had 15 Superfund sites listed in the Environmental Protection Agency's National Priorities List. These include several smelters, such as Jacobs Smelter in Stockton, and Hill Air Force Base in Ogden. Utah's Carbon County is home to one of the largest landfills in the United States.

6 Population

In 2011, Utah ranked 34th in the United States in population with an estimated total of 2,817,222 residents. The population is projected to reach 3.2 million by 2025. Utah's population density in 2010 was 34.3 persons per square mile (13.2 persons per square kilometer).

The median age in 2011 was only 29.6 years of age, considerably younger than the national average of 37.3. In 2011, about 31% of all Utah residents were under 18 while only 9% were 65 and older.

Salt Lake City is Utah's most populous city, with a 2011 estimated population of 189,899 (metro area 1,145,905). Other major cities include West Valley City, 131,942; Provo, 115,321; West Jordan, 105,675; Orem, 90,727; Sandy, 89,200, and Ogden, 83,949. In 2010, 78% of the state's residents lived in metropolitan areas.

7 Ethnic Groups

According to the 2010 Census, Hispanics and Latinos are the largest ethnic minority in Utah, with an estimated 358,340 people or 13% of the total population in the state. Native Americans/ Alaska Natives numbered about 32,927, with residents primarily of the Uintah, Ouray, and Navajo tribes. About 55,285 Asians resided in the state as of 2010. Utah also had an estimated African American population of 29,287.

In 2010, about 218,000 or 8.2% of Utah residents were foreign born, compared to a US average of 12.7%. Among persons reporting at least one specific ancestry in 2010, 719,448 persons claimed English descent, 323,135 German, 155,362 Danish, 164,050 Irish, and 108,734 Swedish.

8 Languages

Utah English is primarily a merger of Northern and Midland dialects brought into the west by the Mormons, who were originally from New York. Conspicuous in Mormon speech in the central valley, although less frequent now in Salt Lake City, is a reversal of vowels, so that *farm* and *barn* sound like *form* and *born* and, conversely, *form* and *born* sound like *farm* and *barn.*

In 2011, 85.1% of all state residents five years of age or older spoke only English at home. Other languages spoken at home, and the percentage of people who spoke them, included Spanish (10.1%), other Indo-European languages (2%), and Asian and Pacific Islander languages (2.1%).

9 Religions

According to a 2008 survey by the Pew Forum on Religion & Public Life, the dominant religious group in Utah, accounting for 58% of the state population, is the Church of Jesus Christ of Latter-day Saints, popularly known as the Mormons. The church was founded by Joseph Smith Jr. in 1830, the same year he published the *Book of Mormon,* the group's sacred text. In 1847, the Mormons made a long pilgrimage from the East to Utah to escape religious persecution. Today, the Mormon Church and its leadership continue to play a central role in the state's political, economic, and cultural institutions.

Roman Catholics formed the second-largest group, with about 10% of the population, followed by Evangelical Protestants with 7%, and mainline Protestants, with 6%. Around 1% of

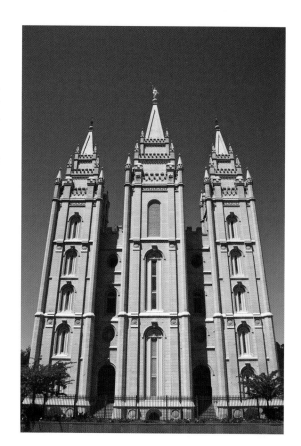

Many Mormons settled in Utah. Work on the Salt Lake Temple, which is made of granite, was started in 1853. It is the centerpiece of the Church of Jesus Christ of Latter-day Saints. © ACTION SPORTS PHOTOGRAPHY/SHUTTERSTOCK.COM.

the population was affiliated with historically black Protestant churches. All other religions were represented by less than 0.5% of the population. About 16% of the population identified themselves as unaffiliated with any religious organization.

10 Transportation

Utah, where the golden spike was driven in 1869 to mark the completion of the first Transcontinental Railroad in the United States, had 2,067 rail miles (3,327 kilometers) of track in 2009. There were eight freight railroads in the state that year, including two Class I railroads. Amtrak provides passenger service to Salt Lake City, Provo, Helper, and Green River.

The Utah Transit Authority, created in 1970, provides bus service for Salt Lake City, Provo, and Ogden. In 2008, Utah had over 44,705 miles (71,946 kilometers) of public roads and streets, of which 5,841 miles (9,400 kilometers) were state highways. In 2009, there were 1,687,306 licensed drivers in the state. That year, there were 1,180,000 cars, 58,000 motorcycles, and 1,228,000 trucks registered in the state. The main east–west and north–south routes—I-80 and I-15, respectively—intersect at Salt Lake City.

Utah had 88 airports and 49 heliports in 2009. By far the busiest airport was Salt Lake City International Airport, with 9,901,447 passenger enplanements in 2009, making it the 24th-busiest airport in the nation that year.

11 History

Utah's historic Native American groups are primarily Shoshonean: the Ute branch in the

At the Golden Spike National Historic Site, which celebrates the completion of the Transcontinental Railroad, replicas of the historic locomotives re-enact the setting in which the two trains met. Pictured here is the replica Jupiter steam locomotive. © GARY WHITTON/SHUTTERSTOCK.COM.

eastern two-thirds of the state, the Goshute of the western desert, and the Southern Paiute of southwestern Utah. The Athapaskan-speaking Navajo of southeastern Utah migrated from western Canada, arriving not long before the Spaniards. White settlement from 1847 led to wars between whites and Native Americans in 1853–54 and 1865–68, with many Native Americans finally removed to reservations.

Native American rock art is found throughout Utah. Here, the petroglyphs on Newspaper Rock depict people, horses, other animals, human feet, and even a wagon wheel. © GEIR OLAV LYNGFJELL/SHUTTERSTOCK.COM.

Mexicans and Spaniards entered Utah in 1765. In July 1776, a party led by two Franciscan priests, Francisco Atanasio Domínguez and Silvestre Vélez de Escalanta, explored the region. Trade between Santa Fe, the capital of the Spanish province of New Mexico, and the tribes of Utah was fairly well established by the early 1800s. Until 1848, the 1,200-mile (1,900-kilometer) Spanish Trail, the longest segment of which lies in Utah, was the main route through the Southwest.

When Joseph Smith Jr., founder of the Church of Jesus Christ of Latter-day Saints (Mormons), was lynched in 1844, Brigham Young and other Mormon leaders decided to move west. By April 1847, a pioneer company of Mormons was on its way to Utah. The church organization served as the first government.

Deseret After the Treaty of Guadalupe-Hidalgo (1848) gave the United States title to much of the Southwest, the Mormons established the provisional state of Deseret. Congress refused to admit Deseret to the Union, choosing instead to create the Utah Territory, which encompassed, in addition to present-day Utah, most of Nevada and parts of Wyoming and Colorado. By the 1860s, Utah was assigned its present boundaries.

The territorial period lasted for 46 years, marked by immigration, growth, and conflict.

Mormon militia clashed with federal troops in the so-called Utah War of 1857–58, which left Mormon leaders hostile to federal authorities. Almost 98% of Utah's total population was Mormon until after 1870, and the Mormon way of life dominated politics, economics, and social and cultural activities. As church president, Brigham Young remained the principal figure in the territory until his death in 1877.

In 1863, with the discovery of silver-bearing ore in Bingham Canyon, a boom in precious metals began and those connected with mining—mostly non-Mormons—began to exert influence in the territory. Several factors made the non-Mormon minority fearful of Mormon domination. These included the lack of free public schools, new immigration by Mormon converts, the mingling of church and state, and—most notably—the Mormon practice of polygamy (having multiple wives). This practice was finally renounced by the Mormons in 1890. Nevertheless, even in the 21st century, fundamentalist Mormon sects, not recognized by the main church, continue to practice polygamy, mostly in small communities scattered throughout the Southwest.

Statehood A constitutional convention was held in 1895, and statehood became a reality on 4 January 1896. The early 20th century saw further growth of the mineral industry. Gradually, modern cities emerged, along with power plants, interurban railroads, and highways. By 1920, nearly half of the population lived along the Wasatch Front. The influx of various ethnic groups diversified the state's social and cultural life, and the proportion of Mormons in the total population declined to about 68% by 1920.

Utah businesses enjoyed the postwar prosperity of the 1920s. However, mining and agriculture were depressed throughout the 1920s and 1930s, decades marked by increased union activity, particularly in the coal and copper industries. The Great Depression of the 1930s hit Utah especially hard. Severe droughts hurt farmers in 1931 and 1934, and high freight rates limited the expansion of manufacturing. With the coming of World War II (1939–45), increased demand for food revived Utah's agriculture, and important military installations and war-related industries brought new jobs to the state.

In the years after World War II, the state's population doubled. Politics generally reflect prevailing Mormon attitudes and tend to be conservative. The state successfully opposed plans for storing nerve-gas bombs in Utah.

Utah's economy was among the strongest of all the states in the early 21st century. A major issue facing state leaders is balancing protection of the environment with residential and commercial development. In 2002, Utah hosted the Winter Olympic Games in and around Salt Lake City.

Wildfires and serious drought conditions plagued Utah in the early 2000s. By 2005, however, the Utah Center for Climate and Weather had declared Utah's six-year drought to be over.

Since 2000, Utah has continued to diversify its economy, particularly in the high-technology sectors. Population growth has followed this new economy, with the state becoming the third-fastest growing in the United States, by percentage, between 2000 and 2010. The state also has continued a trend begun in the 1970s of increased ethnic and racial diversity.

Utah Governors: 1896–2013

1896–1905	Heber Manning Wells	Republican
1905–1909	John Christopher Cutler	Republican
1909–1917	William Spry	Republican
1917–1921	Simon Bamberger	Democrat
1921–1925	Charles Rendell Mabey	Republican
1925–1933	George Henry Dern	Democrat
1933–1941	Henry Hooper Blood	Democrat
1941–1949	Herbert Brown Maw	Democrat
1949–1957	Joseph Bracken Lee	Republican
1957–1965	George Dewey Clyde	Republican
1965–1977	Calvin Lewellyn Rampton	Democrat
1977–1985	Scott Milne Matheson	Democrat
1985–1993	Norman Howard Bangerter	Republican
1993–2003	Michael Okerlund Leavitt	Republican
2003–2005	Olene Walker	Republican
2005–2009	Jon M. Huntsman, Jr.	Republican
2009–	Gary R. Herbert	Republican

12 State Government

The state legislature consists of a 29-member senate and a 75-seat house of representatives. Senators serve for four years, representatives for two. The chief executive officers, all elected for four-year terms, include the governor, lieutenant governor (who also serves as secretary of state), attorney general, treasurer, and auditor. There are no gubernatorial term limits. The governor's vetoes may be overridden by two-thirds of the elected members of each house of the legislature.

In 2012, legislators received $117 during regular sessions per day and the governor received $109,900 per year.

13 Political Parties

In November 2008, Utah residents cast 62% of their presidential votes for Republican John McCain and 35% for Democrat Barack Obama. These numbers were significantly better for the Democratic candidate than in the 2004 election, when Utahns gave Republican George W. Bush 75% of the vote to Democrat John Kerry's 25%. In 2012 Utah voters strongly favored Republican challenger Mitt Romney, a Mormon, over incumbent President Obama. In August 2012, there were an estimated 1,190,072 registered voters in the state. There is no party registration in the state.

Republican Orrin Hatch was reelected to a sixth term in the US Senate in 2006 and a seventh in 2012. Utah's other senator, first-term Republican Mike Lee, was elected in 2010. After the 2012 elections, the delegation to the US House of Representatives consisted of three Republicans and one Democrat. In 2010, the state house had 58 Republicans and 17 Democrats, while the state senate had 22 Republicans and 7 Democrats. That year, there were 12 women serving in the state house and 5 women serving in the state senate. Republican Gary Herbert was elected governor in 2008 and again in 2012.

14 Local Government

Utah has 29 counties, governed by elected commissioners. Other elected county officials include clerk-auditor, sheriff, assessor, recorder, treasurer, county attorney, and surveyor. There were 236 municipal governments in 2010. Larger cities are run by an elected mayor and two commissioners while smaller communities are governed by a mayor and city council. Nonetheless, the state's largest city, Salt Lake City, adopted the mayor-council system. The state had 115 private and public school districts and 300 special districts in 2011. That year, there were 44,529 fulltime and 25,727 parttime state and local government workers.

**Utah Presidential Vote
by Major Political Parties, 1948–2012**

Year	Utah Winner	Democrat	Republican
1948	*Truman (D)	149,151	124,402
1952	*Eisenhower (R)	135,364	194,190
1956	*Eisenhower (R)	118,364	215,631
1960	Nixon (R)	169,248	205,361
1964	*Johnson (D)	219,628	181,785
1968	*Nixon (R)	156,665	238,728
1972	*Nixon (R)	126,284	323,643
1976	Ford (R)	182,110	337,908
1980	*Reagan (R)	124,266	439,687
1984	*Reagan (R)	155,369	469,105
1988	*Bush (R)	207,343	428,442
1992	Bush (R)	183,429	322,632
1996	Dole (R)	221,633	361,911
2000	*Bush, G. W. (R)	203,053	515,096
2004	*Bush, G. W. (R)	241,199	663,742
2008	McCain (R)	327,670	596,030
2012	Romney (R)	251,813	740,600

*Won US presidential election.

Independent candidate Ross Perot received 203,400 votes in 1992 and 66,461 votes in 1996.

15 Judicial System

Utah's highest court is the supreme court, consisting of a chief justice and four other justices. There are approximately 37 district court judges. In 1984, to ease the supreme court's caseload, Utahns approved a constitutional amendment allowing the legislature to create an intermediate court.

In 2010, the FBI reported a violent crime rate (murder, rape, robbery, aggravated assault) in Utah of 212.7 reported incidents per 100,000 inhabitants, among the lowest in the country. The murder and nonnegligent manslaughter rate was 1.9 per 100,000 inhabitants; forcible rape, 34.3; aggravated assault, 130.6; and property crime, 3,179.6.

Prisoners under jurisdiction of state and federal correctional facilities numbered 6,864 as of May 2012. Utah has a death penalty. From 1976 to June 2012, the state carried out seven executions. As of May 2012, Utah had nine inmates on death row. At that time, no prisoner had been executed since 2010.

16 Migration

After the initial exodus of Latter-day Saints from the eastern United States to Utah, Mormon missionaries attracted other immigrants to the state, and some 90,000 foreign converts arrived between 1850 and 1905. Many non-Mormons were recruited from overseas to work in the mines, especially during the early 20th century.

Between 1960 and 2010, the percentage of Utah residents who could be described as belonging to a minority group increased from 2% to 20%, still well below the national average of 36% in 2010. Drawn by the availability of low-wage labor jobs, most of these new residents are Hispanic or Latino immigrants, the largest minority group in the state, constituting 66% of the minority population.

Between 2009 and 2010, the total population (ages one and older) of Utah increased by 19,477, due to the net domestic in-migration (migration within a region or country) of natives (2,493), the net domestic out-migration of immigrants (-254), and the arrival from abroad of natives (9,763) and immigrants (7,475). Of the total foreign-born population in Utah in 2010, 2.9% were from Africa, 16.8% were from Asia, 11.1% were from Europe, and 62.3% were from Latin America. The top three countries of birth of the foreign born in Utah that year were Mexico (46%), Canada (3.2%), and China (2.7%). In comparison, the top three countries of birth in 1990 were Mexico (15.1%), Germany (10.4%), and Canada (10%).

17 Economy

In 2010, Utah's gross state product (GSP) was $116.9 billion, ranking the state 33rd in the nation. Per capita GSP that year was $41,750, ranking the state 34th. During the national recession that began in 2008, the state experienced a large multiyear decline in construction employment. In 2010, Utah's once-booming manufacturing industry also experienced job losses for the third year in a row. The state's largest nonfarm employers were Intermountain Health Care, the University of Utah, the State of Utah, and Brigham Young University. In 2010, there were 68,820 private nonfarm establishments and 191,963 nonemployer establishments in the state.

18 Income

In 2011, Utah had a per capita personal income (including nonmonetary income) of $33,790, 34th in the United States and below the national average of $41,663. The median annual household income for 2008–2010 was $59,857 compared to the national average of $50,022. In 2011, 13.5% of the state's residents lived below the federal poverty level, compared with 15.9% nationwide.

19 Industry

Utah's diversified manufacturing is concentrated in Salt Lake City and in Weber, Utah, and Cache counties. The total estimated value of shipments by manufacturers in 2007 was almost $42.4 billion. Of that total, food manufacturing accounted for the largest share, followed by transportation equipment manufacturing, miscellaneous manufacturing, computer and electronic product manufacturing, and primary metal manufacturing.

20 Labor

In August 2012, the civilian labor force in Utah numbered 1,355,500, with 78,700 people unemployed, for an unemployment rate of 5.8%, compared to the national average of 8.1%. Of those employed in nonfarm industries that month, 66,700 were employed in construction; 117,800 in manufacturing; 235,700 in trade, transportation, and utilities; 72,300 in financial services; 168,800 in professional and business services; 161,900 in health and education; 114,700 in leisure and service industries; and 220,500 in government.

Utah's union movement weakened in the 1980s as mining and heavy manufacturing industries mechanized, which resulted in the elimination of thousands of jobs. In 2011, 82,000 of Utah's employed wage and salary workers were members of unions, representing 7.1% of those so employed. The national average was 13%.

21 Agriculture

Despite a dry climate and unpromising terrain, Utah ranked 37th in the United States in value of agricultural products sold in 2007, with $1.42 billion. Crops accounted for $372 million and livestock and livestock products for $1.04 billion. The first pioneers in Utah settled in fertile valleys near streams, which were diverted for irrigation. Today, Utah farmers and ranchers practice comprehensive soil and water conservation measures to help maximize crop yields and protect the natural resources. A farmland preservation movement is under way to protect valuable food-producing land from urban sprawl. In 2011, there were some 16,600 farms and ranches covering a total of 11,100,000 acres (4,492,010 hectares).

Final agricultural output in 2011 was just under $2 billion, with crops accounting for $525 million. The chief crops that year were hay ($248 million in farm receipts) and greenhouse/nursery crops ($108.2 million). Top export crops in 2011 included wheat and wheat products, with $144.8 million in receipts, and feeds and fodders, with $37.6 million in receipts. The major agricultural counties were Beaver, Utah, Box, Millard, and Cache counties.

22 Domesticated Animals

Livestock and livestock products accounted for $1.1 billion in output in 2011. In 2007, there were an estimated 843,000 cattle and calves, valued at nearly $347.3 million on farms and ranches. During 2007, Utah farms produced $140 million in poultry and eggs, and $292 million in dairy products. In 2011, farm receipts for dairy products amounted to $360.8 million, receipts for cattle and calves were $311.6 million, and receipts for hogs were $209.9 million.

23 Fishing

Fishing in Utah is for recreation only. There are two national fish hatcheries in the state (Ouray and Jones Hole). Fish restoration projects seek to recover razorback sucker and cutthroat trout.

24 Forestry

In 2010, Utah was about 29% forested, with approximately 15,000,000 acres (6,070,284 hectares) of forestland. Approximately 8,189,000 acres (3,314,000 hectares) were in the state's six national forests: Ashley, Dixie, Fishlake, Manti-La Sal, Uinta, and Wasatch-Cache. Only 2,746,000 acres (1,111,000 hectares) were classed as commercial timberland. In 2007, Utah lumber production was 30.3 million board feet, mostly harvested in the Four Corners area. Output from forestry and forest services in 2011 was $363 million.

25 Mining

In 2011, Utah ranked fourth in the nation for value of nonfuel mineral production at $4.57 billion in value, 6.17% of the US total. Approximately 60% of the value came from metals, which included copper, gold, iron, magnesium, molybdenum, and silver. In addition, Utah mines produced significant quantities of beryllium, cement, magnesium compounds, sand and gravel, and salt.

In 2010, 5.3 million metric tons of crushed stone were mined in the state, valued at $42.6 million; along with 28.4 million metric tons of sand and gravel, valued at $155 million; and 33.7 million metric tons of aggregate, valued at $198 million.

26 Energy and Power

Since 1980, electrical consumption in Utah has averaged a 3.3% increase, outpacing its population rate of growth of 2.1%. Utah exports about 33% of its electrical production to other states. Utah's five refineries process crude oil primarily from Utah, Colorado, Wyoming, and Canada. Utah has a voluntary goal of 20% of net electricity generation from cost-effective renewable energy

Copper is one of the metals still mined in Utah. © BOYKOV/SHUTTERSTOCK.COM.

resources by 2025. In 2011, 4.7% of net electricity generation came from renewable resources.

Crude oil production has experienced a surge in Utah in the 21st century. Oil production climbed from 14.6 million barrels in 2004, to 23.4 million barrels in 2011. Production of natural gas experienced a similar trend, with 2010 production rising to 432 billion cubic feet (10.986 billion meters). Production of bituminous coal was estimated at 19 million short tons for 2010, basically flat compared to early 1990s production levels. In 2010, Utah had estimated crude oil reserves of 449 million barrels; reserves of 6.9 trillion cubic feet of natural gas; 132 million barrels of natural gas plant liquids; and 210 million short tons of recoverable coal.

As of June 2012, total net electricity generation was 3,358,000 megawatt hours (MWh). This included 3,000 MWh generated by petroleum-fired plants; 579,000 MWh by natural-gas fired plants; 2,548,000 from coal-fired plants; 100,000 MWh from hydroelectric plants; and 119,000 MWh from other renewable sources. Utah has no nuclear power plants.

27 Commerce

Wholesale sales totaled $25.42 billion in 2007; retail sales were $36.6 billion—all heavily concentrated in the Salt Lake City–Ogden area. In 2008, there were 3,631 wholesale trade establishments and 8,955 retail trade establishments.

Export value of Utah's goods, driven by higher gold prices, rose to $19 billion in 2011. In addition to gold, top exports included electronic integrated circuits and molybdenum.

28 Public Finance

The annual budget is prepared by the State Budget Office and submitted by the governor to the legislature for amendment and approval. The fiscal year runs from 1 July through 30 June.

State revenues for fiscal year 2009 were $11.51 billion and total appropriations equaled that amount. The largest general expenditures were for public and higher education ($4.9 billion), health ($2.1 billion), and transportation ($1.269 billion). The state's debt service for the year was $239,877.

29 Taxation

Utah's personal and corporate income tax is a single bracket 5% rate. The state's general sales and use tax rate is 4.7%, with local sales taxes adding on up to 1.9%. The state also levies a full array of excise taxes covering motor fuels, tobacco products, insurance premiums, public utilities, alcoholic beverages, pari-mutuels, and other selected items. All property taxes are collected at the local level. Property taxes are the primary source of local revenue.

The state collected $5.475 billion in taxes in 2011, of which $2.545 billion came from income taxes, $2.543 billion came from sales and use taxes, and $285 million came from licenses and fees. In 2011, Utah ranked 38th among the states in terms of combined state and local tax burden, which amounted to about $1,944 per capita (per person).

30 Health

In 2011, the infant mortality rate was 4.9 deaths per 1,000 live births. The overall death rate was 5.3 deaths per 1,000 persons. That same year, Utah had the lowest proportion of adult smokers of any state, at only 9.1%, compared to the US rate of 17.2%. Some 57.7% of adults were overweight or obese, and 6.5% had been diagnosed with diabetes. The death rate from diabetes was 21.8 per 100,000 residents in 2009. Death rates from other diseases that year included cancers at 120.6 per 100,000; heart disease at 135.9 per 100,000; and cerebrovascular disease at 35.9 per 100,000. In 2008, there were 2,221 people in Utah living with HIV/AIDS, 0.3% of the US total.

Utah's 35 community hospitals had about 4,344 beds in 2010. The average expense for community hospital care was $2,233 per inpatient day. In 2011, Utah had 208 doctors per 100,000 residents, and in 2011, there were 678 registered nurses per 100,000 residents. In 2007, there were 65 dentists per 100,000 residents. In 2010, approximately 16% of Utah's residents were uninsured.

31 Housing

In 2011, there were an estimated 993,125 housing units in Utah, of which 884,253 (89%) were occupied and 613,449 (69.4%) were owner-occupied. About 68.1% of all units (676,023) were single-family, detached homes, and 3.8% (37,447) were mobile homes. Utility gas was the most common energy source for heating. It was estimated that 4,378 (0.5%) units lacked complete plumbing facilities and 8,349 (0.9%) lacked complete kitchen facilities. The average household size was 3.04 people.

In 2010, 9,171 new privately owned housing units were authorized for construction. The median home value in 2011 was $207,500. The median monthly cost for mortgage owners was $1,418, while renters paid a median of $822 per month.

32 Education

In 2010, 90.6% of Utah residents had graduated from high school and 29.4% had four or more years of college; both figures were higher than the national average.

Total K-12 public school enrollment was estimated at 563,000 in fall 2007. Expenditures for K-12 public education in 2007/08 were estimated at $4.42 billion. Enrollment in private schools in fall 2007 was 16,919.

As of fall 2010, there were 173,016 students enrolled in college or graduate school. In 2010, Utah had 28 degree-granting institutions. Major public institutions include the University of Utah; Utah State University; and Weber State College. Brigham Young University (Provo), founded in 1875 and affiliated with the Latter-day Saints, is the state's best-known private institution.

33 Arts

Music has a central role in Utah's cultural life. The Mormon Tabernacle Choir has won world renown and Ballet West is ranked among the nation's leading dance companies. The Utah Symphony (Salt Lake City) has also gained a national reputation. Opera buffs enjoy the Utah Opera Company, founded in 1976.

The Utah Arts Council sponsors exhibitions, artists in the schools, rural arts and folk arts programs, and statewide arts competitions in cooperation with arts organizations throughout the state. In addition, the partially state-funded Utah Arts Festival is held each year in Salt Lake City.

Utah has several art museums and galleries. Living Traditions: A Celebration of Salt Lake's Folk and Ethnic Arts, is an annual festival that takes place on the weekend before Memorial Day. The three-day event, which celebrated its 25th anniversary in 2010, attracts as many as 50,000 people and offers continuous music and dance on two stages, as well as crafts demonstrations and sales. The Sundance Institute, founded by Robert Redford in 1981, presents the annual Sundance Film Festival, which is widely regarded as one of the nation's most influential gatherings for independent filmmakers.

The Utah Arts Council supports many programs with the help of state and federal funding. The Utah Humanities Council was established in 1975 and promotes several literacy and history-related programs and exhibits.

34 Libraries and Museums

In 2012, Utah had 112 public libraries and bookmobiles. The systems had a total of over 6 million volumes and a circulation of over 24 million. The Salt Lake County library system and the Weber County system were the largest. The leading academic libraries are the University of Utah (Salt Lake City) and Brigham Young University (Provo). Other collections are the Latter-day Saints' Library-Archives (Family History Museum) and the Utah State Historical Society Library, both in Salt Lake City.

In 2012, Utah had approximately 224 public and private museums, notably the Utah Museum of Natural History, the Utah Museum of Fine Arts, the Hill Aerospace Museum near Ogden, the College of Eastern Utah Prehistoric Museum, and the Museum of Peoples and Cultures in Provo. Some homes are maintained as museums, including Beehive House and Wheeler Historic Farm in Salt Lake City and Brigham Young's winter home in St. George. The John Wesley Powell River History Museum in Green River traces the one-armed explorer's exploration of the Colorado and Green rivers in the mid-1800s. The small city of Blanding houses the Dinosaur Museum, which includes skeletons, footprints, fossilized skin, and other specimens as well as an extensive collection of movie posters featuring dinosaurs and other beasts.

35 Communications

In 2010, 82.3% of homes had Internet access, and 79.7% had broadband access. That same year, there were approximately 140 AM and FM radio stations, as well as 18 television stations.

36 Press

In 2010, Utah had 35 newspapers that printed at least once a week. Leading daily newspapers with their 2012 daily circulation were the Salt Lake City *Tribune* (105,746 daily, 122,782 Sundays), the *Deseret News* (79,000 daily, 160,617 Sundays), and the Ogden *Standard-Examiner* (63,000 daily, 68,000 Sundays).

37 Tourism, Travel, and Recreation

In 2010, the state estimated that it hosted about 20.2 million visitors spending a total of around $6.5 billion. About 75% of all trips were made by residents from the western United States. International visitors account for about 3.6% of all

travel to the state. The top international sources are Canada, United Kingdom, Mexico, Japan, Germany, the Netherlands, France, and South Korea. Also in 2010, nearly 4.7 million visitors came to state parks and 6.3 million came to national parks. Skier visits totaled 4.2 million. The ski industry supports over 122,800 jobs.

The top five tourist attractions in 2009 (by attendance) were Temple Square, Salt Lake City (5 million); Zion National Park (2.74 million); Glen Canyon National Recreation Center (approximately 600,000); Wasatch Mountain State Park (342,000); and Lagoon Amusement Park. Pioneer Trail State Park and Hogle Zoo are leading attractions of Salt Lake City, about 11 miles (18 kilometers) east of the Great Salt Lake. At the Bonneville Salt Flats, experimental automobiles have set world land speed records.

Utah has 43 state parks, 5 national parks, and 6 national monuments. Utah is known for its vibrant red rock canyons, naturally created stone arches, unusual rock formations, and Native American rock art. Among Utah's state parks are Fremont Indian State Park and Museum, which preserves various petroglyphs from an earlier civilization; Snow Canyon State Park with its vibrant red and white sandstone cliffs; and Goblin Valley State Park, where thousands of sandstorm formations (called hoodoos) resemble goblins. The Golden Spike National Historic Site recalls the 1869 completion of the first Transcontinental Railroad in the United States, which joined the nation.

The majestic Monument Valley, part of the Navajo National Tribal Park, is situated on the Utah/Arizona border. The area was featured in many western movies over the years, including the classic John Wayne movie *Stagecoach*. Scenes from *2001: A Space Odyssey*, *Forrest Gump*, and *Mission Impossible: II* were also filmed there.

The Great Salt Lake contains too much salt to make it habitable for fish. © MARCO REGALIA/SHUTTERSTOCK.COM.

Photographers, hikers, mountain bikers, climbers, and others swell the population of the city of Moab for most of the year as they participate in recreational activities. Moab is located near several national parks, including Arches and Canyonlands. The latter park is a favorite for many off-road vehicle enthusiasts. Bryce Canyon National Park and Cedar Breaks National Monument, near the small town of Panguitch, are known for their orange-colored spiral formations. Capitol Reef National Park is famous for its waterpocket fold, a geologic feature that the National Park Service calls "a wrinkle on the earth."

Mountain and rock climbing, skiing, fishing, and hunting are major forms of recreation. Raft trips down the Colorado River are popular with tourists.

The state fair is held each year in Salt Lake City. Other top annual events include the Sundance Film Festival, the Moab Music Festival, and the Moab Folk Festival.

38 Sports

Utah has two major league professional sports teams, the Utah Jazz of the National Basketball Association, which moved from New Orleans to Salt Lake City at the close of the 1979 season; and Real Salt Lake of Major League Soccer. Salt Lake City is also home to minor league baseball and hockey teams.

Utah is popular with rock climbers, off-road vehicle enthusiasts, and hikers. Many visitors to Arches National Park outside the city of Moab take a hike along a sandstone formation to visit one of the state's most iconic landmarks—Delicate Arch. The site is so popular it is featured on Utah license plates. © DARREN J. BRADLEY/SHUTTERSTOCK.COM.

Other annual sporting events include the Easter Jeep Sandhill Climb in Moab, the Ute Stampede (a rodeo) in Nephi in July, and various skiing events at Utah's world-class resort in Park City. Salt Lake City hosted the Winter Olympics in 2002.

39 Famous Utahns

George Sutherland (b. England, 1862–1942) served as an associate justice of the US Supreme Court (1922–1938). Other important federal officeholders from Utah include Ezra Taft Benson (b. Idaho, 1899–1994), President Dwight Eisenhower's secretary of agriculture and leader of the Mormon Church from 1985 until his death. Jacob "Jake" Garn (1932–), first elected to the US Senate in 1974, was launched into space aboard the space shuttle in 1985.

The dominant figure in Utah history is Brigham Young (b. Vermont, 1801–1877), leader of the Mormons for more than 30 years. Notorious outlaw Robert LeRoy Parker (1866–1937?), better known as "Butch Cassidy," was born in Beaver, Utah. The state's most important scientist is John A. Widtsoe (b. Norway, 1872–1952), whose pioneering research in dryland farming revolutionized agricultural practices. Frank Zamboni (1901–1988) invented the ice-resurfacing machine bearing his name.

Utah's artists and writers include sculptor Mahonri M. Young (1877–1957); painter Henry L. A. Culmer (b. England, 1854–1914); author-critic Bernard A. DeVoto (1897–1955); and novelist Edward Abbey (1927–1989). Businessman, management consultant, and author Stephen R. Covey (1932–2012) was born in Salt Lake City. Donald "Donny"

Brother and singer duo, Donny and Marie Osmond, are among Utah's most famous celebrities. © EVERETT COLLECTION INC / ALAMY.

Osmond (1957–) and his sister Marie (1959–) are Utah's best-known popular singers. Comedienne Roseanne Barr (1952–) and actor James Woods (1947–) are also natives. Actor, director, and environmentalist Robert Redford (1936–) founded the Sundance Institute near Park City, Utah.

Maurice Abravanel (b. Greece, 1903–1993) conducted the Utah Symphony for many years. Sports figures of note are former world middleweight boxing champion Gene Fullmer (1931–); Merlin Olsen (1940–2010),

a tackle on the Los Angeles Rams who went on to become an actor; and Steve Young (1961–), former quarterback for the San Francisco 49ers.

40 Bibliography

BOOKS

Bancroft, Hubert Howe, and Alfred Bates. *History of Utah, 1540–1886.* San Francisco, CA: The History Company, 1889. Reprint, Charleston, SC: Nabu Press, 2010.

Bristow, M. J. *State Songs of America.* Westport, CT: Greenwood Press, 2000.

Brown, Jonatha A. *Utah.* Milwaukee, WI: Gareth Stevens, 2007.

D'Arc, James. *When Hollywood Came to Town: A History of Moviemaking in Utah.* Layton, UT: Gibbs Smith, 2010.

Francaviglia, Richard V. *Over the Range: A History of the Promontory Summit Route of the Pacific Railroad.* Logan, UT: Utah State University Press, 2008.

Jabado, Salwa. *Fodor's Utah: With Zion, Bryce, Arches, Capitol Reef & Canyonlands National Parks,* 4th ed. New York: Random House, 2010.

Murray, Julie. *Utah.* Edina, MN: Abdo Publishing, 2006.

WEB SITES

"State and County QuickFacts: Utah." *US Bureau of the Census.* http://quickfacts.census.gov/qfd/states/49000.html (accessed on October 25, 2012).

"State of Utah." *Utah.gov.* www.utah.gov (accessed on October 25, 2012).

"Utah." *National Park Service.* http://www.nps.gov/state/ut/index.htm?program=all (accessed on October 25, 2012).

Utah Office of Tourism. http://travel.utah.gov/research_and_planning/index.html (accessed on October, 2012).

Utah.com. www.utah.com (accessed on October 25, 2012).

Vermont

State of Vermont

ORIGIN OF STATE NAME: Derived from the French words *vert* (green) and *mont* (mountain).

NICKNAME: The Green Mountain State.

CAPITAL: Montpelier.

ENTERED UNION: 4 March 1791 (14th).

OFFICIAL SEAL: Bisecting Vermont's golden seal is a row of wooded hills above the state name. The upper half has a spearhead, pine tree, cow, and two sheaves of wheat, while two more sheaves and the state motto fill the lower half.

FLAG: The coat of arms on a field of dark blue.

COAT OF ARMS: Rural Vermont is represented by a pine tree in the center, three sheaves of grain on the left, and a cow on the right, with a background of fields and mountains. A deer crests the shield. Below are crossed pine branches and the state name and motto.

MOTTO: Freedom and Unity.

SONG: "Hail Vermont."

FLOWER: Red clover.

TREE: Sugar maple.

ANIMAL: Morgan horse.

BIRD: Hermit thrush.

FISH: Brook trout (cold water) and walleye pike (warm water).

INSECT: Honeybee.

BEVERAGE: Milk.

LEGAL HOLIDAYS: New Year's Day, 1 January; birthday of Martin Luther King Jr., 3rd Monday in January; Presidents' Day, 3rd Monday in February; Town Meeting Day, 1st Tuesday in March; Memorial Day, last Monday in May; Independence Day, 4 July; Bennington Battle Day, 16 August; Labor Day, 1st Monday in September; Veterans Day, 11 November; Thanksgiving Day, 4th Thursday in November and the day following; Christmas Day, 25 December.

TIME: 7 a.m. EST = noon GMT.

Location and Size

Situated in the northeastern United States, Vermont is the second largest of the six New England states, and ranks 43rd in size among the 50 states. Vermont's total area is 9,614 square miles (24,900 square kilometers), including 9,249 square miles (23,955 square kilometers) of land and 365 square miles (945 square kilometers) of inland water. Its maximum east–west extension is 90 miles (145 kilometers). Its maximum

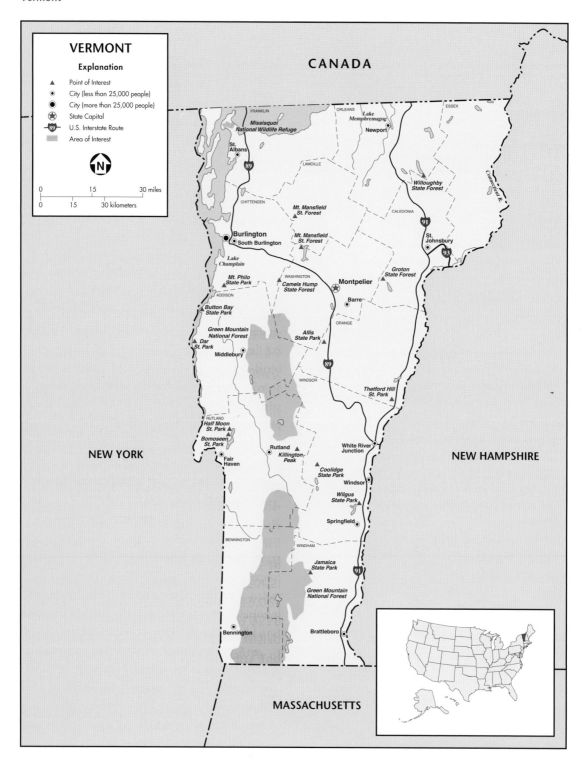

VERMONT

Explanation

▲ Point of Interest
◉ City (less than 25,000 people)
● City (more than 25,000 people)
✪ State Capital
—89— U.S. Interstate Route
▨ Area of Interest

◈N

0   15   30 miles
0   15   30 kilometers

CANADA

FRANKLIN

Missisquoi
National Wildlife Refuge

ORLEANS

Lake
Memphremagog

Newport

ESSEX

St.
Albans

LAMOILLE

Willoughby
State Forest

CHITTENDEN

Mt. Mansfield
St. Forest

CALEDONIA

Burlington
South Burlington

Mt. Mansfield
St. Forest

St.
Johnsbury

Lake
Champlain

Mt. Philo
State Park

WASHINGTON

Camels Hump
State Forest

Montpelier

Groton
State Forest

ADDISON

Barre

Button Bay
State Park

Green Mountain
National Forest

▲ Dar
St. Park

Allis
State Park

Middlebury

ORANGE

WINDSOR

Thetford Hill
St. Park

RUTLAND

Half Moon
St. Park

Bomoseen
St. Park

Rutland

Killington
Peak

White River
Junction

NEW YORK

Fair
Haven

Coolidge
State Park

NEW HAMPSHIRE

Windsor

Wilgus
State Park

Springfield

BENNINGTON

WINDHAM

Jamaica
State Park

Green Mountain
National Forest

Bennington

Brattleboro

MASSACHUSETTS

north–south extension is 158 miles (254 kilometers). Vermont's total boundary length is 561 miles (903 kilometers). The state's territory includes several islands and the lower part of a peninsula jutting south into Lake Champlain.

2 Topography

The Green Mountains are Vermont's most prominent physical feature. Extending north–south from the Canadian border to the Massachusetts state line, the Green Mountains contain the highest peaks, including Mansfield at 4,393 feet (1,340 meters), the highest point in Vermont. A much lower range, the Taconic Mountains, straddles the New York–Vermont border for about 80 miles (129 kilometers). To the north is the narrow Valley of Vermont and farther north is the Champlain Valley, a lowland between Lake Champlain (site of the state's lowest point, 95 feet/29 meters above sea level) and the Green Mountains. The Vermont piedmont is a narrow corridor of hills and valleys stretching to the east of the Green Mountains. The Northeast Highlands consist of an isolated series of peaks near the New Hampshire border.

Vermont's major inland rivers are the Missisquoi, Lamoille, and Winooski. The state includes about 66% of Lake Champlain on its western border and about 25% of Lake Memphremagog on the northern border.

3 Climate

In Burlington, mean temperatures range from 18°F (-7°C) in January to 70°F (21°C) in July. Winters are generally colder and summer nights cooler in the higher elevations of the Green Mountains. The record high temperature for the state is 105°F (41°C), registered at Vernon on 4 July 1911. The record low, -50°F (-46°C), occurred at Bloomfield on 30 December 1933.

The average annual precipitation is 40 inches (102 centimeters). Annual snowfall ranges from 55 inches (140 centimeters) in the lowlands to 125 inches (318 centimeters) in the mountain areas.

4 Plants and Animals

Common trees of Vermont include the commercially important sugar maple (the state tree), ash, butternut, white pine, and the poplar. Other native plants include 15 types of conifer, 192 sedges, and 130 grasses. In 2012, two plant species, Jesup's milk-vetch and northeastern bulrush, were listed by the US Fish and Wildlife Service as endangered.

Native mammals include coyote, red fox, and snowshoe hare. Characteristic birds include the raven and Canada jay. In 2012, the US Fish and Wildlife Service listed three Vermont animal species as threatened or endangered. These were the Indiana bat, Canada lynx, and dwarf wedgemussel.

5 Environmental Protection

All natural resource regulation, planning, and operation are coordinated by the Department of Environmental Conservation. Several dams on the Winooski and Connecticut rivers help control flooding of the river basins. In an effort to reduce roadside litter, the use of throwaway beverage containers was banned in 1972. Billboards were banned in 1968.

In 2012, Vermont had 11 hazardous waste sites listed in the Environmental Protection Agency's National Priorities List. These included five landfills and three mines. As of 2012, about 5% of the state was designated as wetlands and the government had established the Vermont Wetlands Conservation Strategy.

6 Population

In 2011, Vermont ranked 49th among the 50 states in population with an estimated total of 626,431 residents. Population density was 67.73 inhabitants per square mile (26.15 per square kilometer) in 2010. The population was projected to reach 703,288 by 2025. The median age in 2011 was 42 years. That year, about 15% of all residents were 65 or older while 20.1% were under 18.

In 2011, the largest cities in Vermont were Burlington (42,645 people), South Burlington (18,017), and Rutland (16,399). Montpelier, with less than 8,000 residents, is the smallest state capital, by population, in the United States. In 2010, 32% of the state's population lived in metropolitan areas.

7 Ethnic Groups

According to the 2010 Census, there were 50,683 (8.1%) residents in Vermont reporting French Canadian ancestry and 47,807 (7.6%) listing their ancestry as Italian. Hispanics and Latinos numbered 9,208. Among those who listed only one race on the Census, 7,947 marked Asian, 6,277 marked black or African American, and 2,207 marked American Indian/ Alaska Native. About 24,837 residents were foreign born.

Vermont Population Profile

Total population per Census 2010:	625,741
Population change, 2006–10:	0.3%
Hispanic or Latino†:	1.5%
Population by race	
One race:	98.3%
White:	95.3%
Black or African American:	1.0%
American Indian/Alaska Native:	0.4%
Asian:	1.3%
Native Hawaiian/Pacific Islander:	0.0%
Some other race:	0.3%
Two or more races:	1.7%

Population by Age Group, Census 2010

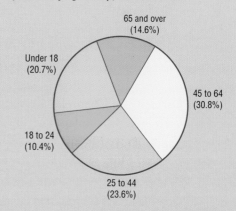

65 and over (14.6%)
Under 18 (20.7%)
45 to 64 (30.8%)
18 to 24 (10.4%)
25 to 44 (23.6%)

Major Cities by Population, 2011 Estimates

City	Population	% change 2005–11
Burlington	42,645	10.7
South Burlington	18,017	6.0
Rutland	16,399	-3.8
Essex Junction	9,331	5.5
Barre	9,066	-0.7
Montpelier	7,868	-1.7
Winooski	7,312	15.1
St. Albans	6,971	-6.8
Newport	4,579	-12.1
Bellows Falls	3,131	5.0

Notes: †A person of Hispanic or Latino origin may be of any race. NA indicates that data are not available. Percentages may not equal 100 due to rounding.

SOURCE: U.S. Census Bureau. Census 2010 and Population Estimates. www.census.gov/ (accessed July 2012).

Vermont Population by Race
CENSUS 2010

This table shows the number of people who are of one, two, or three or more races. For those claiming two races, the number of people belonging to the various categories is listed. The U.S. government conducts a census of the population every 10 years.

	Number	Percent
Total population	625,741	100.0
One race	614,988	98.3
Two races	10,143	1.6
White *and* Black or African American	2,353	0.4
White *and* American Indian/Alaska Native	4,535	0.7
White *and* Asian	2,112	0.3
White *and* Native Hawaiian/Pacific Islander	148	—
White *and* some other race	549	0.1
Black or African American *and* American Indian/Alaska Native	116	—
Black or African American *and* Asian	53	—
Black or African American *and* Native Hawaiian/Pacific Islander	21	—
Black or African American *and* some other race	63	—
American Indian/Alaska Native *and* Asian	24	—
American Indian/Alaska Native *and* Native Hawaiian/Pacific Islander	7	—
American Indian/Alaska Native *and* some other race	37	—
Asian *and* Native Hawaiian/Pacific Islander	33	—
Asian *and* some other race	82	—
Native Hawaiian/Pacific Islander *and* some other race	10	—
Three or more races	610	0.1

SOURCE: U.S. Census Bureau. Census 2010. www.census/gov/ (accessed July 2012). A dash (—) indicates that the percent is less than 0.1.

8 Languages

Vermont English, although typical of the Northern dialect, differs from that of New Hampshire in several respects, including retention of the final *r* and use of *eavestrough* in place of *eavespout* or *gutters*.

In 2011, 95.1% of the population age five and over spoke only English at home. Other languages spoken at home included Spanish (1%), other Indo-European languages (3.1%), and Asian and Pacific Islander languages (0.7%).

9 Religions

According to a 2008 survey by the Pew Forum on Religion & Public Life, 29% of the people in New Hampshire and Vermont, which were counted together, said they were Catholic. Another 23% identified as mainline Protestant, while 11% were affiliated with Evangelical Protestant traditions. Judaism, Buddhism, and the Mormonism were the religion of 1% or less of the population. In this region, 26% of people said they were unaffiliated with any religious faith.

Notably, Vermont was the birthplace of both Joseph Smith and Brigham Young, founders of the Church of Jesus Christ of Latter-day Saints (Mormons).

10 Transportation

In 2009, there were approximately 600 rail miles (965 kilometers) of track operated by eight freight railroads. In 2012, Amtrak provided passenger service to 11 stations in the state.

There were 14,436 miles (23,232 kilometers) of public streets, roads, and highways in 2009. Hundreds of miles of roads were damaged in 2011 by Hurricane Irene. A total of 208,000 automobiles, 256,000 trucks, 29,000 motorcycles, and 1,000 buses were registered in the state in 2009, when there were 506,977 licensed drivers.

In 2012, Vermont had 62 airports, 16 heliports, and 6 seaplane bases. Burlington International Airport is the state's major air terminal. In 2009, there were 702,301 passenger enplanements in the entire state.

Autumn in Vermont brings a great bounty of colors, as shown here along a country road. © ENFI/SHUTTERSTOCK.COM.

11 History

Algonquian-speaking Abnaki settled along Lake Champlain and in the Connecticut Valley, and Mahican settled in the southern counties of what is now Vermont between 1200 and 1790. The region, however, had shown evidence of continuous habitation for the last 10,000 years. In 1609, Samuel de Champlain became the first European explorer of Vermont. From the mid-17th to the mid-18th centuries, there was regular traffic through the state and attempts at settlement by the French. Fort Dummer, built in 1724 near present-day Brattleboro, was the first permanent settlement.

Governor Benning Wentworth of New Hampshire, claiming that his colony extended as far west as did Massachusetts and Connecticut, had granted 131 town charters in the territory by 1764. In that year, the crown declared that New York's northeastern boundary was the Connecticut River. Owners of New Hampshire titles, fearful of losing their land, prevented New York from enforcing its jurisdiction. The Green Mountain Boys, organized by Ethan Allen in 1770–1771, scared off the defenseless settlers under the New York title and scorned the New York courts.

Shortly after the outbreak of the Revolutionary War, Ethan Allen's Green Mountain Boys helped capture Fort Ticonderoga. There were several British raids on Vermont towns during the war. After the Revolution, most Vermonters wanted to join the United States, but members of the dominant Allen faction refused in order to protect their large landholdings. Vermont declared itself an independent republic with the name "New Connecticut." Following the political defeat of Allen and his followers in 1789, Vermont sought statehood and was admitted to the Union on 4 March 1791.

State Development Vermonters of the next generation developed towns and villages with water-powered mills, charcoal-fired furnaces, general stores, newspapers, craft shops, churches, and schools. In the War of 1812, Vermont soldiers fought in the Battle of Plattsburgh, New York. The Mexican War (1846–1848) was unpopular in the state, but Vermont, which had strongly opposed slavery, was an enthusiastic supporter of the Union during the Civil War.

The opening of the Champlain–Hudson Canal in 1823, and the building of the early railroad lines in 1846–1853, made Vermont more vulnerable to competition from the West, destroying many small farms and businesses. Immigration by the Irish and French Canadians, however, soon stabilized the population and the expansion of light industry bolstered the economy.

During the 20th century and especially after World War II, manufacturing prospered in valley villages, and Vermont's picturesque landscape began to attract city buyers of second homes. New highways made the cities and rural areas more accessible, and Vermont absorbed an influx of young professionals from New York and Massachusetts.

Longtime Vermonters enjoy their state's natural beauty. As of 2010, Vermont was the nation's second most rural state, behind only Maine. Slightly more than 61% of Vermont residents live in areas designated as rural. In 1993, Vermont passed legislation barring smoking in all public buildings.

In 2000, Vermont was the first state to allow same-sex civil unions, and in 2009, the legislature voted to allow gay marriages, becoming the fourth state in the United States to do so.

Parts of Vermont were severely damaged by flooding related to Hurricane Irene in August 2011. The flooding was the worst the state had seen in 83 years and repair costs were expected to exceed $1 billion.

12 State Government

The general assembly consists of a 150-member house of representatives and a 30-member senate. State elective officials include the governor, lieutenant governor (elected separately), treasurer, and secretary of state. The governor may serve unlimited two-year terms. All bills require a majority vote in each house for passage. Bills can be vetoed by the governor, and vetoes can be overridden by a two-thirds vote of each legislative house.

The legislative salary as of 2011 was $604.79 per week and the governor's salary in 2010 was $142,542.

13 Political Parties

The Republican Party gained control of Vermont state offices in 1856 and kept it for more than 100 years. No Democrat was elected governor from 1853 until 1962.

In June 2012, there were 444,550 registered voters; there is no party registration in the state. Democrat Howard Dean was elected governor in 1991, and was reelected in 1994, 1996, 1998, and 2000. (The state has no term limit for the office of governor.) Although Dean gained early support in his run for the Democratic presidential nomination in 2003, he withdrew from the

Vermont Governors: 1778–2013

1778–1789	Thomas Chittenden	—	1890–1892	Carroll Smalley Page		Republican
1789–1790	Moses Robinson	Dem-Rep	1892–1894	Levi Knight Fuller		Republican
1790–1797	Thomas Chittenden	—	1894–1896	Urban Andrain Woodbury		Republican
1797	Paul Brigham	Dem-Rep	1896–1898	Josiah Grout		Republican
1797–1807	Isaac Tichenor	Federalist	1898–1900	Edward Curtis Smith		Republican
1807–1808	Israel Smith	Dem-Rep	1900–1902	William Wallace Stickney		Republican
1808–1809	Isaac Tichenor	Federalist	1902–1904	John Griffith McCullough		Republican
1809–1913	Jonas Galusha	Dem-Rep	1904–1906	Charles James Bell		Republican
1813–1815	Martin Chittenden	Federalist	1906–1908	Fletcher Dutton Proctor		Republican
1815–1820	Jonas Galusha	Dem-Rep	1908–1910	George Herbert Prouty		Republican
1820–1823	Richard Skinner	Dem-Rep	1910–1912	John Abner Mead		Republican
1823–1826	Cornelius P. Van Ness	Dem-Rep	1912–1915	Allen Miller Fletcher		Republican
1826–1828	Ezra Butler	Dem-Rep	1915–1917	Charles Winslow Gates		Republican
1828–1831	Samuel Chandler Crafts	Nat-Rep	1917–1919	Horace French Graham		Republican
1831–1835	William Adams Palmer	Anti–Mason Dem	1919–1921	Percival Wood Clement		Republican
1835–1841	Silas Hemenway Jennison	Whig	1921–1923	James Hartness		Republican
1841–1843	Charles Paine	Whig	1923–1925	Redfield Proctor, Jr.		Republican
1843–1844	John Mattocks	Whig	1925–1927	Frankin Swift Billings		Republican
1844–1846	William Slade	Whig	1927–1931	John Eliakim Weeks		Republican
1846–1848	Horace Eaton	Whig	1931–1935	Stanley Calef Wilson		Republican
1848–1850	Carlos Coolidge	Whig	1935–1937	Charles Manley Smith		Republican
1850–1852	Charles Kilborn Williams	Whig	1937–1941	George David Aiken		Republican
1852–1853	Erastus Fairbanks	Whig	1941–1945	William Henry Wills		Republican
1853–1854	John Staniford Robinson	Democrat	1945–1947	Mortimer Robinson Proctor		Republican
1854–1856	Stephen Royce	Whig, Republican	1947–1950	Ernest William Gibson, Jr.		Republican
1856–1858	Ryland Fletcher	Know Nothing	1950–1951	Harold John Arthur		Republican
1858–1860	Hiland Hall	Republican	1951–1955	Lee Earl Emerson		Republican
1860–1861	Erastus Fairbanks	Whig	1955–1959	Joseph Blaine Johnson		Republican
1861–1863	Frederick Holbrook	Whig Republican	1959–1961	Robert Theodore Stafford		Republican
1863–1865	John Gregory Smith	Republican	1961–1963	Frank Ray Keyser, Jr.		Republican
1865–1867	Paul Dillingham, Jr.	Republican	1963–1969	Philip Henderson Hoff		Democrat
1867–1869	John Boardman Page	Republican	1969–1973	Deane Chandler Davis		Republican
1869–1870	Peter Thacher Washburn	Republican	1973–1977	Thomas Paul Salmon		Democrat
1870	George Whitman Hendee	Republican	1977–1985	Richard Arkwright Snelling		Republican
1870–1872	John Wolcott Stewart	Republican	1985–1991	Madeleine May Kunin		Democrat
1872–1874	Julius Converse	Republican	1991	Richard Arkwright Snelling		Republican
1874–1876	Asahel Peck	Republican	1991–2003	Howard Dean		Democrat
1876–1878	Horace Fairbanks	Republican	2003–2011	James Douglas		Republican
1878–1880	Redfield Proctor, Sr.	Republican	2011–	Peter Shumlin		Democrat
1880–1882	Roswell Farnham	Republican				
1882–1884	John Lester Barstow	Republican				
1884–1886	Samuel Everett Pingree	Republican	Anti–Mason Democrat – Anti–Mason Dem			
1886–1888	Ebenezer Jolls Ormsbee	Republican	Democratic Republican – Dem-Rep			
1888–1890	William Paul Dillingham	Republican	National Republican – Nat-Rep			

race in early 2004. He later became the chairman of the Democratic National Committee. Republican James Douglas was elected governor of Vermont in 2002, and was reelected in 2004 and 2006. He announced he would not run for reelection in 2010, and Peter Shumlin, a Democrat, won the governor's seat.

Following the 2010 elections, Democrats controlled the state senate, with 20 seats out of 30. In the state house of representatives, the Democrats held 94 seats; the Republicans had 48; Independents had 3 seats; and the Vermont Progressive Party had 5 seats. Vermont is one of the only states with a third party that has such a significant presence. In 2012, women held 59 seats in the state house and 11 seats in the state senate.

Democrat Patrick Leahy has served the state as US senator since 1975. In 2001, Senator James Jeffords, after winning reelection in 2000 as a Republican, became an Independent. His move shifted control of the evenly divided Senate to the Democrats. Jeffords announced his retirement in 2005. In 2006, veteran congressman Bernie Sanders, an Independent, widely supported by the Vermont Progressive Party, ran for and won the seat in the US Senate vacated by Jeffords. He has caucused with the Democrats. Sanders easily won re-election in 2012. Vermont's delegation to the House of Representatives consisted of one Democrat, Peter Welch, as of 2012.

Vermont has often shown its independence in national political elections. In 2000, the state gave 51% of the vote to Democratic nominee Al Gore and 41% to Republican George W. Bush. In 2004, Democrat John Kerry won 59% of the vote in Vermont to President Bush's 39%. In 2008, Democrat Barack Obama took the state with 67.5% of the vote against Republican John McCain's 30.6%. President Obama again won the state in 2012, solidly beating Republican challenger Mitt Romney.

14 Local Government

In 2010, there were 14 counties, 9 cities, and 237 townships in Vermont, as well as 360 public school districts. In 2007, there were 144 special districts in the state. County officers, operating out of shire towns (county seats), include the probate courts judge, county clerk, state's attorney, and treasurer. All cities have mayor-council systems. Towns are governed by selectmen; larger towns also have town managers. The town meeting remains an important part of government in the state. In 2011, there were 35,021 full-time and 12,214 part-time state and local government employees in Vermont.

15 Judicial System

Vermont's highest court is the supreme court, which consists of a chief justice and four associate justices. Other courts include the superior and district courts. In 2010, the courts were restructured to unify all of the state courts under the supreme court, streamlining the judicial process in the state.

In 2010, Vermont had one of the lowest reported violent crime rates in the nation, at 130.2 reported incidents per 100,000 residents. The murder and nonnegligent manslaughter rate

Vermont Presidential Vote by Major Political Parties, 1948–2012			
Year	Vermont Winner	Democrat	Republican
1948	Dewey (R)	45,557	75,926
1952	*Eisenhower (R)	43,299	109,717
1956	*Eisenhower (R)	42,540	110,390
1960	Nixon (R)	69,186	98,131
1964	*Johnson (D)	108,127	54,942
1968	*Nixon (R)	70,255	85,142
1972	*Nixon (R)	68,174	117,149
1976	Ford (R)	77,798	100,387
1980	*Reagan (R)	81,891	94,598
1984	*Reagan (R)	95,730	135,865
1988	*Bush (R)	115,775	124,331
1992	*Clinton (D)	133,592	88,122
1996	*Clinton (D)	137,984	80,532
2000	Gore (D)	149,022	119,775
2004	Kerry (D)	184,067	121,180
2008	*Obama (D)	219,262	98,974
2012	*Obama (D)	199,239	92,698

*Won US presidential election.

Independent candidate Ross Perot received 65,991 votes in 1992 and 31,024 votes in 1996.

was 1.1 per 100,000 inhabitants; forcible rape, 21.1; aggravated assault, 96.2; and property crime, 2,282.3. As of 31 December 2009, a total of 2,220 prisoners were being held in Vermont's state and federal prisons. Vermont no longer has the death penalty; the state abolished it in 1964.

16 Migration

The earliest Vermont settlers were farmers from southern New England and New York. Most were of English descent although some Dutch settlers moved to Vermont from New York. French Canadians began arriving in the 1830s. As milling, quarrying, and mining grew during the 19th century, other Europeans arrived—small groups of Italians and Scots in Barre, and Poles, Swedes, Czechs, Russians, and Austrians in the Rutland quarry areas. Irish immigrants built the railroads in the mid-19th century. Steady out-migrations during the 19th and early 20th centuries kept population increases down.

Between 2009 and 2010, the total population (ages one and older) of Vermont increased by 6,976, due to the net domestic in-migration (migration within a region or country) of natives (4,200), the net domestic out-migration of immigrants (-51), and the arrival from abroad of natives (2,200) and immigrants (627). Of the total foreign-born population in Vermont in 2010, 7.6% were from Africa, 28.1% were from Asia, 30.5% were from Europe, and 10.1% were from Latin America. The top three countries of birth of the foreign born in Vermont that year were Canada (23.4%), United Kingdom (6%), and Vietnam (5.6%). In comparison, the top three countries of birth in 1990 were Canada (38.1%), Germany (9.1%), and the United Kingdom (8.2%).

17 Economy

After World War II, agriculture was replaced by manufacturing and tourism as the backbone of the economy. Durable goods manufacturing (primarily electronics and machine parts), construction, wholesale and retail trade, and other service industries showed the largest growth in employment during the 1990s.

In 2010, Vermont's gross state product (GSP) was $26.4 billion, ranking it last among the US states. Per capital GSP was $44,000, ranking the state 30th. In 2010, there were 21,451 private nonfarm establishments and 59,945 nonemployer establishments in the state.

18 Income

In 2010, Vermont ranked 19th among the 50 states and the District of Columbia with a median per capita personal income (including nonmonetary income) of $41,832. The median annual household income for 2008–2010 was $53,409, ranking the state 22nd in the nation. In 2011, 11.5% of Vermont residents lived below the federal poverty level, compared to 15.9% nationwide.

19 Industry

Leading industry groups were electrical and electronic equipment, food products, printing and publishing, paper and allied products, fabricated metal products, and industrial machinery and equipment. Scales, machine tools, and electronic components are important manufactured items.

20 Labor

In August 2012, the civilian labor force in Vermont numbered 356,700. That month, 19,000 people were unemployed, for an unemployment rate of 5.3%, compared to the national average of 8.1%. That same month, nonfarm wage and salaried employment included: 13,600 workers employed in construction; 30,900 in manufacturing; 56,400 in trade, transportation and utilities; 12,200 in financial activities; 26,500 in business and professional occupations; 32,800 in leisure and hospitality; and 52,800 in government.

In 2011, 39,000 of Vermont's employed wage and salary workers were members of unions, representing 13.5% of those so employed. The national average was 13%.

21 Agriculture

Although Vermont is one of the nation's most rural states, only 20.9% of the land was farmland in 2007. Total agricultural output from Vermont's 7,000 farms was $826.4 million in 2011, with just $120 million coming from crops. Maple products were the leading crop,

Many of the earliest settlers in Vermont were farmers. Today, there are some 7,000 farms in the state. © REBVT/SHUTTERSTOCK.COM.

with $39.9 million in farm receipts in 2011, followed by greenhouse and nursery products, with $24.6 million in receipts. Leading exports that year were seeds ($6.9 million in receipts), feeds and fodders ($4.7 million), and fruits and fruit preparations ($3.6 million). Leading agricultural counties are Addison, Franklin, Orleans, Orange, and Rutland counties.

22 Domesticated Animals

The merino sheep and the Morgan horse (a breed developed in Vermont) were common sights on pastures more than a century ago, but today they have been for the most part replaced by dairy cattle. Total output from domesticated animals was $626.57 million in 2011. Dairy was the largest contributor to farming revenue in the state in 2011, producing $445 million in sales. Cattle and calves added $71 million. Top exports that year included $27.4 million in dairy products receipts.

23 Fishing

Sport fishermen can find ample species of trout, perch, walleye pike, bass, and pickerel in Vermont's waters, many of which are stocked by the Department of Fish and Game. There are two national fish hatcheries in the state (Pittsford and White River). There is very little commercial fishing.

24 Forestry

The Green Mountain State is covered by 4,628,000 acres (1,873,000 hectares) of forestland, which is 78% of the state's total land area. Much of it is owned or leased by lumber companies. Output from forestry and farm services was $80 million in 2011.

The largest forest reserve in Vermont is the Green Mountain National Forest, with 391,862 acres (158,587 hectares) in 2005. It is managed by the US Forest Service.

25 Mining

The value of nonfuel mineral production in Vermont in 2011 was estimated to be $123 million, 0.17% of the US total, and ranking the state 44th in the nation. Crushed stone, dimension stone, gemstones, and construction sand and gravel were the main nonfuel mineral commodities, with crushed stone and dimension stone accounting for 71% of Vermont's production. In 2010, 10.2 million metric tons of crushed stone were mined in the state, valued at $101 million; along with 4.4 million metric tons of sand and gravel, valued at $36.5 million; and 7.3 million metric tons of aggregate, valued at $58.9 million.

26 Energy and Power

Because of the state's lack of fossil fuel resources, utility bills are higher in Vermont than in most states. Vermont has no marketable resources of crude oil, coal, or natural gas. As of June 2012, total net electricity generation was 446,000 megawatt hours (MWh). This included 326,000 MWh generated in nuclear power plants; 79,000 MWh in hydroelectric plants; and 41,000 MWh from other renewable resources. Vermont has one nuclear power plant, Vermont Yankee.

27 Commerce

In 2008, there were 851 wholesale establishments in the state employing 11,000 people and providing a payroll of $509 million. Retail establishments included 3,734 businesses, employing 41,000 people with a payroll of $964 million. In 2011, Vermont exported $4.25 billion in goods. Top exports that year included electronic circuits and machine parts.

28 Public Finance

The budgets for two fiscal years are submitted by the governor to the Vermont General Assembly for approval during its biennial session. The fiscal year runs from 1 July to 30 June.

The total revenues for 2008 were $5.1 billion. Expenditures were $5.2 billion. The highest general expenditures were for education ($832 million), public welfare ($1.25 billion), and highways ($268 million). The total debt was $3.37 billion.

29 Taxation

In 2012, Vermont's personal income tax five-bracket schedule ranged from 3.6% to 9.5%. Corporations are taxed at rates ranging from 7% to 8.9%. The state sales and use tax rate is 6%, with basics, including food and medicines, exempted, and local sales taxes limited to 1%. The state also imposes a full array of excise taxes covering motor fuels, tobacco

The capitol building of Vermont is in Montpelier. © JEFFREY M. FRANK/SHUTTERSTOCK.COM.

products, insurance premiums, public utilities, alcoholic beverages, parimutuels, and other selected items.

The state collected $2.68 billion in taxes in 2011, of which $955 million came from state property taxes, $661 million from income taxes, $99.8 million came from licenses and fees, and $661 million came from sales taxes and gross receipts. In 2011, Vermont ranked fourth highest in the United States for per capita state tax burden, with per capita tax of $4,291.

30 Health

In 2011, the infant mortality rate was 4.8 per 1,000 live births. The crude death rate in 2008 was 7.2 deaths per 1,000 people. In 2010, 15.4% of Vermont adults smoked, compared to the US rate of 17.2%. That year, 58.5% of adults were overweight or obese, and 6.8% had been diagnosed with diabetes. The death rate from diabetes was 19.2 per 100,000 residents in 2009. Death rates from other diseases that year included cancers at 168.8 per 100,000; heart disease at 156 per 100,000; and cerebrovascular disease at 29.6 per 100,000. In 2008, there were 350 people in Vermont living with HIV/AIDS, less than 0.01% of the US total.

Vermont's 14 hospitals had approximately 2.1 beds per 1,000 in population in 2010. The average expense for community hospital care was $1,656 per inpatient day in 2010. Vermont had 333 doctors per 100,000 residents in 2008 and 1,017 registered nurses per 100,000 residents in 2011. The state had 365 dentists in 2012. In 2010, about 9% of the population was uninsured.

31 Housing

As rustic farmhouses gradually disappear, modern units (many of them vacation homes for both Vermonters and nonresidents) are being built to replace them. In 2011, there were an estimated 324,385 housing units in Vermont, 257,358 (79.3%) that were occupied and 183,452 (71.3%) that were owner-occupied. About 66.8% (216,849) of all units were single-family, detached homes, and 6.9% (22,318) were mobile homes. About 29% of all housing was built in 1939 or earlier. Fuel oil was the most common energy source for heating. It was estimated that 1,136 (0.5%) units lacked complete plumbing facilities and 2,172 (0.8%) lacked complete kitchen facilities. The average household size of owner-occupied units was 2.46 people, while the average household size of renter-occupied units was 2.03 people.

In 2011, median home value was $213,700. The median monthly cost for mortgage owners was $1,487. Renters paid a median of $849 per month. Vermont had the second-highest percentage of seasonal, recreational, and occasional use homes at 15.6%, behind only Maine.

32 Education

In 2010, 90.6% of Vermont residents age 25 and older were high school graduates and 20.2% had obtained a bachelor's degree or higher.

Total public school enrollment was estimated at 86,000 at the end of the 2009 school year. Expenditures for public education were $1.36 million or $18,913 per student in 2009, making Vermont the state that spent the most per student on public education that year.

As of 2008, there were 43,000 students enrolled in college or graduate school, and Vermont had 25 degree-granting institutions. The state college system includes colleges at Castleton, Johnson, and Lyndonville; a technical college at Randolph Center; and the Community College of Vermont system with 12 branch campuses. The University of Vermont is a state-supported institution combining features of both a private and a state facility. Founded in 1791, it is the oldest higher educational institution in the state.

Notable private institutions include Bennington College, Champlain College, Landmark College (serving students with ADHD and learning disabilities), Marlboro College, and Norwich University, the oldest private military college in the United States. The School for International Training is the academic branch of the Experiment in International Living, a student exchange program. Other notable institutions include St. Michael's College and Trinity College.

33 Arts

The Vermont State Crafts Centers at Frog Hollow (Middlebury), Burlington, and Manchester display the works of Vermont artisans. Marlboro College is the home of the summer Marlboro Music Festival, cofounded by famed pianist Rudolf Serkin, who directed the festival from 1952 to 1992. Among the summer theaters in the state are those at Dorset and Weston. The Middlebury College Bread Loaf Writers' Conference, founded in 1926, meets each August in Ripton.

The Flynn Center for the Performing Arts in Burlington serves as a major performance center for the area. It is home to the Lyric Stage, the Vermont Symphony Orchestra, the Vermont Stage Company, and the Burlington Discover Jazz Festival. Other musical performance and education venues include the Vermont Jazz Center in Brattleboro and the Vergennes Opera House, which presents concerts, films, dance and theater presentations, and various literary readings, as well as operas.

The Vermont Council on the Arts supports a number of programs with the help of state and federal funds. The Vermont Humanities Council supports literacy and history-related programs, as well as sponsoring annual Humanities Camps at schools throughout the state.

34 Libraries and Museums

During the 2009/10 fiscal year, the state's public libraries held 2.94 million books, and had a total of 3.25 million items in all formats (except for periodicals and electronic media) as well as a combined circulation of 4.69 million. The largest academic library was at the University of Vermont (Burlington), with a book stock of over 1.5 million and 2,266 periodical subscriptions in 2009.

Vermont has 89 museums and more than 65 historic sites. Among them are the Bennington Museum, with its collection of Early American glass, pottery, furniture, and Grandma Moses paintings; and the Art Gallery–St. Johnsbury Athenaeum, featuring 19th-century American artists.

The Shelburne Museum, housed in restored Early American buildings, contains collections of American primitives and Native American artifacts. The Vermont Museum, in Montpelier, features historical exhibits concerning Native

Americans, the Revolutionary War, rural life, and railroads and industry. Old Constitution House in Windsor offers exhibits on Vermont history.

35 Communications

In 2010, 74.7% of residents had access to the Internet at home and 69.2% had broadband. In 2012, there were 95 radio stations in the state, including 5 major AM and 19 major FM radio stations, as well as 7 major television stations.

36 Press

In 2012, the leading daily was the *Burlington Free Press* (30,558 readers). *Vermont Life* magazine is published quarterly.

37 Tourism, Travel, and Recreation

With the building of the first ski slopes in the 1930s and the development of modern highways, tourism became a major industry in Vermont. In 2009, direct spending from about 13.7 million visitors totaled $1.42 billion, down significantly due to the recession that began in 2008. The tourism and travel industry supports 33,500 jobs (11.5% of all jobs in the state).

Based on room receipts, winter is the most popular time for visitors, with 37.2% of revenue generated in that season. The state's ski areas offer some of the finest skiing in the East for winter visitors. There are 52 state parks and over 100 campgrounds in the state. Historical sites, including several Revolutionary War battlefields, are popular attractions. Shopping,

One of Vermont's most-sought products is its maple syrup. Here, buckets are attached to trees to catch the sap. © DENNIS DONOHUE/
SHUTTERSTOCK.COM.

particularly for Vermont-made products such as maple syrup, is a major activity for all visitors.

The state fair is held each October in Rutland. Other top annual events include the Stowe Winter Carnival, Vermont Maple Open House Weekend, Dummerston Apple Pie Festival, and Wassail Weekend.

38 Sports

Vermont has no major league professional sports teams. Skiing is, perhaps, the most popular participation sport. Vermont ski areas have hosted national and international ski competitions in both Alpine and Nordic events. World Cup races have been run at Stratton Mountain and the national cross country championships have been held near Putney.

39 Famous Vermonters

Two US presidents, both of whom assumed office on the death of their predecessors, were born in Vermont. Chester Alan Arthur (1829–1886) became the 21st president after James A. Garfield's assassination in 1881 and finished Garfield's term. Calvin Coolidge (1872–1933), 28th president, became president on the death of Warren G. Harding in 1923 and was elected to a full term in 1924.

Important state leaders were Ethan Allen (1738–1789), a frontier folk hero and leader of the Green Mountain Boys; and Ira Allen (1751–1814), the brother of Ethan, who led the fight for statehood.

Vermont's many entrepreneurs and inventors include plow and tractor manufacturer

Among the most popular participation sports in Vermont is skiing. © MARCIO JOSE BASTOS SILVA/SHUTTERSTOCK.COM.

The 28th president, Calvin Coolidge was born in Vermont. He is seen here talking to labor leader Mary Harris "Mother" Jones in 1924. COURTESY OF THE LIBRARY OF CONGRESS.

John Deere (1804–1886) and Elisha G. Otis (1811–1861), inventor of a steam elevator.

Robert Frost (b. California, 1874–1963) maintained a summer home near Ripton, where he helped found Middlebury College's Bread Loaf Writers' Conference. In 1992, Louise Gluck (1943–1997) became the first Vermont woman to win a Pulitzer Prize for poetry. Performer Rudy Vallee (1901–1986), known for his musical skills, was also born in the state.

Skiers Billy Kidd (1943–) and Andrea Mead Lawrence (1932–2009), both Olympic medalists, grew up in Vermont and trained in the state.

40 Bibliography

BOOKS

Bristow, M. J. *State Songs of America.* Westport, CT: Greenwood Press, 2000.

Brown, Jonatha A. *Vermont.* Milwaukee: Gareth Stevens, 2007.

Bushnell, Mark. *It Happened in Vermont.* Guilford, CT: Globe Pequot, 2009.

Duffy, John J., Samuel B. Hand, and Ralph H. Orth, eds. *The Vermont Encyclopedia.* Lebanon, NH: University Press of New England, 2003.

Wilson, Robert F. *Vermont Curiosities: Quirky Characters, Roadside Oddities & Other Offbeat Stuff.* Guilford, CT: Globe Pequot, 2008.

Wilson, Robert F., Barbara Radcliffe Rogers, and Stillman Rogers. *Vermont, Off the Beaten Path,* 8th ed. Guilford, CT: GPP Travel, 2009.

WEB SITES

"Endangered Species Program." *US Fish & Wildlife Service.* http://www.fws.gov/endangered/ (accessed on November 5, 2012).

"State and County QuickFacts: Vermont." *US Bureau of the Census.* http://quickfacts.census.gov/qfd/states/50000.html (accessed on November 5, 2012).

"Vermont: Facts at-a-Glance." *StateHealthFacts.org.* http://www.statehealthfacts.org/profileglance.jsp?rgn=47&rgn=1 (accessed on November 5, 2012).

Vermont Vacation.com: The Official State of Vermont Tourism Site. http://www.vermontvacation.com/ (accessed on November 5, 2012).

Vermont.gov: The Official State Website. www.vermont.gov (accessed on November 5, 2012).

Virginia
Commonwealth of Virginia

ORIGIN OF STATE NAME: Named for Queen Elizabeth I of England, the "Virgin Queen."

NICKNAME: The Old Dominion.

CAPITAL: Richmond.

ENTERED UNION: 25 June 1788 (10th).

OFFICIAL SEAL: OBVERSE: the Roman goddess Virtus, dressed as an Amazon and holding a sheathed sword in one hand and a spear in the other, stands over the body of Tyranny, who is pictured with a broken chain in his hand and a fallen crown nearby. The state motto appears below, the word "Virginia" above, and a border of Virginia creeper encircles the whole. REVERSE: the Roman goddesses of Liberty, Eternity, and Fruitfulness, with the word "Perseverando" (by persevering) above.

FLAG: On a blue field, the state seal is centered on a white circle.

MOTTO: *Sic semper tyrannis* (Thus ever to tyrants).

SONG: "Carry Me Back to Old Virginia" was formally retired from official use in 1997 but has not yet been replaced.

FLOWER: Dogwood.

TREE: Dogwood.

BIRD: Cardinal.

DOG: Foxhound.

BEVERAGE: Milk.

SHELL: Oyster.

LEGAL HOLIDAYS: New Year's Day, 1 January; Lee-Jackson Day, 13 January; birthday of Martin Luther King Jr., 3rd Monday in January; Washington's Birthday, 3rd Monday in February; Memorial Day, last Monday in May; Independence Day, 4 July; Labor Day, 1st Monday in September; Columbus Day, 2nd Monday in October; Veterans' Day, 11 November; Thanksgiving Day, 4th Thursday in November and the day following; Christmas Day, 25 December.

TIME: 7 a.m. EST = noon GMT.

Location and Size

Situated on the eastern seaboard of the United States, Virginia is the fourth largest of the South Atlantic states and ranks 36th in size among the 50 states. The total area of Virginia is 40,600 square miles (105,153 square kilometers), of which land occupies 39,594 square miles (102,547 square kilometers) and inland water 1,006 square miles (2,606 square kilometers).

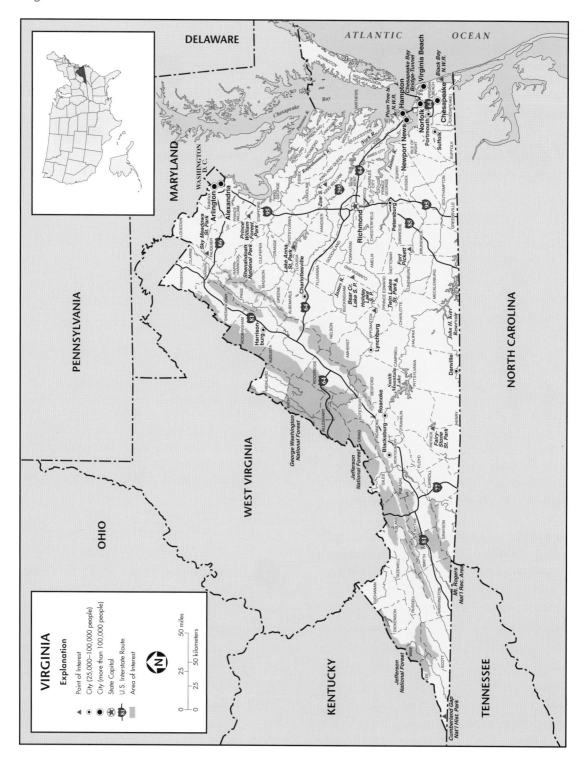

ATLANTIC OCEAN

DELAWARE

MARYLAND

PENNSYLVANIA

WEST VIRGINIA

OHIO

NORTH CAROLINA

KENTUCKY

TENNESSEE

Chesapeake Bay

WASHINGTON D.C.

Arlington
Alexandria

Sky Meadows St. Park
Prince William Forest Park

Shenandoah National Park

Harrison burg

Lake Anna St. Park
Charlottesville

Richmond

Petersburg
Fort Pickett

Bear Cr. Lake S.P.
Holiday Lake S.P.

Twin Lakes St. Park

Lynchburg

Danville

John H. Kerr Reservoir

George Washington National Forest

Smith Mountain Lake

Roanoke

Blacksburg

Fairy Stone St. Park

Jefferson National Forest

Mt. Rogers Nat'l Rec. Area

Cumberland Gap Nat'l Hist. Park

Jefferson National Forest

Newport News
Norfolk
Portsmouth
Suffolk

Hampton
Chesapeake Bay Bridge-Tunnel
Virginia Beach
Black Bay N.W.R.
Chesapeake

Plum Tree Is. N.W.R.

VIRGINIA

Explanation

△ Point of Interest
• City (25,000–100,000 people)
● City (more than 100,000 people)
✱ State Capital
 U.S. Interstate Route
 Area of Interest

N

0   25   50 miles
0   25   50 kilometers

The maximum point-to-point distance from the state's noncontiguous Eastern Shore to the western extremity is 470 miles (756 kilometers). The maximum north–south extension is about 200 miles (320 kilometers). The boundaries of Virginia total 1,356 miles (2,182 kilometers), of which 112 miles (180 kilometers) is general coastline. Virginia's offshore islands in the Atlantic include Chincoteague, Wallops, Cedar, Parramore, Hog Cobb, and Smith.

Virginia is bordered on the northwest by West Virginia; on the northeast by Maryland and the District of Columbia (with the line passing through the Potomac River and Chesapeake Bay); on the east by the Atlantic Ocean; on the south by North Carolina and Tennessee; and on the west by Kentucky. The state's geographic center is in Buckingham County, 5 miles (8 kilometers) southwest of the town of Buckingham.

2 Topography

Virginia consists of three principal areas: the Atlantic Coastal Plain, or Tidewater; the Piedmont Plateau, in the central section; and the Blue Ridge and Allegheny Mountains of the Appalachian chain, in the west and northwest. The long, narrow Blue Ridge Mountains reach a maximum elevation of 5,729 feet (1,746 meters) at Mount Rogers, the state's highest point. Between the Blue Ridge and the Allegheny Mountains of the Appalachian chain in the northwest lies the Valley of Virginia, consisting of transverse ridges and six separate valleys.

The Tidewater has many excellent harbors, notably the deep Hampton Roads estuary. Also in the southeast lies the Dismal Swamp, a drainage basin that includes Lake Drummond, about 7 miles (11 kilometers) long and 5 miles (8 kilometers) wide near the North Carolina border. The artificially created Smith Mountain Lake, at 31 square miles (80 square kilometers), is the largest lake wholly within the state. The John H. Kerr Reservoir, covering 76 square miles (197 square kilometers), straddles the Virginia–North Carolina line. The lowest point of the state is at sea level.

3 Climate

A mild, humid coastal climate is characteristic of Virginia. Temperatures become increasingly cooler with the rising altitudes as one moves westward. The normal daily average temperature at Richmond ranges from 35°F (2°C) in January to 78°F (26°C) in July. The record high, 110°F (43°C), was registered at Balcony Falls (near Glasgow) on 15 July 1954. The record low, -30°F (-34°C), was set at Mountain Lake on 22 January 1985.

The annual average precipitation at Richmond is 42.7 inches (108 centimeters). The average annual snowfall in Richmond is 13.9 inches (35 centimeters). Virginia is also in the path of mid-Atlantic hurricanes and was struck by Hurricane Isobel in 2003 and Hurricane Irene in 2011.

4 Plants and Animals

Native to Virginia are a dozen varieties of oak, five of pine, and two each of walnut, locust, gum, and poplar. Pines predominate in the coastal areas, with numerous hardwoods on slopes and ridges inland. Characteristic wildflowers include trailing arbutus and mountain laurel. In 2012, 15 plant species were listed by the US Fish and Wildlife Service as threatened or endangered in Virginia, including the Virginia round-leaf birch, smooth coneflower, Peter's mountain mallow, and Virginia sneezeweed.

Among native mammals are white-tailed (Virginia) deer, elk, black bear, and bobcat. Principal game birds include the ruffed grouse (commonly called pheasant in Virginia), wild turkey, and bobwhite quail. Tidal waters abound with mussels, gray and spotted trout, and flounder; bass, bream, and bluegill live in freshwater ponds and streams. Native reptiles include such poisonous snakes as the northern copperhead and eastern cottonmouth.

In 2012, the US Fish and Wildlife Service listed 49 animal species as threatened or endangered in Virginia, including the Virginia big-eared bat, red-cockaded woodpecker, northeastern beach tiger beetle, and Virginia northern flying squirrel. Many of the rare or endangered species in the state are found in the Dismal Swamp.

5 Environmental Protection

The Virginia Department of Environmental Quality (DEQ), established in 1993, is under the jurisdiction of the Secretary of Natural Resources. The mission of the DEQ is to protect the environment of Virginia in order to promote the health and wellbeing of the citizens of the Commonwealth. The Commission of Game and Inland Fisheries manages land wildlife and freshwater fish resources, while the Marine Resources Commission manages the wetlands, commercial fishery resources, and the use of the marine environment in the Tidewater area.

Virginia has implemented programs to improve air quality in the Northern Virginia, Richmond, and Hampton Roads regions. The

---

Virginia Population Profile

Total population per Census 2010:	8,001,024
Population change, 2006–10:	4.7%
Hispanic or Latino†:	7.9%
Population by race	
One race:	97.1%
White:	68.6%
Black or African American:	19.4%
American Indian/Alaska Native:	0.4%
Asian:	5.5%
Native Hawaiian/Pacific Islander:	0.1%
Some other race:	3.2%
Two or more races:	2.9%

Population by Age Group, Census 2010

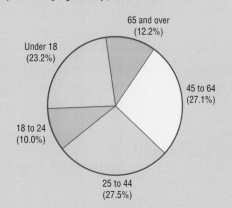

65 and over (12.2%)

Under 18 (23.2%)

45 to 64 (27.1%)

18 to 24 (10.0%)

25 to 44 (27.5%)

Major Cities by Population, 2011 Estimates

City	Population	% change 2005–11
Virginia Beach	442,707	1.0
Norfolk	242,628	4.6
Chesapeake	225,050	2.8
Arlington	207,627	6.0
Richmond	205,533	6.1
Newport News	179,611	-0.2
Alexandria	144,301	6.6
Hampton	136,401	-6.3
Roanoke	96,714	4.4
Portsmouth	95,684	-4.5

Notes: †A person of Hispanic or Latino origin may be of any race. NA indicates that data are not available. Percentages may not equal 100 due to rounding.

SOURCE: U.S. Census Bureau. Census 2010 and Population Estimates. www.census.gov/ (accessed July 2012).

Virginia Population by Race
CENSUS 2010

This table shows the number of people who are of one, two, or three or more races. For those claiming two races, the number of people belonging to the various categories is listed. The U.S. government conducts a census of the population every 10 years.

	Number	Percent
Total population	8,001,024	100.0
One race	7,767,624	97.1
Two races	214,276	2.7
White *and* Black or African American	62,204	0.8
White *and* American Indian/Alaska Native	25,771	0.3
White *and* Asian	59,051	0.7
White *and* Native Hawaiian/Pacific Islander	2,618	—
White *and* some other race	27,658	0.3
Black or African American *and* American Indian/Alaska Native	9,746	0.1
Black or African American *and* Asian	7,056	0.1
Black or African American *and* Native Hawaiian/Pacific Islander	1,151	—
Black or African American *and* some other race	7,226	0.1
American Indian/Alaska Native *and* Asian	1,115	—
American Indian/Alaska Native *and* Native Hawaiian/Pacific Islander	99	—
American Indian/Alaska Native *and* some other race	2,559	—
Asian *and* Native Hawaiian/Pacific Islander	1,943	—
Asian *and* some other race	5,240	0.1
Native Hawaiian/Pacific Islander *and* some other race	839	—
Three or more races	19,124	0.2

SOURCE: U.S. Census Bureau. Census 2010. www.census/gov/ (accessed July 2012). A dash (—) indicates that the percent is less than 0.1.

state has also worked to enhance water quality monitoring for streams and lakes statewide and to continue restoration efforts for the Chesapeake Bay. Voluntary cleanups of contaminated industrial sites have been encouraged.

In 2012, Virginia had 219 hazardous waste sites listed in the Environmental Protection Agency's database, 31 of which were on the National Priorities List. Sites included the Former Nansemond Ordnance Depot, in Suffolk, which had been contaminated during its operation with explosives. About 1 million acres (404,685 hectares) of the state is wetlands.

6 Population

In 2011, Virginia ranked 12th among the 50 states in population with an estimated total of 8,096,604 residents. The population density in 2010 was 196.2 persons per square mile (75.76 persons per square kilometer). In 2011, the median age in Virginia was 37.6 years. About 12.5% of all residents were 65 or older while 22.9% were under 18. The population is projected to reach 9,364,304 by 2025.

The largest city in 2011 was Virginia Beach with 442,707 residents (metro area, 1,679,894). Norfolk was the second largest with 242,628 residents. Other leading cities and their 2011 populations were Chesapeake, 225,050; Arlington, 207,627; Richmond (the capital), 205,533; Newport News, 179,611; Alexandria, 144,301; and Hampton, 136,401. In 2010, 87% of the population lived in metropolitan areas.

7 Ethnic Groups

According to the 2010 Census, there were 1,551,399 African Americans living in Virginia, representing about 19.4% of the total state population. There were also 631,825 Hispanic and Latino residents, chiefly Mexican and Puerto Rican. The state also had 439,890 Asians, including 66,963 Filipinos, 70,577 Koreans, 59,777 Chinese, 53,529 Vietnamese, 103,916 Asian Indians, and 9,471 Japanese. Native Hawaiians and Pacific Islanders numbered 5,980. The Native American population, including Eskimos and Aleuts, numbered 29,225. An estimated 10.8% of Virginians were of foreign birth.

8 Languages

Although the suburban area south of the District of Columbia has many different dialects, the rest of the state has retained its essentially Southern speech features. General terms in use are *batter bread* (a soft corn cake), *batter cake* (pancake), and *polecat* (skunk). Widespread pronunciation features include *greasy* with a *z* sound, *yeast* and *east* as sound-alikes, *creek* rhyming with *peek,* and *can't* rhyming with *paint.*

In 2011, 85.1% of Virginia residents five years of age and over spoke only English at home, 6.7% spoke Spanish, 3.5% spoke another Indo-European language, and 3.4% spoke an Asian or Pacific Islander language.

9 Religions

The Anglican Church (later the Episcopal Church) was the first official church of the colony. In 1785, the Virginia General Assembly of the state adopted the Virginia Statute for Religious Freedom, drafted by Thomas Jefferson, and disestablished the Episcopal Church, making religious tolerance the norm in Virginia.

According to the Pew Forum on Religion & Public Life, in 2008 around 61% of the state's population were Protestant. Around 31% of the population were adherents of Evangelical Protestant traditions; 20% were adherents of mainline Protestant traditions, and 10% belonged to historically black Protestant traditions. Around 10% of the population were Catholic. Jews accounted for around 1% of the population, and Muslims for less than 0.5%. Around 18% of the population were unaffiliated with any religion.

10 Transportation

Virginia was a leader in early railroad development. Rail lines were completed between Richmond and Fredericksburg in 1836, from Portsmouth to Roanoke in 1837, and from Richmond to Washington, D.C., in 1872. Virginia's 1,290 miles (2,076 kilometers) of track formed a strategic supply link for both the Confederate and Union armies during the Civil War. As of 2009, there were nine rail companies operating in the state with a combined trackage of 3,214 miles (5,519 kilometers). Principal (Class I) railroads are Conrail, CSX, and Norfolk Southern. Amtrak passenger trains served 20 communities in 2010.

As of 2009, Virginia had 73,903 miles (117,792 kilometers) of public roads. That year, there were 3.8 million automobiles, 83,000 motorcycles, and 2.6 million trucks registered in the state. In 2009 there were 5,301,182 licensed drivers. Major interstate highways are I-95, I-81, and I-64. The 18-mile (29-kilometer)

Chesapeake Bay Bridge-Tunnel, completed in 1964, connects the Eastern Shore with the southeastern mainland. Popular scenic highways include the Blue Ridge Parkway, Colonial National Historical Parkway, and George Washington Memorial Parkway.

Virginia's District of Columbia suburbs are linked to the nation's capital by the Washington Metropolitan Area Transit Authority's bus and rail systems. Norfolk, Newport News-Hampton, and Richmond have extensive bus systems.

Virginia's Hampton Roads has one of the largest commercial port complexes in the world. Three state-owned general cargo marine terminals—Newport News Marine Terminal, Norfolk International Terminals, and Portsmouth Marine Terminal—share the harbor with more than 20 privately owned bulk terminals. The Hampton Roads harbor has the greatest volume of total tonnage on the US East Coast, handling 15.62 million tons of cargo in 2011. Virginia's ports are located on a naturally deep, ice-free harbor, 18 miles (29 kilometers) from the open sea. In addition to the marine terminals, the Virginia Inland Port (VIP) terminal, just west of Washington, D.C., in Front Royal, Virginia, offers daily rail service to the marine terminals in Hampton Roads and allows direct access to the international trade routes of the 75 international shipping lines calling at the ports.

Virginia had 287 airports, 132 heliports, and 3 seaplane bases in 2009. In 2009, Ronald Reagan National Airport had 8,489,931 passenger enplanements, making it the 26th-busiest airport in the country. At the same time, Dulles International Airport, in Virginia but primarily serving Washington D.C., was the nation's 20th-busiest airport, with 11,122,438 passenger enplanements.

11 History

At the time of English contact, early in the 17th century, Tidewater Virginia was occupied principally by Algonquian-speakers, including the Powhatan and Rappahannock. The piedmont area was the home of the Manahoac, Monacan, and Tutelo, all of Sioux stock. Cherokee lived in Virginia's far southwestern triangle.

The first permanent English settlement in America was established at Jamestown on 13 May 1607. The successful settlement was sponsored by the London Company, chartered by King James I in 1606. The charter defined Virginia as all of the North American coast between 30° and 45°N, and extending inland for 50 miles (80 kilometers). Subsequent charters expanded the territory; the second charter in 1609 extended to the Pacific Ocean while the third charter added Atlantic islands, including Bermuda.

Following early setbacks, the energy, resourcefulness, and military skill of Captain John Smith saved the Jamestown colony from both starvation and destruction. He was taken prisoner by Chief Powhatan, his principal adversary, but was able to work out a fragile peace later cemented by the marriage in 1614 of the chief's favorite daughter, Pocahontas, to John Rolfe, a Jamestown settler. In 1619, the first representative assembly in the New World convened in Jamestown, as self-government through locally elected representatives became a reality in America and an important precedent for the English colonies.

Despite serious setbacks because of Native American massacres in 1622 and 1644, the colony's population expanded rapidly along the James, York, Rappahannock, and Potomac rivers, and along the Eastern Shore. Although originally dependent on indentured servants, in 1662 the colony enacted partus law, a legal doctrine that declared the children of slaves were automatically slaves themselves, thus cementing the plantation slave system.

The 17th century closed on a note of material and cultural progress, as the College of William and Mary, the second institution of higher learning in America, was chartered in 1693. Middle Plantation (renamed Williamsburg in 1722), the site of the college, became the seat of government when the capital was moved from Jamestown in 1699.

18th Century In the decades that followed, the Virginia Colony, bolstered by its main crop of tobacco, became the wealthiest and most populous British colony in North America. Eastern Virginians moving into the Valley of Virginia were joined by Scotch-Irish and Germans moving southward from Maryland and Pennsylvania. Virginians caught up in western settlement lost much of their awe of the mother country during the French and Indian War (1756–63). Virginia, acting independently and with other colonies, repeatedly challenged agents of the Crown. In 1765, the House of Burgesses adopted five resolutions opposing the Stamp Act, through which the British Parliament had sought to tax the colonists for their own defense. In 1769, Virginia initiated a boycott of British goods in answer to the taxation provisions of the hated Townshend Acts.

Virginia joined the other colonies at the First Continental Congress, which met in Philadelphia in 1774 and elected Virginia's Peyton Randolph as president. One native son, Richard Henry Lee, introduced the resolution for independence at the Continental Congress of 1776. Another, Thomas Jefferson, wrote the Declaration of Independence. In the same year, Virginians proclaimed their government a commonwealth and adopted a constitution and declaration of rights, which became the basis for the Bill of Rights in the US Constitution.

Virginians were equally active in the Revolutionary War. George Washington was commander in chief of the Continental Army, and one of the greatest American naval heroes was a Scottish-born Virginian, John Paul Jones. Virginia itself was a major battlefield, and it was on Virginia soil, at Yorktown on 19 October 1781, that British General Charles Cornwallis surrendered to Washington, effectively ending the war.

During the early federal period, Virginia's leadership was as notable as it had been during the American Revolution. James Madison is honored as the "father of the Constitution," and Washington, who was president of the constitutional convention, became the first US president in 1789. Indeed, Virginians occupied the presidency for all but four of the nation's first 28 years.

19th Century During the first half of the 19th century, Virginians became increasingly concerned with the problem of slavery. Nat Turner's slave revolt—which took the lives of at least 55 white men, women, and children in Southampton County in 1831—increased white fears of black emancipation. Nevertheless, legislation to end slavery in Virginia failed adoption by only seven votes the following year.

The first half of the 19th century saw the state become a leading center of scientific, artistic, and educational advancement. This era ended with the coming of the Civil War (1861–65), a conflict about which many Virginians had grave misgivings. A statewide convention, assembled in Richmond in April 1861, adopted an ordinance of secession only after President Abraham Lincoln sought to send troops across Virginia to punish the states that had already seceded and called upon the commonwealth to furnish soldiers for the task. Shortly afterward, Richmond, the capital of Virginia since 1780, became the capital of the Confederacy. Unable to agree to the decision to join the Confederacy, the western counties of the state broke away in 1861 and were recognized by Washington, D.C., in 1863 as the new state of West Virginia.

Robert E. Lee, offered field command of the Union armies, instead resigned his US commission in order to serve his native state as commander of the Army of Northern Virginia and eventually as chief of the Confederate armies. Virginia became the principal battlefield of the Civil War, the scene of brilliant victories won by General Lee's army at Bull Run, Fredericksburg, and Chancellorsville. But the overwhelming numbers and industrial and naval might of the Union compelled Lee's surrender at Appomattox on 9 April 1865.

The war cost Virginia dearly. Richmond was left in ruins, and agriculture and industry throughout the commonwealth were destroyed. In 1867, Virginia was placed under US military rule. After adopting a constitution providing for universal manhood suffrage, Virginia was readmitted to the Union on 26 January 1870.

After a postwar period of unprecedented racial emancipation, Virginia once again moved toward segregation and discrimination as the 19th century neared an end. In 1902, the Virginia constitutional convention enacted a literacy test and poll tax that reduced the black vote to negligible size.

20th Century Two decades later, Harry F. Byrd, a liberal Democrat, defeated G. Walter Mapp in the election of 1925. Immediately after taking office, Byrd launched the state on an era of reform. In a whirlwind 60 days, the Virginia General Assembly revised balloting procedures and adopted measures to lure industry to Virginia. The Anti-Lynch Act of 1927 made anyone present at the scene of a lynching, who did not intervene, guilty of murder.

Following the Great Depression of the 1930s, Virginia became one of the most prosperous states of the Southeast. It profited partly from national defense contracts and military and naval expansion, but also from increased manufacturing and from what became one of the nation's leading tourist industries. Few states made so great a contribution as Virginia to the US effort in World War II (1939–45). More than 300,000 Virginians served in the armed forces; 9,000 lost their lives and 10 were awarded the Medal of Honor.

The postwar period brought many changes in the commonwealth's public life. During the first administration of Governor Mills E. Godwin, Jr. (1966–70), the state enacted a sales tax, expanded funding for four-year colleges, and instituted a system of low-tuition community colleges.

In 1970, A. Linwood Holton Jr. became the first Republican governor of Virginia since the 1800s. Pledging to "make today's Virginia a model in race relations," Holton increased black representation in government. By the mid-1970s, public school integration in Virginia had been achieved to a degree not yet accomplished in many northern states.

The northeast and Virginia Beach/Norfolk area of Virginia boomed in the early 1980s, spurred by an expansion of federal jobs and a national military buildup. In the late 1980s, however, Virginia was hit by a recession. After his inauguration in 1990, Douglas Wilder, the first black governor in the nation and a moderate Democrat, responded to a major shortfall in state revenues by refusing to raise taxes and by insisting on maintaining a $200 million reserve fund. Wilder reduced the budgets and staff of state services and of the state's college and university system.

Wilder, limited by law to one term in office, was succeeded in 1994 by conservative Republican George Allen, who ended 12 years of Democratic rule. He was succeeded in 1998 by another Republican, James S. Gilmore, III, who in turn was succeeded in 2002 by Democrat Mark Warner.

Virginia's economy was strong in the late 1990s into the early 2000s thanks to its diversified base of agriculture, manufacturing, and employment in the federal government agencies in nearby Washington, D.C. Pollution from industry and agriculture remained a significant concern, prompting the state to invest in cleanup efforts for the Chesapeake Bay.

By 2003, Virginia was in the midst of its worst state revenue performance in 40 years. To help overcome massive budget deficits, the state cut funding for higher education by more than 25%. Nearly all state universities raised tuition in response. The State Council of Higher Education estimated that an additional $350 million per year was needed to maintain the quality of public higher education.

In November 2005, Democrat Tim Kaine, who had been serving as lieutenant governor, defeated the Republican nominee, Jerry Kilgore, to become governor of Virginia. In 2008, Democratic presidential candidate Barack Obama

Richmond is one of the principal centers for creative and performing arts. Shown here is a view of the Richmond skyline and the flood wall overlooking the James River. © DMVPHOTOS/SHUTTERSTOCK.COM.

carried the state—the first Democrat presidential candidate to win Virginia since 1964. The recession that began in 2008 did not hit Virginia as hard as other states, in part because Virginia was aided by the high proportion of residents employed by the federal government. In 2010, Republican Robert McDonnell became governor; two years later, Tim Kaine became senator.

12 State Government

The Virginia General Assembly consists of a 40-member senate, elected to four-year terms, and a 100-member house of delegates, serving for two years. The governor, lieutenant governor, and attorney general, all serving four-year terms, are the only officials elected statewide. Most state

Virginia Governors: 1776–2013

1776–1779	Patrick Henry		1869–1874	Gilbert Carlton Walker	Democrat
1779–1781	Thomas Jefferson		1874–1878	James Lawson Kemper	Democrat
1781	William Fleming		1878–1882	Frederick William Hilliday	Democrat
1781	Thomas Nelson		1882–1886	William Ewan Cameron	Readjuster
1781–1784	Benjamin Harrison		1886–1890	Fitzhugh Lee	Democrat
1784–1786	Patrick Henry		1890–1894	Philip Watkins McKinney	Democrat
1786–1788	Edmund Randolph		1894–1898	Charles Triplett O'Ferrall	Democrat
1788–1791	Beverley Randolph		1898–1902	James Hoge Tyler	Democrat
1791–1794	Henry Lee	Federalist	1902–1906	Andrew Jackson Montague	Democrat
1794–1796	Robert Brooke	Dem-Rep	1906–1910	Claude Augustus Swanson	Democrat
1796–1799	James Wood	Federalist	1910–1914	William Hodges Mann	Democrat
1799–1802	James Monroe	Dem-Rep	1914–1918	Henry Carter Stuart	Democrat
1802–1805	John Page	Dem-Rep	1918–1922	Westmoreland Davis	Democrat
1805–1808	William Henry Cabell	Dem-Rep	1922–1926	Elbert Lee Trinkle	Democrat
1808–1811	John Tyler, Sr.	Dem-Rep	1926–1930	Harry Flood Byrd	Democrat
1811	James Monroe	Dem-Rep	1930–1934	John Garland Pollard	Democrat
1811	George William Smith	Dem-Rep	1934–1938	George Campbell Peery	Democrat
1811–1812	Peyton Randolph	Dem-Rep	1938–1942	James Hubert Price	Democrat
1812–1814	James Barbour	AD/S.R.P.	1942–1946	Colgate Whitehead Darden, Jr.	Democrat
1814–1816	Wilson Cary Nicholas	Republican	1946–1950	William Munford Tuck	Democrat
1816–1819	James Patton Preston	Dem-Rep	1950–1954	John Stewart Battle	Democrat
1819–1822	Thomas Mann Randolph	Republican	1954–1958	Thomas Bahnson Stanley	Democrat
1822–1825	James Pleasants	Republican	1958–1962	James Lindsay Almond, Jr.	Democrat
1825–1827	John Tyler, Jr.	Dem-Rep	1962–1966	Albertis Sydney Harrison, Jr.	Democrat
1827–1830	William Branch Giles	Republican	1966–1970	Mills Edwin Godwin, Jr.	Democrat
1830–1834	John Floyd	Democrat	1970–1974	Abner Linwood Holton, Jr.	Republican
1834–1836	Littleton Waller Tazewell	Democrat	1974–1978	Mills Edwin Godwin, Jr.	Republican
1836–1837	Wyndham Robertson	S.R. Dem	1978–1982	John Nichols Dalton	Republican
1837–1840	David Campbell	States Whigs	1982–1986	Charles Spittal Robb	Democrat
1840–1841	Thomas Walker Gilmer	State Rights Whigs	1986–1990	Gerald L. Baliles	Democrat
1841	John Mercer Patton	State Rights Whigs	1990–1994	Lawrence Douglas Wilder	Democrat
1841–1842	John Rutherford	State Rights Whigs	1994–1998	George Felix Allen	Republican
1842–1843	John Munford Gregory	States Whigs	1998–2002	James S. Gilmore, III	Republican
1843–1846	James McDowell	Democrat	2002–2006	Mark Warner	Democrat
1846–1849	William Smith	Confed-Dem	2006–2010	Timothy M. Kaine	Democrat
1849–1852	John Buchanan Floyd	Democrat	2010–	Bob McDonnell	Republican
1852–1856	Joseph Johnson	Democrat			
1856–1860	Henry Alexander Wise	Democrat	Anti–Democrat/State Rights Party – AD/S.R.P.		
1860–1864	John Letcher	Democrat	Confederate Democrat – Confed-Dem		
1864–1865	William Smith	Confed-Dem	Democrat Provisional – Dem-Prov		
1865–1868	Francis Harrison Pierpoint	Unionist	Democratic Republican – Dem-Rep		
1868–1869	Henry Horatio Wells	Dem-Prov	State Rights Democrat – S.R. Dem		

officials are appointed by the governor but must be confirmed by both houses of the legislature. Unique among the states, Virginia prohibits its governors a second consecutive term of office, although former governors are reeligible after four years out of office. Bills become law when signed by the governor or left unsigned for seven days while the legislature is in session. A bill dies if left unsigned for 30 days after the legislature has adjourned. A two-thirds majority in each house is needed to override a governor's veto.

In 2012, the legislative salary was $18,000 for state senators, plus a $135 per diem, and $17,640 for delegates, plus a $178 per diem. The governor's salary was $175,000.

13 Political Parties

The modern Democratic Party traces its origins to the original Republican Party (usually referred to as the Democratic-Republican Party, or the Jeffersonian Democrats), led by two native sons of Virginia, Thomas Jefferson and James Madison. From the end of Reconstruction through the 1960s, conservative Democrats dominated state politics, with few exceptions. During the 1970s, Virginians, still staunchly conservative, turned increasingly to the Republican Party, whose presidential nominees carried the state in every election from 1952 through 2004, except for 1964.

Democrat L. Douglas Wilder was elected governor in 1989 and became the first black governor in US history. Two Republicans, George Allen and James S. Gilmore III, followed, in 1993 and 1997, respectively. They were followed by two Democrats—Mark Warner in 2001 and Tim Kaine in 2005. In 2009, Republican Bob McDonnell was elected.

John Warner, a Republican, was elected to a fifth term in the US Senate in 2002. On his retirement, he was replaced by Democrat Mark Warner. Former Republican Governor George Allen was elected to the US Senate in 2000. He was defeated in the 2006 elections by Democrat James Webb Jr. in a close race. Allen was defeated in another senate bid in 2012, losing to Democrat Tim Kaine. Following the 2012 election, Virginia's delegation to the US House of Representatives consisted of three Democrats and eight Republicans.

As of the 2010 elections, control of the state senate and house was in the hands of the Republicans. Republicans controlled the state house, 59–39, with 2 independents; the state senate was split 20–20 between Republicans and Democrats.

In 2004, Republican George W. Bush won 54% of the vote and Democrat John Kerry won 45%. In 2008, Republican John McCain

Virginia Presidential Vote by Major Political Parties, 1948–2012			
Year	Virginia Winner	Democrat	Republican
1948	*Truman (D)	200,786	172,070
1952	*Eisenhower (R)	268,677	349,037
1956	*Eisenhower (R)	267,760	386,459
1960	Nixon (R)	362,327	404,521
1964	*Johnson (D)	558,038	481,334
1968	*Nixon (R)	442,387	590,319
1972	*Nixon (R)	438,887	988,493
1976	Ford (R)	813,896	836,554
1980	*Reagan (R)	752,174	989,609
1984	*Reagan (R)	796,250	1,337,078
1988	*Bush (R)	859,799	1,309,162
1992	Bush (R)	1,038,650	1,150,517
1996	Dole (R)	1,091,060	1,138,350
2000	*Bush, G. W. (R)	1,217,290	1,437,490
2004	*Bush, G. W. (R)	1,454,742	1,716,959
2008	*Obama (D)	1,959,532	1,725,005
2012	*Obama (D)	1,971,820	1,822,522

*Won US presidential election.

Independent candidate Ross Perot received 348,639 votes in 1992 and 159,861 votes in 1996.

won 46% of the vote and Democrat Barack Obama won 53%. In 2012, President Obama beat his Republican challenger, Mitt Romney, in the state of Virginia. That year, there were 4,653,548 registered voters; there is no party registration in the state.

14 Local Government

As of 2012, Virginia had 95 counties, 39 independent cities, 229 municipal governments, and 135 school districts. In 2007, there were 186 special districts in the state. Independent cities elect their own officials, levy their own taxes, and are unencumbered by any county obligations. Incorporated towns remain part of the counties. In general, counties are governed by elected boards of supervisors, with a county administrator or executive handling day-to-day affairs. Incorporated towns have elected mayors and councils. In 2011, there were 393,488 full-time and 122,144 part-time state and local government employees.

15 Judicial System

The highest judicial body in the commonwealth is the supreme court, consisting of a chief justice and six other justices. The court of appeals has 10 judges. There is a circuit court in each city and county in Virginia. District courts hear all misdemeanors, including civil cases involving $4,500 or less. They also hold preliminary hearings concerning felony cases. Each of the judicial districts has a juvenile and a domestic relations court.

The state's violent crime rate in 2010 was 213.6 reported incidents per 100,000 persons. The murder and nonnegligent manslaughter rate was 4.6 incidents per 100,000 inhabitants; forcible rape, 19.1; aggravated assault, 119.1; and property crime, 2,327.2. Virginia's total prison population in 2011 was 68,834 people. Virginia has the death penalty. From 1976 through 18 August 2011, there were 109 executions, representing the second-highest number in the nation after Texas. In January 2012, there were 12 inmates on death row.

16 Migration

Virginia's earliest European immigrants were English. In the late 17th and early 18th centuries, immigrants came not only from England but also from Scotland, Wales, Ireland, Germany, France, the Netherlands, and Poland. In 1701, about 500 French Huguenots fled Catholic France to settle near the present site of Richmond. Beginning in 1714, many Germans and Scotch-Irish moved from Pennsylvania into the Valley of Virginia.

By the early 19th century, Virginians were moving westward into Kentucky, Ohio, and other states. The Civil War era saw the movement of thousands of blacks to northern states, a trend that accelerated after Reconstruction and again after World War I. Since 1900, the dominant migratory trend has been intrastate, from farm to city. At the same time, the movements of middle-income Virginians to the suburbs and increasing concentrations of blacks in the central cities have been evident in Virginia as in other states.

Between 2009 and 2010, the total population (ages one and older) of Virginia increased by 75,970, due to the net domestic in-migration of natives (24,848), the net domestic in-migration of immigrants (2,657), and the arrival from abroad of natives (23,171) and immigrants (25,294). Of the total foreign-born population in Virginia in 2010, 9.8% were from Africa, 39.7% were from Asia, 11.3% were from Europe, and 37.1% were from Latin America. The top three countries of birth of the foreign born in Virginia in 2010 were El Salvador (9.5%), India (7.2%), and Mexico (7.1%). In comparison, the top three countries of birth in 1990 were Korea (7.6%), the Philippines (7.3%), and El Salvador (6.9%).

17 Economy

Services, trade, and government are important economic areas. Because of Virginia's extensive military installations and the large number of Virginia residents working for the federal government in the Washington, D.C., metropolitan area, the federal government plays a larger role in the Virginia economy than in any other state except Hawaii.

The industries that experienced the most growth in the 1990s were printing, transportation equipment, and electronic and other electrical equipment. Virginia has a high concentration of high-technology industry. The two largest high-tech fields are computer and data processing services and electronic equipment.

In 2010, Virginia's gross state product (GSP) was $427.7 billion, ranking the state ninth in the nation. Per capita GSP was $53,463 that year, also ranking the state ninth. In 2010, there were 193,042 private nonfarm establishments and 510,297 nonemployer establishments in the state.

18 Income

Median per capita personal income (including nonmonetary income) in 2011 was $45,920,

ranking Virginia seventh in the United States. The median annual household income for the period 2008–2010 was $61,544, compared to the national average of $50,022. In 2011, 11.5% of the population lived below the federal poverty level, compared to the national average of 15.9%.

19 Industry

In 2010, the value of shipments by manufacturers was about $92.4 billion. Of that total, beverage and tobacco product manufacturing accounted for the largest share. Richmond is a principal industrial area for tobacco processing, paper and printing, clothing, and food products. Nearby Hopewell is a center of the chemical industry. Newport News, Hampton, and Norfolk are sites for shipbuilding and the manufacture of other transportation equipment. In the western part of the state, Lynchburg is a center for electrical machinery, metals, clothing, and printing; and Roanoke for food, clothing, and textiles. In the south, Martinsville has furniture and textile manufacturing plants.

20 Labor

In August 2012, the civilian labor force in Virginia numbered 4,321,400, with approximately 255,500 workers unemployed, yielding an unemployment rate of 5.9%, compared to the national average of 8.1% for the same period. Those employed in nonfarm wage and salaried jobs that same month included: 175,100 in construction; 225,900 in manufacturing; 634,600 in trade, transportation, and public utilities; 191,800 in financial activities; 665,400 in professional and business services; 483,500 in education and health services; 354,700 in leisure and hospitality services; and 708,700 in government.

In 2010, 198,000 of Virginia's 3,905,300 employed wage and salary workers were members of unions, representing 5.6% of those so employed. The national average was 13%.

21 Agriculture

The commonwealth is an important producer of tobacco, soybeans, peanuts, cotton, tomatoes, potatoes, and peaches. There were an estimated 47,300 farms in 2010, covering 8.1 million acres (3.3 million hectares). Of those, 13,353 acres (5,404 hectares) were certified organic.

In 2011, a total of 550,000 acres (222,577 hectares) were harvested for grain. Soybean production was estimated at 21.5 million bushels; peanut production at 60.8 million pounds; cotton production at 165,000 bales; and tobacco production at 46.8 million pounds (21.23 million kilograms).

Total agricultural output was $4.24 billion in 2011, of which $1.35 billion was crop output. Major crops in 2011 included greenhouse and nursery products, with farm receipts of $266.9 million. Top exports included wheat and wheat products, with $121.1 million in exports; soybeans and soy products, with $93.1 million in exports; and unmanufactured tobacco, with $76.4 million in exports.

The Tidewater is an important farming region, as it has been since the early 17th century. Crops grown include corn, wheat, tobacco, cotton, peanuts, and vegetables. Vegetables and soybeans are cultivated on the Eastern Shore. The Piedmont is known for its apples and other fruits, while the Shenandoah Valley is one of the nation's main apple-growing regions.

22 Domesticated Animals

In 2011, broiler production was Virginia's top farm commodity, with $602 million in cash receipts. Cattle and calves came second, with $452 million in receipts, followed by dairy at $395 million. Horses are also big business in the state, with the total value of all equines in the state placed at $1.2 billion in 2011. There are 215,000 horses in Virginia and around 41,000 horse operations. Top animal exports in 2011 included live animals and meat, with $115.4 million; and poultry, with $114.8 million in exports.

23 Fishing

In 2010, Virginia was the nation's third-largest producer of marine products, behind only Alaska and Louisiana. Total commercial landings in 2010 were more than 80 million pounds (36.3 million kilograms), with a dockside value of around $146 million. Landings at the Reedville port totaled over 394 million pounds (178.7 million kilograms) in 2009, the third-highest volume of all US ports. The port at Hampton Road Area ranked sixth in the nation in catch value at $68.1 million. The bulk of the Virginia commercial catch consists of shellfish such as crabs, scallops, and clams, and finfish such as flounder and menhaden. The sea scallop catch in 2010 was at 9.2 million pounds (4.2 million kilograms), with a total value of more than $70 million.

In 2012, Virginia was home to more than 274 certified seafood and shellfish dealers, with around 6,000 people working on the water. Virginia aquaculture growers in Chesapeake Bay planted nearly 77 million oysters in 2010.

According to the Virginia Department of Agriculture and Consumer Service, Virginia seafood exports totaled $39.4 million in 2010. The top countries where Virginia seafood is exported are Canada, Hong Kong, China, France, Vietnam, Belgium, and Ukraine.

24 Forestry

As of 2010, Virginia had 15.72 million acres (6.36 million hectares) of forestland, representing more than 62% of the state's land area. Around 15.3 million acres (6.19 million hectares) are commercial timberland, and around 500,000 acres (202,342 hectares) are reserved forestland. Hardwood and hardwood-pine type forests make up more than 12 million acres (4.85 million hectares) of the state's forests—more than 78 percent of the total area. Pine forests represent approximately 3 million acres (1.2 million hectares or 19%) of forestland.

State-funded tree nurseries produce more than 25 million seedlings annually. The Division of Forestry's tree seed orchards have developed improved strains of loblolly, shortleaf, white, and Virginia pine for planting in cutover timberland.

For recreational purposes, there were around 2.7 million acres (1.1 million hectares) of forested public lands in 2012, including Shenandoah National Park, Washington and Jefferson National Forests, 24 state parks, and 22 state forests. The US Department of Agriculture Forest Service owns around 1.7 million acres (690,000 hectares) of Virginia's forestland, while the Virginia Department of Forestry owns 67,888 acres (27,473 hectares). The rest is owned by federal, state, and local governments. In 2011, a new state forest—Old Flat—was added to the state's roster.

25 Mining

In 2011, Virginia's nonfuel mining industry ranked 21st in the United States, with a value of $1 billion, 1.4% of the US total. Top minerals mined include crushed stone, kyanite (around 90,000 tons mined per year), iron-oxide pigments, feldspar, heavy mineral sands, and mullite (around 40,000 tons per year). Statewide, in 2012 there were around 460 nonfuel mines covering about 66,000 acres (26,709 hectares) of land. These include quarries, sand and gravel pits, and other surface and underground mining operations.

In 2010, 43.8 million metric tons of crushed stone were mined in the state, valued at $587 million; 7.74 million metric tons of sand and gravel were mined, valued at $86.3 million; and 51.6 million metric tons of aggregates were mined, valued at $673 million.

26 Energy and Power

As of 2010, Virginia had reserves of 3.2 trillion cubic feet of dry natural gas and 337 million short tons of coal, along with a very small amount of crude oil. In June 2012, the state produced 1,000 barrels of crude oil. In 2010, it produced 147 billion cubic feet of marketed natural gas and 22.4 million short tons of coal. As of June 2012, total net electricity generation was 6.6 million megawatt hours (MWh). Of this, 55,000 MWh was generated by petroleum-fired plants; 2.38 million MWh by natural gas-fired plants; 1.5 million MWh by coal-fired plants; 2.46 million MWh by nuclear plants; 71,000 MWh by hydroelectric plants; and 196,000 MWh by other renewable sources. In 2012, Virginia had two nuclear

Virginia's famous Mabry Mill water-powered mill is located on the Blue Ridge Parkway. It is photographed by many tourists, especially in autumn. © JUDY KENNAMER/SHUTTERSTOCK.COM.

power plants in operation, the North Anna plant in Louisa County and the Surry plant near Williamsburg.

The state's only petroleum refinery is located in Yorktown. In April 2007, Virginia established a voluntary renewable energy goal for utilities to generate 12% of their sales from renewable sources by 2022. In 2011, 5.1% of the state's net electricity generation came from renewable energy, over half of which was biomass. In the early 2010s, various firms and the state of Virginia were evaluating the potential to create offshore wind farms near several major cities.

27 Commerce

Output from manufacturing was 30.3 billion in 2010, accounting for 8.4% of the total state economic output. Manufacturing accounted for 83% of the state's exports. Retail sales in 2007 were $105 billion, with per capita retail sales that year of $13,687. The leading types of business in the manufacturing sector were food, beverage, and tobacco products; chemical manufacturing; and transport equipment manufacturing. In 2008, there were 7,659 wholesale trade establishments and 28,872 retail trade establishments in the state. Virginia is a major container shipping center, with almost all shipments handled through the Hampton Roads estuary. Exports in 2011 were valued at around $18 billion.

28 Public Finance

Virginia's budget is prepared by the Department of Planning & Budget, and it is submitted by the governor for approval by the state assembly. The state operates on a biennial budget cycle. The fiscal year begins on 1 July. State revenues for 2011 were $38.8 billion and expenditures were $40.3 billion. The highest general expenditures were for education ($14.8 billion), health and human resources ($11.3 billion), and transportation ($4.1 billion). In 2012, total state

debts, supported and unsupported, amounted to $65.1 billion.

29 Taxation

The personal income tax schedule has four brackets ranging from 2% to 5.75%. The corporate income tax rate is a flat 6%. The state sales tax rate is 4%; local sales tax of 1% may be added. The state imposes selective (excise) taxes on motor fuels, tobacco products, and other selected items. Most property taxes are collected locally.

The state collected $14.8 billion in taxes and fees in 2011/12, of which $9 billion came from individual income taxes, $3 billion from the state sales tax, $209.4 million from excise taxes, $806.5 million from corporate income

The capitol building of Virginia is in Richmond. © ROSE-MARIE HENRIKSSON/SHUTTERSTOCK.COM.

taxes, and the remainder from other taxes and fees. In 2011, Virginia ranked 34th among the states in per capita tax burden, which amounted to about $2,150 per person. The national average was $2,430 per person.

30 Health

In 2011, Virginia's infant mortality rate was 7.3 deaths per 1,000 live births. The overall death rate in 2010 was 7.4 per 1,000 people. In 2009 there were 171.7 deaths per 100,000 residents from heart disease and 176.5 deaths per 100,000 from cancers. There were 42.3 deaths per 100,000 from cerebrovascular diseases in 2009, and 19.6 deaths per 100,000 from diabetes. In 2010, around 8.7% of the adult population had been diagnosed with diabetes, and 61.2% of adults were overweight or obese. Among Virginia's adults ages 18 and older, 18.5% were smokers in 2010, compared to the national rate of 17.2%. At the end of 2008, there were 19,770 people in Virginia living with HIV/AIDS, 2.3% of the US total.

Virginia's 89 hospitals had 2.2 beds per 1,000 residents in 2010. There were 25.5 physicians per 10,000 residents in 2008 and 76.8 nurses per 10,000 in 2011. In 2007, there were 59 dentists per 100,000 residents. The average expense for hospital care was $1,736 per inpatient day in 2010. In 2010, 13 percent of Virginia's residents lacked health insurance.

31 Housing

In 2011, Virginia had an estimated 3,387,801 housing units, 2,990,650 of them occupied; 2,013,595 (67.3%) were owner-occupied. About 2,111,474 (62.3%) of all units were single-family, detached homes, and 176,928 (5.6%) were mobile homes. Electricity and utility gas were the most common energy sources for heating. It was estimated that 15,693 (0.5%) units lacked complete plumbing facilities and 22,106 (0.7%) lacked complete kitchen facilities.

In 2011, the median owner-occupied home value was $243,100. The median monthly cost for mortgage owners was $1,707, while renters paid a median of $1,062 per month.

32 Education

Although Virginia was the first English colony to found a free school (in 1634), the state's public school system developed very slowly. Thomas Jefferson proposed a system of free public schools as early as 1779, but it was not until 1851 that such a system was established and it was for whites only. Free schools for blacks were founded after the Civil War, but they were poorly funded. Opposition by white Virginians to the US Supreme Court's desegregation order in 1954 was marked in certain communities by public school closings and the establishment of all-white private schools. By the 1970s, however, school integration was an accomplished fact throughout the commonwealth.

In 2010, 86.5% of all state residents 25 years of age or older were high school graduates and 34.2% had four or more years of college. Total public school enrollment for all students age three or older was estimated at 2,121,496 in fall 2010. Per pupil expenditures for public education in 2008/09 were estimated at $10,928.

As of 2010, there were 643,379 students enrolled in college or graduate school. Virginia had a total of 82 degree-granting institutions.

The state has had a distinguished record in higher education since the College of William and Mary was founded at Williamsburg (then called Middle Plantation) in 1693. Thomas Jefferson established the University of Virginia at Charlottesville in 1819. In addition to the University of Virginia and the College of William and Mary, public state-supported institutions include Virginia Polytechnic Institute, Virginia Commonwealth University, Virginia Military Institute, Old Dominion University, and George Mason University. Well known private institutions include the Hampton Institute, Randolph-Macon College, University of Richmond, Sweet Briar College, and Washington and Lee University.

33 Arts

Richmond, Norfolk, and the northern Virginia metropolitan area are the principal centers for the creative and the performing arts in Virginia. Richmond's Landmark Theater has been the scene of concerts by internationally famous orchestras and soloists for generations. The Virginia Repertory Theatre presents serious plays and occasionally gives premiere performances of new works.

In Norfolk, the performing arts are housed in Scope, Chrysler Hall, and the Wells Theatre, an ornate building that has hosted such diverse performers as John Philip Sousa, Will Rogers, and Fred Astaire. The internationally recognized Virginia Opera Association gives performances in the Harrison Opera House in Norfolk, the Carpenter Theater in Richmond, and the GMU Center for the Arts in Fairfax.

The Wolf Trap Foundation for the Performing Arts, in northern Virginia, provides theatrical, operatic, and musical performances featuring internationally celebrated performers. The John F. Kennedy Center for the Performing Arts in nearby Washington, D.C., is heavily patronized by Virginians. The College of William and Mary's Phi Beta Kappa Hall in Williamsburg is the site of the Virginia Shakespeare Festival, an annual summer event inaugurated in 1979. Abingdon is the home of the Barter Theatre, the first state-supported theater in the United States, whose alumni included Ernest Borgnine and Gregory Peck. This repertory company has performed widely in the United States and at selected sites abroad.

There are orchestras in Alexandria, Arlington, Fairfax, Lynchburg, Petersburg, and Roanoke. Richmond is home to the Richmond Ballet, Richmond Choral Society, Richmond Jazz Society, Richmond Philharmonic, and the Richmond Symphony. The Virginia Symphony, founded in Charleston in 1920, has been recognized as one of the nation's leading regional symphony orchestras.

The annual Virginia Arts Festival has drawn national attention since its inception in 1997. The annual Shenandoah Valley Music Festival in Orkney Springs features arts and crafts presentations as well as musical performances.

A poet laureate is named to serve a two-year honorary term. In 2010–2012 the state poet laureate was Kelly Cherry. Her books of poetry include *Time Out of Mind* (1994) and *Rising Venus* (2002).

The Virginia Commission on the Arts supports many programs with the help of state and federal funding. The Virginia Foundation for the Humanities was established in 1974 and has since sponsored over 40,000 humanities programs. Virginia has over 500 arts organizations.

34 Libraries and Museums

In 2008, there were 91 public libraries and 2 state libraries, with a book and serial publication stock of over 18.6 million volumes and a combined circulation greater than 69 million. The Virginia State Library in Richmond and the libraries of the University of Virginia (Charlottesville) and the College of William and Mary (Williamsburg) have the personal papers of such notables as Washington, Jefferson, Madison, Robert E. Lee, William H. McGuffey, and William Faulkner. The University of Virginia also has an impressive collection of medieval illuminated manuscripts.

There are about 260 museums in the state. The Virginia Museum of Fine Arts, the first state museum of art in the United States, has a collection that ranges from ancient Egyptian artifacts to mobile jewelry by Salvador Dali. The Science Museum of Virginia has a 280-seat planetarium featuring a simulated excursion to outer space. Norfolk has the Chrysler Museum, with its famous glassware collection, and the Hermitage Foundation Museum, noted for its Oriental art.

The Mariners' Museum in Newport News has a superb maritime collection. Perhaps the most extensive "museum" in the United States is Colonial Williamsburg's mile-long Duke of Gloucester Street, with such remarkable restorations as the

Colonial Williamsburg is one of the most visited historical sites in Virginia. Here, a carriage passes by the governor's mansion.
© MATT MCCLAIN/SHUTTERSTOCK.COM.

Christopher Wren Building of the College of William and Mary, Bruton Parish Church, the Governor's Palace, and the colonial capital.

More historic sites are maintained as museums in Virginia than in any other state. These include Washington's home at Mount Vernon (Fairfax County), Jefferson's residence at Monticello (Charlottesville), and James River plantation houses such as Berkeley, Shirley, Westover, Sherwood Forest, and Carter's Grove. The National Park Service operates a visitors' center at Jamestown.

35 Communications

In 2010, 97.4% of Virginia's occupied housing units had telephones. In 2007, there were over 6.41 million wireless phone subscribers. In 2010, about 73% of residents used the Internet in their home and 69.5% had broadband access.

In 2010, broadcasters operated more than 300 radio stations in Virginia, including more than 20 major AM radio stations and more than 80 major FM stations. In the same year, Virginia had 33 major television stations.

36 Press

USA Today, the nation's second-largest daily newspaper in 2012, is based in McLean, Virginia. In 2011, Virginia had 21 morning dailies and more than 34 nondaily papers. Leading Virginia newspapers in 2012 included the Norfolk *Virginian-Pilot,* Richmond *Times-Dispatch,* and the Newport News *Press.* The newspaper group, Gannett Company, Inc., is based in McLean. This group owns about 80 daily newspapers nationwide, including *USA Today.*

37 Tourism, Travel, and Recreation

In 2010, travelers spent over $19 billion in Virginia. According to the state, the tourism and travel industry supports over 240,000 jobs.

Attractions in the coastal region alone include the Jamestown and Yorktown historic sites, the Colonial Williamsburg restoration, and the homes of George Washington and Robert E. Lee. Also featured are the National Aeronautics and Space Administration's Langley Research Center and the resorts of Virginia Beach.

The interior offers numerous Civil War sites including Appomattox; Thomas Jefferson's Monticello; Booker T. Washington's birthplace near Smith Mountain Lake; and the historic cities of Richmond, Petersburg, and Fredericksburg. In the west, the Blue Ridge Parkway and Shenandoah National Park, traversed by the breathtaking Skyline Drive, are favorite tourist destinations, as are Cumberland Gap and, in the Lexington area, the home of Confederate General Thomas "Stonewall" Jackson.

The state's many recreation areas include state parks, national forests, a major national park, scenic parkways, and thousands of miles of hiking trails and shoreline. Part of the famous Appalachian Trail winds through Virginia's Blue Ridge and Appalachian mountains.

The Virginia State Fair is held each August and September in Mechanicsville. Other top annual attractions include the Old Fiddlers Convention, Richmond Folk Festival, and the International Gold Cup.

38 Sports

Although Virginia has no major league professional sports teams, it does support nine minor

Arlington National Cemetery is located in Virginia. Many tourists visit the national cemetery to pay their respects. Here, a soldier leads a riderless horse during a funeral procession. © DAVID KAY/SHUTTERSTOCK.COM.

league baseball teams, including the Bluefield Blue Jays, the Norfolk Tides, and the Richmond Flying Squirrels. Other minor league baseball teams play in Bristol, Danville, Lynchburg, Pulaski, and Salem. There is also minor league hockey team in Norfolk and Richmond.

Stock car racing is also popular in the state. The Richmond International Raceway and Martinsville Speedway host NASCAR Nextel Cup races each year. Other participant sports popular with Virginians include tennis, golf, swimming, skiing, boating, and water skiing. The state has at least 400 public and private golf courses, including Arnold Palmer's The Signature at West Neck.

39 Famous Virginians

Virginia is the birthplace of eight US presidents. The first president of the United States, George Washington (1732–1799), was unanimously elected president in 1789 and served two four-year terms, declining a third. Thomas Jefferson (1743–1826), the nation's third president, after serving as vice president under John Adams, was elected president of the United States in 1800 and was reelected in 1804.

James Madison (1751–1836) was secretary of state during Jefferson's two terms and then occupied the presidency from 1809 to 1817.

Madison was succeeded as president in 1817 by James Monroe (1758–1831), who was re-elected to a second term starting in 1821 and is best known for the Monroe Doctrine, which has been a part of US policy since his administration. William Henry Harrison (1773–1841) became the ninth president in 1841 but died of pneumonia one month after his inauguration. Harrison was succeeded by his vice president, John Tyler (1790–1862), a native and resident of Virginia.

Another native Virginian, Zachary Taylor (1784–1850), renowned chiefly as a military leader, became the 12th US president in 1849 but died midway through his term. The eighth Virginia-born president, (Thomas) Woodrow Wilson (1856–1924), became the 28th president of the United States in 1913 after serving as governor of New Jersey.

John Marshall (1755–1835) was the third confirmed chief justice of the United States and is generally regarded by historians as the first great American jurist. Five other Virginians have served as associate justices, including Lewis Powell (1908–1998). Distinguished Virginians who have served in the cabinet include Carter Glass (1858–1946), secretary of the Treasury, creator of the Federal Reserve System, and US senator for 26 years.

Other prominent US senators from Virginia include Richard Henry Lee (1732–1794), former president of the Continental Congress; James M. Mason (b. District of Columbia, 1798–1871), who later was the Confederacy's commissioner to the United Kingdom and France; Harry F. Byrd (1887–1966), governor of Virginia from 1926 to 1930 and US senator from 1933 to 1965; and Harry F. Byrd, Jr. (1914–), senator from 1965 to 1982. Some native-born Virginians have become famous as leaders in other nations. Joseph Jenkins Roberts (1809–1876) was the first president of the Republic of Liberia; and Nancy Langhorne Astor (1879–1964) was the first woman to serve in the British House of Commons.

Captain John Smith (b. England, 1580?–1631) was the founder of Virginia and its first colonial governor. Virginia signers of the Declaration of Independence, besides Thomas Jefferson and Richard Henry Lee, included Benjamin Harrison (1726?–1791), father of President William Henry Harrison. Virginia furnished both the first president of the Continental Congress, Peyton Randolph (1721–1775), and the last, Cyrus Griffin (1748–1810).

Notable Virginia governors include Patrick Henry (1736–1799), the first governor of the commonwealth, though best remembered as a Revolutionary orator. Chief among Virginia's great military and naval leaders, besides George Washington and Zachary Taylor, are John Paul Jones (b. Scotland, 1747–1792); Robert E. Lee (1807–1870), the Confederate commander who earlier served during the Mexican War; James Ewell Brown "Jeb" Stuart (1833–1864), commander of Confederate cavalry during the Civil War; George C. Marshall (b. Pennsylvania, 1880–1959); and Douglas MacArthur (1880–1964).

Virginians are also notable in the history of exploration. Daniel Boone (b. Pennsylvania, 1734–1820) pioneered in Kentucky and Missouri. Meriwether Lewis (1774–1809) and William Clark (1770–1838), both native Virginians, led the famous expedition to map the American West. Richard E. Byrd (1888–1957) was both an explorer of Antarctica and a pioneering aviator.

A state memorial honors General Robert E. Lee, who is shown riding his horse, Traveller. © CAITLIN MIRRA/SHUTTERSTOCK. COM.

Virginians Woodrow Wilson and George C. Marshall both received the Nobel Peace Prize, in 1919 and 1953, respectively. Distinguished Virginia-born scientists and inventors include Matthew Fontaine Maury (1806–1873), founder of the science of oceanography; Cyrus H. McCormick (1809–1884), who perfected the mechanical reaper; and Dr. Walter Reed (1851–1902), who proved that yellow fever was transmitted by mosquitoes. Booker T. Washington (1856–1915) was the nation's foremost black educator.

William Byrd II (1674–1744) is widely acknowledged to have been the most graceful writer in English America in his day. Notable 20th-century novelists include Willa Cather (1873–1947), Ellen Glasgow (1874–1945), and James Branch Cabell (1879–1958). Willard Huntington Wright (1888–1939), better known as S. S. Van Dine, wrote many detective thrillers. Twice winner of the Pulitzer Prize for biography, Douglas Southall Freeman (1886–1953) is often regarded as one of the greatest American masters of that genre. Contemporary Virginia authors include novelist William Styron (1925–2006) and journalist Tom Wolfe (Thomas Kennerly Wolfe Jr., 1931–). Celebrated Virginia artists include sculptor Moses Ezekiel (1844–1917) and painters George Caleb Bingham (1811–1879) and Jerome Myers (1867–1940). A protégé of Thomas Jefferson's, Robert Mills (b. South Carolina, 1781–1855), designed the Washington Monument.

The roster of Virginians prominent in the entertainment world includes Bill "Bojangles" Robinson (1878–1949), Joseph Cotten (1905–1994), George C. Scott (1927–1999), Mark Hamill (1951–), Shirley MacLaine (1934–) and her brother Warren Beatty (1937–), Sandra Bullock (1964–), Rob Lowe (1964–), and Wanda Sykes (1964–). Popular musical stars include Kathryn Elizabeth "Kate" Smith (1907–1986), Pearl Bailey (1918–1990), Ella Fitzgerald (1917–1996), Patsy Cline (1932–1963), June Carter Cash (1929–2003), and Wayne Newton (1942–).

Virginia's sports champions include golfers Sam Snead (1912–2002) and Chandler Harper (1914–2004); tennis star Arthur Ashe (1943–1993); football players Bill Dudley (1921–2010) and Francis "Fran" Tarkington (1940–); and baseball pitcher Eppa Rixey (1891–1963). At age 15, Olympic swimming champion Melissa Belote (1957–) won three gold medals. Helen

Chenery "Penny" Tweedy (1922–) is a famous breeder and racer of horses, from whose stables have come Secretariat and other champions.

40 Bibliography

BOOKS

Bristow, M. J. *State Songs of America.* Westport, CT: Greenwood Press, 2000.

Colbert, Judy. *Virginia, Off the Beaten Path.* Guilford, CT: GPP Travel, 2011.

Dubois, Muriel L. *Virginia.* Milwaukee, WI: Gareth Stevens, 2006.

Kent, Deborah. *Virginia.* New York: Children's Press, 2008.

McAuliffe, Bill. *Virginia Facts and Symbols.* Rev. ed. Mankato, MN: Capstone, 2003.

Pederson, Charles E. *The Jamestown Colony.* Edina, MN: Abdo Publishing, 2009.

Wallenstein, Peter. *Cradle of America: Four Centuries of Virginia History.* Lawrence: University Press of Kansas, 2007.

WEB SITES

"Economy at a Glance: Virginia." *US Bureau of Labor Statistics.* http://www.bls.gov/eag/eag. va.htm (accessed on November 16, 2012).

"Endangered Species Program." *US Fish & Wildlife Service.* http://www.fws.gov/endangered/ (accessed on November 16, 2012).

"State & County QuickFacts: Virginia." *US Bureau of the Census.* http://quickfacts.census.gov/qfd/states/ 51000.html (accessed on November 16, 2012).

Virginia General Assembly. http://virginiageneralassembly. gov/ (accessed on November 16, 2012).

"Virginia Is for Lovers." *Virginia Tourism Corporation.* www.virginia.org (accessed on November 16, 2012).

Virginia.gov: Commonwealth of Virginia. www. virginia.gov (accessed on November 16, 2012).

Washington
State of Washington

ORIGIN OF STATE NAME: Named for George Washington.

NICKNAME: The Evergreen State.

CAPITAL: Olympia.

ENTERED UNION: 11 November 1889 (42nd).

OFFICIAL SEAL: Portrait of George Washington surrounded by the words "The Seal of the State of Washington 1889."

FLAG: The state seal centered on a dark green field.

MOTTO: *Alki* (Chinook for "By and by").

SONG: "Washington, My Home."

FLOWER: Coast rhododendron.

TREE: Western hemlock.

BIRD: Willow goldfinch.

FISH: Steelhead trout.

LEGAL HOLIDAYS: New Year's Day, 1 January; birthday of Martin Luther King Jr., 3rd Monday in January; Presidents' Day, 2nd Monday in February; Memorial Day, last Monday in May; Independence Day, 4 July; Labor Day, 1st Monday in September; Veterans' Day, 11 November; Thanksgiving Day, 4th Thursday in November and the day following; Christmas Day, 25 December.

TIME: 4 a.m. PST = noon GMT.

1 Location and Size

Located on the Pacific coast of the northwestern United States, Washington ranks 20th in size among the 50 states. The total area of Washington is 71,298 square miles (184,661 square kilometers), of which land takes up 66,449 square miles (172,103 square kilometers) and water (inland, coastal, and territorial) 4,849 square miles (12,559 square kilometers). The state extends about 360 miles (580 kilometers) from east to west and 240 miles (390 kilometers) from north to south. The state's boundary length totals 1,099 miles (1,769 kilometers), including 157 miles (253 kilometers) of general coastline. Major islands of the San Juan group include Orcas, San Juan, and Lopez. Whidbey is a large island in the upper Puget Sound.

2 Topography

Much of Washington is mountainous. Along the Pacific coast are the Coast Ranges extending northward from Oregon and California. This

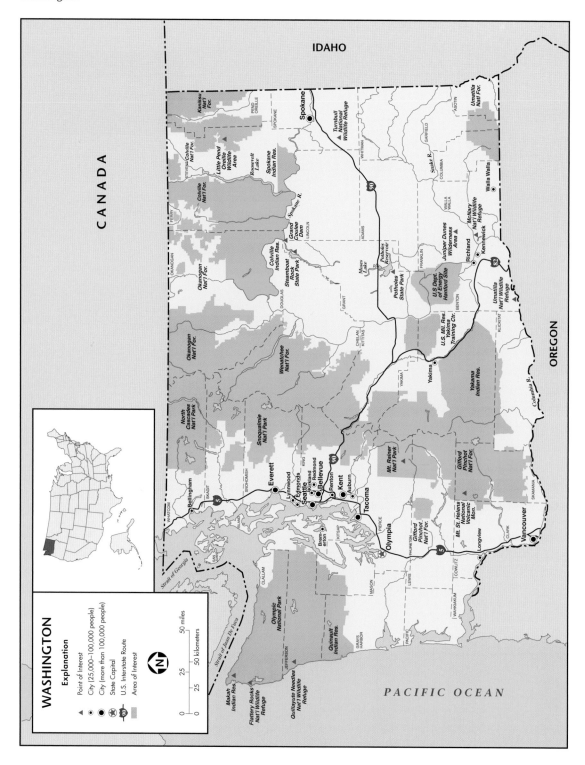

chain forms two groups: the Olympic Mountains in the northwest and the Willapa Hills in the southwest. About 100 miles (160 kilometers) inward from the Pacific coast is the Cascade Range, extending northward from the Sierra Nevada in California. This chain includes Mount Rainier, which at 14,410 feet (4,392 meters) is the highest peak in the state. Between the Coast and Cascade ranges lies the Western Corridor—where most of Washington's major cities are concentrated. Of all the state's other major regions, only the Columbia River basin region of south-central Washington is generally flat.

The Cascade volcanoes were mostly dormant for over 100 years. Early in 1980, however, Mount St. Helens erupted, producing clouds of ash and mudflows. East of the Cascade Range, much of Washington is a plateau underlain by ancient lava flows. In the northeast are the Okanogan Highlands; in the southeast are the Blue Mountains and the Palouse Hills.

Among Washington's numerous rivers, the longest and most powerful is the Columbia, which forms part of the border with Oregon and then flows for more than 1,200 miles (1,900 kilometers) across the heart of the state. Washington's other major river is the Snake. The state has numerous lakes, of which the largest is the artificial Roosevelt Lake, covering 123 square miles (319 square kilometers). One of the largest and most famous dams in the United States is Grand Coulee on the upper Columbia River.

3 Climate

The Cascade Mountains divide Washington into distinct climate zones. Despite its northerly location, western Washington is as mild as the middle and southeastern Atlantic coast, but it is also one of the rainiest regions in the world. Eastern Washington, however, has a much more continental climate, characterized by cold winters, hot summers, and sparse rainfall.

Average January temperatures in western Washington range from 20°F (-7°C) to 48°F (9°C). July temperatures in the same region range from 44°F (7°C) to 80°F (27°C). In the east, the temperatures are much more extreme. In January, temperatures range are from 8°F (-13°C) to 40°F (4°C) and in July, the range is from 48°F (9°C) to 92°F (33°C). The lowest temperature ever recorded in the state was -48°F (-44°C) set at Mazama and Winthrop on 30 December 1968. The highest temperature, 118°F (48°C), was set at Ice Harbor Dam on 5 August 1961.

The average annual precipitation in Seattle is 37 inches (94 centimeters), falling most heavily from October through March. Spokane receives only 17 inches (43 centimeters) of rain per year. The Olympic Rainforest, in Olympic National Park, has an annual rainfall of over 145 inches (368 centimeters). Snowfall in Seattle averages 11.4 inches (29 centimeters) annually. In Spokane, the average snowfall is 49.4 inches (125.5 centimeters). Paradise Ranger Station holds the North American record for the most snowfall in one season, with 1,122 inches (2,850 centimeters) of snow recorded during the winter of 1971–1972. High mountain peaks, such as Mount Adams, Mount Baker, and Mount Rainier, have permanent snowcaps or snowfields of up to 100 feet (30 meters) deep.

4 Plants and Animals

More than 1,300 plant species have been identified in Washington. Sand strawberries and beach peas are found among the dunes. Fennel and spurry grow in salt marshes. Greasewood and sagebrush predominate in the desert regions of the Columbia Plateau. Conifers include Sitka spruce, Douglas fir, and western hemlock. Big-leaf maple, red alder, and western yew are among the common deciduous trees. Wildflowers include the deerhead orchid and wake-robin. The western rhododendron is the state flower. In 2012, there were nine Washington plant species listed as threatened or endangered by the US Fish and Wildlife Service, including the golden paintbrush, Nelson's checker-mallow, Kincaid's lupine, Spalding's catchfly, Ute ladies'-tresses, and water howelia.

Forest and mountain regions support Columbia black-tailed and mule deer, elk, and black bear. Other native mammals are the Canadian lynx, red fox, and red western bobcat. Smaller mammals—raccoon, muskrat, and porcupine—are plentiful. The whistler (hoary) marmot is the largest rodent. Game birds include the ruffed grouse and ring-necked pheasant. Sixteen varieties of owl have been identified; other birds of prey include the prairie falcon, sparrow hawk, and golden eagle. The bald eagle is more numerous in Washington than in any other state except Alaska. Various salmon species thrive in coastal waters and along the Columbia River, and the hair seal and sea lion inhabit Puget Sound.

In 2012, the US Fish and Wildlife Service listed 28 Washington animal species as threatened or endangered, including the short-tailed albatross, brown pelican, pygmy rabbit, humpback whale, eight species of salmon, two species (green and leatherback) of sea turtle, and the killer southern resident whale. These two whale species only pass near Washington waters during their migration periods, but their appearance on the endangered species list allows the state to protect them during this period.

5 Environmental Protection

The mission of the Department of Ecology (established in 1970) is to protect, preserve, and enhance Washington's environment and promote the wise management of its air, land, and water for the benefit of current and future generations. The Department of Ecology directly administers an automobile inspection program for the Seattle, Vancouver, and Spokane areas; an Estuarine Sanctuary program at Padilla Bay; the Conservation Corps employment program; and the Youth Corps litter control program.

Other state agencies with environmental responsibilities are the State Conservation Commission, Environmental Hearings Office, State Parks and Recreation Commission, Department of Health, Department of Fish and Wildlife, and Department of Natural Resources.

Washington state has one of the highest overall recycling rates in the United States. In the mid-1980s, Bellingham began the state's first curbside recycling collection program. Seattle soon started its own program after being forced to close a municipal landfill and facing fierce opposition to construction of a garbage incinerator. In 1989, the state legislature passed the Waste-Not Washington Act, which defined a clear solid waste management strategy and set a recycling goal of 50%.

In 2010, the state had 3,871 reports of hazardous waste, showing a steady decrease since 2006. In 2012, the state had 49 Superfund sites listed on the US Environmental Agency's National Priorities List. These included most of the state's military bases and the Hanford Nuclear Reservation.

6 Population

In 2011, Washington ranked 13th in population among the 50 states with an estimated total of 6,830,038 people. The population is projected to reach 7,996,400 by 2025. The population density in 2010 was 103 persons per square mile (39.6 persons per square kilometer). In 2011, the median age was 37.3. About 12.7% of all residents were 65 or older, while 23.2% were under 18.

In 2010, 92% of the population lived in urban areas. Seattle is the largest city, with an estimated population in 2011 of 620,778 (metro area, 3,500,026). Other large cities are Spokane (210,103), Tacoma (200,678), and Vancouver (164,759).

7 Ethnic Groups

In 2010, the largest minorities in Washington were Hispanics and Latinos, who made up approximately 11.2% of the population. Most of this group came from Mexico. About 7.2% of the population was Asian. Around 1.5% of the population registered as American Indian, and 3.6% registered as black or African American.

8 Languages

Northern and Midland dialects dominate the state's language. Midland is strongest in eastern Washington and the Bellingham area, with Northern strongest elsewhere. In 2011, 81.4% of the population spoke only English at home; 8.1% spoke Spanish; 3.8% spoke another Indo-European language, and 5.6% spoke an Asian or Pacific Islander language.

Washington Population Profile

Total population per Census 2010:	6,724,540
Population change, 2006–10:	5.1%
Hispanic or Latino†:	11.2%
Population by race	
One race:	95.3%
White:	77.3%
Black or African American:	3.6%
American Indian/Alaska Native:	1.5%
Asian:	7.2%
Native Hawaiian/Pacific Islander:	0.6%
Some other race:	5.2%
Two or more races:	4.7%

Population by Age Group, Census 2010

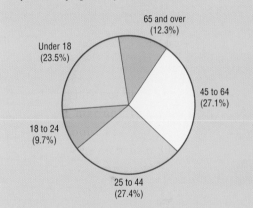

- 65 and over (12.3%)
- Under 18 (23.5%)
- 45 to 64 (27.1%)
- 18 to 24 (9.7%)
- 25 to 44 (27.4%)

Major Cities by Population, 2011 Estimates

City	Population	% change 2005–11
Seattle	620,778	8.2
Spokane	210,103	6.7
Tacoma	200,678	2.4
Vancouver	164,759	4.6
Bellevue	124,798	6.5
Kent	120,916	47.8
Everett	104,295	8.0
Renton	92,812	58.6
Yakima	92,512	13.9
Federal Way	91,085	9.6

Notes: †A person of Hispanic or Latino origin may be of any race. NA indicates that data are not available. Percentages may not equal 100 due to rounding.

SOURCE: U.S. Census Bureau. Census 2010 and Population Estimates. www.census.gov/ (accessed July 2012).

Washington Population by Race
CENSUS 2010

This table shows the number of people who are of one, two, or three or more races. For those claiming two races, the number of people belonging to the various categories is listed. The U.S. government conducts a census of the population every 10 years.

	Number	Percent
Total population	6,724,540	100.0
One race	6,411,614	95.3
Two races	282,352	4.2
White *and* Black or African American	51,624	0.8
White *and* American Indian/Alaska Native	66,769	1.0
White *and* Asian	83,994	1.2
White *and* Native Hawaiian/Pacific Islander	9,817	0.1
White *and* some other race	34,488	0.5
Black or African American *and* American Indian/Alaska Native	5,458	0.1
Black or African American *and* Asian	6,290	0.1
Black or African American *and* Native Hawaiian/Pacific Islander	1,407	—
Black or African American *and* some other race	3,251	—
American Indian/Alaska Native *and* Asian	2,773	—
American Indian/Alaska Native *and* Native Hawaiian/Pacific Islander	734	—
American Indian/Alaska Native *and* some other race	2,261	—
Asian *and* Native Hawaiian/Pacific Islander	7,209	0.1
Asian *and* some other race	5,000	0.1
Native Hawaiian/Pacific Islander *and* some other race	1,277	—
Three or more races	30,574	0.5

SOURCE: U.S. Census Bureau. Census 2010. www.census/gov/ (accessed July 2012). A dash (—) indicates that the percent is less than 0.1.

9 Religions

According to the Pew Forum on Religion & Public Life in 2008, 25% of Washington residents identified as Evangelical Protestants; 23% as mainline Protestants; 16% as Roman Catholics; and 2% as Mormons. About 1% were affiliated with historically black Protestant churches. One percent of the population was Jewish, 1% Buddhist, and 1% Jehovah's Witnesses. No other religion had more than 0.5% of the population. Around 23% of the state's residents were unaffiliated with any religious organization.

10 Transportation

In 2009, Washington had 764 miles (1,230 kilometers) of state highway interstate. Principal interstate highways include I-90, connecting Spokane and Seattle, and I-5, proceeding north–south from Vancouver, British Columbia, through Seattle and Tacoma to Vancouver, Washington, and Portland, Oregon, and on through California. The total roadway miles for 2009 amounted to 83,505 miles (134,388 kilometers). In 2010, Washington had a total of 460 fatalities due to collisions, out of around 57.2 billion miles traveled. In 2009, the state had 4,075,764 licensed drivers. That year, 3.3 million automobiles and 2.6 million trucks were registered in the state.

In 2009, the Seattle-Tacoma airport had 15,242,175 passenger enplanements, making it the nation's 16th-busiest airport that year. In 2009, there were 366 airports, 160 heliports, and 17 seaplane bases in the state.

Washington's principal ports include Seattle, Tacoma, and Anacortes, all part of the Puget Sound area and belonging to the Seattle Customs District. Longview, Kalama, and Vancouver, along the Columbia River, are ports within the Portland (Oregon) Customs District. In 2010, the ferry system of Washington made a total of $208.6 million in revenues.

There are 22 freight railroads in Washington, including 2 Class I freight railroads, and 3,652 miles (5,877 kilometers) of freight track.

11 History

The Cascade Mountains prevented most communication between Native Americans of the coast and those of the eastern plateau, and their cultures evolved differently. The coastal tribes used timber to construct dugout canoes, wooden dwellings, and some stationary wooden furniture. They emphasized rank based on wealth, and warfare between villages was fairly common. The plateau (or "horse") tribes, on the other hand, paid little attention to class distinctions; their social organization was simpler and intertribal warfare less frequent. After the horse reached Washington around 1730, the plateau tribes became largely nomadic, traveling long distances in search of food.

The first Europeans known to have sailed along the Washington coast were Spaniards, who explored the coastline to the southern tip of Alaska in 1774 and 1775. English Captain James Cook arrived in the Pacific Northwest in

A view of downtown Seattle shows the Space Needle on the left and the volcanic Mt. Rainier in the background on the right. Seattle ranks among the country's largest ports. © ANDY Z./SHUTTERSTOCK.COM.

1778 while searching for a northwest passage across America. Cook was the first of numerous British explorers and traders to be attracted by the valuable fur of the sea otter, and the maritime fur trade began to prosper.

American interest in the area increased after Meriwether Lewis and William Clark's expedition to inspect the Louisiana Purchase. They first sighted the Pacific Ocean in 1805 from the north bank of the Columbia River. As reports of the trip became known, a host of British and American fur traders followed portions of their route to the Pacific coast, and the formation of missionary settlements encouraged other Americans to journey to the Pacific Northwest.

Statehood As early as 1843, an American provisional government had been established in the region. Three years later, a US-Canada boundary along the 49th parallel was established by agreement with the British. Oregon Territory, including the present state of Washington, was organized in 1848. In 1853, the land north of the Columbia River gained separate territorial status as Washington (which included part of present-day Idaho).

Although a series of treaties with the tribes of the Northwest had established a system of reservations, bloody uprisings by the Yakima, Nisqualli, and Cayuse were not suppressed until the late 1850s. On the economic front, discoveries of gold in the Walla Walla area and in Idaho brought prosperity to the entire region. The completion in 1883 of the Northern Pacific Railroad line from the eastern United States to Puget Sound encouraged immigration, and Washington's population swelled to 357,232 by 1890.

Cattle- and sheep-raising, farming, and lumbering were all established by the time

Washington became the 42nd state in 1889. In 1909, Seattle staged the Alaska-Yukon-Pacific Exposition, celebrating the Alaska gold rush and Seattle's new position as a major seaport. World War I (1914–18) brought the state several major new military installations, and the Puget Sound area thrived as a shipbuilding center. The war years also saw the emergence of radical labor activities, especially in the shipbuilding and logging industries.

1930s to 1990s Washington's economy was in dire straits during the Great Depression of the 1930s, when the market for forest products and field crops tumbled. The New Deal era brought numerous federally funded public works projects, notably the Bonneville and Grand Coulee dams on the Columbia River. They provided hydroelectric power for industry and water for the irrigation of desert lands. During World War II, Boeing led the way in establishing the aerospace industry as Washington's primary employer. Also during the war, the federal government built the Hanford Reservation nuclear research center. This was one of the major contractors in the construction of the first atomic bomb and later became a pioneer producer of atomic-powered electricity.

The 1960s and 1970s witnessed the growth of increasing public concern for protection of the state's unique natural heritage. An unforeseen environmental hazard emerged in May 1980 with the eruption of Mount St. Helens and the resulting widespread destruction.

Washington experienced a deep recession in 1979. The logging and lumber industries, competing with mills in the Southeast and in Canada, were particularly hard hit. Nuclear waste also became an issue when it was confirmed in 1990

Despite the devastation wrought when Mount St. Helens erupted in 1980, the area has seen a tremendous amount of rebirth.
© TUSHARKOLEY/SHUTTERSTOCK.COM.

that plutonium produced at the Hanford Reservation bomb fuel facility had leaked into the nearby Columbia River. The state and federal governments launched a cleanup program that cost hundreds of millions of dollars and still continues.

The state's economy was strengthened by the expansion of Microsoft Corporation, Boeing, and Weyerhauser Paper, but was still hampered by falling agricultural prices and weakness in the timber industry.

In 1996, Democrat Gary Locke was elected to the governorship, making him the nation's first governor of Chinese ancestry. In 2000, Locke won reelection. Under his administration education spending was increased and the

welfare system reformed, which cut the state's welfare rolls by one-third.

In late 1999, the city of Seattle hosted a World Trade Organization (WTO) conference that was protested by 40,000 to 50,000 demonstrators. The protesters were concerned about sustainable economies, fair trade, the environment, workers's rights, globalization, corporate greed, and a host of other issues. Although most demonstrators were peaceful, some rioting occurred. This prompted a heavy police response that included pepper-spraying numerous protesters as well as many arrests. In the aftermath, some of the protesters sued the city over various legal violations, and the city paid money to settle the lawsuits.

Washington Governors: 1889–2013

1889–1893	Elisha Peyre Ferry	Republican
1893–1896	John Hart McGraw	Republican
1896–1901	John Rankin Rogers	Popular Democrat
1901–1905	Henry McBride	Republican
1905–1909	Albert Edward Mead	Republican
1909	Samuel Goodlove Cosgrove	Republican
1909–1913	Marion E. Hay	Republican
1913–1919	Earnest Lister	Democrat
1919–1925	Louis Folwell Hart	Republican
1925–1933	Roland Hill Hartley	Republican
1933–1941	Clarence Daniel Martin	Democrat
1941–1945	Arthur Bernard Langlie	Republican
1945–1953	Monrad Charles Wallgren	Democrat
1953–1957	Arthur Bernard Langlie	Republican
1957–1965	Albert Dean Rosellini	Democrat
1965–1977	Daniel Jackson Evans	Republican
1977–1981	Dixy Lee Ray	Democrat
1981–1985	John D. Spellman	Republican
1985–1993	Booth Gardner	Democrat
1993–1997	Michael Edward Lowry	Democrat
1997–2005	Gary Locke	Democrat
2005–2013	Christine Gregoire	Democrat
2013–	Jay Inslee	Democrat

In the 1990s, Washington experienced robust economic growth, fueled by the high-tech computer and aerospace sectors. However, by the early 2000s these two sectors would become the source of serious economic problems for the state.

21st Century In 2001, Boeing announced it was relocating its headquarters to Chicago, Illinois. In that same year, the dot-com bubble on Wall Street burst, and on 11 September 2001 the terrorist attacks on the United States in New York City and in Washington, D.C., took place. These and other lesser economic events severely impacted the state's economy.

A contested 2004 gubernatorial election, eventually decided by the courts, awarded the governorship to Democrat Christine Gregoire. She won out over Republican Dino Rossi, who

declined to appeal the decision. The election was the closest gubernatorial election in US history. Soon afterward Washington was hit by the housing market crash and recession of 2008–09, which put the state in a difficult economic position after its brief period of recovery. Unemployment again grew, and the construction industry faltered. The state began turning to biotechnology, green technologies, and alternative energy ventures in order to bolster its economy. Gregoire won reelection in 2008 and was succeeded by fellow Democrat Jay Inslee in 2013.

In 2012, voters approved ballot proposals legalizing same-sex marriage and the recreational use of marijuana.

 State Government

Washington's constitution of 1889 continues to govern the state. The legislative branch consists of a senate with 49 members elected to four-year terms, and a house of representatives with 98 members serving two-year terms. Executives elected statewide include the governor and lieutenant governor (who run separately), secretary of state, treasurer, attorney general, auditor, superintendent of public education, and officers of insurance and public land. In 2012, the governor was Christine Gregoire, the secretary of state Sam Reed, and the attorney general Rob McKenna. There is no gubernatorial term limit. McKenna, a Republican, took on Democrat Jay Inslee for the governorship in 2012 and narrowly lost.

A bill must first be passed by a majority of the elected members of each house. It then can be signed by the governor, or left unsigned for five days while the legislature is in session or 20 days after it has adjourned. A two-thirds vote of members present in each house is sufficient to override a governor's veto.

In 2010, the average salary of a Washington legislator was $42,106. Salary schedules are set every two years and based on realistic standards as well as the duties of the office. In 2012, the governor of Washington was paid an estimated $166,891 a year, the 10th-highest gubernatorial salary in America.

13 Political Parties

In the early 2000s, Washington largely favored the Democratic Party. The 22nd governor of the state, Christine Gregoire, is a Democrat who defeated the Republican Dino Rossi in 2004 and 2008. She did not seek reelection in 2012 and was succeeded by Democrat Jay Inslee. After the 2012 elections, there were six Democrats and four Republicans in the US House, and both of the state's US senators were Democrats. US senator Maria Cantwell won reelection in 2012, and US senator Patty Murray was reelected in 2010.

Prior to the 2010 election, Democrats held the majority in both the Washington state senate and house. However, continuing economic distress led to a slight party shift in 2010. Democrats maintained control, but with smaller majorities. In 2011, the state senate had a 27 to 22 Democratic majority and the state house had a 56 to 42 Democratic majority. That year there were 29 women serving in the state house and 18 women serving in the state senate.

Washington holds 11 electoral votes. In the 2004 presidential election, Democrat John Kerry took 52.8% of the vote to Republican George W. Bush's 45.6%. In the 2008 presidential election, the state voted for Democrat Barack

Obama with 57.3% of the vote to Republican John McCain's 40.48%. In 2012, Washington voters supported President Obama over Republican challenger Mitt Romney. As of August 2012, there were 3,731,742 voters registered in the state. There is no party registration in the state.

14 Local Government

As of 2007, Washington had 39 counties and 1,845 local governments, including 1,229 special districts. There were 281 subcounty general purpose governments, 281 municipal governments, and no township governments. The municipalities were divided into three different classes, with the first class having more than 10,000 people, the second class having between 1,500 and 10,000 people and no home rule charter, and the third class having no charter

Washington Presidential Vote by Major Political Parties, 1948–2012			
Year	Washington Winner	Democrat	Republican
1948	*Truman (D)	476,165	386,315
1952	*Eisenhower (R)	492,845	599,107
1956	*Eisenhower (R)	523,002	620,430
1960	Nixon (R)	599,298	629,273
1964	*Johnson (D)	779,699	470,366
1968	Humphrey (D)	616,037	588,510
1972	*Nixon (R)	568,334	837,135
1976	Ford (R)	717,323	777,732
1980	*Reagan (R)	650,193	865,244
1984	*Reagan (R)	807,352	1,051,670
1988	Dukakis (D)	933,516	903,835
1992	*Clinton (D)	993,037	731,234
1996	*Clinton (D)	1,123,323	840,712
2000	Gore (D)	1,247,652	1,108,864
2004	Kerry (D)	1,510,201	1,304,894
2008	*Obama (D)	1,750,848	1,229,216
2012	*Obama (D)	1,755,396	1,290,670

*Won US presidential election.

Independent candidate Ross Perot received 541,780 votes in 1992 and 201,003 votes in 1996.

and fewer than 1,500 inhabitants. In 2011, there were 285,361 full-time and 138,939 part-time state and local government employees in Washington.

15 Judicial System

There are four levels to the judicial court system in Washington. The supreme court, located in Olympia, is at the head of the system, followed by the court of appeals, the superior courts, and finally the courts of limited jurisdiction such as district courts. The supreme court hears appeals from the court of appeals and administers the overarching court system, but has little to do with any unrelated civil or criminal cases. Minor civil and criminal cases are decided by the courts of limited jurisdiction, while major cases are heard by the superior courts. The supreme court, in addition to making key decisions, occasionally travels to hear cases in other cities, visit colleges, or take part in various events.

In 2010, Washington had a violent crime rate of 313.8 reported incidents per 100,000 people. The murder and nonnegligent manslaughter rate was 2.3 incidents per 100,000 inhabitants; forcible rape, 38.1; aggravated assault, 185.3; and property crime, 3,706.6. That year, there were 30,905 prisoners in the state's prisons and jails. The state imposes the death penalty, of which the condemned can choose hanging or lethal injection. In 2012, there were seven offenders sentenced to the death penalty in the state.

16 Migration

The first overseas immigrants to reach Washington were Chinese laborers, imported during the 1860s. The 1870s and 1880s brought an influx of immigrants from western Europe, especially Germany, Scandinavia, and the Netherlands, and from Russia and Japan.

Between 1990 and 1998, Washington had net gains of 374,000 in domestic migration and 121,000 in international migration. In the period 2000–05, net international migration was 134,242 people, while net domestic migration for that same year was 80,974, for a net gain of 215,216 people.

Throughout the 1990s and the early 2000s, the Hispanic migration to Washington increased. Between 2000 and 2010, the foreign-born population of the state increased by 44%, and in 2010 about 13.1% of the population was composed of immigrants, compared to only 6.6% in 1990. About 45.5% of the foreign born in the state were US citizens in 2010. Immigrants for that year made up 17.3% of working-age adults. The largest source of immigrants continued to be Asia, although Latin America was a close second.

Between 2009 and 2010, the total population (ages one and older) of Washington increased by 83,251, due to the net domestic in-migration of natives (25,993), the net domestic out-migration of immigrants (-371), and the arrival from abroad of natives (23,438) and immigrants (34,191). Of the total foreign-born population in Washington in 2010, 4.8% were from Africa, 40.2% were from Asia, 16.8% were from Europe, and 31.3% were from Latin America. The top three countries of birth of the foreign born in Washington in 2010 were Mexico (26.3%), the Philippines (7.3%), and Vietnam (6.3%). In comparison, the top three countries of birth in 1990 were Mexico (14.3%), Canada (13.7%), and the Philippines (8.5%).

17 Economy

Key Washington industries include aerospace, forest products, global health and life sciences, information and communication technology, manufacturing, marine technology, agriculture, and tourism.

Due to growth in stable industries such as software and technology, Washington was one of the first states to show signs of recovery from the recession of 2008–09. Washington and Seattle received numerous accolades in 2010 and 2011, including reaching *US News & World Report*'s top spots for best state to start a business, best city for technology growth and employees, city with the strongest economy, and best state for software publishing employment.

In 2010, Washington's gross state product (GSP) was $351 billion, ranking the state 14th. Per capita GSP was $52,403 that year, ranking the state 10th. In 2010, there were 175,914 private nonfarm establishments and 405,256 nonemployer establishments in the state.

18 Income

Per capita personal income (including nonmonetary income) in 2011 was $44,294, ranking Washington 14th in the United States. The median annual household income for the period 2008–2010 was $58,330, compared to the national average of $50,022. In 2011, 13.9% of the population lived below the federal poverty level, compared to the national average of 15.9%

19 Industry

Washington has a long history of strong aerospace growth, and by 2011 was still a vital location for aerospace research, with more than 650 aerospace companies and more than 83,000 workers in the industry. Clean energy is a far newer field, but the state has 64% more clean tech jobs than the national average. Forest products represent more than 15% of the manufacturing industry in the state. In life sciences and global health studies, Washington has 200 businesses in the field. Closer to the state's natural resources, the marine sector and agricultural industries are also especially strong.

Washington is especially noted for its large software companies. Intel, Hewlett-Packard, Oracle, Adobe, and Google had research and development plants in the state in 2012, and Microsoft has had its headquarters in Redmond since 1986. Tourism is also an important part of the state's industry focus. In 2010, more than 143,000 jobs were supported by tourism.

20 Labor

In August 2012, the civilian labor force in Washington numbered 3,497,900, with approximately 302,100 workers unemployed, yielding an unemployment rate of 8.6%, compared to the national average of 8.1% for the same period. Those employed in nonfarm wage and salaried jobs that same month included: 141,300 in construction; 287,800 in manufacturing; 540,200 in trade, transportation, and public utilities; 103,100 in information; 139,600 in financial activities; 345,800 in professional and business services; 391,600 in education and health services; 276,800 in leisure and hospitality; and 536,300 people in government.

In 2011, 557,000 of Washington's employed wage and salary workers were members of unions, representing some 20.4% of those so

Skagit Valley is the home of an annual tulip festival that brings in more than 1 million visitors. © KARAMYSH/SHUTTERSTOCK.COM.

employed. The national average was 13%. In 2012, Washington had the highest minimum wage at $9.04 per hour, followed by neighboring state Oregon. In 2013 the rate in Washington increased to $9.19 per hour.

21 Agriculture

In 2007, Washington had more than 14.9 million acres devoted to farmland, with an average farm size of 381 acres. In 2011, there were 39,500 farms in the state. Total agricultural output that year was $9.67 billion, with field crops accounting for $6.4 billion in output. Fruits and nuts, wheat, potatoes, specialty products like floriculture products and Christmas trees,

vegetables, and berries were all major sources of revenue. Apples were the leading crop in 2011, with farm receipts of $1.56 billion; farm receipts for wheat amounted to $1 billion; and receipts from potatoes were $710.8 million. Other major crops included hops, corn, and grasses.

Top exports in 2011 included fruits and fruit preparations ($1 billion in exports) and vegetables and vegetable preparations ($682.4 million in exports). Major agricultural counties included Yakima, Grant, Benton, Franklin, and Walla Walla.

22 Domesticated Animals

Total domesticated animals output in 2011 was $2.38 billion. Dairy products were the most profitable sector, with $1.27 billion in farm receipts. Receipts from sale of cattle and calves were $701.6 million that year. Eggs were another key product, bringing $120 million in 2010. Mink pelts were another source of revenue for the state, which ranked ninth in mink farms in 2010.

In December 2003, a cow in Washington tested positive for bovine spongiform encephalopathy, also known as mad cow disease. As a result, various cows were quarantined and tested for the disease. It was the first reported case in the United States.

23 Fishing

Approximately 3.7 million salmon were caught in Washington in 2010, generating more than $40 million in revenue. While this is one of the most valuable single species, general commercial fishing numbers were much higher. For example, all shellfish and marine catches in total had a value of $274 million in 2010. That year, trout sales amounted to 3.4% of total US sales and put the state in sixth place for trout production.

Westport, Ilwaco–Chinook, and Bellingham are the major ports in the state. In the early 2010s, key concerns for the fishing industry included keeping invasive species out of Washington waters and carefully managing the fishing of salmon species in Washington rivers to encourage a regrowth of salmon populations. On the coast, private shellfishing and crabbing are popular activities in a wide variety of locations. In 2009, the Fish and Wildlife Commission began a new policy of reform for hatcheries and fisheries within the state, designed to meet new conservation goals for salmon and steelhead

by encouraging more harvesting of hatchery-bred fish instead of their wild counterparts.

24 Forestry

More than 52% of the land was forested in 2006. Federal forests covered 43% of the state, followed by State Trust Lands, Native American Lands, and country forests. Private forests accounted for 36% of the total forestland. The largest federal forests are Wenatchee, Mount Baker–Snoqualmie, and Okanogan. In 2010, there were 877 forest fires recorded, one of the lowest numbers in decades in the state. However, more acres were burned in 2010 than in 2009 (40,942 to 24,053), indicating that on average the fires were larger in size.

Washington uses replanting tactics every year to create sustainable timber cycles. Clear-cutting is used to harvest timber, but is limited by law to 120 acres without a special license. In 2010, 2.7 billion board feet were harvested, most on private lands. Popular softwoods included Douglas fir, hemlock, true firs, and Ponderosa pine. Red alder was the primary popular hardwood.

25 Mining

In 2011, nonfuel mineral production in Washington amounted to $727 million, accounting for 0.98% of the US total and ranking the state 30th. Major nonfuel minerals mined in the state included gold, diatomite, sand and gravel, and crushed stone.

By 2010, there were only 5,900 workers in the natural resources and mining industry, marking a steady decrease throughout the early 2000s as attention shifted toward other employment opportunities. Surface mining reclamation projects, on the other hand, continued to grow as reclamation of the 1,200 permitted mines in the state continued.

26 Energy and Power

Along with Oregon, Washington is one of the largest users of hydroelectricity in the nation. In 2009, hydroelectric power accounted for almost three-fourths of the power used by the state, and the Grand Coulee hydroelectric power plant on the Columbia River was the highest-capacity plant of its kind in the nation. Washington also had five oil and gas refineries, making it a key refinery sector for the Northwest area. The state's Energy Independence Act requires large electric utilities to obtain 15% of their electricity from new renewable energy resources by 2020 and to undertake cost-effective energy conservation.

Washington has no reserves of crude oil, coal, or natural gas. Electric power industry net summer generating capacity in 2010 was 30,477,700 megawatts. As of June 2012, total net electricity generation was 11,375,000 megawatt hours (MWh). Of this, 165,000 MWh was generated by natural gas-fired plants; 1,000 MWh by coal-fired plants; 716,000 MWh by nuclear plants; 9.65 million MWh by hydroelectric plants; and 799,000 MWh by other renewable sources. In 2012, Washington had one nuclear power plant in operation, the Columbia Generating Station at the Hanford nuclear reservation.

Windy conditions along the Columbia River make it a prime spot for wind turbines. © LONNIE GORSLINE/SHUTTERSTOCK.COM.

27 Commerce

In 2008, there were 9,717 wholesale trade establishments and 22,481 retail trade establishments. In 2011, total exports from Washington equaled $64.6 billion, making the state the fifth largest for overall exports. Biggest exports were aircraft and aircraft parts in terms of value, while the largest imports sector was industrial machinery. Since Canada is so close, trade with the northern country is easy, and Canada had been the largest trading partner of Washington until the early 2000s, when China supplanted it.

Retail sales in 2011 reached $57.1 billion, with auto and general merchandise sales topping the list. E-commerce showed the strongest growth in the past decade, with a 15.2% growth rate between 2001 and 2011. Total retail sales for the state grew at around 0.6% annually for the past decade.

In 2010, the top export markets for the state included China, Canada, Japan, South Korea, Indonesia, and Germany.

28 Public Finance

Washington's biennial budget is prepared by the Office of Financial Management and submitted by the governor to the legislature for amendment and approval. The fiscal year runs from 1 July through 30 June. The 2011/13 budget planned on using $35 billion, continuing a steady increase in the state budget.

29 Taxation

Washington is one of six states without individual or corporate income taxes. The biggest source of state revenue is the general sales and use tax, set at 6.5% with local sales taxes adding on another 2.4%. Food purchased for consumption off premises (such as at home) is exempt. The state also imposes excise taxes on gasoline and cigarettes. There is also a state property tax, which accounts for about 30% of total tax revenue.

In 2011, Washington state collected $17.41 billion in state taxes. This included $1.87 billion in state property taxes; $14.1 billion in sales taxes and gross receipts; and $931 million in license taxes and fees. The per capita state tax burden that year was $2,549, compared with a national average of $2,430, and giving Washington the 19th-highest state tax burden in the nation.

30 Health

In 2011, Washington's infant mortality rate was 5.1 deaths per 1,000 live births. The overall death rate in 2009 was 709.8 per 100,000. There were 154.4 deaths per 100,000 residents from heart disease in 2009; and 174.9 deaths per 100,000 from cancers. There were 38.7 deaths per 100,000 from cerebrovascular diseases and 22.8 deaths per 100,000 from diabetes. In 2010, around 7.6% of the adult population had been diagnosed with diabetes at some point, and 61.8% of adults were overweight or obese. Among Washington adults ages 18 and older, 15.2% were smokers in 2010, compared to the national rate of 17.2%. At the end of 2008, there were 10,252 Washingtonians living with HIV/AIDS, 1.2% of the US total.

Washington's 86 community hospitals had about 1.7 beds per 100,000 in 2010. The average expense for community hospital care was $2,810 per inpatient day in 2010. Washington had 251 physicians and 798 registered nurses in

2008 and 70 dentists in 2007 per 100,000 residents. In 2010, 13% of Washington residents lacked health insurance.

31 Housing

Washington suffered from the housing market crash, which began to show itself in 2006 with falling home sales. Sales continued to fall until 2009 when they went through a period of sharp volatility, rising and plummeting from quarter to quarter before stabilizing at the end of 2011 with very little growth at all. By the end of 2011, the state had seen house prices fall overall for the previous four years, and the median selling price was $224,200, more than 9% lower than in 2010. By the start of 2012, there were 77,000 seriously delinquent mortgages in the state, which had a foreclosure rate of about 5,000 houses per quarter.

In 2011, there were an estimated 2,907,605 housing units, 90.5% (2,632,621) of which were occupied and 62.8% (1,653,712) of which were owner-occupied. About 63.3% (1,841,873) of all units were single-family, detached homes; 201,937 (6.9%) were mobile homes. Utility gas and electricity were the most common energy sources for heating. It was estimated that 14,897 units (0.6%) lacked complete plumbing facilities and 30,300 (1.2%) lacked complete kitchen facilities.

The median home value in 2011 was $256,300. The median monthly cost for mortgage owners was $1,733, while renters paid a median of $930.

32 Education

In 2010, Washington had 1,661,690 students over three years of age enrolled in schools. In the years 2006–2010, 89.6% of the state's population over the age of 25 had graduated from high school, while 31% had a bachelor's degree or higher. Total school revenue from all sources equaled $9.9 billion in 2010. The teachers and administrators in the public K–12 school system had an average salary of $56,197.

Annual tuition fees for the 2011/12 higher education year were around $3,542 per student for public community and technical colleges. The largest institutions are the University of Washington (founded in 1861) and Washington State University. Other public institutions include the following: Eastern Washington University, Central Washington University, Western Washington University, and Evergreen State College. Private institutions include Gonzaga University, Pacific Lutheran University, Seattle University, Seattle Pacific University, University of Puget Sound, Walla Walla University, and Whitworth University.

33 Arts

The focus of professional performance activities in Washington is Seattle, home of the Seattle Symphony, Pacific Northwest Ballet Company, and Seattle Repertory Theater. Tacoma and Spokane have notable local orchestras.

Seattle is also the birthplace of grunge music. Hitting the mainstream in the early 1990s, grunge brought fame to Nirvana (lead singer, Kurt Cobain), Pearl Jam (lead singer, Eddie Vedder), Soundgarden (lead singer, Chris Cornell), Alice in Chains (lead singer, Layne Staley), and other bands.

The Seattle Cherry Blossom and Japanese Cultural Festival has been a popular community event since its inception in 1975. The annual Diwali Festival, also in Seattle, is sponsored in part by the regional Confluence of Festivals in India and the Washington State Arts Commission. It includes performances of traditional dance, music, and drama.

Among Washington's many museums, universities, and other organizations exhibiting works of art on a permanent or periodic basis are the Seattle Art Museum and the Henry Art Gallery of the University of Washington at Seattle. Others include the Whatcom Museum of History and Art, the State Capitol Museum, and the Northwest Museum of Arts and Culture in Spokane.

By 2012, the state art collection held by the government included 45,000 pieces of art from more than 35 years of acquisition. Washington also manages a Public Artist Roster for all professional visual artists interested in acquiring some of the grants offered by the Arts Commission. In 2008, Washington had over 100,000 jobs directly related to creative arts, and over 1,000 arts-related organizations. These organizations produced $673 million in revenue for that year.

34 Libraries and Museums

In 2010, there were 62 public libraries, many of which had multiple branch libraries. By 2010,

At Boeing's Museum of Flight in Seattle, visitors can view more than 150 historic planes and spacecraft. © KANWARJIT SINGH BOPARAI/SHUTTERSTOCK.COM.

nearly all of these libraries had public web sites. Libraries in high population areas include the Fort Vancouver Regional Library District, the King County Library System, and the Seattle Public Library. The principal academic libraries are at the University of Washington (Seattle) and Washington State University (Pullman). Olympia is the home of the Washington State Library.

In 2010, the state had 4 art museums, 1 youth-oriented museum, 2 culturally specific museums, 6 historic houses, 24 general history museums, 5 multidisciplinary museums, 1 natural history museum, 5 science and technology museums, and 6 randomly classified museums. The Washington State Historical Society Museum (Tacoma) features Native American and other pioneer artifacts. Mount Rainer National Park displays zoological, botanical, geological, and historical collections. The Pacific Science Center (Seattle) concentrates on aerospace technology. The Seattle Aquarium is a leading attraction of Waterfront Park. Also in Seattle is Woodland Park Zoological Gardens and the Burke Museum of Natural History and Culture. Tacoma has the Point Defiance Zoo and Aquarium as well as the Glass Museum.

35 Communications

By 2006, the cable industry was serving 1.5 million Washington households for television, Internet, and telephone services. The availability of high-speed Internet services increased Internet use throughout the state. By 2010, 79.7% of the population had access to the Internet at home, and 76.7% had broadband access. In 2012, Washington had 36 television stations and more than 100 radio stations.

36 Press

In 2012, the Washington Newspaper Publishers Association had a membership of 130 community newspapers. Key publications included the *Seattle Times,* the *Seattle Post-Intelligencer,* the *Olympian,* and the *Tacoma News Tribune Ledger.* With the increasing popularity of online news sites, newspaper circulations began to drop in the early 2000s. In a six-month period in 2008, average weekday circulation fell by 7.8% for the *Post-Intelligencer* and 7.7% for the *Seattle Times.* These two papers were combined on Sundays, and Sunday circulation fell by 9% in the same period. In March 2009 the *Post-Intelligencer* ceased its print publication, significantly reduced its staff, and moved to an all-digital newspaper—the first major daily metro newspaper to do so. Other papers also suffered smaller subscription losses. In 2008, all the major daily newspapers in the state saw revenue losses in the latter half of the year, due to lower income from advertisers.

37 Tourism, Travel, and Recreation

Tourism is the fourth-largest industry in Washington state, behind software, aerospace, and agriculture. In 2010, the industry provided citizens with more than 150,000 jobs and $4.5 billion in earnings. In six counties, jobs in the industry count for more than 10% of total employment. Total direct visitor spending in 2011 was $16.4 billion, and visitors paid nearly $1 billion in various taxes in 2010. Hotel and motel taxes support convention centers, art institutions, low-income housing, and transportation projects across the state.

Seattle Center—featuring the 605-foot (184-meter) Space Needle tower, EMP Museum (containing the Science Fiction Museum and Hall of Fame), and Pacific Science Center—helps make Washington's largest city one of the most exciting on the West Coast. Nevertheless, scenic beauty and opportunities for outdoor recreation are Washington's principal attractions for tourists from out of state.

Mount Rainier National Park, covering 235,404 acres (95,265 hectares), encompasses the state's highest peak. Glaciers, lakes, and mountain peaks are featured at North Cascades National Park, while Olympic National Park is famous as the site of Mount Olympus and the Olympic Rainforest. Washington also offers two national historic parks, two national historic sites (Fort Vancouver and the Whitman Mission), and three national recreation areas (Coulee Dam, Lake Chelan, and Ross Lake).

The German-themed town of Leavenworth is popular with families, especially during the holiday season. Whale-watching excursions, which take spectators near the Puget Sound's resident orca pods, are enjoyed by residents and out-of-state visitors alike.

The Western Washington State Fair is held in Puyallup each September. Other top annual

A group of orcas surface as they swim in the San Juan Islands area, with Washington's Mt. Baker in the background. © MONIKA WIELAND/SHUTTERSTOCK.COM.

events in the state include the Bumbershoot Festival, Ellensburg Rodeo, the Lentil Festival, and the Snoqualmie Pass Music Festival.

38 Sports

Washington is home to several professional major league sports teams, which play in Seattle. These include the Mariners of Major League Baseball; the Seahawks, of the National Football League; the Storm, of the Women's National Basketball Association; and the Seattle Sounders FC of Major League Soccer.

Skiing, boating, and hiking are popular sports. Annual sporting events include outboard hydroplane races in Electric City in June and the Ellensburg Rodeo in September.

39 Famous Washingtonians

Washington's most distinguished public figure was US Supreme Court Justice William O. Douglas (b. Minnesota, 1898–1980), whose 37-year tenure on the court was the longest. Other federal officeholders from Washington include Lewis B. Schwellenbach (b. Wisconsin, 1894–1948), secretary of labor under Harry S Truman; and Brockman Adams (b. Georgia, 1927–2004), secretary of transportation under Jimmy Carter. Serving in the US Senate from 1945 to 1981, Warren G. Magnuson (b. Minnesota, 1905–1989) chaired the powerful Appropriations Committee. A fellow Democrat, Henry M. "Scoop" Jackson (1912–1983), was influential on the Armed Services Committee and ran unsuccessfully for his party's presidential nomination in 1976. Thomas Stephen Foley (1929–) was Speaker of the House from 1987 until his defeat in the 1994 elections.

Dixy Lee Ray (1914–1993), governor from 1977 to 1981, was the first female governor in the state's history. Bertha Knight Landes (b. Massachusetts, 1868–1943), elected mayor of Seattle in 1926, was the first woman to be elected mayor of a large US city.

Famous entrepreneurs from Washington include merchandiser Eddie Bauer (1899–1986) and William Henry "Bill" Gates III (1955–), cofounder of the Microsoft Corporation.

Hans Georg Dehmelt (b. Germany, 1922–) was a recipient of the 1989 Nobel Prize for physics as a member of the University of Washington faculty. William E. Boeing (b. Michigan, 1881–1956) pioneered Washington's largest single industry, aerospace technology.

Washington authors have made substantial contributions to American literature. Mary McCarthy (1912–1989) was born in Seattle, and one of her books, *Memories of a Catholic Girlhood* (1957), describes her early life there. University of Washington faculty member Theodore Roethke (b. Michigan, 1908–1963), won the Pulitzer Prize for poetry in 1953. Max Brand (Frederick Schiller Faust, 1892–1944) wrote hundreds of Western novels. Native American author Sherman Alexie (1966–) also hails from Washington state.

Washington has also been the birthplace of several prominent cartoonists, including Chuck Jones (1912–2002), who created the Road Runner and other animated characters; Hank Ketcham (1920–2001), who created the comic strip *Dennis the Menace;* and Gary Larson (1950–), creator of *The Far Side.*

Singer-actor Harry Lillis "Bing" Crosby (1904–1977), born in Tacoma, remained a loyal alumnus of Spokane's Gonzaga University. Modern dance choreographer Merce

Washington's Apolo Anton Ohno is a speed skater who won eight Olympic medals, making him the most decorated American in Winter Olympic Game history as of 2010. © ZUMA WIRE SERVICE / ALAMY.

Cunningham (1919–2009) was a Washington native, along with ballet pioneer Robert Joffrey (1930–1988). Modern artist Robert Motherwell (1915–1991) was born in Aberdeen. Washington's contributions to popular music include rock guitarist Jimi Hendrix (James Marshall Hendrix, 1942–1970) and Nirvana frontman Kurt Cobain (1967–1994). Actors born in Washington include Blair Underwood

(1964–), Craig T. Nelson (1944–), and Jean Smart (1951–).

Olympic medalist in speed skating and *Dancing with the Stars* champion Apolo Anton Ohno (1982–) was also born in Washington.

40 Bibliography

BOOKS

Bristow, M. J. *State Songs of America.* Westport, CT: Greenwood Press, 2000.

Crutchfield, James A. *It Happened in Washington.* 2nd ed. Guilford, CT: TwoDot, 2008.

Ernst, Chloe. *Washington, Off the Beaten Path,* 9th ed. Guilford, CT: GPP Travel, 2013.

McAuliffe, Emily. *Washington Facts and Symbols.* Rev. ed. Mankato, MN: Capstone, 2003.

Ritter, Harry. *Washington's History: The People, Land, and Events of the Far Northwest.* Portland, OR: Westwinds Press, 2003.

Stein, R. Conrad. *Washington.* New York: Children's Press, 2009.

WEB SITES

"Economy at a Glance: Washington." *US Bureau of Labor Statistics.* http://www.bls.gov/eag/eag. wa.htm (accessed on November 16, 2012).

"Endangered Species Program." *US Fish & Wildlife Service.* http://www.fws.gov/endangered/ (accessed on November 16, 2012).

"Experience Washington." *Washington Tourism Alliance.* www.experiencewashington.com/ (accessed on November 16, 2012).

"State & County QuickFacts: Washington." *US Bureau of the Census.* http://quickfacts. census.gov/qfd/states/53000.html (accessed on November 16, 2012).

Access Washington: State of Washington. http://access. wa.gov/ (accessed on November 16, 2012).

Washington State Historical Society. http://www.wshs. org/ (accessed on November 16, 2012).

West Virginia

State of West Virginia

ORIGIN OF STATE NAME: The state was originally the western part of Virginia.

NICKNAME: The Mountain State.

CAPITAL: Charleston.

ENTERED UNION: 20 June 1863 (35th).

OFFICIAL SEAL: The same as the coat of arms.

FLAG: The flag has a white field bordered by a strip of blue, with the coat of arms in the center, wreathed by rhododendron leaves; across the top of the coat of arms are the words "State of West Virginia."

COAT OF ARMS: A farmer stands to the right and a miner to the left of a large ivy-draped rock bearing the date of the state's admission to the Union. In front of the rock are two hunting rifles, upon which rest a Cap of Liberty. The state motto is beneath and the words "State of West Virginia" above.

MOTTO: *Montani semper liberi* (Mountaineers are always free).

SONG: "The West Virginia Hills"; "West Virginia, My Home Sweet Home"; "This Is My West Virginia."

FLOWER: Rhododendron.

TREE: Sugar maple.

ANIMAL: Black bear.

BIRD: Cardinal.

FISH: Brook trout.

COLORS: Old gold and blue.

LEGAL HOLIDAYS: New Year's Day, 1 January; birthday of Martin Luther King Jr., 3rd Monday in January; Presidents' Day, 3rd Monday in February; Memorial Day, last Monday in May; West Virginia Day, 20 June; Independence Day, 4 July; Labor Day, 1st Monday in September; Columbus Day, 2nd Monday in October; Veterans' Day, 11 November; Thanksgiving Day, 4th Thursday in November and the day following; Christmas Day, 25 December.

TIME: 7 a.m. EST = noon GMT.

Location and Size

Located in the South Atlantic region of the eastern United States, West Virginia ranks 41st in size among the 50 states. The area of West Virginia totals 24,230 square miles (62,755 square kilometers), including 24,038 square miles (62,258 square kilometers) of land and 192 square miles (497 square kilometers) of inland water. The state extends 265 miles (426 kilometers) from east to west and 237 miles (381

149

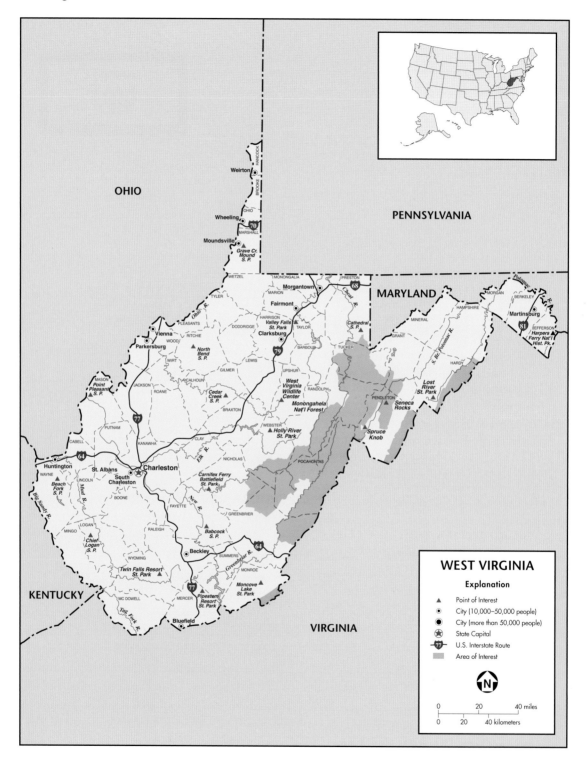

kilometers) from north to south. Its total boundary length is 1,180 miles (1,899 kilometers).

2 Topography

Most of West Virginia's eastern panhandle, crossed by the Allegheny Mountains, is in the Ridge and Valley region of the Appalachian Highlands. The remainder is part of the Allegheny Plateau. The state's highest point, Spruce Knob, towers 4,861 feet (1,483 meters) above sea level. Major lowlands lie along the rivers, especially the Potomac, Ohio, and Kanawha. A point on the Potomac River near Harpers Ferry has the lowest elevation, only 240 feet (73 meters) above sea level. West Virginia has no natural lakes. Subterranean streams have carved out numerous caverns—including Seneca Caverns, Smoke Hole Caverns, and Organ Cave—from limestone beds.

3 Climate

West Virginia has a humid continental climate with hot summers and cool to cold winters. The climate of the eastern panhandle is influenced by its proximity to the Atlantic slope and is similar to that of nearby coastal areas. Mean annual temperatures vary from 56°F (13°C) in the southwest to 48°F (9°C) in higher elevations. The highest recorded temperature is 112°F (44°C), set at Martinsburg on 10 July 1936. The lowest temperature, -37°F (-38°C), occurred at Lewisburg on 30 December 1917.

Annual precipitation averages around 44 inches (112 centimeters). Average annual snowfall in the state is about 12 inches (31 centimeters) in the southwestern lowlands. Higher elevations can receive more than 72 inches (183 centimeters). Snowfall is heaviest in the eastern part of the state, with Snowshoe averaging around 51 days of snow per year, or 159 inches (404 centimeters). Beckley, in the western part of the state, averages around 62 inches (157.5 centimeters), while Clarksburg averages around 25 inches (63.5 centimeters) per year.

4 Plants and Animals

West Virginia provides a natural habitat for more than 3,200 species of plants. Oak, maple, poplar, and softwoods such as hemlock and pine are common forest trees in West Virginia. Rhododendron, dogwood, and pussy willow are among the more than 200 flowering trees and shrubs. The Cranberry Glades, an ancient lake bed similar to a glacial bog, contains the bog rosemary and other plant species common in more northern climates. As of 2012, six plant species were listed as threatened or endangered, including the northeastern bulrush, running buffalo clover, and shale barren rock cress.

The white-tailed (Virginia) deer, black bear, and wildcat are still found in the deep timber of the Allegheny ridges. Common birds include the cardinal, scarlet tanager, and catbird. Major game birds are the wild turkey, bobwhite quail, and ruffed grouse. Notable among more than 100 species of fish are smallmouth bass, rainbow trout, and brook trout (the state fish). The copperhead and rattlesnake are both numerous and poisonous.

In 2012, the US Fish and Wildlife Service listed 13 animal species as threatened or endangered in West Virginia, including three species of bat (gray, Indiana, and Virginia big-eared), fanshell, snuffbox mussel, and the Virginia northern flying squirrel.

Environmental Protection

The Division of Environmental Protection (DEP) was established in October 1991 and became West Virginia's leading environmental agency in July 1992, with the consolidation of the state's major environmental regulatory programs. A new DEP program is the Office of Environmental Advocate. The office was created to improve public access and input into DEP functioning.

Environmental issues confronting the state of West Virginia include the restoration of about 2,000 miles (3,218 kilometers) of streams impacted by acid mine damage. To combat the problem, the state has created the Stream Restoration Program, which is using a variety of treatment methods to improve water quality. In 2011, the ongoing program completed restoration of Beaver Creek, an important habitat for native brook trout. In 2012, less than 1% (102,000 acres/41,300 hectares) of West Virginia's land was designated wetlands.

West Virginia mandates that cities with populations of 10,000 or more must develop recycling programs. As of 2012, West Virginia had nine hazardous waste sites listed on the Environmental Protection Agency's National Priorities List. These included the Alleghany Ballistics Laboratory and the 107-acre Sharon Steel Corporation.

 Population

In 2011, West Virginia had an estimated total population of 1,855,364, ranking the state 37th in the country in terms of population. The population is expected to shrink to 1,801,112 by 2020. The population density in 2010 was

---

West Virginia Population Profile

Total population per Census 2010:	1,852,994
Population change, 2006–10:	1.9%
Hispanic or Latino†:	1.2%
Population by race	
One race:	98.5%
White:	93.9%
Black or African American:	3.4%
American Indian/Alaska Native:	0.2%
Asian:	0.7%
Native Hawaiian/Pacific Islander:	0.0%
Some other race:	0.3%
Two or more races:	1.5%

Population by Age Group, Census 2010

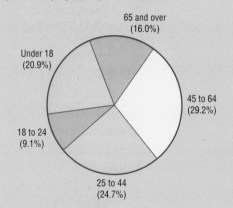

65 and over (16.0%)
Under 18 (20.9%)
45 to 64 (29.2%)
18 to 24 (9.1%)
25 to 44 (24.7%)

Major Cities by Population, 2011 Estimates

City	Population	% change 2005–11
Charleston	51,177	0.0
Huntington	49,253	0.1
Parkersburg	31,557	-1.4
Morgantown	30,293	7.1
Wheeling	28,355	-4.3
Weirton	19,651	0.5
Fairmont	18,764	-1.5
Beckley	17,675	4.4
Martinsburg	17,487	9.3
Clarksburg	16,649	1.3

Notes: †A person of Hispanic or Latino origin may be of any race. NA indicates that data are not available. Percentages may not equal 100 due to rounding.

SOURCE: U.S. Census Bureau. Census 2010 and Population Estimates. www.census.gov/ (accessed July 2012).

West Virginia Population by Race
CENSUS 2010

This table shows the number of people who are of one, two, or three or more races. For those claiming two races, the number of people belonging to the various categories is listed. The U.S. government conducts a census of the population every 10 years.

	Number	Percent
Total population	1,852,994	100.0
One race	1,825,852	98.5
Two races	25,650	1.4
White *and* Black or African American	11,602	0.6
White *and* American Indian/Alaska Native	7,728	0.4
White *and* Asian	3,086	0.2
White *and* Native Hawaiian/Pacific Islander	432	—
White *and* some other race	1,350	0.1
Black or African American *and* American Indian/Alaska Native	592	—
Black or African American *and* Asian	181	—
Black or African American *and* Native Hawaiian/Pacific Islander	52	—
Black or African American *and* some other race	236	—
American Indian/Alaska Native *and* Asian	66	—
American Indian/Alaska Native *and* Native Hawaiian/Pacific Islander	17	—
American Indian/Alaska Native *and* some other race	36	—
Asian *and* Native Hawaiian/Pacific Islander	85	—
Asian *and* some other race	163	—
Native Hawaiian/Pacific Islander *and* some other race	24	—
Three or more races	1,492	0.1

SOURCE: U.S. Census Bureau. Census 2010. www.census/gov/ (accessed July 2012). A dash (—) indicates that the percent is less than 0.1.

77.1 persons per square mile (29.8 persons per square kilometer). The median age in 2011 was 41.4 years. About 16.2% of all residents were 65 or older, while 20.7% were under 18.

In 2011, Charleston had an estimated 51,177 residents. Other major cities include Huntington (49,253), Parkersburg (31,557), Morgantown (30,293), and Wheeling (28,355). Around 57% of West Virginians lived in urban areas in 2010, compared to an average of 84% in the United States.

7 Ethnic Groups

According to the 2010 Census, about 3,787 Native Americans were living in West Virginia. About 63,124 residents were black Americans.

There were 22,268 Hispanics and Latinos and 12,406 persons of Asian origin. Of those who reported at least one specific ancestry group, English, German, Irish, and Dutch were most common. In 2010, around 335,477 reported having German ancestry, 205,530 English ancestry, 267,713 Irish ancestry, and 85,848 Italian ancestry.

8 Languages

West Virginia generally maintains Midland speech, but there are speech differences between the northern and southern halves of the state. For instance, in the northern part, the words *sat* and *sight* sound very much alike and specific terms include *run* for creek and *teetertotter* for seesaw. In the southern half, *can't* and *aunt* rhyme with *paint,* a creek is called a *branch,* and *tinter* means teeter.

In 2011, 97.7% of the population five years of age and over spoke only English at home. Other languages spoken at home included Spanish (0.91%), other Indo-European languages including French and German (0.9%), and Asian and Pacific Islander languages (0.4%).

9 Religions

Throughout its history, West Virginia has been overwhelmingly Protestant. Most settlers before the American Revolution were Anglicans, Presbyterians, Quakers, or members of German sects, such as Lutherans, German Reformed, Dunkers, and Mennonites. The Great Awakening had a profound effect on these settlers and they avidly embraced its evangelism, emotionalism, and emphasis on personal religious experience.

According to the Pew Forum on Religion & Public Life, in 2008, 36% of the state's population were Evangelical Protestants; 32% were mainline Protestants; and 2% were adherents of historically black Protestant traditions. At the same time, around 7% of the state's population were Catholic; 1% were Jewish; 1% were Hindu; and less than 0.5% were Muslim. Around 19% of the state's population were unaffiliated with any religion.

10 Transportation

The first major pre-Civil War railroad line was the Baltimore and Ohio (B&O), completed to Wheeling in 1852. Today, the railroads still play an important part in coal transportation.

In 2010, CSX and Norfolk Southern were the state's Class I operators. In the same year, total rail mileage was 2,231 miles (5,390 kilometers). As of 2010, Amtrak provided passenger service to 10 communities.

In 2011, there were 38,646 miles (62,195 kilometers) of public roads under the state system. The West Virginia Turnpike was completed from Charleston to Princeton in 1955. There were 687,000 automobiles and 684,000 trucks registered in the state in 2009 and 1,328,992 licensed drivers.

Major navigable inland rivers are the Ohio, Kanawha, and Monongahela. Each has locks and dams. In 2010, West Virginia had 74 airports and 35 heliports. Yeager Airport in Charleston is the state's main air terminal. There were 374,883 total enplanements in the state in 2009; no foreign carriers serve the state.

11 History

When European settlers arrived in present-day West Virginia, only a few Shawnee, Tuscarora, and Delaware Indian villages remained, but the area was still actively used as hunting and warring grounds, and European possession was hotly contested.

The fur trade stimulated early exploration by both the English and French. England prevailed following the French and Indian War. It is thought that the first settlement in West Virginia was founded at Bunker Hill in 1731. By 1750, several thousand settlers were living in the eastern panhandle, and there was movement into the Greenbriar, Monongahela, and the upper Ohio River valleys after 1769, although wars with Native Americans occurred sporadically until the 1790s. The area that is now West

Virginia was still part of Virginia when the state entered the Union on 25 June 1788.

Serious differences between eastern and western Virginia developed after the War of 1812. Eastern Virginia was dominated by large plantations that used slave labor, while small diversified farms and infant industries predominated in western Virginia. Westerners resented property qualifications for voting, inadequate representation in the Virginia legislature, and undemocratic county governments. They were dissatisfied with the quality of government operations. In 1859, abolitionist John Brown led a raid at Harpers Ferry, seizing the US Armory. Brown was captured, convicted, and ultimately hanged for treason, which made him a hero of the abolitionist movement.

Statehood When Virginia seceded from the Union in 1861, western counties remaining loyal to the Union set up the Reorganized Government and consented to the separation of present West Virginia from Virginia. After approval by Congress and President Abraham Lincoln, West Virginia entered the Union on 20 June 1863 as the 35th state.

Following the Civil War (1861–65), West Virginia began developing its mineral resources, such as coal, limestone, and calcium nitrate

An aerial view shows the town of Harpers Ferry, which is now a national historical park. © STEVE HEAP/SHUTTERSTOCK.COM.

(used in gunpowder). Both Democratic and Republican governors after the Civil War sought to improve transportation, foster immigration, and provide tax structures attractive to business. Republican governors of the early 20th century, attuned to Progressive ideas, were instrumental in the adoption of the direct primary, safety legislation for the coal mines, revision of corporate tax laws, and improvements in highways and education.

During the Great Depression of the 1930s, West Virginia suffered significantly. The economic trouble ushered in a Democratic era. West Virginians embraced the liberal philosophies of presidents Franklin D. Roosevelt and Harry S Truman. World Wars I (1914–18) and II (1939–45) produced significant changes in the state, particularly through stimulation of the chemical, steel, and textile industries, which lessened its dependence on mining, historically the backbone of its economy.

After World War II After World War II, mechanization and strip mining displaced thousands of miners and resulted in a large exodus to other states. By 1960, West Virginia was considered one of the most economically depressed areas of the country, primarily because of conditions in the mining regions. Antipoverty programs of the John F. Kennedy and Lyndon B. Johnson administrations provided some relief, but much of it was temporary.

Over the next several decades, West Virginia's manufacturing and mining sectors shrank dramatically. Automation, foreign competition, and the recession of the early 1980s caused employment in steel, glass, chemical manufacturing, and coal mining to drop by one-third between 1979 and 1985. However, tourism, centered on skiing and whitewater rafting, provided West Virginia with a growing source of income.

The same technological advances that forced a restructuring of the economy produced social change. Electronic communications largely eliminated the cultural isolation long felt by West Virginia residents. In the 1990s, the state won a number of federal projects, including the FBI's fingerprint identification division, aided by the tenure of Senator Robert C. Byrd, who was chairman of the US Senate Appropriations Committee from 1988 to 1995 and from 2001 to 2005.

In 2002, West Virginia began programs to attract retirees to the state. In 2004, Democrat Joe Manchin III was elected as governor to replace Bob Wise, who chose not to run for reelection that year. Manchin's election marked the first time since 1964 that two persons of the same political party followed one another in the governor's office. Manchin resigned in 2010, following his election to the US Senate, and was replaced by Democrat Earl Ray Tomblin.

The global recession that began in 2008 affected West Virginia, along with the rest of the country, and the state had an uneven recovery. While the government, education, and health sectors recovered by 2010, manufacturing and construction lagged behind. The state received a larger share of federal dollars than many larger states, and this aided recovery.

12 State Government

Since becoming a state, West Virginia has had two constitutions. The 1872 constitution had been amended 17 times as of January 2012. The legislature consists of a senate with 34 members and a house of delegates with 100 members. Senators serve four-year terms, and delegates serve two-year terms. Elected officials of the executive branch of government include the governor, secretary of state, auditor, and attorney general. There is no lieutenant governor. The governor is limited to two consecutive terms, but is reeligible after four years out of office. Bills passed by the legislature become law when signed by the governor. Those the governor vetoes may become law if majorities of both house memberships override the veto—except for revenue and appropriations bills, which require a two-thirds majority of both houses.

The legislative salary in 2012 was $20,000 per year plus $131 per diem; the governor's salary was $150,000 per year.

13 Political Parties

In 2010, there were 1,216,000 registered voters. In 2010, 54% of registered voters were Democratic, 29% Republican, and 17% unaffiliated or members of other parties. Since the 1930s, Republican presidential candidates have carried West Virginia in 1956, 1972, 1984, 2000, 2004, and 2008. Democrat Robert Byrd began his service in the US Senate in 1959 and was majority leader from 1977 to 1980. He was reelected to his ninth term in 2006. On his death in 2010, he was replaced by the former governor, Democrat Joe Manchin. Midway through his second gubernatorial term, Manchin resigned to take up his seat in the Senate and he was replaced as governor by Democrat Earl Ray Tomblin, who was elected in a special election in 2010. Both Manchin and Tomblin won reelection in 2012.

West Virginia Governors: 1863–2013		
1863–1869	Arthur Inghram Boreman	Republican
1869	Daniel Duane Farnsworth	Republican
1869–1871	William Erskine Stevenson	Republican
1871–1877	John Jeremiah Jacob	Dem/Indep
1877–1881	Henry Mason Matthews	Democrat
1881–1885	Jacob Beeson Jackson	Democrat
1885–1889	Emanuel Willis Wilson	Democrat
1889–1893	Aretas Brooks Fleming	Democrat
1893–1897	William Alexander MacCorkle	Democrat
1897–1901	George Wesley Atkinson	Republican
1901–1905	Albert Blakeslee White	Republican
1905–1909	William Mercer Owens Dawson	Republican
1909–1913	William Ellsworth Glasscock	Republican
1913–1917	Henry Drury Hatfield	Republican
1917–1921	John Jacob Cornwell	Democrat
1921–1925	Ephraim Franklin Morgan	Republican
1925–1929	Howard Mason Gore	Republican
1929–1933	William Gustavus Conley	Republican
1933–1937	Herman Guy Kump	Democrat
1937–1941	Homer Adams Holt	Democrat
1941–1945	Matthew Mansfield Neely	Democrat
1945–1949	Clarence Watson Meadows	Democrat
1949–1953	Okey Leonidas Patteson	Democrat
1953–1957	William Casey Marland	Democrat
1957–1961	Cecil Harland Underwood	Republican
1961–1965	William Wallace Barron	Democrat
1965–1969	Hulett Carlson Smith	Democrat
1969–1977	Arch Alfred Moore, Jr.	Republican
1977–1985	John Davidson Rockefeller IV	Democrat
1985–1989	Arch Alfred Moore, Jr.	Republican
1989–1997	Gaston Caperton	Democrat
1997–2000	Cecil Underwood	Republican
2000–2005	Bob Wise	Democrat
2005–2010	Joe Manchin III	Democrat
2010–	Earl Ray Tomblin	Democrat

Democrat/Independent – Dem/Indep

Senator John D. Rockefeller IV, reelected to his fifth term in 2008, is also a Democrat. Following the 2012 elections, West Virginia's US representatives consisted of two Republicans and one Democrat. Following the 2010 elections, there were 28 Democrats and 6 Republicans in the state senate (2 of them women), and 65 Democrats and 35 Republicans in the state house (22 of them women).

In the 2004 presidential elections, Republican George W. Bush won 56% of the vote while

West Virginia Presidential Vote by Major Political Parties, 1948–2012

Year	West Virginia Winner	Democrat	Republican
1948	*Truman (D)	429,188	316,251
1952	Stevenson (D)	453,578	419,970
1956	*Eisenhower (R)	381,534	449,297
1960	*Kennedy (D)	441,786	395,995
1964	*Johnson (D)	538,087	253,953
1968	Humphrey (D)	374,091	307,555
1972	*Nixon (R)	277,435	484,964
1976	*Carter (D)	435,914	314,760
1980	Carter (D)	367,462	334,206
1984	*Reagan (R)	328,125	405,483
1988	Dukakis (D)	341,016	310,065
1992	*Clinton (D)	331,001	241,974
1996	*Clinton (D)	327,812	233,946
2000	*Bush, G. W. (R)	295,497	336,475
2004	*Bush, G. W. (R)	326,541	423,778
2008	McCain (R)	303,857	397,466
2012	Romney (R)	238,230	417,584

*Won US presidential election.

Independent candidate Ross Perot received 108,829 votes in 1992 and 71,639 votes in 1996.

Democratic challenger John Kerry won 43%. In 2008, Republican John McCain won 55.7% of the vote, while Democrat Barack Obama won 42.6%. In 2012, West Virginia voters opted for Republican candidate Mitt Romney over President Barack Obama.

14 Local Government

West Virginia has 55 counties. The chief county officials are the three commissioners, who serve on the county court; the sheriff, assessor, county clerk, and prosecuting attorney; and the five-member board of education. There were 106 cities as of 2012, of which four had populations greater than 30,000. There were 57 public school districts in 2012 and 321 special districts in the state in 2007. In 2011, there were 95,112 full-time and 23,649 part-time people employed in state and local government.

15 Judicial System

The highest court in West Virginia, the supreme court of appeals, has five justices, including the chief justice. The court has broad appeals jurisdiction in both civil and criminal cases, and original jurisdiction in certain other cases. West Virginia's general trial court is the circuit court. Circuit courts had jurisdiction over juvenile, domestic relations, and administrative proceedings. Local courts include the county magistrate and municipal courts.

In 2010 the state had a violent crime rate of 314.6 reported incidents per 100,000 persons, representing a 5% increase in violent crimes from the previous year. The murder and nonnegligent manslaughter rate was 3.3 per 100,000 inhabitants; forcible rape, 19.1; aggravated assault, 247.5; and property crime, 2,239.6. As of 2011, the total prison population in the state was 10,719. West Virginia does not practice capital punishment; the state abolished the death penalty in 1965.

16 Migration

West Virginia has considerable national and ethnic diversity. Settlers before the Civil War consisted principally of English, German, Scotch-Irish, and Welsh immigrants, many of whom came by way of Pennsylvania. A second wave of immigration from the 1880s to the 1920s brought thousands of Italians, Poles, Austrians, and Hungarians to the coal mines and industrial towns, which also attracted many blacks from the South.

Between 1990 and 1998, West Virginia had net gains of 8,000 in domestic migration and 3,000 in international migration. In the period

1995–2000, some 138,487 people moved into the state and 149,241 moved out, for a net loss of 10,754, many of whom moved to Ohio. For the period 2000–05, net international migration was 3,691 and net internal migration was 10,518 for a net gain of 14,209 people. Between 2009 and 2010, 2,633 people moved to West Virginia from abroad, and 39,609 people moved from another state. At the same time, a total of 49,349 people left the state, for a net outward migration of 9,740.

Of the total foreign-born population in West Virginia in 2010, 8.2% were from Africa, 43.8% from Asia, 19% from Europe, and 23.6% from Latin America. The top three countries of birth of the foreign born in West Virginia were Vietnam (6.7%), the Philippines (6%), and Mexico (5.4%). In contrast, the top three countries of foreign birth in 1990 were the United Kingdom (10.5%), Germany (9.5%), and Italy (9.2%). In 2010, the foreign born made up just 1.2% of the state's population.

17 Economy

Agriculture was the backbone of West Virginia's economy until the 1890s, when coal, oil, natural gas, and timber began to play a major role. World War I stimulated important industries such as chemicals, steel, glass, and textiles. The beauty of West Virginia's mountains and forests has attracted an increasing number of tourists, but the state's rugged terrain and relative isolation from major markets continue to hamper its economic development.

West Virginia did not participate substantially in the high technology boom of the 1990s, even as the long-term decline of its coal mining industry continued. The state weathered the worldwide downturn that began in 2008 better than many, as it saw strong growth in coal, but it is heavily reliant on federal programs such as Medicare, which increased during the recession. From December 2007 to April 2012, West Virginia lost only 0.1% of its jobs, compared to the national average of 3.6%. In 2010, the state had a gross state product (GSP) of $66.6 billion, ranking the state 40th in the nation. That year, the state's per capita GSP was $35,053, ranking the state 49th in the nation.

In 2009, there were around 38,990 private nonfarm establishments and 88,081 nonemployer establishments in the state.

18 Income

In 2010, West Virginia had a gross state product (GSP) of $64.6 billion and a median per capita income (including nonmonetary income) of $21,232, with a median annual income of $40,824, compared to the national median of $50,022, ranking the state 48th in the nation. In 2011, 18.6% of the population lived below the federal poverty level compared to 15.9% nationwide.

19 Industry

West Virginia is known for its rich natural resources and strong industrial presence. The value of shipments by manufacturers in 2010 totaled just over $25 billion. Major industries included coal, organic chemicals, primary metals, fabricated metal products, and lumber and wood products.

Major industrial areas are the Kanawha, Ohio, and Monongahela valleys and the eastern panhandle. The largest industrial corporations with operations in West Virginia include E.I.

du Pont de Nemours, American Electric Power, ArcelorMittal, and General Electric Plastics. The largest private employers in 2010 were Walmart, West Virginia United Health System, Charleston Area Medical Center, Kroger, and Consolidation Coal Company.

20 Labor

In August 2012, the total civilian labor force in West Virginia numbered 798,200, with approximately 59,700 workers unemployed, yielding an unemployment rate of 7.5%, compared to the national rate of 8.1%. That same month, nonfarm wage and salaried employment included: 36,200 workers in construction; 47,200 in manufacturing; 132,400 in trade, transportation, and public utilities; 27,300 in financial activities; 62,900 in professional and business services; 127,200 in education and health services; 73,300 in leisure and hospitality services; and 150,700 in government.

Important milestones in the growth of unionism were the organization of the state as District 17 of the United Mine Workers of America (UMWA) in 1890 and the formation of the State Federation of Labor in 1903. The coal miners fought to gain union recognition by coal companies and instances of violence were not uncommon in the early 1900s. Wages, working conditions, and benefits for miners improved rapidly after World War II.

In 2011, 102,000 people, or 14.8%, belonged to a union, compared to a national average of 13%.

21 Agriculture

With a total estimated farm export value of $68.7 million in 2010, West Virginia ranked

45th among the 50 states. Total farm marketings in 2009 were $496 million, of which $91 million was in crop production and the remainder was in livestock and livestock products. That year, the four major farm products were broilers, cattle, calves, and turkeys. In 2008, 285 acres (114 hectares) were certified as under organic cultivation.

In 2007, the state had 3.7 million acres (1.45 million hectares), or 24% of the total land, devoted to farming. Of this, approximately 942,000 acres (381,000 hectares) was cropland. West Virginia's approximately 23,000 farms (in 2010) averaged 157 acres (63.6 hectares) in size. Major farm sections are the eastern panhandle, a tier of counties along the Virginia border, the upper Monongahela Valley, and the Ohio Valley. Leading crops produced in 2007 were hay (1.1 million tons), corn for grain (3.4 million bushels in 2008), soybeans (738,000 bushels in 2008), apples (85 million pounds/38.5 kilograms in 2008), and tobacco.

22 Domesticated Animals

In 2008, there were an estimated 415,000 cattle and calves in the state, valued at $113.5 million. During 2008, the state had 7,000 hogs and pigs; poultry farmers produced 85.7 million broilers valued at $165.2 million, and 3.8 million turkey, valued at $57 million. The dairy industry yielded 181 million pounds (82 million kilograms) of milk, valued at $33.7 million, and 247 million eggs, valued at $30.4 million.

23 Fishing

West Virginia fishing has little commercial importance. In 2010, there were around 30

The state has approximately 23,000 farms. Hay, shown here rolled in bales, is one of West Virginia's leading crops. © JORGE MORO/ SHUTTERSTOCK.COM.

pay lakes providing trout fishing. In addition, the Palestine Hatchery and the Apple Grove Hatchery, in Mason County, are operated by the state's Division of Natural Resources. These hatcheries provide walleye, musky, tiger musky, catfish, and bass to the states' lakes and streams. In 2006, there were 291,000 licensed anglers in the state.

24 Forestry

In 2010, West Virginia was a heavily forested state, with forests covering 78% (12.0 millions acres/4.9 million hectares) of the state's 15.4 millions acres (6.2 million hectares) of land.

Of this, 11.75 million acres (4.75 million hectares) were classified as timberland. About 92% of West Virginia forest species are hardwoods, with approximately 71% of the timberland being of the oak-hickory forest type. In all, West Virginia's forests contain more than 100 species of trees.

Around 30,000 people are employed in the forest industry in West Virginia. The state is encouraging the professional management of its forests so they will continue to produce a sustained array of benefits, such as wood products, jobs, clean water, oxygen, scenery, and diverse recreational opportunities like hunting, hiking, and tourism.

25 Mining

The value of nonfuel mineral production in 2011 was about $350 million—about 0.47% of the US total. That year, West Virginia ranked 35th in the United States in nonfuel mineral production. In 2010, the state produced 15.1 million metric tons of crushed stone, worth $148 million; and 402,000 metric tons of sand and gravel, worth $3.3 million.

26 Energy and Power

West Virginia has long been an important supplier of energy in the form of electric power and fossil fuels.

Major coal mining regions lie within a north–south belt some 60 miles (97 kilometers) wide through the central part of the state and include the Fairmount, New River-Kanawha, Pocahontas, and Logan-Mingo fields. In 2011, West Virginia was the country's second-largest coal-producing state, after Wyoming, with total recoverable reserves in active mines at 1.97 billion short tons—11% of the US total. Crude oil reserves in 2010 were 17 million barrels. The state also had reserves of 7 trillion cubic feet of dry natural gas and 122 million barrels of liquid natural gas in 2010. West Virginia ranked third among the states in total energy production in 2010, producing 5.3% of the nation's total.

As of May 2012, total net electricity generation was 5.76 million megawatt hours (MWh), of which 13,000 MWh was produced in petroleum-fired plants; 27,000 (MWh) in natural gas-fired plants; 5.5 million MWh in coal-fired plants; and 149,000 MWh in hydroelectric plants. Net summer capacity in 2010 was 16.5 million megawatts.

Coal is shown being moved on barges on the Kanawha River.
© SPIRIT OF AMERICA/SHUTTERSTOCK.COM.

27 Commerce

Merchant wholesaler sales totaled $11.3 billion in 2007; retail sales were $20.5 billion in the same year. In 2007, manufacturer shipments amounted to $25 billion, while retail sales per capita were $11,340. Major manufacturing industries in the state in 2010 included chemical manufacturing ($2.5 billion in output), primary metal manufacturing ($483 million in output), and fabricated metal products ($469 million). Total state foreign exports in 2011 amounted to $3.4 billion, about 0.3% of the US total.

In 2008, there were 1,576,000 wholesale trade establishments in the state and 6,846,000 retail establishments.

28 Public Finance

The governor is responsible for submitting a budget to the legislature each year. The fiscal year is from 1 July to June 30. In 2012, the budget totaled $11.4 billion. The highest general expenditures were for education ($1.97 billion),

The capitol building of West Virginia is in Charleston. A statue of General Thomas "Stonewall" Jackson stands on the capitol grounds. © TODD TAULMAN/SHUTTERSTOCK.COM.

health and human resources ($808.5 million), and higher education ($447.8 million). As of March 2012, the state's net tax-supported debt totaled $1.86 billion, and non-tax-supported debt was $6 billion.

29 Taxation

In 2012, personal income taxes ranged from 3% to 6.5% in five tax brackets. The corporate income tax is 7.75% and consumer sales taxes are 6% on goods and services. The tax on food and food ingredients is being phased out. In 2012, that tax was reduced from 3% to 2%. Counties and localities mainly tax real estate and personal property. There are selective (excise) taxes on items such as gasoline and cigarettes.

The state collected $5.1 billion in taxes in 2011, of which $6 million came from property taxes, $2.4 billion from sales tax and gross receipts, $1.97 billion from income tax, and $150 million from licenses. In 2011, West Virginia ranked 39th among the states in terms of per capita tax burden, which amounted to about $2,772 per person, compared to the national average of $2,430 per person.

30 Health

In 2011, West Virginia's infant mortality rate was 7.6 per 1,000 live births. The overall death rate was 95.9 per 100,000 population in 2008. Death rates in 2008 for major causes of death (per 100,000 resident population) included heart disease, 228.1; cancer, 201.6; and cerebrovascular diseases, 47.2. In 2008, there were 1,507 people in the state living with HIV/AIDS (0.2% of the US total). In 2010, 26.8% of adults were smokers, compared to a national rate of 17.2%. Around 67.9% of adults were overweight or obese, and 11.7% had diabetes. Pneumoconiosis (black lung) is an occupational hazard among coal miners.

West Virginia's 56 hospitals had 3.9 beds per 1,000 residents in 2010. Average per capita health spending in 2009 was $7,667. Average cost per inpatient day was $1,323. There were 23.3 physicians per 10,000 residents in 2008 and 985 nurses per 100,000 in 2011. In 2012, there were a total of about 894 dentists in the state. In 2010, at least 14% of West Virginia's residents lacked medical insurance.

Medical education is provided by medical schools at West Virginia University and Marshall University and at the West Virginia School of Osteopathic Medicine.

31 Housing

In 2010, West Virginia had an estimated 882,213 housing units, of which 741,940 were occupied. That year, 28% were in multi-unit structures and 74.6% were owner-occupied. About 70.2% of all units were single-family, detached homes; 16.1% were mobile homes. Utility gas and electricity were the most common energy sources for heating. It was estimated that 5,009 units lacked complete plumbing facilities and 4,834 lacked complete kitchen facilities.

In 2010, the median home value was $95,100. The median monthly cost for mortgage owners was $918, while renters paid a median of $571 per month.

32 Education

West Virginia has generally ranked below national standards in education. In 2010, 83.2% of adult West Virginians were high school graduates and 17.5% had completed four or more years of college.

Total school enrollment for those three years of age and older, including college and university, was estimated at 427,552 in fall 2010. Per pupil education expenditure in 2010 was $10,615.

As of fall 2010, there were 121,784 students enrolled in college or graduate school. In 2010, West Virginia had more than 40 degree-granting institutions. Public universities include West Virginia University, Marshall University, West Virginia State University, and the West Virginia College of Graduate Studies (all offering graduate work), as well as three medical schools. Private colleges include the University of Charleston and Mountain State University.

33 Arts

West Virginia is known for the quilts, pottery, and woodwork of its mountain artisans. Huntington Galleries, the Sunrise Foundation at Charleston, and Oglebay Park in Wheeling are major art centers. The Clay Center for the Arts and Sciences at Charleston includes a performing arts center that hosts the annual Stretched Strings Festival. Other musical attractions include the West Virginia Symphony Orchestra in Charleston, the Charleston Ballet, Charleston Light Opera Guild, the Wheeling Symphony, and a country music program at Wheeling. The Charleston Stage Company and the Children's Theater of Charleston are also popular. The Mountain State Art and Craft Fair is held each summer at Ripley.

The West Virginia Department of Education's Division of Culture and History sponsors many programs with the help of state and federal funds. The West Virginia Humanities Council sponsors an active speaker's bureau and the History Alive! program. The state has more than 150 arts associations and 30 local arts groups.

34 Libraries and Museums

In 2001, West Virginia had 79 branch libraries and 97 central libraries, holding 4,968,735 volumes in print and serving more than 6 million visitors a year. The largest library system is the Kanawha County Public Library system at Charleston, with 523,663 volumes. Of college and university libraries, the largest collection was at West Virginia University.

There were more than 50 museums in the state in 2012, including the State Museum and the Sunrise Museum in Charleston, the Children's Discovery Museum in Morgantown, and the Oglebay Institute-Mansion Museum in Wheeling. Historic sites include Point Pleasant, which marks the site of a battle between colonists and Native Americans, and Harpers Ferry, which was the site of John Brown's raid.

35 Communications

In 2010, there were 1,296,905 Internet users in West Virginia, around 70.5% of the population. In 2012, the state passed a law banning texting or using a cell phone without a hands-free device while driving.

In 2012, broadcasting facilities included more than 65 AM and more than 150 FM radio stations throughout the state, as well as 13 major television stations.

36 Press

In 2012, West Virginia had 17 daily newspapers and 9 nondaily newspapers. Leading West Virginia newspapers include the Charleston *Gazette,* the Charleston *Mail,* and the Huntington *Herald-Dispatch.*

37 Tourism, Travel, and Recreation

In 2007, around 54.6 million tourists visited West Virginia. Direct travel spending in 2007 generated around $3.97 billion.

Whitewater rafting enthusiasts flock to the New River and Gauley River, and around 1 million skiers venture down the slopes of the Appalachian Mountains each year. Major attractions are Harpers Ferry National Historical Park, Canaan Valley State Park in Tucker County, and White Sulphur Springs, a popular mountain resort.

The state fair is held in August in Lewisburg. Other major yearly events include the Strawberry Festival, the Mountain State Arts and Crafts Fair, the Upper Ohio Valley Italian festival, and the Winter Festival of Lights.

There are 51 state parks and forests, including Cass Scenic Railroad, which includes a restoration of an old logging line, and Prickett's Fort, with recreations of pioneer life.

38 Sports

No major league professional teams are based in West Virginia, but there are several minor league baseball teams: the West Virginia Power, which plays in Charleston and is affiliated with the Pittsburgh Pirates; the Princeton

The scenic Glade Creek Grist Mill is part of Babcock State Park. It was built in 1976 as a re-creation of an earlier mill.
© JORGE MORO/SHUTTERSTOCK.COM.

Rays and the Bluefield Orioles, which play in Mercer County in the Appalachian league; and the West Virginia Miners, a Beckley team that plays in the Prospect League, a collegiate wooden-bat league. There is also minor league hockey in Wheeling. In college football, West Virginia produced a string of national contenders in the late 1980s and early 1990s. West Virginia football teams play in the Atlantic Coast Conference.

Horse racing tracks operate in Chester and Charles Town. Greyhound races are run in Wheeling and Charleston. Other popular sports are skiing and whitewater rafting.

39 Famous West Virginians

Newton D. Baker (1871–1937) was secretary of war during World War I. Lewis L. Strauss (1896–1974) was commerce secretary and chairman of the Atomic Energy Commission and Cyrus R. Vance (1917–2002) served as secretary of state. John W. Davis (1873–1955), an ambassador to Great Britain, ran as the Democratic presidential nominee in 1924. Prominent members of the US Senate have included Robert C. Byrd (1917–2010) and John D. "Jay" Rockefeller IV (b. New York, 1937–).

Major state political leaders, all governors (though some have held federal offices), have included E. Willis Wilson (1844–1905), Henry D. Hatfield (1875–1962), and Arch A. Moore Jr. (1923–).

Brigadier General Charles E. "Chuck" Yeager (1923–), a World War II ace, became the first person to fly faster than the speed of sound.

The state's only Nobel Prize winner was Pearl S. Buck (1893–1973), who won the Nobel Prize for literature for her novels about China. Alexander Campbell (b. Ireland, 1788–1866), with his father, founded the Disciples of Christ Church. Major labor leaders have included Walter Reuther (1907–1970), president of the United Auto Workers; and Arnold Miller (1923–1985), president of the United Mine Workers.

Entertainers include musician George Crumb (1929–), a Pulitzer Prize-winning composer; opera singers Eleanor Steber (1916–1990) and Phyllis Curtin (1922–); country

Pilot Chuck Yeager set many flight speed records during his career. © EVERETT COLLECTION INC. / ALAMY.

singers Kathy Mattea (1959–) and Brad Paisley (1972–); and comedy actor Don Knotts (1924–2006). Documentary maker Morgan Spurlock (1970–) was born in the state. Educator and author Booker Taliaferro Washington (1856–1915) was also a West Virginian. Important writers of the modern period include Mary Lee Settle (1918–2005) and John Knowles (1926–2001).

Baseball great George Brett (1953–) was born in the state; Jerry West (1938–) was a collegiate and professional basketball star as well as

a pro coach after his playing days ended; Rod Hundley (1934–) and Hal Greer (1936–) also starred in the National Basketball Association. Mary Lou Retton (1968–) won a gold medal in gymnastics at the 1984 Olympics. Another West Virginian of note is Anna Jarvis (1864–1948), founder of Mother's Day.

40 Bibliography

BOOKS

Adkins, Leonard M. *An Explorer's Guide: West Virginia,* 2nd ed. Woodstock, VT: The Countryman Press, 2011.

Bristow, M. J. *State Songs of America.* Westport, CT: Greenwood Press, 2000.

Clauson-Wicker, Su. *West Virginia, Off the Beaten Path,* 7th ed. Guilford, CT: GPP Travel, 2009.

Fenney, Kathy. *West Virginia Facts and Symbols.* Rev. ed. Mankato, MN: Capstone, 2003.

Swick, Gerald. *Historic Photos of West Virginia.* Nashville, TN: Turner Publishing, 2010.

WEB SITES

"Economy at a Glance: West Virginia." *US Bureau of Labor Statistics.* http://www.bls.gov/eag/eag.wv.htm (accessed on November 9, 2012).

"Endangered Species Program." *US Fish & Wildlife Service.* http://www.fws.gov/endangered/ (accessed on November 9, 2012).

"State & County QuickFacts: West Virginia." *US Bureau of the Census.* http://quickfacts.census.gov/qfd/states/54000.html (accessed on November 9, 2012).

"State of West Virginia." *WV.gov.* www.wv.gov (accessed on November 9, 2012).

West Virginia Secretary of State. www.sos.wv.gov (accessed on November 9, 2012).

Wisconsin

State of Wisconsin

ORIGIN OF STATE NAME: Probably from the Ojibwa word *wishkonsing,* meaning "place of the beaver."

NICKNAME: The Badger State.

CAPITAL: Madison.

ENTERED UNION: 29 May 1848 (30th).

OFFICIAL SEAL: Coat of arms surrounded by the words "Great Seal of the State of Wisconsin" and 13 stars below.

FLAG: A dark-blue field, fringed in yellow on three sides, surrounds the state coat of arms on each side, with "Wisconsin" in white letters above the coat of arms and "1848" below.

COAT OF ARMS: Surrounding the US shield is the shield of Wisconsin, which is divided into four parts symbolizing agriculture, mining, navigation, and manufacturing. Flanking the shield are a sailor, representing labor on water; and a yeoman or miner, representing labor on land. Above is a badger and the state motto; below, a horn of plenty and a pyramid of pig lead.

MOTTO: Forward.

SONG: "On, Wisconsin!"

FLOWER: Wood violet.

TREE: Sugar maple.

ANIMAL: Badger; white-tailed deer (wildlife); dairy cow (domestic).

BIRD: Robin.

FISH: Muskellunge.

INSECT: Honeybee.

DOG: American water spaniel.

FOSSIL: Trilobite.

MINERAL: Galena.

ROCK OR STONE: Red granite.

BEVERAGE: Milk.

LEGAL HOLIDAYS: New Year's Day, 1 January; birthday of Martin Luther King, Jr., 3rd Monday in January; Presidents' Day, 3rd Monday in February; Good Friday, Friday before Easter, March or April; Memorial Day, last Monday in May; Independence Day, 4 July; Labor Day, 1st Monday in September; Primary Day, 2nd Tuesday in September in even-numbered years; Columbus Day, 2nd Monday in October; Election Day, 2nd Tuesday in November in even-numbered years; Veterans Day, 11 November; Thanksgiving Day, 4th Thursday in November; Christmas Day, 25 December.

TIME: 6 a.m. CST = noon GMT.

1 Location and Size

Located in the eastern north-central United States, Wisconsin ranks 26th in size among the

Lake Superior

Apostle Islands
National Lakeshore

Big Bay
State Park

Superior

BAYFIELD

DOUGLAS

ASHLAND

Chequamegon
National
Forest

IRON

MICHIGAN

Bad River
Indian
Reservation

Lac du
Flambeau
Ind. Res.

BURNETT

WASHBURN

SAWYER

VILAS

St. Croix
N. S. W.

PRICE

FOREST

FLORENCE

Chequamegon
National
Forest

Lac Courte Oreilles
Indian
Reservation

ONEIDA

POLK

BARRON

RUSK

LINCOLN

MARINETTE

Nicolet
National
Forest

Chequamegon
National
Forest

LANGLADE

OCONTO

St. Croix R.

Chippewa R.

TAYLOR

Interstate
St. Park

ST. CROIX

DUNN

CHIPPEWA

Lake
Wissota
St. Park

CLARK

Wolf R.

MENOMINEE

Menominee
Indian
Reservation

Willow River
St. Park

94

MARATHON

Rib
Mountain
St. Park

Wausau

Stockbridge
Indian
Reservation

SHAWANO

Newport
St. Park

PIERCE

EAU CLAIRE

Kinnickinnic
St. Park

Eau Claire

Black R.

Pota-
watomi
S.P.

Whitefish Dunes
State Park

PEPIN

WOOD

PORTAGE

WAUPACA

BROWN

DOOR

GREEN BAY

BUFFALO

TREMPEALEAU

Mississippi R.

MINNESOTA

JACKSON

Necedah
Wildlife
Refuge

Hartman Creek
State Park

Appleton

Oneida
Indian
Reservation

Green
Bay

MANITOWOC

KEWAUNEE

Black
River
S. F.

JUNEAU

ADAMS

WAUSHARA

WINNEBAGO

CALUMET

Point Beach
State Forest

43

MONROE

Fox R.

MARQUETTE

GREEN
LAKE

High Cliff
St. Park

Lake
Winnebago

Manitowoc

LA CROSSE

La Crosse

90

Fort McCoy
Military
Reservation

94

Wisconsin R.

Oshkosh

FOND DU LAC

SHEBOYGAN

Sheboygan

Lake Michigan

VERNON

Wildcat Mountain
State Park

SAUK

COLUMBIA

Wisconsin Dells

DODGE

Fond
du Lac

Horicon National
Wildlife Refuge

Kettle
Moraine
St. Forest

IOWA

Mirror Lake
State Park

Devils Lake
State Park

RICHLAND

CRAWFORD

Wisconsin R.

IOWA

DANE

JEFFERSON

WASHINGTON

West
Bend

OZAUKEE

Menomonee
Falls

WAUKESHA

Wauwatosa

MILWAUKEE

GRANT

Governor Dodge
State Park

Madison

90

Rock R.

94

Brookfield

Waukesha

New Berlin

West Allis

Milwaukee

Green-
field

Upper Mississippi
Wildlife and
Fish Refuge

LAFAYETTE

GREEN

ROCK

WALWORTH

RACINE

Racine

Janesville

43

KENOSHA

Kenosha

Beloit

ILLINOIS

WISCONSIN

Explanation

▲ Point of Interest

◉ City (25,000–100,000 people)

⬤ City (more than 100,000 people)

✪ State Capital

〔94〕 U.S. Interstate Route

▦ Area of Interest

N

0   25   50 miles

0   25   50 kilometers

50 states. The total area of Wisconsin is 65,496 square miles (169,634 square kilometers), of which 54,157 square miles (140,268 square kilometers) is land and 11,338 square miles (29,366 square kilometers) is covered by water. The state extends 295 miles (475 kilometers) from east to west and 320 miles (515 kilometers) from north to south. The state's boundaries have a total length of 1,379 miles (2,219 kilometers). Important islands belonging to Wisconsin are the Apostle Islands in Lake Superior and Washington Island in Lake Michigan.

2 Topography

Wisconsin can be divided into four main geographical regions, each covering roughly one quarter of the state's land area. The most highly elevated of these is the Superior Upland, along the state's 156 miles (251 kilometers) of coastline along Lake Superior. This region has heavily forested rolling hills but no high mountains. A second upland region, called the Driftless Area, has a more rugged terrain. The third region is a large, crescent-shaped plain in central Wisconsin. Finally, in the east and southeast, along 407 miles of Lake Michigan shoreline, lies a large, lowland plain. This topography includes the Door County peninsula, which extends into Lake Michigan and forms Green Bay.

Timms Hill, in north-central Wisconsin, is the state's highest point, at 1,951 feet (595 meters). The lowest elevation is 579 feet (177 meters), along the Lake Michigan shoreline. There are nearly 14,000 inland lakes in Wisconsin, with more than 9,000 lakes located in the northern region. Lake Winnebago, in eastern Wisconsin, covering an area of 215 square miles (557 square kilometers), is the second-largest freshwater lake in the United States.

The Mississippi River, which forms part of the border with Minnesota and the entire border with Iowa, is the main navigable river. The Wisconsin River is the major river flowing through the state on a south-southwest course for 430 miles (692 kilometers) before meeting the Mississippi at the Iowa border. Other tributaries of the Mississippi are the St. Croix, Chippewa, and Black rivers. Located on the Black River are Big Manitou Falls, at 165 feet (50 meters) the highest of the state's many waterfalls.

3 Climate

Wisconsin has a continental climate with hot, humid summers and cold winters. The average annual temperature ranges from 39°F (4°C) in the north to about 50°F (10°C) in the south. The statewide average in 2011 of 44°F (6°C) was above normal, as many states in the eastern half of the country experienced warmer than average temperatures that year. Average daily temperatures in Milwaukee have ranged from 13°F (-10°C) to 27°F (-2°C) in January and from 62°F (16°C) to 79°F (26°C) in July. The lowest temperature ever recorded in Wisconsin is -55°F (-48°C) at Couderay on 4 February 1996. The highest temperature, 114°F (46°C), occurred at Wisconsin Dells on 13 July 1936.

Annual precipitation in the state ranges from about 34 inches (86 centimeters) for parts of the northwest to about 28 inches (71 centimeters) in the south-central region and the areas bordering Lake Superior and Lake Michigan. Annual snowfall can vary from about 30 inches (76 centimeters) at Beloit in the south to over 100 inches (154 centimeters) in the north, where snowfall may begin in early November. The annual average snowfall in Milwaukee is 47 inches (118 centimeters). Statewide average precipitation of 30 inches (76 centimeters) in 2011 was fairly close to normal. Although the state is known for dairy farming, the annual precipitation during the growing season makes the area ideal for growing corn and other crops.

4 Plants and Animals

Common trees of Wisconsin include oaks, black cherry, and hickory. Pines, yellow birch, and moosewood are among the trees that grow in the north. Characteristic of southern Wisconsin are sugar maple (the state tree), white elm, and basswood. Prairies are thick with grasses. Forty-five varieties of orchid have been identified, as well as 20 types of violet, including the wood violet (the state flower). In 2012, there were seven plant species listed by the US Fish and Wildlife Service as threatened, including the eastern prairie fringed orchid, prairie bush-clover, dwarf lake iris, Pitcher's thistle, Fassett's locoweed, and northern wild monkshood.

White-tailed deer (the state wild animal), black bear, and chipmunk are mammals typical of forestlands. The striped skunk and red and gray foxes are characteristic of upland fields, while wetlands harbor such mammals as the muskrat, mink, and river otter. Game birds include the ring-necked pheasant, bobwhite quail, and ruffed grouse. Some 336 bird species are native to Wisconsin. Reptiles include 23 varieties of snake, 13 types of turtle, and 4 kinds of lizard. Muskellunge (the state fish), northern pike, and brook trout are found in Wisconsin waterways.

In 2012, the US Fish and Wildlife Service listed nine Wisconsin animal species as threatened or endangered, including the Canada lynx, Karner blue butterfly, Hine's emerald dragonfly, piping plover, and gray wolf. In June 2007, the bald eagle was removed from the list of threatened and endangered species nationwide.

5 Environmental Protection

The present Department of Natural Resources (DNR), organized in 1967, brings together conservation and environmental protection responsibilities. The department supervises air, water, and solid waste pollution control programs and deals with the protection of forest, fish, and wildlife resources.

Pulp and paper mills, cheese factories, and canneries have taken major steps to control and prevent harmful water pollution. Communities have built new or upgraded existing sewage treatment plants to reduce the flow of sewage into rivers and streams. Pulp and paper mills have spent millions of dollars to reduce suspended solids and other pollutants in their industrial effluent.

Contaminated stormwater and runoff from agriculture, development, and other sources remain the most serious threats to Wisconsin's lakes, rivers, and streams. Wetland protection regulations were upgraded in the late 1980s, and in 1991 the state became the first in the nation to legislate wetlands protection. Between 1992 and 1998, approximately 11,312 acres of wetlands were restored.

In 2012, there were 43 sites in Wisconsin listed on the US Environmental Protection Agency's National Priorities List (NPL) of hazardous waste sites. These included the Janesville Ash Beds, in Janesville, an ash bed landfill contaminated with hazardous substances.

6 Population

According to the US Census Bureau, Wisconsin ranked 20th in population among the 50 states in 2011. The state had 5,711,767 residents that year. The population is projected to reach 6,088,374 in 2025. In 2011, the median age for the state was 38.7. About 13.9% of all residents were 65 or older, while 23.2% were under 18. Average population density in 2010 was 105 persons per square mile (40.5 persons per square kilometer).

In 2011, Milwaukee, the largest city in Wisconsin, had a population of 597,867 (metro area, 1,562,216). Other large cities (with their populations) were Madison, 236,901 (metro area, 576,467), and Green Bay, 105,809 (metro area, 309,469). In 2010, 75% of the population lived in metropolitan areas.

7 Ethnic Groups

According to the 2010 Census, the African American population was 359,148 residents, or about 6.3% of the state total. Hispanics and Latinos were the next-largest minority with 336,056 residents, or 5.9% of Wisconsinites. The Asian population of 129,234 represented 2.3% of the total. Native Hawaiians/Pacific Islanders numbered 1,827, and Native Americans numbered 54,526. The principal tribes were Chippewa, Oneida, Menominee, and Ho-Chunk. From 2006 to 2010, foreign-born residents averaged 4.6% of the total population compared to the national average of 12.7%.

8 Languages

Wisconsin English is almost entirely Northern, similar to the areas that provided Wisconsin's

Wisconsin Population Profile

Total population per Census 2010:	5,686,986
Population change, 2006–10:	2.3%
Hispanic or Latino†:	5.9%
Population by race	
One race:	98.2%
White:	86.2%
Black or African American:	6.3%
American Indian/Alaska Native:	1.0%
Asian:	2.3%
Native Hawaiian/Pacific Islander:	0.0%
Some other race:	2.4%
Two or more races:	1.8%

Population by Age Group, Census 2010

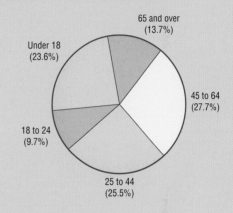

65 and over (13.7%)
Under 18 (23.6%)
45 to 64 (27.7%)
18 to 24 (9.7%)
25 to 44 (25.5%)

Major Cities by Population, 2011 Estimates

City	Population	% change 2005–11
Milwaukee	597,867	3.3
Madison	236,901	6.9
Green Bay	105,809	4.6
Kenosha	99,738	4.7
Racine	78,853	-0.7
Appleton	73,243	4.3
Waukesha	70,867	4.7
Eau Claire	66,623	6.5
Oshkosh	66,344	4.5
Janesville	63,479	2.4

Notes: †A person of Hispanic or Latino origin may be of any race. NA indicates that data are not available. Percentages may not equal 100 due to rounding.

SOURCE: U.S. Census Bureau. Census 2010 and Population Estimates. www.census.gov/ (accessed July 2012).

Wisconsin Population by Race
CENSUS 2010

This table shows the number of people who are of one, two, or three or more races. For those claiming two races, the number of people belonging to the various categories is listed. The U.S. government conducts a census of the population every 10 years.

	Number	Percent
Total population	5,686,986	100.0
One race	5,582,669	98.2
Two races	97,512	1.7
White *and* Black or African American	32,590	0.6
White *and* American Indian/Alaska Native	22,491	0.4
White *and* Asian	16,578	0.3
White *and* Native Hawaiian/Pacific Islander	1,157	—
White *and* some other race	14,396	0.3
Black or African American *and* American Indian/Alaska Native	3,025	0.1
Black or African American *and* Asian	1,032	—
Black or African American *and* Native Hawaiian/Pacific Islander	249	—
Black or African American *and* some other race	2,135	—
American Indian/Alaska Native *and* Asian	565	—
American Indian/Alaska Native *and* Native Hawaiian/Pacific Islander	45	—
American Indian/Alaska Native *and* some other race	721	—
Asian *and* Native Hawaiian/Pacific Islander	679	—
Asian *and* some other race	1,500	—
Native Hawaiian/Pacific Islander *and* some other race	349	—
Three or more races	6,805	0.1

SOURCE: U.S. Census Bureau. Census 2010. www.census/gov/ (accessed July 2012). A dash (—) indicates that the percent is less than 0.1.

first settlers—Michigan, northern Ohio, New York State, and western New England. Common terms include the Northern *pail*, and *angleworm* (earthworm). In Milwaukee, a drinking fountain is called a *bubbler.*

According to the US Census Bureau in 2011, 91.3% of Wisconsin's population five years old and older spoke only English in the home, 4.4% spoke Spanish; 2.3% spoke other Indo-European languages, and 1.6% spoke Asian and Pacific Islander languages.

 Religions

The first Catholics to arrive were Jesuit missionaries seeking to convert the Huron Indians in the 17th century. Protestant settlers and missionaries of different sects, including large numbers of German Lutherans, came during the 19th century, along with Protestants from the east. Jews settled primarily in the cities.

According to the Pew Forum on Religion & Public Life, in 2008, 24% of Wisconsin residents identified as Evangelical Protestants; 23% were affiliated with mainline Protestant churches; 29% were Roman Catholic; 3% were affiliated with historically black Protestant churches; and 1% were Orthodox. No other religion had more than 0.5% of the population. Around 16% of the state's residents were unaffiliated with any religious organization.

10 Transportation

According to the Wisconsin Department of Transportation, there were 10 freight railroads

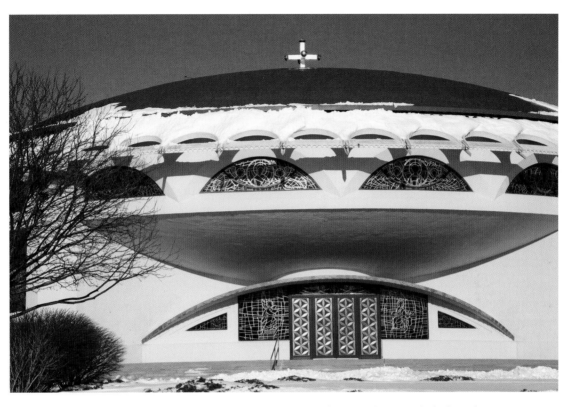

The Annunciation Greek Orthodox Church in Milwaukee was designed by famous architect Frank Lloyd Wright. © HENRYK SADURA/SHUTTERSTOCK.COM.

operating on 3,500 rail miles (5,633 kilometers) of track in 2010. Amtrak's long-distance passenger train service originating in Chicago included six stops in Wisconsin as well as commuter service in the Chicago-Milwaukee corridor that operated seven days a week.

As of January 2010, Wisconsin had 114,800 miles (184,753 kilometers) of public roadway. The state had just over 4 million licensed drivers in 2009, along with 2.6 million automobiles, 310,000 motorcycles, and 2.28 million registered trucks. In 2011, there were 569 traffic fatalities in Wisconsin.

Wisconsin had 81 public bus and shared-ride taxi systems as of 2012. There were nine private bus companies providing scheduled service between cities and major airports in Wisconsin and neighboring states. Two companies offered ferry service across Lake Michigan from Milwaukee or Manitowoc. Additionally, the Merrimac Ferry crosses the Wisconsin River and the Cassville Ferry crosses the Mississippi River into Iowa. Ferries also operated to Madeline Island in Lake Superior and Washington Island in Lake Michigan.

Wisconsin is bordered on three sides by commercial waterways (Lake Superior to the north, Lake Michigan to the east, and the Mississippi River to the west) that make transportation of freight by water a viable alternative. The opening of the St. Lawrence Seaway in 1959 allowed oceangoing vessels access to Wisconsin and 16 other states via the five Great Lakes. Additionally, the Upper Mississippi River System links Wisconsin and four other states to the Gulf Coast. As of 2012, Wisconsin had 28 commercial ports or harbors. The Port of Duluth-Superior (shared with Duluth, Minnesota) on Lake Superior is the busiest of all Great Lakes ports. Other important Wisconsin ports, all on Lake Michigan, are Milwaukee, Green Bay, Port Washington, Oak Creek, Manitowoc, and Sturgeon Bay; coal is the chief commodity. On the Mississippi River, Prairie du Chien and La Crosse are the main ports.

As of 2009, Wisconsin had 436 airports, 95 heliports, and 17 seaplane bases, including eight major airports, in Appleton, Green Bay, Eau Claire, La Crosse, Madison, Milwaukee, Mosinee, and Rhinelander. Milwaukee's General Mitchell International Airport is the state's main air terminal, with 3,814,053 passenger enplanements in 2009, making it the nation's 47th-busiest airport that year.

11 History

During the 17th century, the Ojibwa, Sauk, Fox, Potawatomi, Kickapoo, and other tribes came to the area that is now Wisconsin. These tribes engaged in agriculture, hunting, and fishing, but with the arrival of Europeans became increasingly dependent on the fur trade. The first European believed to have reached Wisconsin was the Frenchman Jean Nicolet, who in 1634 landed on the shores of Green Bay. After 1673, Jesuits established missions, and French fur traders opened up posts. The French were succeeded by the British after the French and Indian War. Although ceded to the United States in 1783, the region remained British in all but name until 1816, when the United States built forts at Prairie du Chien and Green Bay.

Under the Ordinance of 1787, Wisconsin became part of the Northwest Territory; it was subsequently included in the Indiana Territory, the Territory of Illinois, and then the Michigan Territory. The Wisconsin Territory was formed in 1836. In the 1830s, the region's population and economy began to expand rapidly. Wisconsin voters endorsed statehood in 1846, and on 29 May 1848, President James K. Polk signed the bill that made Wisconsin the 30th state.

Wisconsinites took a generally abolitionist stand. In the Civil War (1961–65), 96,000 Wisconsin men fought on the Union side and 12,216 died. During the late 19th century, Wisconsin was generally prosperous; dairy products, food processing, and lumbering emerged as major industries, and Milwaukee grew into an important industrial center.

20th Century Under Republican governor Robert "Fighting Bob" La Follette in the early 20th century, the legislature passed a law providing for the nation's first direct statewide primary. Other La Follette measures included increased taxation of railroads, regulation of lobbyists, creation of a civil service, and the establishment of a railroad commission to regulate rates.

After La Follette left the governor's office to become a US senator, his progressivism was carried on by his Republican successors. During one session in 1911, legislators enacted the first state income tax in the United States and one of the first workers' compensation programs.

Between the world wars, Wisconsin's tradition of reform continued. A pioneering old-age pension act was passed in 1925; seven years later, Wisconsin enacted the nation's first unemployment compensation act. In the 1930s, La Follette's son, Philip, serving as governor, successfully pressed for the creation of state agencies to develop electric power, arbitrate labor disputes, and set rules for fair business competition. His so-called Little New Deal corresponded to the New Deal policies of the Franklin Delano Roosevelt administration.

After World War II, the state continued a trend toward increased urbanization, and its industries prospered. The major figure on the national scene in the postwar era was Senator Joseph R. McCarthy, who began unsubstantiated attacks in 1950 on alleged Communists and other subversives in the federal government. After McCarthy's censure by the US Senate in 1954 and his death in 1957, the progressive tradition began to recover strength, and the liberal Democratic Party grew increasingly influential in state politics.

During the 1960s and early 1970s, there was student unrest at the University of Wisconsin and a growing discontent among Milwaukee's African American population. In 1984, the Milwaukee school board filed suit in federal court against the state and Milwaukee's suburbs, charging that the policies of the state and suburban schools had resulted in an unconstitutionally segregated school system. Two years later, the Milwaukee School Board and nine suburban districts agreed on a plan in which 2,700 city minority students would transfer voluntarily to the nine suburbs, and 9,000 to 10,000 suburban students would attend Milwaukee schools.

Wisconsin's economy remained stable through the 1980s and 1990s. In 1993, the Mississippi River flooded, causing four deaths and an estimated $900 million in damage in 47 Wisconsin counties.

Milwaukee is the largest city in Wisconsin, with a population of 597,867 in 2011. © HENRYK SADURA/SHUTTERSTOCK.COM.

In 2002, Jim Doyle became the first Democratic governor to be elected in Wisconsin in 16 years. He advocated abortion rights, gun control, and environmental protection. Doyle was at odds with the Republican-controlled state legislature over issues of state spending on education and health care, and on raising taxes. Although Wisconsin faced a $3.2 billion two-year budget deficit in 2003, Doyle subsequently managed to balance the budget, while holding the line on taxes, and as a result, state taxes as a percentage of income were by 2005 the lowest in 34 years in the state. Doyle was reelected and held office until January 2011 when Republican Scott Walker took over.

Government worker protests that began in February 2011 gained national attention, as newly elected Walker forged ahead with plans to cut the state's $3.6 billion budget deficit by enacting a law that would curtail the collective bargaining rights of public sector unions. As a result, public workers would have to pay more for their health insurance and pensions. After the law was passed in March, opponents forced a recall election. During the next year, membership in public employee unions in Wisconsin dropped by more than half, and Walker won the recall election in June 2012 by a 7% margin.

12 State Government

The Wisconsin legislature consists of a senate with 33 members elected for four-year terms,

and an assembly of 99 representatives elected for two-year terms. There are six elected state officers—governor and lieutenant governor (elected jointly), secretary of state, state treasurer, attorney general, and superintendent of public instruction—serving four-year terms. There are no gubernatorial term limits. As the chief executive officer, the governor exercises authority by the power of appointment, by presenting a budget bill and major addresses to the legislature, and by the power to veto bills and call special legislative sessions.

A bill may be introduced in either house of the legislature but must be passed by both houses to become law. The governor has six days (Sundays excluded) to sign or veto a measure. If the governor fails to act and the legislature is still in session, the bill automatically becomes law. Vetoes can be overridden by a two-thirds majority of both houses.

Wisconsin Governors: 1848–2013

1848–1852	Nelson Dewey	Democrat	1921–1927	John James Blaine	Republican
1852–1854	Leonard James Farwell	Whig	1927–1929	Fred R. Zimmerman	Republican
1854–1856	William Augustus Barstow	Democrat	1929–1931	Walter Jodok Kohler, Sr.	Republican
1856	Arthur MacArthur	Democrat	1931–1933	Philip Fox LaFollette	Republican
1856–1858	Coles Bashford	Republican	1933–1935	Albert George Schmedeman	Democrat
1858–1862	Alexander Williams Randall	Republican	1935–1939	Philip Fox LaFollette	Progressive
1862	Louis Powell Harvey	Republican	1939–1943	Julius Peter Heil	Republican
1862–1864	Edward P. Salomon	Republican	1943–1947	Walter Samuel Goodland	Republican
1864–1866	James Taylor Lewis	Republican	1947–1951	Oscar Rennebohm	Republican
1866–1872	Lucius Fairchild	Republican	1951–1957	Walter Jodok Kohler, Jr.	Republican
1872–1874	Cadwallader Colden Washburn	Republican	1957–1959	Vernon Wallace Thompson	Republican
1874–1876	William Robert Taylor	Democrat	1959–1963	Gaylord Anton Nelson	Democrat
1876–1878	Harrison Ludington	Republican	1963–1965	John Whitcome Reynolds	Democrat
1878–1882	William E. Smith	Republican	1965–1971	Warren Perley Knowles	Republican
1882–1889	Jeremiah McLain Rusk	Republican	1971–1977	Patrick Joseph Lucey	Democrat
1889–1891	William Dempster Hoard	Republican	1977–1979	Martin James Schreiber	Democrat
1891–1895	George Wilbur Peck	Democrat	1979–1983	Lee Sherman Dreyfus	Republican
1895–1897	William Henry Upham	Republican	1983–1987	Anthony Scully Earl	Democrat
1897–1901	Edward Scofield	Republican	1987–2001	Tommy George Thompson	Republican
1901–1906	Robert Marion LaFollette	Republican	2001–2003	Scott McCallum	Republican
1906–1911	James Ole Davidson	Republican	2003–2011	Jim Doyle	Democrat
1911–1915	Francis Edward McGovern	Republican	2011–	Scott Walker	Republican
1915–1921	Emanuel Lorenz Philipp	Republican			

As of 2012, the legislators' salary was $49,943 and the governor's salary was $144,423.

13 Political Parties

Beginning in the late 1850s, the newly founded Republican Party held sway in Wisconsin for over 100 years. The Democrats held a substantial edge at the state level in the 1970s and 1980s. Socialist parties have won some success in Wisconsin's political history. In 1910, Emil Seidel was elected mayor of Milwaukee, becoming the first Socialist mayor of a major US city; and Victor Berger became the first Socialist ever elected to Congress.

Democratic candidate Al Gore won Wisconsin by a narrow margin of 5,396 votes in the 2000 presidential election. He and Republican George W. Bush both received 48% of the vote in Wisconsin. In the presidential election of 2004, Democratic challenger John Kerry won 49.8% of the vote in Wisconsin, compared to incumbent President Bush's 49.4%. Democrat Barack Obama won the state in the 2008 presidential election with 56.2% of the vote, to Republican John McCain's 42.3%. President Obama easily defeated Republican Mitt Romney in Wisconsin, which was considered a battleground state, in the 2012 election. Republican Scott Walker was elected governor in 2010.

Wisconsin's US senators are Republican Ron Johnson and Democrat Tammy Baldwin. Senator Johnson won the 2010 election against Senator Russell Feingold, who had been re-elected in 2004. Senator Baldwin won her 2012 contest against Republican Tommy Thompson, who had served as U.S. Secretary of Health and Human Services during the George W. Bush administration. In 2013, Wisconsin's

US representatives consisted of five Republicans and three Democrats. In 2012, there were 18 Republicans and 15 Democrats in the state senate and 59 Republicans and 39 Democrats in the state assembly. That same year, there were 23 women serving in the state house and 9 women serving in the state senate. In July 2011, there were 3,285,704 registered voters in the state of Wisconsin.

14 Local Government

As of 2010, Wisconsin had 72 counties, 190 cities, 1,257 towns, 404 villages, and 427 school districts. Each county is governed by a board of supervisors. Some counties, including Milwaukee County, have elected county executives. Other county officials include district attorneys, sheriffs, clerks, treasurers, and coroners. Most cities are

Wisconsin Presidential Vote by Major Political Parties, 1948–2012

Year	Wisconsin Winner	Democrat	Republican
1948	*Truman (D)	647,310	590,959
1952	*Eisenhower (R)	622,175	979,744
1956	*Eisenhower (R)	586,768	954,844
1960	Nixon (R)	830,805	895,175
1964	*Johnson (D)	1,050,424	638,495
1968	*Nixon (R)	748,804	809,997
1972	*Nixon (R)	810,174	989,430
1976	*Carter (D)	1,040,232	1,004,967
1980	*Reagan (R)	981,584	1,088,845
1984	*Reagan (R)	995,740	1,198,584
1988	Dukakis (D)	1,126,794	1,047,499
1992	*Clinton (D)	1,041,066	930,855
1996	*Clinton (D)	1,071,971	845,029
2000	Gore (D)	1,242,987	1,237,279
2004	Kerry (D)	1,489,504	1,478,120
2008	*Obama (D)	1,677,211	1,262,393
2012	*Obama (D)	1,620,985	1,410,966

*Won US presidential election.

Independent candidate Ross Perot received 544,479 votes in 1992 and 227,339 votes in 1996.

governed by a mayor-council system. Executive power in a village is vested in an elected president, who presides over an elected board but has no veto power. Wisconsin towns are generally governed by a board of supervisors. Wisconsin has 12 federally recognized American Indian areas. In 2011, there were 233,031 full-time and 151,027 part-time state and local government employees.

15 Judicial System

The judicial branch is headed by a supreme court consisting of seven justices who are elected to 10-year terms. The supreme court, which is the final authority on state constitutional questions, hears appeals at its own discretion and has original jurisdiction in limited areas. The state's next highest court is the court of appeals, whose decisions may be reviewed by the supreme court. Circuit courts are Wisconsin's trial courts and have original jurisdiction in civil and criminal cases. Wisconsin's 252 municipal courts have jurisdiction over violations of local ordinances.

According to the Federal Bureau of Investigation, in 2010 Wisconsin had a violent crime rate of 248.7 reported incidents per 100,000 population. The murder and nonnegligent manslaughter rate was 2.7 incidents per 100,000 inhabitants; forcible rape, 20.9; aggravated assault, 145.9; and property crime, 2,507.7. Inmates in Wisconsin federal and state prisons totaled 35,116 at the beginning of 2010. Wisconsin does not have a death penalty; it was abolished in 1853.

16 Migration

Until the early 19th century, Wisconsin was inhabited mainly by Native Americans. In the 1820s, southerners began to arrive from the lower Mississippi and in the 1830s easterners poured in from New York, Ohio, Pennsylvania, and New England. Foreign immigrants began arriving in the 1820s, either directly from Europe or after temporary settlement in eastern states. Most of the early immigrants were from Ireland and England.

After the Black Hawk War in 1832, Native Americans were forced to cede most of their lands to the federal government, and many were forced to move west of the Mississippi River. In 1836, the state's population was approximately 11,000, a number that ballooned to over 200,000 by 1850. Germans began to arrive in large numbers after the Revolution of 1848, and by 1860 they were predominant in the immigrant population. The state soon became a patchwork of ethnic communities—Germans in the counties near Lake Michigan, Norwegians in southern and western Wisconsin, Dutch in the lower Fox Valley and near Sheboygan, and other groups in other regions.

After the Civil War, and especially in the 1880s, immigration reached new heights with Wisconsin receiving a large share of Germans and Scandinavians. The proportion of Germans declined, however, as new immigrants arrived from Finland, Russia, and southern and eastern Europe. Poverty and political oppression in Poland led many to immigrate to Wisconsin, where they became the second-largest ethnic group.

When US entry into World War II led to a shortage of laborers, the federal government formed the Emergency Farm Labor Program in 1942. Wisconsin growers began importing temporary workers from Mexico, Jamaica, the Bahamas, and British Honduras. Consequently, millions of Mexican farm laborers came to the state until the program was discontinued in 1964.

During the Vietnam war, a guerrilla army, comprising primarily Hmong militia, fought alongside US troops in Laos. After US military forces pulled out of Vietnam in 1975, the Hmong of North Vietnam were forced to flee to refugee camps in Thailand. Thousands of Hmong refugees began to arrive in Wisconsin and other states beginning in 1975. Over the next 20 years, 100,000 Hmong refugees fled to the United States. As of 2010, the Hmong remained the largest Asian population in both Wisconsin and Minnesota. The Wisconsin Hmong population of nearly 50,000 in 2010 was the third-largest in the nation, behind California and Minnesota.

Between 2009 and 2010, the total population (ages one and older) of Wisconsin decreased by 3,681, due to the net domestic out-migration of natives (-19,759), the net domestic in-migration of immigrants (1,584), and the arrival from abroad of natives (7,429) and immigrants (7,065). Of the total foreign-born population in Wisconsin in 2010, 3% were from Africa, 32.7% were from Asia, 18.2% were from Europe, and 43.3% were from Latin America. The top three countries of birth of the foreign born in Wisconsin in 2010 were Mexico (34.8%), India (6%), and China (4.9%). In comparison, the top three countries of birth in 1990 were Germany (13.8%), Laos (10.5%), and Mexico (8.7%).

17 Economy

Wisconsin's industries are diversified, with nonelectrical machinery and food products as the leading items. Other important industries are paper and pulp products, transportation equipment, electrical and electronic equipment, and fabricated metals. Economic growth has been concentrated in the southeast. There, soils and climate are favorable for agriculture; a skilled labor force is available to industry; and capital, transportation, and markets are most readily accessible.

Wisconsin's and the nation's economy shrank during the global recession that began in 2008. Wisconsin's exports were 8.5% of gross state product (GSP) in 2008, but fell to 7.5% in 2009 as international trade dropped off. Like most other states, Wisconsin's GSP declined during the recession, only reaching $239 billion in 2009. Manufacturing accounted for $42.3 billion (17.7% of GSP), followed by the real estate sector, at $30.1 billion (12.6% of GSP). Two other sectors—health care and social assistance, and finance and insurance—each represented about $22 billion, or 9% of GSP.

In 2010, Wisconsin's GSP was $251.4 billion, ranking the state 20th in the nation. Per capita GSP was $44,105 that year, ranking the state 29th. In 2010, there were 139,554 private nonfarm establishments and 331,692 nonemployer establishments in the state.

18 Income

Median per capita personal income (including nonmonetary income) in 2011 was $40,073, ranking Wisconsin 25th in the United States. From 2008 to 2010, the median annual household income in Wisconsin was $51,484, compared to the national average of $50,022. In 2011, 13.1% of the state's residents lived below the federal poverty level, as compared with 15.9% nationwide.

19 Industry

The total value of shipments by manufacturers was $163 billion in 2007, compared to nearly $137 billion in 2004. Of that total, food products (especially cheese, meat, and canned fruits and vegetables), industrial machinery and equipment, paper and allied products, and transportation equipment were most important.

Industrial activity is concentrated in the southeast, especially in the Milwaukee metropolitan area. Major corporations based in Milwaukee include Johnson Controls and Rockwell Automation–Allen-Bradley, makers of electric and electronic components; and Harley-Davidson, best known for its touring and custom motorcycles. In September 2003, over 250,000 motorcycle enthusiasts gathered in Milwaukee to celebrate the 100th anniversary of Harley-Davidson.

20 Labor

In August 2012, the civilian labor force in Wisconsin numbered 3,061,200, with approximately 229,100 workers unemployed, yielding an unemployment rate of 7.5%, compared to the national average of 8.1% for the same period. Those employed in nonfarm wage and salaried jobs that same month included: 82,100 in construction; 446,700 in manufacturing; 509,700 in trade, transportation, and public utilities; 153,500 in financial activities; 282,400 in professional and business services; 418,200 in education and health services; 238,000 in leisure and hospitality services; and 411,300 in government.

Labor began to organize in the state after the Civil War. The Knights of St. Crispin, a shoemakers' union, grew into what was at that time the nation's largest union, before it collapsed during the Panic of 1873. In 1887, unions of printers, cigarmakers, and iron molders organized the Milwaukee Federated Trades Council and in 1893 the Wisconsin State Federation of Labor was formed. A statewide union for public employees was established in 1932. In 2011, 358,000 of Wisconsin's employed wage and salary workers were members of unions, representing 14.1% of those so employed. The national average was 13%. The hourly minimum wage for the state in 2011 was $7.25, which was equivalent to the federal minimum wage rate.

21 Agriculture

According to the US Department of Agriculture, there were 15.2 million acres (6.2 million hectares) of land, nearly 50% of the state's total land area, distributed among 78,000 Wisconsin farms in 2010. The average farm size was 195 acres (79 hectares). Wisconsin's total agricultural output was $13 billion in 2011. Leading field crops were corn, soybeans, hay, and potatoes. Farmland is concentrated in the southern two-thirds of the state, especially in the southeast. Potatoes are grown mainly in central Wisconsin, cranberries in the Wisconsin River Valley, and cherries in the Door Peninsula.

Top crops in 2011 included corn ($2 billion in farm receipts), soybeans ($845 million), and potatoes ($253 million). Top Wisconsin agricultural exports that year included soybeans and soybean products ($546.1 million in export receipts), feed grains and products ($442.7 million), and vegetables and vegetable preparations ($180 million). Major agricultural counties in the state are Dane, Grant, Marathon, Dodge, and Fond du Lac counties.

22 Domesticated Animals

Aided by the skills of immigrant cheesemakers and by the encouragement of dairy farmers who emigrated from New York, Wisconsin turned to dairy farming in the late 19th century. In 2011, output from domesticated animals was almost $6 billion. According to the US Department of Agriculture, the state had 1.26 million milk cows that produced over 26 billion pounds (11.8 billion kilograms) of milk as of 2010. Dairy products were the state's top agriculture commodity in 2011, with farm receipts of $5.24 billion. Dairy farms are prominent in nearly all regions, but especially in the Central Plains and Western Uplands. Wisconsin ranchers also raise livestock for meat production.

With 3.45 million cattle and calves on Wisconsin farms, cattle was the state's next most important animal commodity. Sales exceeded $1.23 billion in 2011. Wisconsin farms also had about 340,000 hogs and pigs, and 90,000 sheep.

23 Fishing

In 2010, Wisconsin ranked third among the Great Lakes states (behind Michigan and Ohio) in the quantity and value of its commercial fishing, with 3.5 million pounds (1.6 million kilograms) valued at $3.7 million.

The muskellunge is the premier game fish of Wisconsin's inland waters; Coho and chinook salmon, introduced to Lake Michigan, now

A Wisconsin dairy farm is shown. The state is famous for its cheese products. © NANCY GILL/SHUTTERSTOCK.COM.

thrive there as well. Lake trout, rainbow trout, and brown trout are other cold-water dominant species. Walleye, smallmouth bass, and northern pike thrive in warm-water areas. Lake sturgeon is a rare species in the United States, but the largest concentration is in Wisconsin's Lake Winnebago. Lake sturgeon occurs naturally in the Mississippi, Lake Michigan, and Lake Superior drainage basins; and the species has been released in many Wisconsin lakes. Wisconsin's Department of Natural Resources (DNR) operates 17 state fish hatcheries, which raise millions of fish to be released in lakes and rivers where there is little or no natural reproduction.

24 Forestry

In 2012, Wisconsin had 15,965,000 acres (6,461,000 hectares) of forest, covering 46% of the state's land area. About 70% of all forestlands are privately owned. Hardwoods make up about 80% of the sawtimber. The most heavily forested region is in the north. According to the DNR, the harvesting of timber in Wisconsin declined to 5.2 million standard cords (mainly aspen and maple) in 2006, the first decline in five years. About half of the harvest is used to produce pulpwood (for paper production), while the remainder is used in lumber and veneer production. In 2006, pulpwood production decreased 33% to 2.2 million standard cords. By 2008, production had dropped another 9% to 2 million cords. At that time, about 550,000 cords of red oak, maples, and other species were harvested for residential fuelwood. This trend continued as the recession of 2008–2009 and subsequent housing downturn caused lumber production nationwide to reach the lowest levels nationwide since the recession in 1982.

In addition to commercial purposes, Wisconsin's woods have recreational value. Two national forests (Chequamegon and Nicolet), both located in northern Wisconsin, cover 1,396,000 acres (564,941 hectares). The 10 state forests cover 931,000 acres (376,762 hectares), approximately half of which lie in the Northern Highland American Legion State Forest. County forests cover 1,982,000 acres (802,086 hectares). In 2010, only about 7,800 acres were harvested in the national forests and 55,000 acres in state and county lands. Forest management and fire control programs are directed by the DNR. The US Forest Service operates a Forest Products Laboratory at Madison, in cooperation with the University of Wisconsin.

25 Mining

The US Geological Survey's estimated value of nonfuel mineral commodities produced in Wisconsin was $599 million in 2011, representing only about 0.81% of the national output. Production had increased from $372 million a decade prior. During this period, crushed stone and construction sand and gravel continued to be the leading mineral commodities produced in Wisconsin. In 2010, 24.3 million metric tons of crushed stone were mined in the state, valued at $206 million; 26.5 million metric tons of sand and gravel were mined, valued at $128 million; and 50.8 million metric tons of aggregates were mined, valued at $333 billion.

26 Energy and Power

The state's first hydroelectric plant was built at Appleton in 1882. Many others were built later, especially along the Wisconsin River. Wisconsin has no coal mines; however, coal fuels about two-thirds of Wisconsin's power plants. The state has two nuclear power stations: Point Beach, operated by Wisconsin Electric Power Company; and the Kewaunee plant, operated by the Wisconsin Public Service Company. Point Beach is one of the oldest operating reactors in the United States. Hydropower is a significant source of electricity generation in the paper industry and for electric utility generation.

Electric power industry net summer generating capacity in 2010 was 17,835,900 megawatts. As of June 2012, total net electricity generation was 6 million megawatt hours (MWh). Of this, 3,000 MWh was generated by petroleum-fired plants; 1.45 million MWh by natural gas-fired plants; 2.9 million MWh by coal-fired plants; 1.23 million MWh by nuclear plants; 264,000 MWh by hydroelectric plants; and 229,000 MWh by other renewable sources.

27 Commerce

Wholesale sales totaled $60 billion in 2007, compared to $68.5 billion in 2002. Retail sales were $72.3 billion, or $12,904 per capita, in 2007, compared to $59.9 billion five years earlier. In 2008, there were 7,194 wholesale trade establishments and 20,542 retail trade establishments. Although exports shrank in Wisconsin and nationally during the recession in 2009, exports rebounded in 2010. According to the Wisconsin Department of Revenue, the state's exports in 2011 increased 18.3% to $22 billion, ranking it 19th in the nation. This compared to about $15 billion in exports in 2005 and $20.6 billion in 2008. Machinery, computers and electronics, automotive parts, processed foods, paper, and chemicals were major exports. Canada

received $6 billion, or 30%, of Wisconsin's exports, while Mexico received 10%. China, Japan, and Germany were also important export markets. Foreign trade is conducted through the Great Lakes ports of Superior-Duluth, Milwaukee, Green Bay, and Kenosha.

28 Public Finance

Budget estimates are prepared by various departments and sent to the governor or governor-elect in the fall of each even-numbered year. The following January, the governor presents a

The capitol building of Wisconsin is in Madison. © HENRYK SADURA/SHUTTERSTOCK.COM.

biennial budget to the legislature, which passes a budget bill, often after many amendments. The fiscal year begins 1 July and ends June 30.

Total revenues for 2010 were $48 billion and expenditures were $38.6 billion. The largest expenditures in 2009 were $11.1 billion on education and $8.3 billion on public welfare. Other major expenditures were $2.3 billion on highways, $1.1 billion on hospitals, and $1.1 billion on corrections. State debt exceeded $22 billion.

29 Taxation

General purpose tax revenues include personal income tax, corporate tax, general sales tax, selective sales tax (on alcoholic beverages, insurance premiums, and public utilities), license tax, and other taxes on severance, documentary and stock transfers, and death and gift income. The largest single source of state revenue is the income tax on individuals. Personal income tax rates on net taxable income in Wisconsin range from 4.6% to 7.75%. The corporate tax rate is 7.9% of net income. The general sales tax is 5%. In 2010, Wisconsin collected $14.4 billion of general purpose taxes. Nearly $6 billion was from personal income taxes, and $4 billion was from general sales taxes.

Local tax revenue is collected from property taxes, licenses and permits, fines and penalties, and fees for government services, among other sources. In 2011, Wisconsin collected $5.2 billion in property taxes from counties, cities, towns, and villages. Total revenue collected was $13.7 billion. Major expenditures included $4.2 million for health and human services, $1.6 million for law enforcement, and $1.5 million for government operations. Per capita state tax collections were $2,687 in 2011, compared to a national per capita of $2,430, giving Wisconsin the 16th-highest state tax burden that year.

30 Health

In 2011, Wisconsin's infant mortality rate was 6.7 deaths per 1,000 live births. The overall death rate in 2009 was 708.9 per 100,000. There were 164.7 deaths per 100,000 residents from heart disease in 2009 and 171 deaths per 100,000 from cancers. There were 38 deaths per 100,000 from cerebrovascular diseases and 17.3 deaths per 100,000 from diabetes. In 2010, around 7.1% of the adult population had been diagnosed with diabetes, and 63.6% of adults were overweight or obese. Among Wisconsin adults ages 18 and older, 19.1% were smokers in 2010, compared to the national rate of 17.2%. At the end of 2008, there were 4,867 people in Wisconsin living with HIV/AIDS, 0.6% of the US total.

Wisconsin's 124 community hospitals had about 2.4 beds per 100,000 in 2010. The average expense for community hospital care was $1,953 per inpatient day in 2010. In 2009, Wisconsin had 246 physicians, along with 988 registered nurses (2011 figure), and 57 dentists (2007 figure) per 100,000 residents. In 2010, 9% of Wisconsin's residents lacked health insurance.

31 Housing

In 2011, there were an estimated 2,634,806 housing units, 86.4% (2,275,352) that were occupied and 67.9% (1,543,908) that were owner-occupied. About 66.7% (1,757,502) of all units were single-family, detached homes; 100,260 (3.8%) were mobile homes. Utility gas was the most common energy source for heating. It was estimated that 13,146 (0.6%) lacked complete plumbing facilities and 24,313 (1.1%) lacked complete kitchen facilities.

The median home value in 2011 was $166,700. The median monthly cost for mortgage owners was $1,402, while renters paid a median of $739.

32 Education

The first kindergarten in the state was established in Watertown in 1856. As of 2010, Wisconsin had 2,292 public schools and 872,436 students. The US Census Bureau estimated that from 2006 to 2010, 89.4% of all Wisconsinites 25 years or older had completed high school. In 2010, 26% had obtained a bachelor's degree or higher and 36% had an associate's degree or higher, compared to 18% and 25%, respectively, a decade prior.

For the 2008/09 school year, the US National Center for Education noted Wisconsin's public school enrollment was at 872,000. State expenditures for public education at that time were estimated at $9.7 billion. In 2008, there were 353,000 students enrolled in college or graduate school, including 228,000 full-time students, at the state's 77 degree-granting institutions. The University of Wisconsin (UW) campus in Madison had 42,595 students enrolled in the fall of 2010, including 28,297 undergraduates. The statewide UW system had 182,000 students enrolled for the same school year. Approximately 370,000 were enrolled in the Wisconsin Technical College System.

The UW system comprises 13 degree-granting campuses, 13 two-year centers, and the University of Wisconsin-Extension, which has outreach and continuing education activities on all 26 UW campuses and in all 72 Wisconsin counties. There were 20 private four-year institutions in 2011, including such leading institutions as Marquette University, Lawrence University, Ripon College, and Beloit College. The Wisconsin Technical College System has 49 campuses in 16 college districts, which offer two-year associate degrees, one and two-year technical diplomas, and short-term technical diplomas.

33 Arts

Wisconsin offers numerous facilities for drama, music, and other performing arts, including Marcus Center for the Performing Arts in Milwaukee and the Alliant Energy Center in Madison. Milwaukee has a repertory theater and there are many other theater groups around the state. Summer plays are performed at an unusual garden theater at Fish Creek in the Door Peninsula. There is also an annual music festival at that site.

The Pro Arte String Quartet in Madison and the Fine Arts Quartet in Milwaukee have been sponsored by the University of Wisconsin, which has also supported many other musical activities. Milwaukee is the home of the Milwaukee Ballet Company, and the Milwaukee Symphony. Madison is home to the Madison Symphony, the Madison Opera, and the Wisconsin Chamber Orchestra.

The Wisconsin Arts Board aids artists and performing groups and assists communities in developing arts programs. The Wisconsin Humanities Council was founded in 1972.

34 Libraries and Museums

In 2009, Wisconsin's 380 public libraries had more than 65 million books. The Milwaukee Public Library, founded in 1878, and the

Madison Public Library were two of the largest regional systems. The largest academic library is that of the University of Wisconsin at Madison. The best-known special library is that of the State Historical Society of Wisconsin at Madison, with 3.6 million books and numerous government publications and documents.

In 2012, the Wisconsin Department of Tourism had more than 600 listings for museums and cultural and historical sites. The State Historical Society maintains a historical museum on the Capitol Square in Madison and 10 other historical sites and museums around the state. The Milwaukee Public Museum contains collections on history, natural history, and art. The Milwaukee Art Center and the Madison Art Center have large collections of the visual arts. Other leading art museums include the Chazen Museum of Art in Madison and the Theodore Lyman Wright Art Center at Beloit College. There are nine children's museums in the state.

The Circus World Museum at Baraboo occupies the site of the original Ringling Brothers Circus. Other museums of special interest include the Robert C. Williams Paper Museum (Appleton), the National Railroad Museum (Green Bay), and the Green Bay Packer Hall of Fame. More than a thousand species of animals are on exhibit at the Milwaukee County Zoo; Madison and Racine also have zoos. Historical sites are Old World Wisconsin, a working pioneer community near Eagle with 60 historic structures, and the Taliesin estate of architect Frank Lloyd Wright in Spring Green.

35 Communications

In 2010, 73.7% of Wisconsin households had Internet access, with 73.5% having broadband access. According to the Federal Communications Commission, there were 111 licensed daytime AM radio stations and 236 licensed full-service FM radio stations in Wisconsin in 2011.

36 Press

Founded in 1882 by Lucius Nieman, the *Milwaukee Journal* (now known as the *Milwaukee Journal Sentinel*) won a Pulitzer Prize in 1919 for distinguished public service and remains the state's largest-selling and most influential newspaper.

In 2012, Wisconsin had 28 daily newspapers. Two publications had circulations that were among the top 100 in the United States in 2011: the *Milwaukee Journal Sentinel* (194,436 daily, 333,999 Sunday) and the *Wisconsin State Journal* (87,629 daily, 119,382 Sunday). Because of the prevalence of online news sources, the daily circulation of these two papers had declined 33,000 and 14,000, respectively, since 2005.

37 Tourism, Travel, and Recreation

The Wisconsin Department of Tourism estimated tourism revenue of $16 billion in 2011, which was up from $14.8 billion in 2010. There were 95 million visitors to the state, compared to 84.5 million in 2010 and 77.6 million in 2009. The tourism industry directly and indirectly supports 1 in 13 jobs in the state.

The state has ample scenic attractions and outdoor recreational opportunities. In addition to the famous Wisconsin Dells gorge, visitors are attracted to the Cave of the Mounds at Blue Mounds, the sandstone cliffs along the Mississippi River, the lakes and forests of the Rhinelander and Minocqua areas in the north, and Lake Geneva, a resort, in the south.

Wisconsin has nearly 50 state parks, including Willow River State Park located on the western edge of the state. © JOSEPH SCOTT PHOTOGRAPHY/SHUTTERSTOCK.COM.

There are three national parks in Wisconsin: Apostle Islands National Lakeshore, on Lake Superior, and the St. Croix and Lower St. Croix scenic riverways. There are 48 state parks, covering 65,483 acres (26,193 hectares).

The Wisconsin State Fair takes place each August in West Allis. Other top annual events include the Lumberjack World Championships, the Cranberry Festival, and the Apple Festival.

38 Sports

Wisconsin has three major league teams: the Milwaukee Brewers of Major League Baseball, the Green Bay Packers of the National Football League, and the Milwaukee Bucks of the National Basketball Association. The Milwaukee Brewers had their franchise-best record in 2011, when they advanced to the National League Championship Series but lost in six games to the St. Louis Cardinals. As of 2012, the Green Bay Packers had won the Super Bowl four times, including in 2011 against the Pittsburgh Steelers. There are also numerous minor league baseball, basketball, and hockey teams in the state.

The University of Wisconsin (UW) Badgers compete in the Big Ten Conference. Badger ice hockey teams have won the National Collegiate Athletic Association (NCAA) championship six times. In football, they won the Rose Bowl in 1994, 1999, and 2000. The Badgers lost the 2012 Rose Bowl to the Oregon Ducks. The UW Badger's men's basketball team lost in the NCAA Final Four in 2000 but advanced to the Sweet Sixteen in 2003, 2008, 2011, and 2012.

Milwaukee is the site of the Greater Milwaukee Open in professional golf. Winter sporting events include ski jumping tournaments in Iola, Middleton, and Wetsby; the World Championship Snowmobile Derby in Eagle River in January; and the American Birkebeiner Cross-Country Race, the largest cross-country ski marathon in North America.

39 Famous Wisconsinites

Wisconsinites who have won prominence as federal judicial or executive officers include Jeremiah Rusk (b. Ohio, 1830–1893), a Wisconsin governor selected as the first head of the Agriculture Department in 1889; Melvin Laird (b. Nebraska, 1922–1992), a congressman who served as secretary of defense from 1969 to 1973; and William Rehnquist (1924–2005), named to the Supreme Court in 1971 and the 16th chief justice from 1986 to 2005.

Joseph R. McCarthy (1908–1957) won attention in the Senate and throughout the nation for his anti-Communist crusade. William Proxmire (b. Illinois, 1915–2005), a Democrat, succeeded McCarthy in the Senate and eventually chaired the powerful Senate Banking Committee.

Wisconsin was the birthplace of several Nobel Prize winners, including Herbert S. Gasser (1888–1963), who shared a 1944 Nobel Prize for research into nerve impulses; John Bardeen (1908–1991), who shared the physics award in 1956 for his contribution to the development of the transistor; and Herbert A.

Simon (1916–2001), who won the 1978 prize in economics.

Thornton Wilder (1897–1975), a novelist and playwright, heads the list of literary figures born in the state. He is best known for *The Bridge of San Luis Rey* (1927), *Our Town* (1938), and *The Skin of Our Teeth* (1942), each of which won a Pulitzer Prize. Hamlin Garland (1860–1940), a novelist and essayist, was also a native, as was the poet Ella Wheeler Wilcox (1850–1919). The novelist Edna Ferber (b. Michigan, 1887–1968) spent her early life in the state. Laura Ingalls Wilder (1867–1957), author of *Little House on the Prairie,* was born in Wisconsin.

Harry Houdini, the master escape artist, was born in Budapest, Hungary, but spent his childhood in Wisconsin.
© LORDPRICE COLLECTION / ALAMY.

Wisconsin is the birthplace of architect Frank Lloyd Wright (1869–1959) and the site of his famous Taliesin estate (Spring Green). The artist Georgia O'Keeffe (1887–1986) was born in Sun Prairie.

Wisconsin natives who have distinguished themselves in the performing arts include Spencer Tracy (1900–1967), Orson Welles (1915–1985), Chris Noth (1954–), Mark Ruffalo (1967–), Tyne Daly (1946–), Heather Graham (1970–), and Tony Shalhoub (1953–). Pianist and entertainer Liberace (1919–1987) was born in West Allis. Steve Miller (1943–) of the Steve Miller Band is from Milwaukee. Comedian Chris Farley (1964–1997) was born and raised in Madison. Magician and escape artist Harry Houdini (Ehrich Weiss, b. Hungary, 1874–1926) was raised in the state.

Speed-skater Eric Heiden (1958–), a five-time Olympic gold medalist in 1980, was born in Madison. First female Indycar Series winner Danica Patrick (1982–) was born in Beloit. Dallas Cowboys quarterback Tony Romo (1982–) was born in San Diego but raised in Burlington, Wisconsin.

40 Bibliography

BOOKS

Allen, Terese, and Bobbie Malone. *The Flavor of Wisconsin for Kids.* Madison, WI: Wisconsin Historical Society Press, 2012.

Blashfield, Jean F. *Wisconsin.* New York: Children's Books, 2007.

Bristow, M. J. *State Songs of America.* Westport, CT: Greenwood Press, 2000.

Hart, Joyce. *Wisconsin,* 2nd ed. New York: Marshall Cavendish Benchmark, 2006.

Hintz, Martin. *Wisconsin, Off the Beaten Path,* 10th ed. Guilford, CT: GPP Travel, 2012.

Janik, Erika. *A Short History of Wisconsin.* Madison, WI: Wisconsin Historical Society Press, 2010.

McAuliffe, Emily. *Wisconsin Facts and Symbols.* Rev. ed. Mankato, MN: Capstone, 2003.

WEB SITES

"Economy at a Glance: Wisconsin." *US Bureau of Labor Statistics.* http://www.bls.gov/eag/eag.wi.htm (accessed on November 16, 2012).

"Endangered Species Program." *US Fish & Wildlife Service.* http://www.fws.gov/endangered/ (accessed on November 16, 2012).

"State & County QuickFacts: Wisconsin." *US Bureau of the Census.* http://quickfacts.census.gov/qfd/states/55000.html (accessed on November 16, 2012).

Wisconsin Department of Tourism. http://www.travelwisconsin.com (accessed on November 16, 2012).

Wisconsin Historical Society. http://www.wisconsinhistory.org (accessed on November 16, 2012).

Wisconsin.gov: State of Wisconsin. http://www.wisconsin.gov/state/index.html (accessed on November 16, 2012).

Wyoming

State of Wyoming

ORIGIN OF STATE NAME: Derived from the Native American words *maugh-wau-wa-ma,* meaning "large plains."

NICKNAME: The Equality State; The Cowboy State.

CAPITAL: Cheyenne.

ENTERED UNION: 10 July 1890 (44th).

OFFICIAL SEAL: A female figure holding the banner "Equal Rights" stands on a pedestal between pillars topped by lamps symbolizing the light of knowledge. Two male figures flank the pillars, on which are draped banners that proclaim "Livestock," "Grain," "Mines," and "Oil." At the bottom is a shield with an eagle, star, and Roman numerals XLIV, flanked by the dates 1869 and 1890. The whole is surrounded by the words "Great Seal of the State of Wyoming."

FLAG: A blue field with a white inner border and a red outer border (symbolizing, respectively, the sky, purity, and the Native Americans) surrounds a bison with the state seal branded on its side.

MOTTO: Equal Rights.

SONG: "Wyoming."

FLOWER: Indian paintbrush.

TREE: Cottonwood.

ANIMAL: Bison.

BIRD: Western meadowlark.

FISH: Cutthroat trout.

GEM: Jade.

FOSSIL: Knightia.

COIN: Golden Sacajawea Dollar.

SPORT: Rodeo.

INSECT: Sheridan's Green Hairstreak Butterfly.

DINOSAUR: Triceratops.

LEGAL HOLIDAYS: New Year's Day, 1 January; birthday of Martin Luther King Jr. and Wyoming Equality Day, 3rd Monday in January; Presidents' Day, 3rd Monday in February; Memorial Day, last Monday in May; Independence Day, 4 July; Labor Day, 1st Monday in September; Veterans' Day, 11 November; Thanksgiving Day, 4th Thursday in November; Christmas Day, 25 December. Special observances are made on Arbor Day, last Monday in April; Native American Day, 2nd Friday in May; Juneteenth, 3rd Saturday in June; birthday of Nellie Tayloe Ross, 29 November; Pearl Harbor Remembrance Day, 7 December; Wyoming Day, 10 December.

TIME: 5 a.m. MST = noon GMT.

1 Location and Size

Located in the Rocky Mountain region of the northwestern United States, Wyoming ranks

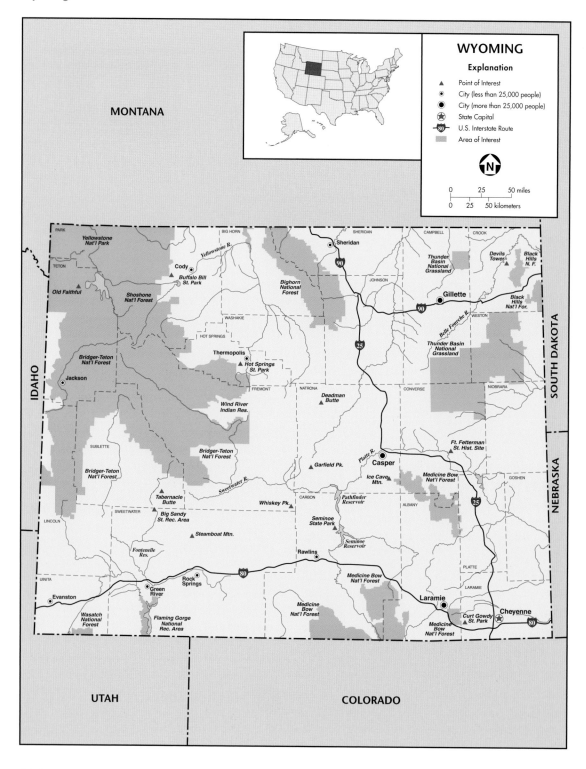

ninth in size among the 50 states. The total area of Wyoming is 97,809 square miles (253,325 square kilometers), of which land comprises 96,989 square miles (251,201 square kilometers) and inland water 820 square miles (2,124 square kilometers). The state has a maximum east–west extension of 365 miles (587 kilometers). Its extreme distance from north to south is 265 miles (426 kilometers). The state's boundary length is 1,269 miles (2,042 kilometers).

2 Topography

The eastern third of Wyoming forms part of the Great Plains; the remainder belongs to the Rocky Mountains. Extending diagonally across the state from northwest to south is the Continental Divide, which separates the generally eastward-flowing drainage system of North America from the westward-flowing drainage of the Pacific states.

Gannett Peak, in western Wyoming, at 13,804 feet (4,210 meters), is the highest point in the state. The lowest point in the state, 3,099 feet (945 meters), occurs in the northeast, on the Belle Fourche River.

Wyoming's largest lake, Yellowstone, lies in the heart of Yellowstone National Park. In Grand Teton National Park to the south are two smaller lakes, Jackson and Jenny. Major rivers include the Green, Yellowstone, Big Horn, Powder, Snake, Belle Fourche, and Cheyenne.

3 Climate

Wyoming is generally semiarid with localized desert conditions. Daily temperatures in Cheyenne range from 15°F (-9°C) to 38°F (3°C) in

The Grand Tetons offer spectacular scenery in Wyoming. In the foreground is the T. A. Moulton Barn, which is part of Mormon Row. The barn with its scenic backdrop is popular with photographers. © EASTVILLAGE IMAGES/SHUTTERSTOCK.COM.

January and from 54°F (12°C) to 83°F (28°C) in July. The record low temperature, -66°F (-54°C), was set on 9 February 1933 at Riverside. The record high, 114°F (46°C), occurred at Basin on 12 July 1900.

The average annual precipitation in Cheyenne is 14.5 inches (36 centimeters). The average annual snowfall in Cheyenne is 51.2 inches (130 centimeters).

4 Plants and Animals

Wyoming has more than 2,000 species of ferns, conifers, and flowering plants. Prairie grasses dominate the eastern third of the state, while desert shrubs (primarily sagebrush) cover the Great Basin in the west. Rocky Mountain forests consist largely of pine, spruce, and fir. Game mammals include the mule deer, elk, and moose. The jackrabbit and antelope are plentiful. Wild turkey and sage grouse are leading game birds. There are 78 species of fish, of which rainbow trout is the favorite game fish.

In 2012, there were four Wyoming plant species on the US Fish and Wildlife Service's list of threatened or endangered species. These were the Colorado butterfly plant, Ute ladies' tresses, blowout penstemon, and desert yellowhead. That year, there were six Wyoming animal species listed as threatened or endangered. These were the Preble's meadow jumping mouse, the Wyoming toad, the grizzly bear, the Kendall Warm Springs dace, the black-footed ferret, and the Canada lynx.

In 2011, the US Fish and Wildlife Service, together with the Wyoming Game and Fish Commission, removed the gray wolf from the endangered animal listing for the state. Evidence showed that gray wolf populations were thriving, although a full state wolf management plan had yet to be approved by the state government. In 2012, similar plans were made to remove the grizzly bear from the state endangered species list, due to their prevalence (and the increased number of attacks on people) in Yellowstone Park. In 2012, wolf hunting was allowed in the state for the first time since 1974.

5 Environmental Protection

The state's principal environmental concerns are conservation of scarce water resources and preservation of air quality. The Department of Environmental Quality, which was established in 1973 and reorganized in 1992, enforces measures to prevent pollution of Wyoming's surface water and groundwater and administers 21 air-monitoring sites to maintain air quality.

By 2010, the Wyoming Department of Environmental Quality was dealing with abandoned mining lands, build permits, drinking water standards, and a number of various energy concerns. Wyoming coal producers pay a reclamation fee of 35 cents per ton of surface mined coal to help reclaim such environments after mines are closed.

In 2012, there were two sites listed on the US Environmental Agency's National Priorities List of Superfund sites. These were the F.E. Warren Air Force Base in Cheyenne and Mystery Bridge Road/US Highway 20 in Evansville.

6 Population

Wyoming has one of the lowest population densities in the United States (5.85 people per square mile/2.26 per square kilometer), and ranks with

Alaska, Montana, and similar sparsely populated areas that have a large number of small, rural towns. Its estimated population in 2011 was 568,158. About 23.7% of the population was under the age of 18, while 12.7% was over the age of 65. The median age was 36.8 years. The largest cities in the state in 2011 were Cheyenne (population 60,096), Casper (55,988), and Laramie (31,312). Just 30% of the population lived in urban areas in 2010.

7 Ethnic Groups

In 2010, about 90.7% of the population of Wyoming were Caucasian, and 8.9% were of Hispanic descent. (Hispanics can be of any race.) Around 2.4% of residents were American Indians and Alaska Natives. About 0.8% of the population was African American and 0.8% were Asian Americans. Many members of the population cite German (nearly 30%), English, and Irish (around 15% each) ancestry.

8 Languages

Generally, Wyoming English is North Midland with some South Midland elements, especially along the Nebraska border. In 2011, 93.6% of the population spoke only English at home; 4.8% spoke Spanish; 0.6% spoke another Indo-European language; and 0.6% spoke an Asian or Pacific Islander language.

9 Religions

The religiously active population in Wyoming is split between Protestants, Catholics, and Mormons. According to the Pew Forum on Religion & Public Life, in 2008 some 26% of

Wyoming Population Profile

Total population per Census 2010:	563,626
Population change, 2006–10:	9.4%
Hispanic or Latino†:	8.9%
Population by race	
One race:	97.8%
White:	90.7%
Black or African American:	0.8%
American Indian/Alaska Native:	2.4%
Asian:	0.8%
Native Hawaiian/Pacific Islander:	0.1%
Some other race:	3.0%
Two or more races:	2.2%

Population by Age Group, Census 2010

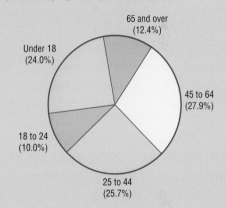

Major Cities by Population, 2011 Estimates

City	Population	% change 2005–11
Cheyenne	60,096	7.8
Casper	55,988	8.2
Laramie	31,312	20.2
Gillette	29,389	29.6
Rock Springs	23,229	23.7
Sheridan	17,517	7.2
Green River	12,622	7.1
Evanston	12,282	7.2
Riverton	10,867	15.2
Jackson	9,710	5.4

Notes: †A person of Hispanic or Latino origin may be of any race. NA indicates that data are not available. Percentages may not equal 100 due to rounding.

SOURCE: U.S. Census Bureau. Census 2010 and Population Estimates. www.census.gov/ (accessed July 2012).

Wyoming Population by Race
CENSUS 2010

This table shows the number of people who are of one, two, or three or more races. For those claiming two races, the number of people belonging to the various categories is listed. The U.S. government conducts a census of the population every 10 years.

	Number	Percent
Total population	563,626	100.0
One race	551,265	97.8
Two races	11,770	2.1
White *and* Black or African American	1,900	0.3
White *and* American Indian/Alaska Native	4,466	0.8
White *and* Asian	1,737	0.3
White *and* Native Hawaiian/Pacific Islander	298	0.1
White *and* some other race	2,498	0.4
Black or African American *and* American Indian/Alaska Native	121	—
Black or African American *and* Asian	61	—
Black or African American *and* Native Hawaiian/Pacific Islander	11	—
Black or African American *and* some other race	138	—
American Indian/Alaska Native *and* Asian	50	—
American Indian/Alaska Native *and* Native Hawaiian/Pacific Islander	20	—
American Indian/Alaska Native *and* some other race	232	—
Asian *and* Native Hawaiian/Pacific Islander	100	—
Asian *and* some other race	96	—
Native Hawaiian/Pacific Islander *and* some other race	42	—
Three or more races	591	0.1

SOURCE: U.S. Census Bureau. Census 2010. www.census/gov/ (accessed July 2012). A dash (—) indicates that the percent is less than 0.1.

Wyoming and Montana residents (they were counted together in the survey) identified as Evangelical Protestants; 21% were affiliated with mainline Protestant churches; 23% were Roman Catholic; 5% were Mormons; 2% were Jehovah's Witnesses; and 1% were Buddhist. No other religion had more than 0.5% of the population. Around 20% of the state's residents were unaffiliated with any religious organization.

10 Transportation

Wyoming had 28,105 miles (45,231 kilometers) of public roads in 2008. In 2009, there were 4 freight railroads, including 2 Class I freight railroads, in the state. Wyoming is served chiefly by the Burlington Northern/Santa Fe and Union Pacific railroads. That year, there were 1,886 miles (3,035 kilometers) of freight railroad track in the state. There is no Amtrak service to Wyoming.

In 2009, there were 404,489 licensed drivers in Wyoming. That year, there were 255,000 automobiles, 31,000 motorcycles, and 384,000 trucks registered in the state. The state had about 17,735 miles driven per capita for 2009, the highest ratio in the nation at that time. There were 15,278 traffic crashes in 2009. The Wyoming Department of Transportation had total revenue of more than $654 million the same year, bolstered by the federal economic stimulus bills passed that year. By 2012, the state had a $3.3 billion funding deficit for its transportation system, with many bridges and roadways in need of repair.

As of 2009, there were 93 airports and 26 heliports in the state. The largest airport was Jackson Hole Airport. Wyoming airports had 402,030 total passenger enplanements in 2009.

11 History

The first noted explorer of Wyoming was François Louis Verendrye in the early 1740s, who entered the territory as he explored pelt-trading options. Another exploration of the area was made by American fur trader John Colter, who traversed the northwestern part of the state in 1807–08, probably crossing what is now Yellowstone Park. After Colter, trappers and fur traders crisscrossed Wyoming.

Between 1840 and 1867, thousands of Americans crossed Wyoming on the Oregon Trail, bound for Oregon or California. Very few, however, settled in this harsh region. The event that brought population as well as territorial status to Wyoming was the coming of the Union Pacific Railroad. In 1868, Wyoming was organized as a territory; in the following year, 1869, Wyoming became the first territory or state that allowed women to vote. (Women did not receive the right to vote nationally until 1920.)

Wyoming became a center for cattle ranchers and foreign investors who hoped to make a fortune from free grass and the high price of cattle. The struggle between the large landowners and small ranchers culminated in the so-called Johnson County War of 1891–92.

Statehood Wyoming became a state in 1890, but growth remained slow. Attempts at farming proved unsuccessful in this high, arid region, and Wyoming to this day remains a sparsely settled ranching state. What growth has occurred has been primarily through the minerals industry, especially the development of coal, oil, and natural gas resources during the 1970s national energy crisis. However, the worldwide oil glut in the early 1980s slowed the growth of the state's energy industries.

In 1984, the growth of the state's nonfuel mineral industry slowed as well. Since then, the state has looked to tourism as an effective means of expanding its economy. In the summer of

Yellowstone National Park draws in many tourists every year. Of particular interest is Old Faithful geyser, one of the most popular geothermal attractions in the United States. © LEE PRINCE/SHUTTERSTOCKCOM.

1988, forest fires raged across Yellowstone National Park, devastating about one-third of the park's area.

Wyoming's small towns were struggling to keep their young people from moving away. In 2000, Wyoming's population was aging faster than any other state: there were more people over age 35 than 34 or under.

By the end of the first decade of the 21st century, the state was attempting to draw in more business through tourism, but was struggling with issues such as transportation and energy. The highways of Wyoming, many of them rural, were old and needed widespread repair, but the state budget did not have the necessary funding. Part of this was due to energy losses. In the early 2000s, the state had experienced an energy boom as large shale deposits were discovered and mined, bringing in large amounts of revenue for the state. However, shale mining for natural gas quickly grew complicated in the face of new regulations, and companies began to pull out of the area until, by the start of the 2010s, natural gas prices had fallen, the energy boom was over, and Wyoming had used up most of its extra funds.

12 State Government

The Wyoming legislature consists of a 30-member senate and a 60-member house of representatives. Senators are elected to four-year terms and representatives for two-year terms. Heading the executive branch are the following elected officials: the governor, secretary of state, auditor, treasurer, comptroller, commissioner of finance, and superintendent of public instruction. There is no lieutenant governor. The governor is restricted to two terms, serving no more than 8 out of any 16 years. A bill passed by the legislature becomes law if signed by the governor, if left unsigned by the governor for three days while the legislature is in session (or 15 days after it has adjourned), or if passed over the governor's veto by two-thirds of the members of each house.

In 2012, the governor of the state was Matt Mead, in office until 2015. The president of the senate was Jim Anderson, and the speaker of the house was Edward Buchanan. All three were Republicans.

In 2010, Wyoming legislators were paid $150 each day of work, plus $109 per diem. That year, the governor of Wyoming was paid

Wyoming Governors: 1890–2013		
1890	Francis Emroy Warren	Republican
1890–1893	Amos Walker Barber	Republican
1893–1895	John Eugene Osborne	Democrat
1895–1899	William Alford Richards	Republican
1899–1903	DeForest Richards	Republican
1903–1905	Fenimore Chatterton	Republican
1905–1911	Bryant Butler Brooks	Republican
1911–1915	Joseph Maull Carey	Republican
1915–1917	John Benjamin Kendrick	Democrat
1917–1919	Frank L. Houx	Democrat
1919–1923	Robert Davis Carey	Republican
1923–1924	William Bradford Ross	Democrat
1924–1925	Franklin Earl Lucas	Republican
1925–1927	Nellie Tayloe Ross	Democrat
1927–1931	Frank Collins Emerson	Republican
1931–1933	Alonzo Monroe Clark	Republican
1933–1939	Leslie Andrew Miller	Democrat
1939–1943	Nels Hanson Smith	Republican
1943–1949	Lester Calloway Hunt	Democrat
1949–1951	Arthur Griswold Crane	Republican
1951–1953	Frank Aloysius Barrett	Republican
1953–1955	Clifford Joy Rogers	Republican
1955–1959	Milward Lee Simpson	Republican
1959–1961	John Joseph Hickey	Democrat
1961–1963	Jack Robert Gage	Democrat
1963–1967	Clifford Peter Hansen	Republican
1967–1975	Stanley Knapp Hathaway	Republican
1975–1987	Edgar J. Herschler	Democrat
1987–1995	Michael John Sullivan	Democrat
1995–2003	Jim Geringer	Republican
2003–2011	Dave Freudenthal	Democrat
2011–	Matt Mead	Republican

$105,000 a year, the 40th-highest gubernatorial salary in America.

13 Political Parties

The Republicans have dominated Wyoming politics at the federal and state level for many years. In 2012, the governor, both US senators (Mike Enzi and John Barrasso), and US representative Cynthia Lummis were Republicans. In the state house of representatives there were 50 Republicans and 10 Democrats in 2012, while the senate had 26 Republicans and 4 Democrats. That year, there were 12 women serving in the state house and 1 woman serving in the state senate.

In the 2004 presidential election, Republican George W. Bush took 68.8% of the vote, while Democratic challenger John Kerry took 29% of the vote. In the 2008 presidential election, the state voted for Republican

Wyoming Presidential Vote by Major Political Parties, 1948–2012

Year	Wyoming Winner	Democrat	Republican
1948	*Truman (D)	52,354	47,947
1952	*Eisenhower (R)	47,934	81,049
1956	*Eisenhower (R)	49,554	74,573
1960	Nixon (R)	63,331	77,451
1964	*Johnson (D)	80,718	61,998
1968	*Nixon (R)	45,173	70,927
1972	*Nixon (R)	44,358	100,464
1976	Ford (R)	62,239	92,717
1980	*Reagan (R)	49,427	110,700
1984	*Reagan (R)	53,370	133,241
1988	*Bush (R)	67,113	106,867
1992	Bush (R)	68,160	79,347
1996	Dole (R)	77,934	105,388
2000	*Bush, G. W. (R)	60,481	147,947
2004	*Bush, G. W. (R)	70,776	167,629
2008	McCain (R)	82,868	164,958
2012	Romney (R)	69,286	170,962

*Won US presidential election.

Independent candidate Ross Perot received 51,263 votes in 1992 and 25,928 votes in 1996.

John McCain by 64.78% to Democrat Barack Obama's 32.54%. In 2012, the state again supported the Republican challenger (Mitt Romney) over President Obama. As of July 2012, there were 215,113 voters registered in the state.

14 Local Government

As of 2010, Wyoming was subdivided into 23 counties, 99 municipalities, and 61 public school districts. It also had 549 special districts and authorities (2007 figure). County officials include a clerk, treasurer, assessor, sheriff, attorney, three commissioners, and from one to five county judges. Municipalities may decide their own form of government, including mayor-council and council-manager. Special districts include cemetery districts, county improvement districts, drainage districts, and fire protection districts, all areas under frequent change. In 2011, there were 46,085 full-time and 17,970 part-time state and local government employees in Wyoming.

15 Judicial System

Wyoming's judicial branch consists of a supreme court with a chief justice and four other justices, a district court in every county, and justice of the peace courts. District courts try felony criminal cases, large civil cases, juvenile cases, and probate cases. A court reporter is assigned to each district court. The supreme court, located in Cheyenne, is a final arbiter for appeals from the district courts. The Wyoming court system undertakes independent projects to promote justice and knowledge in the state, including the Children's Justice Project, which had a conference in mid-2012 to discuss child welfare, neglect, and abuse.

In 2010, Wyoming had a violent crime rate of 195.9 reported incidents per 100,000 people. The murder and nonnegligent manslaughter rate was 1.4 incidents per 100,000 inhabitants; forcible rape, 29.1; aggravated assault, 151.9; and property crime, 2,461.6. That year, there were 3,663 prisoners in the state's prisons and jails. Wyoming has the death penalty, but as of 2012 had only executed one person since 1976 (that execution occurred in 1992). As of 2012, there was one person on death row in the state.

16 Migration

In 2010, 96.9% of the population of Wyoming was native to the state and 3.1% was foreign born. Out of the foreign-born population, 35.5% were naturalized US citizens, while 64.5% were not US citizens. Approximately 20,000 people in the state had been born outside the United States in 2010. Most had entered before 2000, but nearly 41% had entered the state after 2000. Although some 58% of the foreign-born population was from Latin America, both Europe and Asia had strong contingents as well.

Between 2009 and 2010, the total population (age one and older) of Wyoming increased by 1,899, due to the net domestic in-migration of natives (777), the net domestic out-migration of immigrants (-917), and the arrival from abroad of natives (1,035) and immigrants (1,004). Of the total foreign-born population in Wyoming in 2010, 1.9% was from Africa, 18.4% was from Asia, 16% was from Europe, and 56.9% was from Latin America. The top three countries of birth of the foreign born in Wyoming in 2010 were Mexico (42.7%), the Philippines (8.6%), and Canada (5.4%). In comparison, the top three countries of birth in 1990 were Mexico (26.3%), the United Kingdom (13.3%), and Germany (11.9%).

17 Economy

The economic life of Wyoming is largely sustained by agriculture (chiefly feed grains and livestock), mining (including petroleum and gas production), and tourism. In the early 2000s, an energy boom and the growth of the natural gas industry provided continuing capital for the state, but by the 2010s the recession had slowed down economic growth for the state. In 2010, Wyoming's gross state product (GSP) was $38.2 billion, ranking the state 48th in the nation. Per capita GSP was $63,667 that year, ranking the state sixth. In 2010, there were 20,231 private nonfarm establishments and 45,614 nonemployer establishments in the state.

18 Income

Per capita personal income (including nonmonetary income) in 2011 was $47,301, ranking Wyoming sixth in the nation. For the period 2008–2010, the median annual household income in Wyoming was $53,236, compared to the national average of $50,022. In 2011, 11.3% of the state's residents lived below the federal poverty level, compared with 15.9% nationwide.

19 Industry

The primary industries of Wyoming are mineral extraction, tourism, and agriculture. The mineral extraction industry brought in $14.5 billion in tax dollars in 2007 alone, followed by $1 billion in tax revenue for tourism. While it does not have such a strong effect on state decisions, agriculture is a mainstay of Wyoming business. In 2007, agricultural products such as livestock and hay had a total value of $1.02 billion. In the retail and restaurant trade, sales in 2010 equaled $9.23 billion.

20 Labor

In 2010, the average annual pay for a worker in Wyoming was $41,963, making it the 29th-highest-paying state in the nation. The minimum wage was one of the lowest, at $5.15 per hour.

In August 2012, the civilian labor force in Wyoming numbered 306,300, with approximately 17,400 workers unemployed, yielding an unemployment rate of 5.7%, compared to the national average of 8.1% for the same period. Those employed in nonfarm wage and salaried jobs that same month included: 27,600 in mining and logging; 20,200 in construction; 8,800 in manufacturing; 53,400 in trade, transportation, and utilities; 10,900 in financial activities; 17,400 in professional and business services; 27,200 in education and health services; 34,200 in leisure and hospitality; and 75,300 in government.

In 2011, 21,000 of Wyoming's employed wage and salary workers were members of unions, representing 8.4% of those so employed. The national average was 13%.

21 Agriculture

In 2010, Wyoming had 11,000 farms and ranches, with an average of 2,745 acres per farm. On average these are very large numbers, due to the largely rural nature of much of the state. In 2007, 48.6% of the state was farmland. Final crop output for 2011 was $356.7 million, out of a total agricultural sector output of $1.9 billion. Hay, at farm receipts of $148 million, was the leading crop in 2011, followed by sugar beets, with receipts of $59.6 million, and corn, with receipts of $41.8 million. Feeds, seeds, feed grains, and wheat products were also key crops.

Top crop exports in 2011 included feeds and fodders, with $63.1 million in exports; seeds, with $17.2 million in exports; feed grains and products, with $14.3 million in exports; and wheat and wheat products, with $12.3 million in exports. Major agricultural counties were Goshen, Laramie, Platte, Fremont, and Park counties.

22 Domesticated Animals

In 2011, Wyoming had 1.3 million cattle and calves, along with 365,000 sheep and 99,000 hogs and pigs. Final animal output came to $1.16 billion in 2011. Cattle and calves brought in farm receipts of $863.8 million, followed by hogs, with receipts of $117.3 million. Live animal and meat exports were valued at $9.8 million that year.

23 Fishing

There is no important commercial fishing in Wyoming. Fishing is largely recreational, and fish hatcheries and fish-planting programs keep the streams well stocked. The state also has thousands of lakes and reservoirs suitable for fishing. Some of the most highly recommended rivers include Bear River, Big Horn River, and Encampment River. Popular lakes include the

Big Sandy Reservoir, the Deaver Reservoir, and Grassy Lake. Most species sought in the state are trout, such as the cutthroat, rainbow, or golden varieties. However, Kokanee salmon and mountain whitefish are also available. In 2012, a resident fishing license cost $24, while a non-resident license cost $92. Lake trout limits were six, while stream limits were three.

24 Forestry

Wyoming has 10,995,000 acres (4,450,000 hectares) of forested land, equal to 17.8% of the state's land area. Of this, 5,739,000 acres (2,323,000 hectares) are usable as commercial timberland. Ponderosa pine accounts for about 50% of the annual cut and lodgepole pine most of the rest. The remainder consists of Douglas fir, larch, Engelmann spruce, and other species.

The state has eight national forests. Big-horn National forest holds 1.1 million acres and sports the Cloud Peak Wilderness area. Black Hills National Forest spans eastern Wyoming and South Dakota. Bridger-Teton National Forest, the second-largest national forest outside of Alaska, has more than 3.4 million acres. Medicine Bow National Forest has more than a million acres and also includes grassland areas. Shoshone National Forest has more than 2.4 million acres and is a very popular spot for recreation and tourism. Caribou-Targhee National Forest is primarily in Idaho but extends into portions of Wyoming.

25 Mining

In 2011, Wyoming ranked 11th nationally in the value of nonfuel mineral production, with a value of $1.95 billion, 2.63% of the US total.

Wyoming ranked first in the nation in soda ash and bentonite production; the state also ranked highly in the production of gypsum. Major uses of Wyoming bentonite were as pet waste absorbent, drilling mud, pelletizing iron ore, in foundry sand, and as a waterproof sealant.

Wyoming also led the nation in soda ash production from the world's largest known resource of trona, a natural sodium carbonate-bicarbonate. Trona mined in Wyoming was used to produce soda ash, caustic soda, sodium sulfite, sodium bicarbonate, sodium cyanide, and calcined trona. Wyoming is also known to have deposits of gold and silver, diamonds, copper, and metals belonging to the platinum group.

26 Energy and Power

The Powder River Basin is the largest coal production area in the nation, accounting for 40% of all coal in the United States. Half the energy the state uses comes from coal products, followed by 21% from petroleum and 17% from natural gas. Renewable energy has only a small presence in the state.

Proven reserves in 2010 included 567 million barrels of crude oil; 35 trillion cubic feet of dry natural gas; 1 billion barrels of natural gas plant liquids (2008 figure); and 6.6 billion short tons of coal. Energy production in 2010 included 4.8 million barrels of crude oil; 2.3 trillion cubic feet of marketed natural gas; and 442.5 million short tons of coal.

As of June 2012, total net electricity generation was 3.76 million megawatt hours (MWh). Of this, 9,000 MWh was generated by petroleum-fired plants; 3.2 million MWh by coal-fired plants; 148,000 MWh by hydroelectric plants; and 301,000 MWh by other renewable sources.

In 2011, total energy spending on energy-efficiency programs reached $4.5 million, about 0.8% of all utility revenues. There are no mandatory statewide energy codes.

27 Commerce

In 2007, Wyoming made $6.3 billion in wholesale revenue. Total retail sales came to $8.9 million, with Laramie County coming in first. In 2008, there were 830 wholesale trade establishments and 2,862 retail trade establishments in the state. In 2011, exports amounted to $1.2 billion. Top exports included sodium bicarbonate and crude oil.

28 Public Finance

Wyoming's biennial budget is prepared by the governor and submitted to the state legislature at the beginning of each even-numbered calendar year. The fiscal year is from 1 July to 30 June.

Between 2001 and 2011, the state budget of Wyoming doubled in size, due in large part to the energy boom in the state. However, the recession beginning in 2008 caused the legislature to make several reductions in standard budgets for 2011 in order to control spending. On 8 March 2012, Governor Matt Mead signed a $3.2 billion budget bill that called for maintaining a flat level of state spending for fiscal years 2012 and 2013. The budget maintained spending for state agencies but also included a provision requiring agencies to present plans to cut their budgets by 4% in 2013 in response to falling natural gas prices. In 2012, Wyoming

The capitol building of Wyoming is in Cheyenne. A statue of women's rights activist Esther Hobart Morris in on the grounds. Morris was the first female justice of the peace in the United States. © CAITLIN MIRRA/SHUTTERSTOCK.COM.

had a total state debt of approximately $6.9 billion when calculated by adding the total of outstanding official debt, pension, and other postemployment benefits (OPEB) liabilities, Unemployment Trust Fund loans, and the 2013 state budget gap.

29 Taxation

The sales tax in Wyoming is 4%. Other taxes include those on cigarettes and gasoline, in addition to other taxes such as those on minerals. Wyoming has no personal or corporate income tax. Property taxes are based on local assessments, and agricultural land value is based on productivity instead of fair market value.

Wyoming collected $2.46 billion in state taxes in 2011. This included $284.3 million in property taxes, $987.2 million in sales taxes and gross receipts, $141 million in license taxes and fees, and $1 billion in other taxes. Per capita state tax collections were $4,333 in 2011, compared to a national per capita of $2,430, giving Wyoming the third-highest state tax burden that year.

30 Health

In 2011, Wyoming's infant mortality rate was 7.2 deaths per 1,000 live births. The overall death rate in 2009 was 772 per 100,000. There were 173 deaths per 100,000 residents from heart disease in 2009 and 168.3 deaths per 100,000 from cancers. There were 42.5 deaths per 100,000 from cerebrovascular diseases and 18.3 deaths per 100,000 from diabetes. In 2010, around 7.2% of the adult population had been diagnosed with diabetes, and 63.8% of adults were overweight or obese. Among Wyoming adults ages 18 and older, 19.5% were smokers in 2010, compared to the national rate of 17.2%. At the end of 2008, there were 224 people in Wyoming living with HIV/AIDS, less than 0.01% of the US total.

Wyoming's 24 community hospitals had about 3.5 beds per 100,000 in 2010. The average expense for community hospital care was $1,103 per inpatient day in 2010. In 2009, Wyoming had 187 physicians; in 2011 it had 845 registered nurses; and in 2007 it had 51 dentists per 100,000 residents. In 2010, 14% of Wyoming's residents lacked health insurance.

31 Housing

Housing in Wyoming went through several transitions in the early 2000s, as urban areas saw high levels of growth due to new economic opportunities (especially in areas bolstered by the energy industry). This led to high demand and housing shortages. However, the housing market collapse and the recession beginning in 2008 reversed this trend and brought the housing market nearly to a standstill. In 2010, Wyoming issued 2,298 residential building permits.

In 2011, there were an estimated 265,554 housing units, 83.8% (222,539) of which were occupied and 70.6% (157,223) of which were owner-occupied. About 67.2% (178,546) of all units were single-family, detached homes; 36,337 (13.7%) were mobile homes. Utility gas and electricity were the most common energy sources for heating. It was estimated that 1,336 (0.6%) units lacked complete plumbing facilities and 2,220 (1%) lacked complete kitchen facilities.

The median home value in 2011 was $179,900. The median monthly cost for mortgage owners was $1,269, while renters paid a median of $759.

32 Education

In 2010, 92.3% of the population older than 25 were high school graduates, and 24.1% had a bachelor's degree. The student-to-teacher ratio in schools in 2009 was 12.5, and the high school graduation rate was 80.4%. There were 393 public schools, with more than 85,000 students.

Rodeos are popular in Wyoming. © SASCHA BURKARD/
SHUTTERSTOCK.COM.

In 2012, Wyoming had nine degree-granting institutions and seven community colleges. The state controls and funds the University of Wyoming in Laramie, as well as the seven community colleges. The University of Wyoming had 13,476 students in 2009 and offered 190 areas of study.

33 Arts

The Grand Teton Music Festival (formerly the Jackson Hole Fine Arts Festival) was established in 1962 and has continued to present an annual program of symphonic and chamber music performed by some of the nation's top artists. The Cheyenne Civic Center serves as a venue for a variety of musical and theatrical groups, including the Cheyenne Symphony Orchestra. Cheyenne is also home to the Cheyenne Little Theater Players, a community theater group that marked its 80th anniversary in 2010.

The Wyoming Council on the Arts funds local activities and organizations in the visual and performing arts, including painting, music, theater, and dance. The Wyoming Council for the Humanities has an active roster of speakers and ongoing history programs, and it also sponsors a Native American Language Preservation program.

34 Libraries and Museums

In 2011, the public libraries of Wyoming were visited about 3.8 million times. The state spent about $52.09 per capita on library services and provided nearly 2.8 million books and audio materials. Public libraries added 29 Internet access computers in 2011 for a total of 805. In total, more than 10,000 child programs were hosted, and employees numbered 655.

The state has several notable historical sites and museums, including the Wyoming State Museum in Cheyenne; the Buffalo Bill Historical Center (Cody), which exhibits paintings by Frederic Remington; and the anthropological, geological, and art museums of the University of Wyoming at Laramie.

35 Communications

In 2010, 74.4% of the population had access to the Internet at home and 70.5% had access to broadband. In 2011, Wyoming became the first state to use Google Apps for all its government administrative needs. By 2012, text messaging was prohibited for drivers, but handheld cell phone use was still allowed.

In 2012, there were 188 radio stations and 6 television stations in the state.

36 Press

In 2012, there were some 19 newspapers in the state, including the *Mini*, of Buffalo, the *Campbell County Observer*, and the *Bighorn Mountain Express*. The largest circulation belonged to the *Casper Star-Tribune*. These papers, along with many others, had developed a strong online presence, and digital news publications, such as *Wyoming Webworks News*, were on the rise in the state.

37 Tourism, Travel, and Recreation

Along with mining, tourism is a key industry for the state, which features many famous parks and natural destinations. In 2008, Wyoming had more than 2.5 million visitors to its state parks and historic sites, a 9% increase from 2007. Yellowstone had the most visitors, followed by Grand Teton.

There are two national parks in Wyoming (Yellowstone and Grand Teton) and eight national forests. Yellowstone National Park is the oldest and largest national park in the United States, featuring some 3,000 geysers and hot springs, including the celebrated Old Faithful. The thermal waters of Yellowstone are popular with tourists from the United States and across the globe.

Just to the south of Yellowstone is Grand Teton National Park with its majestic peaks

Devils Tower National Monument, shown here with the red glow of sunset, was featured in several movies, including Steven Spielberg's Close Encounters of the Third Kind.
© WILDNERDPIX/SHUTTERSTOCK.COM.

and scenic lakes. Adjacent to Grand Teton is the National Elk Refuge, the feeding range of the continent's largest known herd of elk. Devils Tower and Fossil Butte are highly visited national monuments in the state.

Among the state's national historic sites is Fort Laramie, which was among the most important forts on the Oregon Trail. In Guernsey are found some of the best-preserved examples of trail ruts made by wagons traveling the Oregon-California Trail in the 1800s. The many wagons that passed over the soft sandstone left ruts that in some places measure 5-feet (1.5 meters) deep.

The Fort Bridger State Museum and Historic Site, named after famous mountain man and trapper Jim Bridger, provides interpretive displays. The city of Thermopolis offers the Wyoming Dinosaur Center with more than 30 skeletons. The Buffalo Bill Historical Center in

Cody has displays on William F. Cody's Wild West Show. Its Gallery of Western Art showcases a wide range of artwork, from landscapes and wildlife to Native Americans and cowboys. The Cody Firearms Museum, also at the center, displays American-made guns. Also of interest is the Chinese Joss House Museum in Evanston that pays tribute to the many Chinese who lived in the area and worked on the railroads and in the mines, laundries, and stores.

The Wyoming State Fair is held each August in Douglas. Other top annual events include the International Pedigree Stage Stop Sled Dog Race, Woodchopper's Jamboree & Rodeo, Buffalo Bill's Wild West Days, 1838 Mountain Man Rendezvous, Cody Stampede, and Cheyenne Frontier Days.

38 Sports

There are no major league professional sports teams in Wyoming, and the state sport has officially been declared as rodeo. Participation sports in Wyoming are typically Western. Skills developed by ranch hands in herding cattle are featured at rodeos held throughout the state. Cheyenne Frontier Days is the largest of these rodeos. Skiing is also a major sport, with Jackson Hole being the largest, best-known resort.

In collegiate sports, the University of Wyoming competes in the Mountain West Conference.

39 Famous Wyomingites

Important federal officeholders from Wyoming include Willis Van Devanter (b. Indiana, 1859–1941), who served on the US Supreme Court from 1910 to 1937. Richard "Dick" Cheney (b. Nebraska, 1941–), Wyoming's US representative from 1979 to 1989 and the US secretary of defense from 1989 to 1992, was elected vice president on the Republican ticket with George W. Bush in 2000 and 2004. Nellie Tayloe Ross (b. Missouri, 1876–1977) became the first female governor of any state in 1925, serving later as director of the US Mint from 1933 to 1953.

Many of Wyoming's better-known individuals are associated with the frontier. William F. "Buffalo Bill" Cody (b. Iowa, 1846–1917)

Actor Harrison Ford is one of Wyoming's most well-known residents. He owns a large ranch near Jackson. © FEATUREFLASH / SHUTTERSTOCK.COM.

established the town of Cody. A number of outlaws made their headquarters in Wyoming. The most famous were "Butch Cassidy" (Robert Leroy Parker, b. Utah, 1866–1909?) and the "Sundance Kid" (Harry Longabaugh, 1863?–1909?). Wyoming's most famous entrepreneur was James Cash Penney (b. Missouri, 1875–1971), whose early experience with J.C. Penney department stores was in Wyoming. Jackson Pollack (1912–1956), known for his Impressionistic "all-over drip style" painting, was born in Cody.

Other famous people with Wyoming ties are famous sportscaster Curt Gowdy (1919–2006), who has a state park named after him near Cheyenne; nationally known attorney and author Gerry Spence (1929–); and actor Harrison Ford (1942–), who owns a large ranch near Jackson and has successfully used his private helicopter to help law enforcement locate several lost hikers.

40 Bibliography

BOOKS

Bristow, M. J. *State Songs of America.* Westport, CT: Greenwood Press, 2000.

Davis, John W. *Wyoming Range War: The Infamous Invasion of Johnson County.* Norman: University of Oklahoma Press, 2012.

DuBois, Muriel L. *Wyoming Facts and Symbols.* Rev. ed. Mankato, MN: Capstone, 2003.

Hanson-Harding, Alexandra. *Wyoming.* New York: Children's Press, 2009.

McCoy, Michael. *Wyoming, Off the Beaten Path,* 7th ed. Guilford, CT: GPP Travel, 2010.

Murray, Julie. *Wyoming.* Edina, MN: Abdo Publishing, 2006.

Prentzas, G.S. *Wyoming.* New York: Children's Press, 2009.

Thomas, William. *Wyoming.* Milwaukee, WI: Gareth Stevens, 2007.

WEB SITES

"Economy at a Glance: Wyoming." *US Bureau of Labor Statistics.* http://www.bls.gov/eag/eag.wy.htm (accessed on November 16, 2012).

"Endangered Species Program." *US Fish & Wildlife Service.* http://www.fws.gov/endangered/ (accessed on November 16, 2012).

"State & County QuickFacts: Wyoming." *US Bureau of the Census.* http://quickfacts.census.gov/qfd/states/56000.html (accessed on November 16, 2012).

"Wyoming 2012—Just the Facts." *State of Wyoming.* http://eadiv.state.wy.us/Wy_facts/facts2012.pdf (accessed on November 16, 2012).

Wyoming State Historical Society. http://www.wyshs.org/ (accessed on November 16, 2012).

"Wyoming's Official State Travel Website." *Wyoming Travel and Tourism.* www.wyomingtourism.org (accessed on November 16, 2012).

District of Columbia

ORIGIN OF STATE NAME: From "Columbia," a name commonly applied to the United States in the late 18th century, ultimately derived from Christopher Columbus.

OFFICIAL SEAL: In the background, the Potomac River separates the District of Columbia from the Virginia shore, over which the sun is rising. In the foreground, Justice, holding a wreath and a tablet with the word "Constitution," stands beside a statue of George Washington. At the left of Justice is the Capitol; to her right, an eagle and various agricultural products. Below is the District motto and the date 1871; above are the words "District of Columbia."

FLAG: The flag, based on George Washington's coat of arms, consists of three red stars above two horizontal red stripes on a white field.

MOTTO: *Justitia omnibus* (Justice for all).

FLOWER: American Beauty rose.

TREE: Scarlet oak.

BIRD: Wood thrush.

LEGAL HOLIDAYS: New Year's Day, 1 January; birthday of Martin Luther King Jr., 3rd Monday in January; Washington's Birthday, 3rd Monday in February; Emancipation Day, 16 April; Memorial Day, last Monday in May; Independence Day, 4 July; Labor Day, 1st Monday in September; Columbus Day, 2nd Monday in October; Veterans Day, 11 November; Thanksgiving Day, 4th Thursday in November; Christmas Day, 25 December.

TIME: 7 a.m. EST = noon GMT.

BECAME US CAPITAL: The Residence Act, passed by Congress on 16 July 1790, established the capital in the District of Columbia. The capital was first used officially when Congress opened its session on 17 November 1800.

 Location and Size

Located in the South Atlantic region of the United States, the District of Columbia has a total area of 68 square miles (177 square kilometers), of which land takes up 61 square miles (158 square kilometers) and inland water 7 square miles (11 square kilometers).

 Topography

The District of Columbia lies wholly within the Atlantic Coastal Plain. The major physical features are the Potomac River and its nearby

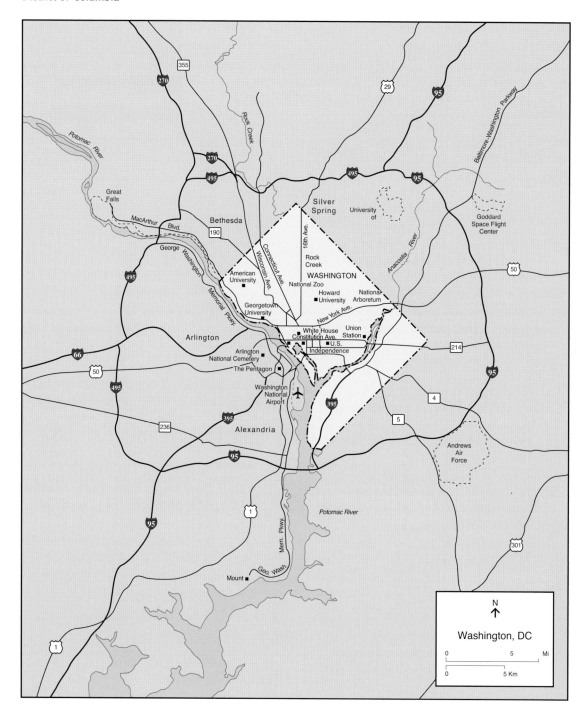

marshlands; the Anacostia River; Rock Creek; and the gentle hills of the north. The District's average elevation is about 150 feet (46 meters). The highest point, at 410 feet (125 meters), is in the northwest, a grassy knoll known as Reno Hill in Fort Reno Park, Tenleytown. The lowest point is the Potomac, just above sea level.

3 Climate

The climate of the nation's capital is characterized by chilly, damp winters and hot, humid summers. The mean average temperature is 58°F (14°C). Monthly averages range from lows of 29°F (-2°C) in January, the coldest month, to 71°F (22°C) in July, the warmest month; while average highs range from 43°F (6°C) in January to 88°F (32°C) in July. The record low, -15°F (-26°C), was set on 11 February 1899. The record high, 106°F (41°C), was set on 20 July 1930. Annual precipitation is an average of 39.74 inches (100 centimeters) annually during 1981–2000. Annual snowfall averages 14.5 inches (43 centimeters). The average humidity is 75% at 7 a.m. and 53% at 1 p.m.

4 Plants and Animals

Most of the original plant life of the District of Columbia was destroyed by urbanization. However, the District has long been known for its beautiful parks, which have about 1,800 varieties of flowering plants and 250 varieties of shrubs and trees. Boulevards are shaded by stately sycamores, pine and red oaks, American lindens, and black walnut trees. Famous among the introduced species are the flowering Japanese cherry trees around the Tidal Basin. Magnolia, dogwood, and gingko are also characteristic.

The District's animal life includes squirrels, cottontails, English sparrows, and starlings. In the early 21st century, the US Fish and Wildlife Service listed two species (Hay's Spring amphipod and the Eastern puma) as endangered and one species (the bald eagle) as threatened. The Eastern puma has since been declared extinct.

5 Environmental Protection

The Environmental Regulation Administration (ERA) administers district and federal laws, regulations, and mayoral initiatives governing the environment and natural resources of the District of Columbia and the surrounding metropolitan area. Its main duty is the protection of human health and the environment as they relate to pesticides, hazardous waste, underground storage tanks, water, air, soils, and fisheries programs. As of 2012, the Environmental Protection Agency's database listed one hazardous waste site on the national priorities list—the 71.5-acre Washington Navy Yard. The Navy Yard is the oldest continuously operated Navy facility in the United States and is contaminated largely by waste generated by ordinance production.

Air quality is generally good but can become hazardous in the summer months due to a build-up of ozone and particulate matter from vehicle emissions.

6 Population

In 2011, the District of Columbia had an estimated population of 617,996 residents. The population is 100% urban. The population density in 2010 was 9,857 persons per square mile. If considered as a state, the District would rank 50th in the nation, behind Wyoming. Considered as a city, the District ranked 24th in the nation in 2010. In 2011, the median age was 33.4 years old. That same year, of all residents, 11.4% were 65 years old or older, while 17% were under 18.

District of Columbia Population Profile

Total population per Census 2010:	601,723
Population change, 2006–10:	3.5%
Hispanic or Latino†:	9.1%
Population by race	
One race:	97.1%
White:	38.5%
Black or African American:	50.7%
American Indian/Alaska Native:	0.3%
Asian:	3.5%
Native Hawaiian/Pacific Islander:	0.1%
Some other race:	4.1%
Two or more races:	2.9%

Population by Age Group, Census 2010

Under 18 (16.8%)
65 and over (11.4%)
45 to 64 (23.2%)
18 to 24 (14.5%)
25 to 44 (34.1%)

Major Cities by Population, 2011 Estimates

City	Population	% change 2005–11
Washington	617,996	12.3

Notes: †A person of Hispanic or Latino origin may be of any race. NA indicates that data are not available. Percentages may not equal 100 due to rounding.

SOURCE: U.S. Census Bureau. Census 2010 and Population Estimates. www.census.gov/ (accessed July 2012).

7 Ethnic Groups

In the 2010 Census, African Americans were the largest ethnic or racial group in the District of Columbia, accounting for 50.7% of the population. Whites made up the next largest ethnic group, at 38.5% of the population. Hispanics (who can be of any race) made up 9.1% of the District's population. According to the 2010 Census, 13% of the District's residents were foreign born. In addition, there are many foreign-born residents attached to foreign embassies and missions, contributing to the District's ethnic diversity.

8 Languages

Many different dialects of English are spoken in the Washington, D.C., area. In 2011, 85.0% of all District of Columbia residents five years of age or older spoke only English at home. The most common non-English language spoken at home was Spanish, which was spoken at home by 7.2% of residents five years of age or older. Around 4.5% of the population spoke another Indo-European language, and 1.8% spoke an Asian or Pacific Islander language at home.

9 Religions

According to the Pew Forum on Religion & Public Life, in 2008 around 18% of the District's population were Roman Catholic. Mainline Protestants were next in numbers with around 20% of the population, while Evangelical and black Protestant traditions together had around 33% of the population. The population was also around 5% Jewish, while 17% of the population were unaffiliated with any religious organization.

District of Columbia Population by Race
CENSUS 2010

This table shows the number of people who are of one, two, or three or more races. For those claiming two races, the number of people belonging to the various categories is listed. The U.S. government conducts a census of the population every 10 years.

	Number	Percent
Total population	601,723	100.0
One race	584,407	97.1
Two races	15,273	2.5
White *and* Black or African American.	3,476	0.6
White *and* American Indian/Alaska Native	904	0.2
White *and* Asian.	3,736	0.6
White *and* Native Hawaiian/Pacific Islander.	121	—
White *and* some other race	2,068	0.3
Black or African American *and* American Indian/Alaska Native . . .	1,787	0.3
Black or African American *and* Asian.	900	0.1
Black or African American *and* Native Hawaiian/Pacific Islander. . .	226	—
Black or African American *and* some other race . . .	1,047	0.2
American Indian/Alaska Native *and* Asian	57	—
American Indian/Alaska Native *and* Native Hawaiian/Pacific Islander . . .	10	—
American Indian/Alaska Native *and* some other race. . . .	145	—
Asian *and* Native Hawaiian/Pacific Islander.	143	—
Asian *and* some other race	333	0.1
Native Hawaiian/Pacific Islander *and* some other race. . . .	320	0.1
Three or more races	2,043	0.3

SOURCE: U.S. Census Bureau. Census 2010. www.census/gov/ (accessed July 2012). A dash (—) indicates that the percent is less than 0.1.

The Washington National Cathedral was established by Congress through an 1893 charter with the Protestant Episcopal Cathedral Foundation. The charter was signed by President Benjamin Harrison, and the building was completed in 1912.

10 Transportation

Union Station, located north of the Capitol, is the District's rail terminal, from which Amtrak provides passenger service to the northeast corridor and southern points. As of 2012, Amtrak operated services from Union Station to major destinations including New York, Chicago, New Orleans, Atlanta, Boston, Seattle, Portland, San Francisco, Oklahoma City, and Toronto (Canada). The Washington Metropolitan Area Transit Authority, or Metro, operates bus and subway transportation within the city and its suburbs in Maryland and Virginia.

In 2008, there were 167,000 automobiles, 1,000 motorcycles, and 43,000 trucks registered in the District, and 373,735 licensed drivers.

Three major airports handle the District's commercial air traffic: Ronald Reagan Washington National Airport, just south of the city in Virginia; Dulles International Airport in Virginia; and Baltimore/Washington International Thurgood Marshall Airport in Maryland. In 2011, total passengers for the three airports were: 18.8 million for Reagan Washington National; 23.2 million for Dulles; and 21.9

million for Thurgood Marshall. There were 16 heliports serving the District in 2011.

11 History

The English founded the Jamestown, Virginia, settlement in 1607. Originally part of the Maryland Colony, the region of the present-day capital had been carved up into plantations by the latter half of the 17th century. After the US Constitution (1787) provided that a tract of land be reserved for the seat of the federal government, Congress authorized George Washington to choose a site along the Potomac River in 1791. Washington made his selection and appointed Andrew Ellicott to survey the area. He then employed Pierre Charles L'Enfant, a French military engineer, to draw up plans for the federal city.

L'Enfant's design called for a wide roadway (now called Pennsylvania Avenue) to connect the Capitol with the president's house (the White House), a mile away. L'Enfant was dismissed before completion of the work, and Ellicott carried out the plans. Although construction was delayed by lack of adequate financing, President John Adams and some 125 government officials moved into the District in 1800. The plaster on the walls of the White House was still wet when Adams moved in.

On 3 May 1802, the city of Washington was incorporated, with an elected council and a mayor appointed by the president. In August 1814, during the War of 1812, British forces invaded and burned the Capitol building, the White House, and other public buildings. They spared the residential areas, and out of respect also spared the home of the commandant of the US Marines. After Dr. William Thornton,

superintendent of patents, pleaded with the British officers not to burn the Patent Office and the Post Office, those buildings were also saved. All of the buildings destroyed were rebuilt within five years. At the request of its residents, Virginia took back its portion of the District in 1846, confining the District to the eastern shore of the Potomac.

The Civil War (1861–65) brought a large influx of Union soldiers, workers, and freed slaves, expanding the city of Washington to include almost all of the District of Columbia. The District's population rose sharply, spurring the development of modern Washington. Slaves owned in Washington were emancipated on 16 April 1862, nine months before Lincoln's Emancipation Proclamation of 1 January 1863. In 1874, a new form of government was established, headed by three commissioners appointed by the president.

The 1930s brought a rise in public employment, growth of federal facilities, and the beginnings of large scale public housing construction. The White House was completely renovated in the late 1940s, and a huge building program coincided with the expansion of the federal bureaucracy during the 1960s.

Post-World War II Era In more recent years, the District's form of government has undergone significant changes. The 23rd Amendment to the US Constitution, ratified on 3 April 1961, permitted residents to vote in presidential elections. Beginning in 1971, the District was allowed to send a nonvoting delegate to the US House of Representatives, and a local school board was also elected. Local self-rule began in 1975, when an elected mayor and council took office. There was a movement for statehood

Over the years, the District of Columbia has been the site of many protests and marches. During the quest for universal women's suffrage, groups of female activists protested in front of the White House and the Capitol. Here, women stage a protest in 1917 asking the president for help. They were ultimately successful three years later when women got the right to vote nationally.
COURTESY OF THE LIBRARY OF CONGRESS.

which won local approval, but was defeated by the US Senate in 1992, when they refused to consider the bill.

The District has both prospered and suffered in recent decades. An expanding economy increased the city's office space but at the same time, the city has been wracked by drug-related crime and by corruption in high places. In 1990, the District's mayor of 12 years, Democrat Marion Barry, was convicted of possessing cocaine. Barry was succeeded that year by lawyer Sharon Pratt Dixon, the first African American woman to lead a major US city. Dixon promised to clean house "with a shovel, not a broom."

In 1994, Marion Barry, returning to political life after serving a six-month jail term for his drug conviction, defeated Republican Carol Schwartz in the mayoral contest. By the following year the city was nearly insolvent and Congress was forced to create the District of Columbia Financial Control Board to oversee all municipal spending. In the election of 1998, Anthony A. Williams was elected mayor. He ushered in a period of urban renewal and budget surpluses and in 2001 the District regained control over its finances.

In 2002, Mayor Williams was reelected. Williams did not seek reelection in 2006 and was succeeded by Adrian Fenty, who pledged to overhaul the city's underperforming public schools. In 2010, Fenty lost to former council chair Vincent Gray, who pledged to provide greater economic opportunities to the city's many underserved areas. As of 2012, Eleanor Holmes Norton serves as the District's delegate to the House of Representatives.

Colorful fireworks surround the US Capitol Building during a July 4th celebration. © GARY718/SHUTTERSTOCK.COM.

The recession that began in 2008 largely passed over Washington, D.C. This was primarily due to an increase in federal employment and spending. During the recession, the District was the only metropolitan area in the country to see an increase in growth.

12 State Government

The District of Columbia is the seat of the federal government and houses the principal parts of the legislative, executive, and judicial branches.

The District of Columbia committees of the US Senate and House of Representatives oversee affairs within Washington, D.C. The District elects a delegate to the US House who participates in discussions and votes on bills within the District of Columbia Committee, but who may not vote on measures on the actual floor of the House. The District has no representation in the Senate. Within the District, there is wide public support for statehood, but in 1992 Congress rejected District statehood by 63 votes. The bill for statehood, however, can be reintroduced.

The Council of the District of Columbia, the legislative body for the District, has 13 representatives who serve four-year terms. The mayor and council members are elected by District voters. As of 2011, council members earned an annual salary of $125,538. Council members receive annual cost-of-living increases to their salaries. There is no governor.

13 Political Parties

Both the Democratic and Republican parties, the nation's major political organizations, have headquarters in the District. Voters in the District itself are overwhelmingly Democratic, unfailingly casting their votes for the Democratic nominee in every election since 1964. In May 2012 there were 465,971 registered voters, of whom 30,772 were registered as Republicans. In the 2004 presidential election, 89.2% of residents voted for John Kerry (Democrat), while 9.3% voted for George W. Bush (Republican). In 2008, 92.5% of residents voted for Barack Obama (Democrat), and 6.5% voted for John McCain (Republican). In 2012, most DC voters threw their support behind incumbent President Obama as he took on Republican challenger Mitt Romney. As of 2012, the District had three electoral votes. Eleanor Holmes Norton has been the District's nonvoting member of the House of Representatives since 1991.

14 Local Government

In 1973, Congress provided the District with a home-rule charter, allowing residents to elect their own mayor and a city council of 13 members, all serving four-year terms. The mayor is the District's chief executive, and the council

D.C. Presidential Vote by Major Political Parties, 1964–2012

Year	D.C. Winner	Democrat	Republican
1964	*Johnson (D)	169,796	28,801
1968	Humphrey (D)	139,566	31,012
1972	McGovern (D)	127,627	35,226
1976	*Carter (D)	137,818	27,873
1980	Carter (D)	124,376	21,765
1984	Mondale (D)	180,408	29,009
1988	Dukakis (D)	159,407	27,590
1992	*Clinton (D)	192,619	20,698
1996	*Clinton (D)	158,220	17,339
2000	Gore (D)	171,923	18,073
2004	Kerry (D)	202,970	21,256
2008	*Obama (D)	245,800	17,367
2012	*Obama (D)	267,070	21,381

*Won US presidential election.

Independent candidate Ross Perot received 9,681 votes in 1992 and 3,611 votes in 1996.

is the legislative branch. Under constitutional authority, however, Congress can enact laws on any subject affecting the District, and all legislation enacted by the District is subject to congressional veto. In 2007, a bill was passed in the US Congress allowing the District's mayor to take direct control of the D.C. Public School Board, the superintendent position, and the school budget. All District charter schools are governed by a separate school board—the D.C. Public Charter School Board. The District has one metropolitan district, one school district, and one special district. In 2011, there were 41,246 full-time and 2,172 part-time state and local government employees in D.C.

15 Judicial System

The US Court of Appeals for the District of Columbia functions in a manner similar to that of a state supreme court. It also has original jurisdiction over federal crimes. The Superior Court of the District of Columbia serves as a trial court. The District of Columbia is the only US jurisdiction where the US Attorney's Office, and not the local government, prosecutes criminal offenders for nonfederal crimes.

According to the FBI Crime Index, the violent crime (murder/nonnegligent homicide, forcible rape, robbery, aggravated assault) rate in the District was 1,330.2 incidents per 100,000 population in 2010. The murder and nonnegligent manslaughter rate was 21.9 per 100,000 inhabitants; forcible rape, 31.1; aggravated assault, 558.4; and property crime, 4,778.9. Prisoners sentenced to serve more than one year fall under the jurisdiction of the Bureau of Prisons. In 2010, there were 3,552 prisoners in the District's jails.

The District of Columbia no longer has the death penalty; D.C. abolished it in 1981. The last execution there took place in 1957. When the issue was revisited in 1992, District residents voted 2–1 against the death penalty.

16 Migration

The principal migrations have been an influx of Southern blacks after the Civil War and, more recently, the rapid growth of the Washington, D.C., metropolitan area. In the period 2000 to 2010, the District's total population increased by 5.2%, to 601,723 people, from 572,059 in 2000. According to the US Census Bureau, 50.7% of the District's residents in 2010 were African American, and 13% were foreign born.

The District's population tends to remain fairly steady. Between 2009 and 2010, the total population (ages one and older) increased by 2,253. During that time, 4,082 native-born

residents and 726 foreign immigrants moved out of the District; 44,579 native-born residents moved into the District from a US state; 48,661 native born left the District of Columbia for a US state; and 3,127 natives and 3,934 foreign immigrants moved into the District from abroad. Around 39.7% of the foreign-born residents of the District were citizens in 2010.

17 Economy

The District's economy tends to rise and fall with federal spending patterns. In 2011 and 2012, the Washington, D.C., area ranked as the nation's strongest local economy, if considered as a city. The total number of firms in 2007 was 55,887, with a high proportion of these being African American-owned (28.2%, as compared to 7.1% nationally) or woman-owned (34.5%, as compared with 28.8% nationally).

In 2008, the gross state product (GSP) of the Washington, D.C.-Arlington-Alexandria metropolitan area totaled $425 billion, ranking it as the fourth-largest metropolitan economy in the United States. The District itself had a GSP of $104.7 billion in 2010, ranking it 35th as a state. That year, per capita GSP was $174,500, ranking the District first if considered as a state. Professional and business services contributed $92.9 billion, or 23.5% of the total economic output; followed by government at $83.1 billion, or 21%; real estate at $57.6 billion, trade at $28.5 billion, and health and education at $23.7 billion.

18 Income

In the years 2008 to 2010, the median per capita household income (including nonmonetary income) in the District of Columbia was $55,280, compared to the national median of $50,022, ranking the District 39th if considered as a state. In 2011, 18.7% of the District's residents lived below the federal poverty level compared to 15.9% nationwide.

19 Industry

The federal government is the District's largest employer. Although not known as a manufacturing center, the District does have a small manufacturing sector. The Government Printing Office operates one of the largest printing plants in the United States. Also in the District is the Washington Post Company, publisher of the newspaper of that name and of the *Herald* magazine. The company also owns several television stations, the Slate Group, and Kaplan Inc.

In 2007, the shipment value of all manufactured products in the District totaled $332.8 million. In that same year, 2,015 people in the District worked in the manufacturing sector.

20 Labor

In August 2012, the District's civilian labor force stood at 354,000, with 31,200 of those unemployed. The unemployment rate was 8.8%, as compared to the national rate of 8.1%. Of the 725,400 people who were employed in nonfarm occupations, 234,800 worked in government; 122,900 worked in education and health services; 147,700 in professional and business services; 13,900 in mining, logging, and construction; and 63,300 in leisure and hospitality.

The District of Columbia serves as the headquarters of many labor organizations. In 2011, a total of 23,000 of the District's employed wage and salary workers were members of a union, representing 8.3% of those so employed, as compared to the 2011 national average of 11.8%.

21 Agriculture

There is no commercial farming in the District of Columbia.

22 Domesticated Animals

The District of Columbia has no livestock industry.

23 Fishing

There is no commercial fishing in the District of Columbia. Recreational fishing is accessible via a boat-launching facility on the Anacostia River.

24 Forestry

There is no forestland or forest products industry in the District of Columbia.

25 Mining

There is no mining in the District of Columbia, although a few mining firms have offices there.

26 Energy and Power

The only generation of electricity in the District of Columbia has been from two small, 35-year-old, petroleum-fired electric power plants that have been used only a few hours per year; both were scheduled for closure in 2012. In April

2012, they produced 2,000 megawatt hours (MWh) of electricity. One of the largest solar power panel installations in Washington, D.C., is located on the roof of the US Department of Energy's headquarters building and generates about 230,000 kilowatt hours of electricity per year. In 2012, the District of Columbia's total net generating capability was 199,858 megawatt hours, with an average retail price of 13.35 cents per kilowatt hour.

Ranking the District as a state would make its electricity service the ninth most expensive in the nation. The District has no proven reserves of crude petroleum and natural gas, nor does it have any refining capacity. All fossil fuel needs are supplied by the states of Maryland and Virginia.

27 Commerce

As of 2007, the District of Columbia's wholesale trade sector had sales totaling $2.1 billion, while the retail trade sector had sales that same year of $3.84 billion. Retail sales per capita were $6,555. As expected for a tourism and travel center, retail and wholesale sectors were dwarfed by accommodation and food and beverage sales, at $4.28 billion. In 2009, the District had 21,200 private nonfarm establishments and 41,143 nonemployer establishments. The District has very little manufacturing, and its primary exports are all knowledge-based, in areas such as scientific research and public policy research. Exports in 2010 were around $300 million.

28 Public Finance

The budget for the District of Columbia is prepared in conjunction with the mayor's office and reviewed by the city council, but is subject to review and approval by Congress. The fiscal year runs from 1 October through 30 September. The District of Columbia Financial Responsibility and Management Assistance Authority was created in 1995 in order to deal with the District's massive debt, and it is in charge of its budget and financial planning. The 2013 budget, approved in 2012, totaled $9.9 billion. Of this, the D.C. government expected tax revenues of $6.75 billion. The largest portion of the budget ($3.36 billion; 27%) was earmarked for human services and low-income programs, while $1.6 billion (25% of the budget) was earmarked for education, and $988 million (15%) for public safety.

29 Taxation

As of 1 January 2012, the District of Columbia had four individual income tax brackets, ranging from 4% to 8.95%. However, those who work in the District but live in the suburbs are not taxed. The corporate income tax rate was a flat 9.975%. The District levies a 6% general sales and use tax, although food purchased for consumption off premises (such as at home) is exempt. There are also excise taxes on gasoline and cigarettes.

The local tax base is marked by a shortage of taxable real estate, since much of the District is occupied by government buildings. Also, the District cannot tax the incomes of those who work inside the district, but live in the suburbs. Consequently, much of the tax base is derived from taxes on business property.

30 Health

Health conditions in the nation's capital are mixed. In October 2011, the infant mortality rate was estimated at 11.9 per 1,000 live births, almost twice the national average. The crude death rate in 2009, according to the Centers for Disease Control and Prevention, was 806 per 100,000 population. In 2010, Washington, D.C., also had the highest HIV infection rate in the nation, at 3%. The death rate of 229.2 (per 100,000 people) from heart disease in 2008 was also in the bottom quartile of the United States. The death rate from cerebrovascular disease was 36 per 100,000, compared to a national rate of 40.7; while the cancer death rate was 192.1, compared to a national rate of 175.3.

However, in 2010 the American Fitness Index report, published by the American College of Sports Medicine, ranked D.C. as among the nation's fittest, citing low rates of diabetes (6.7% of the area's population, as opposed to 8.7% nationwide); low smoking rates of 14.8%, compared to a national rate of 17.2%; low levels of obesity, at 57.5% compared to a national rate of 63.8%; and a high proportion of people buying fresh fruits and vegetables.

The District of Columbia's eight community hospitals had about 2,752 beds in 2011. Average expenses per inpatient day were $2,434, higher than the national rate of $1,910 per day. In 2011, there were 486 physicians per 100,000 people, and 104 dentists. There were 142 nurses per 100,000 in 2011. The per capita health spending in the District was $10,849 as of 2011 and approximately 7.6% of all District residents lacked medical insurance.

31 Housing

In 2010, the District of Columbia had an estimated 296,836 housing units, of which 43.5% were owner-occupied, ranking the District as having one of the lowest number of homeowners in the nation. About 61.7% of all units were in multi-unit buildings, as compared with an average of 26% in the United States as a whole. Just 0.1% (294) were mobile homes. Buildings with 20 or more units accounted for 104,000, or 35% of the total units. Only 12% of all units were single-family, detached homes. Just over 39% of all housing units in the District were built in 1939 or earlier. It was estimated that about 8,233 units were without telephone service, 1,843 lacked complete plumbing facilities, and 2,423 lacked complete kitchen facilities. Most households relied on gas and electricity for heating.

In 2010, the median home value of owner-occupied units was $426,900, making the District one of the nation's six most expensive housing markets. Median monthly cost for mortgage owners was $2,297, while median rents were $1,198 per month.

32 Education

The District of Columbia's first public schools were opened in 1805. Between 2006 and 2010, of all residents 25 years of age or older, 86.5% were high school graduates and some 49.2% were college graduates.

Total enrollment in public schools was estimated at 46,517 in fall 2011. Enrollment in private schools in fall 2011 was around 21,000.

The District of Columbia has a number of prominent degree-granting institutions, both private and public. Some of the best-known private universities are American University, Georgetown University, George Washington University, and Howard University. The University of the District of Columbia, created in

1976 from the merger of three institutions, has an open admissions policy for District freshman undergraduate students. It has five academic colleges. The US Department of Agriculture Graduate School also operates within the District.

33 Arts

The District of Columbia Commission on the Arts and Humanities was founded in 1968 and is a partner with the Mid-Atlantic Arts Foundation. The Humanities Council of Washington, D.C., was established in 1980 and acts in support of local programs.

The John F. Kennedy Center for the Performing Arts, opened in 1971, is the District's principal performing arts center. Its five main halls, including the Opera House, Concert Hall, Eisenhower Theater, Terrace Theatre, and American Film Institute Theater, display gifts from at least 30 foreign governments, ranging from stage curtains and tapestries, to sculptures and crystal chandeliers. Major theatrical productions are also presented at the Arena Stage–Kreeger Theater, National Theatre, Folger Theatre, and Ford's Theatre. REP Inc. is one of the few professional African American theaters in the United States. The New Playwrights' Theatre of Washington is a nonprofit group presenting new plays by American dramatists.

The District's leading symphony is the National Symphony Orchestra, which performs at the Concert Hall of the Kennedy Center. The Washington Opera performs at the Kennedy Center's Opera House.

During the summer months, the Carter Barron Amphitheater presents popular music and jazz. Concerts featuring the US Army, US Navy, and US Marine Corps bands and the Air

People are shown picnicking near the Washington Monument during the area's Cherry Blossom Festival. © LISSANDRA MELO/ SHUTTERSTOCK.COM.

Force Symphony Orchestra are held throughout the District.

Throughout the year, many of the organizations based in the District, such as the Smithsonian and the Sierra Club, hold talks and lecture series. Embassies of foreign governments are also a source of cultural events throughout the year.

34 Libraries and Museums

Washington, DC, is the site of the world's largest library, the Library of Congress, with a 2012 collection of more than 152 million items on approximately 838 miles of bookshelves, including 34.5 million books and print materials. The library, which is also the cataloging and bibliographic center for libraries throughout the United States, has permanent displays of the 1455 Gutenberg Bible, Thomas Jefferson's first draft of the Declaration of Independence, and Abraham Lincoln's first two drafts of the Gettysburg Address.

In addition, the Folger Shakespeare Library contains rare Renaissance manuscripts and a full-size recreation of an Elizabethan theater. The District's own public library system has a main library and 24 branches, and it also provides downloadable books, music, and other materials.

The District of Columbia is home to numerous museums. The Smithsonian Institution—endowed in 1826 by British citizen James Smithson, who had never visited the United States—operates a vast museum and research complex that includes the National Air and Space Museum, National Museum of Natural History, National Museum of History and Technology, many of the District's art museums, and the National Zoological Park. The Smithsonian National Gallery of Art houses one of the world's outstanding collections of Western art from the 13th century to the present.

The Library of Congress is one of the largest libraries in the world. Shown here is the scientific library reading room. © GALINA MIKHALISHINA/SHUTTERSTOCK.COM.

Among the capital's other distinguished art collections are the Phillips Collection, the oldest museum of modern art in the United States; the Museum of African Art, located in the Frederick Douglass Memorial Home; and the Corcoran Gallery of Art, devoted primarily to American paintings, sculpture, and drawings of the last 300 years. The US National Arboretum, US Botanic Garden, and National Aquarium are also located in the city.

35 Communications

Washington, D.C., is the home of the US Postal Service. As of 2010, about 96.7% of the District's households had telephones. According to Government Technology, the average overall broadband adoption rate for the District was 65.3% in 2009, but the least affluent wards—wards 5, 7 and 8— all have broadband adoption rates below 40%. In 2012, the District had 7 AM and 13 FM radio stations, and 11 full-power television stations.

36 Press

Because the District of Columbia is the center of US government activity, hundreds of domestic and foreign newspapers maintain permanent news bureaus there. The largest daily newspaper in the District is the *Washington Post,* with a 2012 weekday circulation of 492,600 and a Sunday circulation of 714,600. Other daily papers include the *Washington Times* and the *Washington Examiner.*

The District is also home to several specialty papers, such as *Roll Call, The Hill,* and *Stars and Stripes.*

Press clubs active within the District include the National Press Club, Gridiron Club, American Newspaper Women's Club, Washington Press Club, and White House Correspondents Association.

There are more than 30 major Washington-based periodicals. Among the best known are *National Geographic, U.S. News and World Report, Smithsonian,* and *New Republic.* Important periodicals covering the workings of the federal government are the *Congressional Quarterly* and its companion, *CQ Weekly Report.*

37 Tourism, Travel, and Recreation

As the nation's capital, the District of Columbia is one of the world's leading tourist centers. In 2010, there were over 15.54 million domestic and over 1.74 million international visitors. Visitor spending that year reached almost $5.7 billion, supporting 71,301 jobs.

The most popular sites include the Washington Monument, Lincoln Memorial, Jefferson Memorial, Vietnam Veterans Memorial, White House, Capitol Hill, the Smithsonian Institution, Library of Congress, the National Zoo, the US Holocaust Memorial Museum, and the District's many museums. Across the Potomac in Virginia are Arlington National Cemetery, site of the Tomb of the Unknown Soldier and the grave of John F. Kennedy, and George Washington's home at Mount Vernon.

National holiday celebrations, such as July Fourth and Thanksgiving, are popular in DC. The State Fair is a small event featuring locally grown market garden produce, and it is held in September.

38 Sports

There are several major professional sports teams in Washington, DC, or in nearby Maryland: the Redskins of the National Football League, the

The famous address, 1600 Pennsylvania Avenue, is the location of the White House. It is the official residence of the president as well as the commander in chief's office. The first president to live in the White House was John Adams. © JEFF KINSEY/
SHUTTERSTOCK.COM.

Nationals (formerly the Montreal Expos) of Major League Baseball, the Wizards (formerly the Bullets) of the National Basketball Association, the Mystics of the Women's National Basketball Association, the Capitals of the National Hockey League, and DC United of Major League Soccer.

Hockey and basketball are played in downtown Washington at the MCI Center, which was opened for the 1997–98 season. The Redskins play in the FedEx Field in Landover, Maryland. The Redskins have reached the Super Bowl five times, winning three times. The Bullets won the NBA championship in 1978. The Nationals began playing in newly built Nationals Park in 2008.

In college sports, the Georgetown Hoyas were a dominant force in basketball during the 1980s, reaching the National Collegiate Athletic Association (NCAA) championship game three times and winning the title in 1984. Professional players who began their careers at Georgetown include Allen Iverson, Patrick Ewing, and Reggie Williams.

39 Famous Washingtonians

Although no US president has been born in the District of Columbia, all but George Washington (b. Virginia, 1732–99) lived there while serving as chief executive.

Created by artist Maya Lin, the Vietnam Veterans Memorial in Washington, DC, honors the more than 58,000 American servicemen and women killed during the conflict. © MATTHEW BERGHEISER/SHUTTERSTOCK.COM.

Inventor Alexander Graham Bell (b. Scotland, 1842–1922) was president of the National Geographic Society in his later years. Federal officials born in Washington, D.C., include John Foster Dulles (1888–1959), secretary of state; J. Edgar Hoover (1895–1972), director of the FBI; and Robert C. Weaver (1907–1997), who as secretary of housing and urban development during the administration of President Lyndon B. Johnson was the first African American to hold cabinet rank.

The designer of the nation's capital was Pierre Charles L'Enfant (b. France, 1754–1825), whose grave is in Arlington National Cemetery. Also involved in laying out the capital were surveyor Andrew Ellicott (b. Pennsylvania, 1754–1820) and mathematician-astronomer Benjamin Banneker (b. Maryland, 1731–1806), an African American who was an early champion of equal rights. Washingtonians who achieved military fame include Benjamin O. Davis (1877–1970), the first African American to become an Army general, and his son, Benjamin O. Davis Jr. (1912–2002), who was the first African American to become a general in the Air Force.

Actress Goldie Hawn was born in Washington, DC.
© VIPFLASH/SHUTTERSTOCK.COM.

Among Washingtonians to achieve distinction in the creative arts were John Philip Sousa (1854–1932), bandmaster and composer; composer-pianist-bandleader Edward Kennedy "Duke" Ellington (1899–1974); and singer Marvin Gay (1939–1984).

Other famous Washingtonians include news presenter Connie Chung (1946–); actors Samuel L. Jackson (1948–), Katherine Heigl (1978–), William Hurt (1950–), Christopher Meloni (1961–), and Goldie Hawn (1945–); and tennis player Pete Sampras (1971–).

40 Bibliography

BOOKS

DeFerrari, John. *Lost Washington, D.C.* Charleston, SC: The History Press, 2011.

Elish, Dan. *Washington, D.C.* 2nd ed. New York: Marshall Cavendish Benchmark, 2007.

Feeney, Kathy. *Washington, D.C. Facts and Symbols.* Mankato, MN: Bridgestone Books, 2000.

Gessler, Diana Hollingsworth. *Very Washington DC: A Celebration of the History and Culture of America's Capital City.* Chapel Hill, NC: Algonquin Books, 2009.

Mitchell, Alexander D, IV. *Washington, D.C. Then and Now* San Diego: Thunder Bay Press, 2007.

Powers, Alice L., Ian O'Leary, Kem Knapp Sawyer, et al. *Washington, D.C.* New York: Dorling Kindersley, 2010.

Thompson, John. *National Geographic Traveler: Washington, DC,* 4th ed. Washington, DC: National Geographic, 2011.

WEB SITES

"Destination DC." *Washington DC.* http://washington.org (accessed on November 2, 2012.)

"District of Columbia Electricity Profile 2010." *US Energy Information Administration.* http://www.eia.gov/electricity/state/districtofcolumbia/ (accessed on November 2, 2012).

"District of Columbia Government." *The District of Columbia.* http://www.dc.gov/DC (accessed on November 2, 2012).

"Economy at a Glance: District of Columbia." *US Bureau of Labor Statistics.* http://www.bls.gov/eag/eag.dc.htm (accessed on November 5, 2012).

"State & County QuickFacts." *US Bureau of the Census.* http://quickfacts.census.gov/qfd/states/11000.html (accessed on November 5, 2012).

Puerto Rico

Commonwealth of Puerto Rico

ORIGIN OF STATE NAME: Spanish for "rich port."

NICKNAME: Island of Enchantment.

CAPITAL: San Juan.

OFFICIAL SEAL: In the center of a green circular shield, a lamb holding a white banner reclines on the book of the Apocalypse. Above are a yoke, a cluster of arrows, and the letters "F" and "I," signifying King Ferdinand and Queen Isabella, rulers of Spain at the time of discovery; below is the commonwealth motto. Surrounding the shield, on a white border, are the towers of Castile and lions symbolizing Spain, crosses representing the conquest of Jerusalem, and Spanish banners.

FLAG: From the hoist extends a blue triangle, with one white star; five horizontal stripes—three red, two white—make up the balance.

MOTTO: *Joannes est nomen ejus.* (John is his name.)

SONG: "La Borinquena."

FLOWER: Maga.

TREE: Ceiba.

ANIMAL: Coqui.

BIRD: Reinita.

BECAME A COMMONWEALTH: 25 July 1952.

LEGAL HOLIDAYS: New Year's Day, 1 January; Three Kings Day (Epiphany), 6 January; birthday of Eugenio Maria de Hostos, 2nd Monday in January; birthday of Martin Luther King Jr., 3rd Monday in January; Presidents' Day, 3rd Monday in February; Abolition Day, 22 March; Good Friday, March or April; birthday of José de Diego, 3rd Monday in April; Memorial Day, last Monday in May; Independence Day, 4 July; birthday of Luis Muñoz Rivera, 3rd Monday in July; Constitution Day, 25 July; birthday of José Celso Barbosa, 27 July; Labor Day, 1st Monday in September; Columbus Day, 12 October; Veterans' Day, 11 November; Discovery of Puerto Rico Day, 19 November; Thanksgiving Day, 4th Thursday in November; Christmas Eve, 24 December; Christmas Day, 25 December.

TIME: 8 a.m. Atlantic Standard Time = noon GMT.

Location and Size

Situated on the northeast periphery of the Caribbean Sea about 1,000 miles (1,600 kilometers) southeast of Miami, Florida, Puerto Rico is the easternmost and smallest island of the Greater Antilles group. Its total area is 5,324 square miles (13,790 square kilometers), including 3,425 square miles (8,870 square kilometers) of land and 1,900 square miles (4,921 square

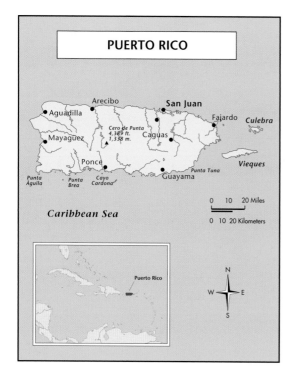

PUERTO RICO

Arecibo • San Juan
• Aguadilla
Fajardo • Culebra
Cero de Punta
4,389 ft.
1,338 m.
Caguas
• Mayagüez
Ponce • Vieques
Punta Tuna
Punta • Punta Cayo Guayama
Águila Brea Cardona

Caribbean Sea

0   10   20 Miles
0 10 20 Kilometers

Puerto Rico

N
W   E
S

kilometers) of water. The main island measures 111 miles (179 kilometers) from east to west and 36 miles (58 kilometers) from north to south.

2 Topography

About 75% of Puerto Rico's land area consists of hills or mountains too steep for intensive commercial cultivation. The Cordillera Central range, separating the northern coast from the semiarid south, has the island's highest peak, Cerro de Punta, at 4,389 feet (1,338 meters). Puerto Rico's best known peak, El Yunque (3,496 feet or 1,066 meters), stands to the east, in the Luquillo Mountains (Sierra de Luquillo). The north coast consists of a level strip about 100 miles (160 kilometers) long and 5 miles (8 kilometers) wide. Principal valleys are located along the east coast, from Fajardo to Cape Mala

Pascua, and around Caguas, in the east-central region. Off the eastern shore are two small islands: Vieques, with an area of 51 square miles (132 square kilometers), and Culebra, covering 24 square miles (62 square kilometers).

The longest river is the Rio Grande de Arecibo, extending 40 miles (65 kilometers) from Cordillera Central just east of Mount Guilarte to an area just east of Arecibo, where it empties into the Atlantic. There are few natural lakes but numerous artificial ones, of which Dos Bocas, south of Arecibo, is one of the most beautiful.

Like many other Caribbean islands, Puerto Rico is the crest of an extinct submarine volcano. About 45 miles (72 kilometers) north of the island lies the Puerto Rico Trench, which at over 28,000 feet (8,500 meters) is one of the world's deepest chasms.

3 Climate

Tradewinds from the northeast keep Puerto Rico's climate steady, although tropical. San Juan has an average annual high temperature of 87.6°F (30.8°C), ranging from 84.3°F (29°C) in January to 90.3°F (32.3°C) in August. The average yearly low is 70.4°F (21.3°C), ranging from 66.5°F (19°C) in February to 73.6°F (23°C) in August. The lowest temperature ever recorded on the island is 39°F (4°C); the highest was 103°F (39°C). The recorded temperature in San Juan has never been lower than 60°F (16°C) or higher than 99°F (37°C).

Rainfall varies by region. Ponce, on the south coast, averages only 32 inches (81 centimeters) a year, while the highlands average 108 inches (274 centimeters); the rain forest on El Yunque receives an annual average of 183 inches (465 centimeters). San Juan's average annual rainfall is 70.8 inches (200 centimeters), with its rainiest months being May through November.

The word "hurricane" derives from *hurakán,* a term the Spanish learned from Puerto Rico's Taino Indians. Several powerful hurricanes have struck Puerto Rico in the recent past, including the devastating Hurricane Georges in 1998 and Hurricane Jeanne in 2004. The latter caused eight deaths and $169.5 million in damages. Following the storm, Puerto Rico was declared a federal disaster area and the name Jeanne was retired from the hurricane naming list.

4 Plants and Animals

During the 19th century, forests covered about three-fourths of Puerto Rico. By the 21st century, however, only one-fourth of the island remained forested. Flowering trees still abound, and the butterfly tree, African tulip, and flamboyán (royal poinciana) add bright reds and pinks to Puerto Rico's lush green landscape. Among hardwoods, now rare, are nutmeg, satinwood, Spanish elm, and Spanish cedar.

The only mammal found by the conquistadores on the island was a kind of barkless dog, now extinct. Virtually all present-day mammals have been introduced, including horses, cattle, cats, and dogs. The only troublesome mammal is the mongoose, brought in from India to control reptiles in the cane fields and now wild in remote rural areas.

Mosquitoes and sand flies are common pests, but the only dangerous insect is the giant centipede, whose sting is painful but rarely fatal.

Perhaps the island's best known inhabitant is the golden coqui, a tiny threatened tree frog. The Puerto Rican crested toad is also on the threatened list. Marine life is extraordinarily abundant, including many tropical fish, crabs, and corals. Puerto Rico has some 200 bird species, many of which live in the rain forest. Thrushes, orioles, grosbeaks, and hummingbirds are common, and the reinita and pitirre are distinctive to the island. Several parrot species are rare, and the Puerto Rican parrot, the iguaca, is endangered. Also on the endangered list are the yellow-shouldered blackbird, the Puerto Rican plain pigeon, and the Puerto Rican whippoorwill. The Mona boa, Puerto Rico boa, and Mona ground iguana are threatened. There are six national wildlife refuges, including one on Vieques and one on Culebra.

5 Environmental Protection

US environmental laws and regulations are applicable in Puerto Rico. Land-use planning, overseen by the Puerto Rico Planning Board, is an especially difficult problem, since residential, industrial, and recreational developers are all competing to use the less than 30 percent of the total land area on an island that is already densely populated. Sewage discharges into the ocean remain a problem.

As of 2012, the island had 16 hazardous waste sites on the National Priorities List, 8 of which involved ground-water contamination. One hazardous waste site was the Atlantic Fleet Weapons Training Area, in Vieques.

6 Population

Puerto Rico's population was estimated at 3,725,789 in 2011, down from 3,808,610 in 2000. With a population density of 1,163 per square mile (449 per square kilometer), Puerto Rico is one of the most densely populated areas of the world.

In 2010, about 24.2% of the population was under the age of 18 and about 14.5% was 65 years old or older. San Juan is Puerto Rico's capital and largest city, with a 2011 population estimate of 389,714, followed by Bayamón, 205,693; Carolina, 175,129; Ponce, 163,727; and Caguas, 142,678.

7 Ethnic Groups

Three main ethnic strands are the heritage of Puerto Rico: the Taino Indians, most of whom fled or perished after the Spanish conquest; black Africans, imported as slaves under Spanish rule; and the Spanish themselves. With an admixture of Dutch, English, Corsicans, and other Europeans, Puerto Ricans today enjoy a distinct Hispanic-Afro-Antillean heritage.

In 2010, about 75.8% of the population was white (primarily of Spanish origin), 12.4% was black, 0.2% was Amerindian, 0.2% was Asian, and 7.8% was of some other race. In 2011, of those islanders indicating an ancestry other than Puerto Rican, 52,556 (1.4% of the total population) gave their ancestry as American; 4,033 (0.1%) as French; 4,573 (0.1%) as Italian; and 3,590 (0.1%) as Sub-Saharan African.

Less than two-thirds of all ethnic Puerto Ricans live on the island. Virtually all the rest reside on the US mainland. In 2010, there were 4.7 million people who identified themselves as Puerto Rican in the 50 states. The State of New York has almost half the US ethnic Puerto Rican population.

8 Languages

Spanish and English are the official languages of Puerto Rico, but Spanish remains dominant

**Puerto Rico
Population Profile**

Total population per Census 2010:	3,725,789
Population change, 2006–10:	-5.1%
Hispanic or Latino†:	99.0%
Population by race	
One race:	96.7%
White:	75.8%
Black or African American:	12.4%
American Indian/Alaska Native:	0.5%
Asian:	0.2%
Native Hawaiian/Pacific Islander:	0.0%
Some other race:	7.8%
Two or more races:	3.3%

Population by Age Group, Census 2010

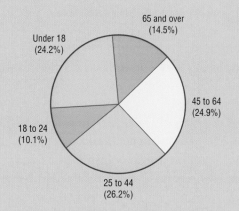

65 and over (14.5%)
Under 18 (24.2%)
45 to 64 (24.9%)
18 to 24 (10.1%)
25 to 44 (26.2%)

Major Cities by Population, 2011 Estimates

City	Population
San Juan	389,714
Bayamón	205,693
Carolina	175,129
Ponce	163,727
Caguas	142,678
Guaynabo	97,280
Arecibo	95,816
Toa Baja	88,799
Mayaguez	87,712
Toa Alta	75,105

Notes: †A person of Hispanic or Latino origin may be of any race. NA indicates that data are not available. Percentages may not equal 100 due to rounding.

SOURCE: U.S. Census Bureau. Census 2010 and Population Estimates. www.census.gov/ (accessed July 2012).

Puerto Rico Population by Race
CENSUS 2010

This table shows the number of people who are of one, two, or three or more races. For those claiming two races, the number of people belonging to the various categories is listed. The U.S. government conducts a census of the population every 10 years.

	Number	Percent
Total population	3,725,789	100.0
One race	3,603,543	96.7
Two races	109,527	2.9
White *and* Black or African American	63,552	1.7
White *and* American Indian/Alaska Native	1,905	0.1
White *and* Asian	1,322	—
White *and* Native Hawaiian/Pacific Islander	324	—
White *and* some other race	24,560	0.7
Black or African American *and* American Indian/Alaska Native	2,359	0.1
Black or African American *and* Asian	494	—
Black or African American *and* Native Hawaiian/Pacific Islander	125	—
Black or African American *and* some other race	10,367	0.3
American Indian/Alaska Native *and* Asian	346	—
American Indian/Alaska Native *and* Native Hawaiian/Pacific Islander	40	—
American Indian/Alaska Native *and* some other race	2,385	0.1
Asian *and* Native Hawaiian/Pacific Islander	30	—
Asian *and* some other race	639	—
Native Hawaiian/Pacific Islander *and* some other race	1,079	—
Three or more races	12,719	0.3

SOURCE: U.S. Census Bureau. Census 2010. www.census/gov/ (accessed July 2012). A dash (—) indicates that the percent is less than 0.1.

among the residents. From 1898 through the 1920s, US authorities unsuccessfully sought to make English the island's primary language. As of 2011, approximately 95.2% of the island's residents over the age of five spoke a language other than English at home. Of these, Spanish was the most common, spoken at home by 95.1% of the population. About 0.1% spoke another Indo-European language at home; while 4.8% spoke English at home. Only 1,210 people spoke an Asian or Pacific Islander language at home.

Taino Indian terms that survive in Puerto Rican Spanish include such place names as Arecibo, Guayama, and Mayagüez, as well as *hamaca* (hammock) and *canoa* (canoe). Among many African borrowings are food terms like *quimbombó* (okra), *guince* (banana), and *mondongo* (a spicy stew).

 Religions

During the first three centuries of Spanish rule, Roman Catholicism was the only religion permitted in Puerto Rico. About 85% of the population was still Roman Catholic in 2008, and the Church maintains numerous hospitals and schools on the island. Most of the remaining Puerto Ricans belong to other Christian denominations, which have been allowed on the island since the 1850s. Pentecostal churches have attracted a significant following, particularly among the urban poor of the barrios.

10 Transportation

Rivers are not navigable, and the only function of narrow-gauge rural railroads is to haul sugarcane to the mills during the harvesting season. Other goods are transported by truck. A few public bus systems provide intercity passenger transport, the largest being the Metropolitan Bus Authority (MBA), a government-owned company serving San Juan and nearby cities. The predominant form of public transportation outside the San Juan metropolitan area is the *público,* a privately owned jitney service of small buses and cars. In many rural areas, this is the only form of public transit.

In 2004, Puerto Rico had 264 miles (424 kilometers) of interstate highways and 15,673 miles (25,217 kilometers) of paved local roads. A rail transit system (the Tren Urbano or Urban Train) began operations in December 2004, connecting San Juan to the surrounding urban areas with 16 stations along a 10.7-mile (17-kilometer), 30-minute route. Ferries link the main island with Vieques and Culebra.

Puerto Rico receives flights from the US mainland and from the Virgin Islands, the British West Indies, Jamaica, and the Dominican Republic, as well as from Great Britain, France, Spain, and the Netherlands. Puerto Rico had 29 airports in 2012, 17 of which had paved runways. Luis Muñoz Marin International Airport had 4,091,898 passenger enplanements in 2009.

11 History

Archaeological finds indicate that at least three Native American cultures settled on the island now known as Puerto Rico long before its discovery by Christopher Columbus on 19 November 1493. The first group, belonging to the Archaic Culture, is believed to have come from Florida sometime between 3000 and 2000 BC and relied on the products of the sea. Later groups came from northern South America and brought agriculture and pottery to the island. The third culture, the Taino, combined fishing with agriculture. A peaceful, sedentary tribe, the Taino were adept at stonework and lived in many parts of the island. To these Indians, the island was known as Boriqúen.

Columbus, accompanied by a young nobleman named Juan Ponce de León, landed at the western end of the island—which he called San Juan Bautista (St. John the Baptist)—and claimed it for Spain. Not until colonization was well under way would the island acquire the name Puerto Rico (literally, "rich port"), with the name San Juan Bautista applied to the capital city. The first settlers arrived on 12 August 1508, under the leadership of Ponce de León, who sought to transplant and adapt Spanish civilization to Puerto Rico's tropical habitat.

The small contingent of Spaniards compelled the Taino, numbering perhaps 30,000, to mine for gold. The rigors of forced labor and the losses from rebellion and disease reduced the Taino population to about 4,000 by 1514, by which time the mines were nearly depleted. With the introduction of slaves from Africa, sugarcane growing became the leading economic activity. Since neither mining or sugarcane was able to provide sufficient revenue to support the struggling colony, the treasury of New Spain began a subsidy that defrayed the cost of the island's government and defense until the early 19th century.

16th to 18th Centuries From the early 16th century onward, an intense power struggle for the control of the Caribbean marked Puerto Rico as a strategic base of the first magnitude. After a French attack in 1528, construction of La Fortaleza (still in use today as the governor's palace) was begun in 1533, and work on El Morro fortress in San Juan commenced six years later. The new fortifications helped repel a British attack led by Sir Francis Drake in 1595. A second force, arriving in 1598 under George Clifford, Earl of Cumberland, succeeded in capturing San Juan, but the British were forced to withdraw by tropical heat and disease.

In 1625, a Dutch attack under the command of Boudewijn Hendrikszoon was repulsed, although much of San Juan was sacked and burned by the attackers. By the 18th century,

Puerto Rico had become a haven for pirates, and smuggling was the major economic activity. A Spanish envoy who came to the island in 1765 was appalled, and his report to the crown inaugurated a period of economic, administrative, and military reform. The creation of a native militia helped Puerto Rico withstand a fierce British assault on San Juan in 1797, by which time the island had more than 100,000 inhabitants.

Long after most of the Spanish colonies in the New World had obtained independence, Puerto Rico and Cuba remained under Spanish rule. Despite several rebellions, most of them inspired by the Latin American liberator Simón Bolivar, Spain's military might halted any revolution on the island.

El Morro fortress, constructed in the 1500s, was built to protect the area from an attack. © ARENA CREATIVE/SHUTTERSTOCK.COM.

Puerto Rico became a shelter for refugees from Santo Domingo, Haiti, and Venezuela who were faithful to Spain, fearful of disturbances in their own countries, or both. As in Cuba, the sugar industry developed in Puerto Rico during this period favored the institution of slavery on the island.

19th Century The 19th century also gave birth, however, to a new Puerto Rican civil and political consciousness. Puerto Rican participation in the short-lived constitutional experiments in Spain (1812–14 and 1820–23) fostered the rise of a spirit of liberalism. The Spanish constitution of 1812 declared that the people of Puerto Rico were no longer colonial subjects but were full-fledged citizens of Spain. Nevertheless, the Spanish crown maintained an alert, centralized, absolutist government in Puerto Rico with all basic powers concentrated in the captain general.

Toward the middle of the 19th century, a *criollo* generation with strong liberal roots began a new era in Puerto Rican history. This group, which called for the abolition of slavery and the introduction of far-reaching economic and political reforms, also developed and strengthened the Puerto Rican literary tradition. The more radical reformers supported the cause of separation from Spain and joined in a propaganda campaign in New York on behalf of Cuban independence. An aborted revolution began in the town of Lares in September 1868 (and coincided with an insurrection in Spain that deposed Queen Isabella II). Though it was soon quelled, this rebellion awakened a dormant sense of national identity among Puerto Ricans.

The major reform efforts after 1868 revolved around abolitionism and *autonomia,* or self-government. Slavery was abolished in 1873 by the First Spanish Republic, which also granted new political rights to the islanders. The restoration of the Spanish monarchy two years later, however, was a check to Puerto Rican aspirations. During the last quarter of the century, leaders such as Luis Muñoz Rivera sought unsuccessfully to secure vast new powers of self-government.

The imminence of war with the United States over Cuba, coupled with autonomist agitation within Puerto Rico, led Spain in November 1897 to grant to the island a charter with broad powers of self-rule. Shortly after an elected government began to function in July 1898, US forces, overcoming Spanish resistance, took over the island. A cease-fire was proclaimed on 13 August, and sovereignty was formally transferred to the United States with the signing of the Treaty of Paris in December, ending the Spanish-American War.

The US government swept aside the self-governing charter granted by Spain and established military rule from 1898 to 1900. Civilian government was restored in 1900 under a colonial law, the Foraker Act, that gave the federal government full control of the executive and legislative branches, leaving some local representation in the lower chamber, or house of delegates. Under the Jones Act of 1917, Congress extended US citizenship to the islanders and granted an elective senate, but still reserved vast powers over Puerto Rico to the federal bureaucracy.

20th Century The early period of US rule saw an effort to Americanize local institutions, including the substitution of English for the Spanish language. In the meantime, American corporate capital took over the sugar industry, developing a plantation economy so pervasive that, by 1920, 75% of the population relied on the cane crop for its livelihood. Glaring irregularities of wealth resulted, sharpening social and political divisions. This period also saw the development of three main trends in Puerto Rican political thinking. One group favored the incorporation of Puerto Rico into the United States as a state; a second group, fearful of cultural assimilation, favored self-government; and a third group wanted independence.

The Great Depression of the 1930s hit Puerto Rico especially hard. With a population approaching two million by the late 1930s and with few occupational opportunities outside the sugar industry, the island's economy deteriorated. Mass unemployment and near-starvation were the results.

Controlling the Puerto Rican legislature from 1932 to 1940 was a coalition of the Socialist Party and the Republican Party. The Socialist Party was led by Santiago Iglesias, a Spanish labor leader who became a protégé of the American Federation of Labor. The Republican Party, which had traditionally supported statehood, had been founded in Puerto Rico by José Celso Barbosa, a black physician who had studied in the United States. The coalition was unable to produce any significant improvement, although under the New Deal a US government effort was made to supply emergency relief for the "stricken island."

Agitation for full political and economic reform or independence gained ground during this period. Great pressure was put on Washington for a change in the island's political status, while social and economic reform was carried to the fullest extent possible within the limitations of the Jones Act. Intensive efforts were made to centralize economic planning, attract new industries through local tax exemptions (Puerto Rico was already exempt from federal taxation), reduce inequalities of income, and improve housing, schools, and health conditions. By 1955, income from manufacturing surpassed agriculture and was five times as great by 1970.

The Popular Democratic Party (PDP), the dominant force in Puerto Rican politics from 1940 to 1968, favored a new self-governing relationship with the United States, distinct from statehood or independence. The party succeeded not only in bringing about significant social and economic change but also in obtaining from Congress, in 1950, a law allowing Puerto Ricans to draft their own constitution with full local self-government. This new constitution, approved in a general referendum on 3 March 1952, led to the establishment on 25 July of the Commonwealth of Puerto Rico (Estado Libre Asociado de Puerto Rico), which was constituted as an autonomous political entity in voluntary association with the United States.

More advanced than most Caribbean countries in education, health, and social development, Puerto Rico suffered from growing political tensions in the early 1980s, with occasional terrorist attacks on US military installations and personnel. These tensions may have been exacerbated by the national recession of 1980–81, which had a particularly severe impact on Puerto Rico. At the same time, the island's economy experienced a structural shift. Whereas 50% of jobs in Puerto Rico had been in agriculture in 1940, by 1989 that figure had dropped to 20%. Manufacturing jobs, in contrast, rose from 5 to 15% of total employment between 1940 and 1989.

In 1989, Hurricane Hugo caused 12 deaths and $1 billion in damage in Puerto Rico. In 1998, Hurricane Georges ravaged the island, causing damage estimated in the billions of dollars. In 2004, Hurricane Jeanne caused eight deaths and led to the island being declared a federal disaster area, qualifying Puerto Rico for more than $40 million in aid.

21st Century In the 2000 elections, Sila M. Calderón was elected the island's first female governor. During Calderón's administration, Puerto Rico was faced with a growing crime rate, fueled by the illegal drug trade. The economy was ailing, made worse by the phasing out of tax breaks that had been given to US companies to set up operations on the island. Calderón did not run for a second term; in 2004, Anibal Acevedo Vila narrowly defeated former governor Pedro Rossello for the office. Political gridlock between the legislature and the governor resulted in the lack of a budget. On 1 May 2006, the government ran out of money. Nearly 100,000 Puerto Rican government employees lost their jobs, some 43 government agencies shut down, and the island's 1,600 public schools were closed.

In 2003, the US Navy withdrew from the island of Vieques, and approximately 15,000 acres of land previously used by the military were turned over to the US Department of the Interior's Fish and Wildlife Service, to be dedicated to a wildlife refuge closed to the public. Over the years, Puerto Ricans had protested the US military presence on Vieques, maintaining that military exercises carried out there were responsible for health and environmental problems. In 1999, an accident on the island during a US military training exercise had killed one Puerto Rican civilian and wounded four others.

In 2008, the governorship was won by Luis Guillermo Fortuño Burset (1960–), president of the New Progressive Party of Puerto Rico (NPP) and a member of the Republican National Committee. He took office during a time of fiscal chaos, as the recession that began in 2008 severely affected the economy of Puerto Rico. Fortuño imposed austerity measures (reductions in benefits and programs) and tax cuts to bring the island's budget deficit under control. However, the unemployment rate climbed to over 17% and the government was forced to lay off more than 13,000 workers amid increasing strikes and protests. In 2012, Fortuño lost his reelection bid to Alejandro Garcia Padilla of the Popular Democratic Party.

The 51st State? Puerto Rico's political status remains a source of controversy. Statehood would give Puerto Rico representation in the US Congress and would make the island eligible for billions of dollars more a year in food stamps, medical insurance, and income support payments, which are currently set at levels far below those of states.

Statehood, however, would also incur the loss of tax benefits. Under current federal tax law for the commonwealth, individuals pay no federal income tax.

In a 1993 plebiscite (direct vote of the people), a slight majority of Puerto Rican voters chose to maintain the island's status as an American commonwealth. The vote was conditioned, however, by a request that Congress modify the terms of the island's commonwealth status. Specifically, Puerto Ricans asked for such "enhancements" as removing the federal ceiling on food stamps and extending Supplemental Security Income, a federal aid program, to elderly and disabled Puerto Ricans. They also requested that federal tax law, recently amended to reduce the exemptions corporations could claim from taxes on profits by 60%, be restored to its original form.

Another plebiscite was held in 1998, in which "none of the above" won a majority of the votes over independence options including statehood, free association, and commonwealth. In November 2012, a plebescite was again held, at the behest of the United Nations Special Committee on Decolonization. The ballot asked whether voters wanted to continue as a territory, become an independent nation, become a state in the United States, or be a nation in free association with the United States. Most voters preferred statehood although as many as 472,000 voters did not make a choice.

12 State Government

Since 1952, Puerto Rico has been a self-governing commonwealth in association with the United States, governed under the Puerto Rican Federal Relations Act and under a constitution based on the US model.

The commonwealth legislature comprises a senate (Senado) of 27 or more members, 2 from each of 8 senatorial districts and 11 elected at large, and a house of representatives (Cámara de Representantes) of 51 members (as of 2012), 1 from each of 40 districts and 11 at large. Each senate district consists of five house districts. Two extra seats are granted in each house to the opposition, if necessary, to limit any party's control to two-thirds. This assures representation for minority parties. The governor, who may serve an unlimited number of four-year terms, is the only elected executive.

Residents of Puerto Rico may not vote in US presidential elections. A Puerto Rican who settles in one of the 50 states automatically becomes eligible to vote for president; conversely, a state resident who migrates to Puerto Rico forfeits such eligibility. Puerto Rico has no vote in the US Senate or House of Representatives, but a nonvoting resident commissioner, elected every four years, may speak on the floor of the House, introduce legislation, and vote in House committees. As of 2012, Democrat Pedro Pierluisi (1959–) was resident commissioner. He was reelected in 2012 for four more years.

13 Political Parties

The Popular Democratic Party (PPD), founded in 1938, favors the strengthening and development of commonwealth status. The New Progressive Party (PNP), created in 1968 as the successor to the Puerto Rican Republican Party, is pro-statehood. Two smaller parties, each favoring independence for the island, are the Puerto Rican Independence Party (PIP), founded in the mid-1940s and committed to democratic socialism, and the more radical Puerto Rican Socialist Party, which has close ties with Cuba. A breakaway group, the Renewal Party, led by the then-mayor of San Juan, Hernán Padilla, left the PNP and took part in the 1984 elections. The Puerto Ricans for Puerto Rico Party was founded in 2003, but lost its certification after it failed to garner the required 3% of the vote in the 2008 elections.

Governor Carlos Romero Barceló of the PNP had pledged to actively seek Puerto Rico's admission to the Union if elected by a large margin. In 1980 he retained the governorship by a plurality of fewer than 3,500 votes. Former governor Rafael Hernández Colón defeated Romero Barceló's bid for reelection in 1984 by more than 54,000 votes. Colon was reelected in 1988 and was succeeded in 1992 by Pedro Rossello, a New Progressive and a supporter of statehood. Rossello was reelected in 1996. In 2000, Sila M. Calderón was elected Puerto Rico's first female governor, with 48.6% of the vote. The 2004 general elections were the second-closest in Puerto Rican history. A recount confirmed the winner, Anibal Acevedo Vila of the PPD. He was the first governor in Puerto Rican history not to have a resident commissioner of his same party, given that Luis Fortuño won the post. Vila was unseated in 2008 by Fortuño by more than 223,000 votes. Fortuño lost his reelection bid in 2012 to Alejandro Garcia Padilla of the Popular Democratic Party.

Although Puerto Ricans living in Puerto Rico have no vote in US presidential elections, the island does send voting delegates to the national conventions of the Democratic and Republican parties.

14 Local Government

The Commonwealth of Puerto Rico had 78 *municipios* (municipalities) in 2012, each governed by a mayor and municipal assembly elected every four years. In fact, these governments resemble US county governments in that they perform services for both urban and rural areas. Many of the functions normally performed by municipal governments in the United States—for instance, fire protection, education, water supply, and law enforcement—are performed by the commonwealth government directly.

15 Judicial System

Puerto Rico's highest court, the supreme court, consists of a chief justice and six associate justices. They are appointed, like all other judges, by the governor with the consent of the senate and serve until compulsory retirement at age 70. The court may sit in separate panels for some purposes, but not in cases dealing with the constitutionality of commonwealth law, for which the entire body convenes. Decisions of the Supreme Court of Puerto Rico regarding US constitutional questions may be appealed to the US Supreme Court.

The Puerto Rico circuit court of appeals consists of 33 justices named by the governor with the consent of the senate. The court was created in 1994 as an intermediary tribunal between the courts of first instance and the supreme court.

The nine superior courts are the main trial courts; superior court judges are appointed to 12-year terms. These courts have original jurisdiction in civil cases not exceeding $10,000 and in minor criminal cases. District courts also hear preliminary motions in more serious criminal cases. Municipal judges, serving for five years, and justices of the peace, in rural areas, decide cases involving local ordinances.

San Juan is the seat of the US District Court for Puerto Rico, which has the same jurisdiction as federal district courts on the US mainland. Six active judges and three senior judges sit in the District of Puerto Rico, assisted by four magistrate judges. Puerto Rico is in the US Court of Appeals First Circuit, which sits in San Juan for two weeks each year.

Puerto Rico's constitution forbids capital punishment, but US prosecutors can seek the

A view of a harbor and the city of San Juan. © SEANPAVONEPHOTO/SHUTTERSTOCK.COM.

death penalty under federal law. As of September 2012, four capital cases have been tried by US authorities since 1988. None of the cases has resulted in a death sentence.

16 Migration

Although migration from Puerto Rico to the US mainland is not a recent phenomenon—several Puerto Rican merchants were living in New York City as early as 1830—there were no more than 70,000 islanders in the United States in 1940. Mass migration, spurred by the booming postwar job market in the United States, began in 1947. The out-migration was particularly large from 1951 through 1959, when the net outflow of migrants from the island averaged more than 47,000 a year.

According to US Census data, the island's population declined by around 2.2%, or 82,821

people between 2000 and 2010. The Census also showed that there were 4.7 million Puerto Ricans living in the United States in 2010, while only 3,725,789 million lived on the island. Puerto Ricans are found in significant numbers in New York, New Jersey, Illinois, Pennsylvania, California, Florida, Connecticut, and Massachusetts.

On the island, there were 112,536 foreign-born residents in 2011. The majority of these (105,015 people) were from Latin America.

17 Economy

The island's most important industrial products are pharmaceuticals, electronics, apparel, and food products. The sugar industry has gradually lost ground to dairy production and other livestock products in the agricultural sector. Tourism is the backbone of a large service industry, and the government sector has also grown. Tourist revenues and remittances from Puerto Rican workers on the US mainland largely counterbalance the island's chronic trade deficit.

The recession in the United States that began in 2008 severely impacted the Puerto Rican economy. Puerto Rico's economy had begun declining years earlier, as tourists and manufacturers were lured away to countries in Latin America and the Caribbean, and the island had come to rely on money from the federal government. With the recession, these funds were cut, and Puerto Rico was forced to trim budgets and lay off public workers. In 2009, unemployment exceeded 16%. By 2012, however, the island's economy was seeing improvement as unemployment was down to 13%–14% and tax revenues had begun increasing for the first time in six years. Puerto Rico's gross domestic product was $96.26 billion in 2010.

18 Income

Median household income in Puerto Rico was $18,314 in 2009, with an average per capita personal income (including nonmonetary income) of around $15,203. This was far lower than in any of the 50 states during that year.

19 Industry

In 2010, the island's net income from manufacturing was $44.6 billion. Chemicals, pharmaceuticals, and machinery are the major manufacturing industries. As of December 2010, there were 57 pharmaceutical plants in Puerto Rico representing many of the world's leading drug and health companies. Companies included Johnson and Johnson (Rio Piedras),

Abbott Chemicals (Barceloneta), Bristol-Myers Squibb (Humacao), Warner-Lambert (Vega Baja), and Schering-Plough (Manati). Baxter International (medical devices) was drawn to the territory in 1976, following passage of the Congressional Tax Reform Act of 1976, which provided incentives to pharmaceutical plants and related industries that opened plants in Puerto Rico. However, when this law, and the incentives, expired in 2006, many companies chose to close their plants.

20 Labor

Puerto Rico's civilian labor force as of August 2012 numbered 1,267,500, while 171,400 were unemployed. That month, unemployment averaged 13.5% compared to the US national average of 8.1%. Those employed in nonfarm wage and salaried jobs that same month included: 79,200 in manufacturing; 33,500 in mining, logging, and construction; 160,700 in trade, transportation, and utilities; 103,700 in professional and business services; 120,400 in education and health services; 71,900 in leisure and hospitality; and 267,400 in government.

Less than 10% of the labor force belongs to trade unions. Wages tend to adhere closely to the US statutory minimum, which applies to Puerto Rico.

21 Agriculture

In 1940, agriculture employed 43% of the work force; by 2010, fewer than 17,000 people worked in the agricultural industry. Nowhere is this decline more evident than in the sugar industry. Production peaked at 1.3 million tons in 1952. The hilly terrain makes mechanization difficult, and manual cutting contributes to production costs that are much higher than elsewhere.

Despite incentives and subsidies, tobacco is no longer profitable, and coffee production—well adapted to the highlands—falls far short of domestic consumption, although about half of the crop is exported. Coffee production in 2010–2011 was valued at around $29.5 million. Plantains (similar to bananas) are also an important crop. Ornamental plants, vegetables, and tropical fruits such as pineapples, mangoes, and bananas are also grown.

22 Domesticated Animals

In early 2011, Puerto Rico had 77,000 head of milk cattle, producing a total value of $219 million in milk products. Chickens for egg production numbered 588,000, with a total egg production of 147 million, valued at $13.7 million. Red meat production amounted to 29.4 million pounds (13.3 million kilograms), while hog production was 41.6 million pounds (18.9 million kilograms). Hog sales amounted to around $6.2 million in 2007.

23 Fishing

Although sport fishing, especially for blue marlin, is an important tourist attraction, the waters surrounding Puerto Rico are too deep to lend themselves to commercial fishery. Tuna brought in from African and South American waters was processed on the western shore, although some plants were closed as tax benefits to companies operating in Puerto Rico were phased out. Species produced by Puerto Rican aquaculture include saltwater shrimp, red snapper, cobia, red tilapia, and ornamental species. In 2007, there were around 40 aquaculture farms in Puerto Rico, with sales of around $833,000.

24 Forestry

Puerto Rico lost its self-sufficiency in timber production by the mid-19th century, as population expansion and increasing demand for food led to massive deforestation. Puerto Rico must import nearly all of its wood and paper products. The public forest system covers 86,095 acres (34,842 hectares), of which 58,249 acres (23,573 hectares) are part of the Puerto Rico State Forest system and 27,846 acres (11,269 hectares) are part of the Caribbean National Forest. The El Yunque Caribbean National Forest is the only tropical rainforest in the US national forest system.

25 Mining

The estimated value of nonfuel mineral commodities produced in Puerto Rico was $98.6 million in 2007. Portland cement, crushed stone, lime, and salt are the most valuable commodities.

At least 11 different types of metallic mineral deposits, including copper, iron, gold, manganese, silver, molybdenum, zinc, lead, and other minerals, are found on the island. Also produced are industrial minerals (cement, stone, clay, and sand and gravel).

26 Energy and Power

Puerto Rico is almost totally dependent on imported crude oil for its energy needs. The island has not yet developed any fossil fuel resources of its own, and its one experimental nuclear reactor, built on the south coast at Rincon in 1964, was shut down after a few years. In 2007, Puerto Rico was the fifth-largest solar thermal power producer in the United States and its territories. Puerto Rico has one petroleum refinery, located in Yabucoa on the southeastern tip of the island.

Inefficiency in the public transport system has encouraged commonwealth residents to rely on private vehicles, thereby increasing the demands for imported petroleum. In 2009, Puerto Rico consumed an estimated 264,000 barrels of oil per day. The vast majority of oil imports came from American and Caribbean suppliers.

Puerto Rico began importing liquefied natural gas in 2000 to supply its gas-fired plant in Penuelas. In 2010, an estimated 27 billion cubic feet (764.5 million cubic meters) was consumed. A coal-fired plant in Guayama was recognized as one of the cleanest coal-fired plants in the world when it became operational in 2002.

In 2010, total net electricity generation was 20.7 billion kilowatt hours. Almost all of this was produced by petroleum, natural gas, or coal-fired plants.

27 Commerce

Wholesale trade in 2008 included some 2,338 establishments and major distributors, and it employed 36,360 people. Retail trade consists mainly of food and apparel stores. In 2008, there were 10,811 retail establishments, employing 131,689 people. Total retail trade amounted to an estimated $36 billion in 2011. Two large shopping centers, Plaza las Americas and Plaza Carolina, are in the San Juan area.

Foreign trade is a significant factor in Puerto Rico's economy. Trade between the United States and Puerto Rico is unrestricted. In 2010, the island's imports were $40 billion and exports were $68.3 billion. Of these, $20.6 billion in imports were from the United States, while $47.6 billion in exports went to the United States.

28 Public Finance

Puerto Rico's annual budget is prepared by the Bureau of Budget and Management and submitted by the governor to the legislature, which has unlimited power to amend it. The fiscal year extends from 1 July to 30 June. In the 2011/12 fiscal year, the budget totaled $28.6 billion. Of this, $14.2 billion was allocated to social development, including health, education, and housing. Protection and safety accounted for $1.6 billion in spending, while $4.3 billion was to be spent on servicing Puerto Rico's debt. In 2010, public debt was approximately $65.2 billion.

29 Taxation

The Puerto Rican Federal Relations Act stipulates that the Commonwealth is exempt from US internal revenue laws. The federal income tax is not levied on permanent residents of Puerto Rico, but federal Social Security and unemployment taxes are deducted from payrolls, and the commonwealth government collects an income tax. Corporations in Puerto Rico are also taxed.

In 2011, the treasury reported total tax revenues of $8.13 billion. About $97.8 million was collected in property taxes. Income tax provided revenues of about $2.2 billion, while revenue

The capitol building of Puerto Rico is in San Juan. © JOSEPH/
SHUTTERSTOCK.COM.

from corporate taxes amounted to $1.677 billion. There are also taxes on room charges at hotels. An excise tax applies for all inbound shipments, there is a tax on sales to foreign corporations with operations in Puerto Rico, and there are taxes on alcohol and motor vehicles as well. Municipalities also impose a municipal license tax, ranging from 27% to 50%, on the gross volume of business each year. Merchandise arriving from the US is subject to a tax of about 6.6%.

Puerto Rico has a 5.5% sales tax. Municipalities have the option of imposing an additional sales tax of up to 1.5%. In addition, in the event that the governor determines an insufficiency in collections for the general fund, an additional 1% to the central government will be imposed.

30 Health

Infant mortality has declined drastically, from 113 deaths per 1,000 live births in 1940 to 7.9 in 2012. That same year, life expectancy was 79 years (75.5 years for males; 82.8 years for females). The leading causes of death were similar to those in most industrialized countries (heart disease, cancer, diabetes mellitus). Alcoholism and drug addiction are among the major public health problems, although suicide occurs less often than it does in most of the states. At the end of 2008, there were an estimated 18,544 residents living with AIDS, and the death rate for HIV was estimated at 10.9 per 100,000 population.

In 2012, Puerto Rico had 54 hospitals with a total of 8,132 staffed beds. In 2004, there were 254 doctors and 1,552 dentists per 100,000 people. In 2005, there were 383 registered nurses per 100,000 population.

31 Housing

In 2011, there were a total of 1,567,959 housing units, 1,256,151 (80.1%) of which were occupied and 876,741 (69.8%) of which were owner-occupied. That year 67.4% of all units (1,057,534) were single-family detached homes and 4,410 (0.3%) were mobile homes. Just over 23% of all units were built between 1970 and 1979. Most homes were heated with electricity. In 2011, 21,391 (1.7%) lacked complete kitchen facilities. The median home value was $120,300. The median monthly cost for units with a mortgage in 2011 was $888 and the median monthly cost for rent was $442.

A row of colorful pastel buildings is shown in Old San Juan. © ARENA CREATIVE/SHUTTERSTOCK.COM.

32 Education

Education is compulsory for children between 6 and 16 years of age, and nearly 2 out of 10 commonwealth budget dollars goes to education. As of 2008, about 90% of the population was literate.

In the fall of 2010, there were 493,300 students attending public primary and secondary school. Instruction is carried out in Spanish, but English is taught at all levels. In 2008, there were 1,114 public primary and secondary schools in Puerto Rico, and per pupil expenditure in 2010 was $7,372.

In 2010, a total of 249,400 students were enrolled in college or university. The primary state-supported institution of higher learning is the University of Puerto Rico, with its main campus at Rico Piedras. The system also includes doctorate-level campuses at Mayagüez and San Juan (for medical sciences), and four-year colleges at Aguadilla, Arecibo, Bayamon, Carolina, Cavey, Humacao, Guayama, Ponce, and Utuado.

The 76 private institutions of higher education in 2012 included the Interamerican University, with campuses at Hato Rey, San German, and other locations; nine seminaries or theological colleges; and seven branches of the Institute of Banking and Commerce.

33 Arts

The Tapia Theater in Old San Juan is the island's major showcase for local and visiting performers, such as the Taller de Histriones group and *zarzuela* (comic opera) troupes from Spain. The Institute of Puerto Rican Culture produces an annual film festival. The Fine Arts Center in San Juan is the largest center of its kind in the Caribbean. It features entertainment ranging from ballet, opera, and symphonies to drama, jazz, and popular music.

Puerto Rico has its own symphony orchestra and conservatory of music. Puerto Rico supports both a classical ballet company (the Ballets de San Juan) and the Areyto Folkloric Group, which performs traditional folk dances. Salsa, a popular style pioneered by such Puerto Rican musicians as Tito Puente, influenced the development of pop music on the US mainland during the 1970s.

34 Libraries and Museums

In 2008, Puerto Rico had a total of 60 public libraries, containing about 920,220 volumes. There were also 70 academic libraries, including the University of Puerto Rico Library at Rio Piedras, and more than 700 school libraries. The library of the Puerto Rico Conservatory of Music, in San Juan, has a collection of music written by Puerto Rican and Latin American composers. Among about 60 museums open in 2012 were the Museo de Arte de Ponce, the Puerto Rico Museum of Contemporary Art, the Arecibo Observatory, and the Marine Station Museum in Mayagüez.

35 Communications

The Puerto Rico Telephone Company was founded in 1914 by the creators of International Telephone and Telegraph (ITT). In 1974, the Puerto Rican government bought the phone company from ITT. In 2011, around 3 million people in Puerto Rico had cell phone accounts, with around 1.3 million using their phone to access the Internet. In 2011, the World Bank reported that around 43% of Puerto Ricans used the Internet.

As of 2012, there were 77 AM and 53 FM radio stations and 24 commercial television channels/networks.

36 Press

Puerto Rico has four major dailies: *El Nuevo Dias,* with the largest circulation in 2011— 178,175 mornings and 212,934 Sundays; *El Voceo; Primera Hora;* and the English-language *Puerto Rico Daily Sun.* There are also two weekly and four regional newspapers.

37 Tourism, Travel, and Recreation

The tourism industry has grown rapidly from 65,000 tourists in 1950 to 1.1 million in 1970 to 4.87 million in 2010. Tourism employed approximately 72,000 workers in May 2012. During 2010, visitors spent $3.6 million in Puerto Rico, compared to $1.4 million in 1990.

Most tourists come for sunning, swimming, deep sea fishing, and the fashionable shops, night clubs, and casinos of San Juan's Condado Strip. Attractions of old San Juan include two fortresses, El Morro and San Cristobal, San Jose Church (one of the oldest in the New World), and La Fortaleza, the governor's palace. The government has encouraged tourists to journey outside of San Juan to destinations such as the rain forest of El Yunque, the Vieques Biobay, and the bird sanctuary and mangrove forest on the shores of Torrecilla Lagoon.

Many tourists and residents catch some sun in Isla Verde Beach in San Juan. © ISRAEL PABON/SHUTTERSTOCK.COM.

There are many annual festivals and events in Puerto Rico, including Fiestas de la Calle San Sebastián, Rincón International Film Festival, Carnival, Dulce Sueño Paso Fino Fair, the International Light Tackle Blue Marlin Tournament, the Festival de los Mascaras, and the Festival de Cafe.

38 Sports

Baseball is very popular in Puerto Rico. There is a six-team professional winter league, in which many ballplayers from American and National league teams participate. Horse racing, boxing, and basketball are also popular. Other annual sporting events include the Copa Velasco Regatta, the first leg of the Caribbean Ocean Racing Triangle, and the International Billfish Tournament in San Juan.

39 Famous Puerto Ricans

Elected to represent Puerto Rico before the Spanish Cortes in 1812, Ramón Power y Giralt (1775–1813), a liberal reformer, was the leading Puerto Rican political figure of the early 19th century. Power, appointed vice president of the Cortes, participated in the drafting of the new Spanish constitution of 1812. Ramón Emeterio Betances (1827–1898) became well known not only for his efforts to alleviate a cholera epidemic in 1855, but also for his crusade to abolish slavery in Puerto Rico and for his leadership in a racial separatist movement.

The dominant political figure in 20th-century Puerto Rico was Luis Muñoz Marin (1898–1980), founder of the Popular Democratic Party in 1938 and president of Puerto

Rico's senate from 1940 to 1948. Muñoz, the first native-born elected governor of the island, devised the commonwealth relationship that has governed the island since 1952.

Women have actively participated in Puerto Rican politics. Ana Roqué de Duprey (1853–1933) led the Asociación Puertorriquena de Mujeres Sufragistas, organized in late 1926, while Milagros Benet de Mewton (1868–1945) presided over the Liga Social Sufragista, founded in 1917. Both groups actively lobbied for the extension of the right to vote to Puerto Rican women, not only in Puerto Rico but in the United States and other countries as well.

Manuel A. Alonso (1822–1889) blazed the trail for a distinctly Puerto Rican literature with the publication in 1849 of *El Gibaro,* the first major effort to depict the traditions and mores of the island's rural society.

In the world of entertainment, Academy Award winners José Ferrer (1912–1992) and Rita Moreno (1931–) are among the most famous. Four-time Tony nominee Raul Juliá (1944–1994) and two-time Tony winner Chita Rivera (1933–) are also from the island. Actor Joaquin Phoenix (1974–) was also born in Puerto Rico. Notable in classical music is cellist-conductor Pablo Casals (b. Spain, 1875–1973), a longtime resident of Puerto Rico. Well-known popular musicians include Tito Puente (b. New York, 1923–2000), José Feliciano (1945–), and Ricky Martin (1971–).

Baseball is a very popular sport in Puerto Rico and a large number of US major league players have come from the islands. Roberto Clemente (1934–1972), one of baseball's most admired performers and a member of the Hall of Fame, played on 12 National League All-Star teams and was named Most Valuable Player in

Singer and guitarist José Feliciano was born in Puerto Rico.
© ZUMA WIRE SERVICE / ALAMY

1966. Outfielder Carlos Beltran (1977–), who signed a $119 million contract with the New York Mets in 2005, third-baseman Mike Lowell (1974–), and Hall of Fame member Orlando Cepeda (1937–) were all from Puerto Rico.

40 Bibliography

BOOKS

Bernthal, Ron. *Puerto Rico, Off the Beaten Path,* 6th ed. Guilford, CT: GPP Travel, 2009.

Brown, Jonatha A. *Puerto Rico.* Milwaukee, WI: Gareth Stevens, 2006.

Feeney, Kathy. *Puerto Rico Facts and Symbols.* Rev. ed. Mankato, MN: Capstone Press, 2003.

Levy, Patricia, and Nazry Bahrawi. *Puerto Rico.* 2nd ed. New York: Marshall Cavendish Benchmark, 2005.

Rigau, Jorge. *Puerto Rico Then and Now.* 2nd ed. San Diego, CA: Thunder Bay Press, 2009.

Rodriquez-Silva, Ileana M. *Silencing Race: Disentangling Blackness, Colonialism, and National Identities in Puerto Rico.* Sydney, Australia: Palgrave Macmillan, 2012.

Stille, Darlene R. *Puerto Rico.* New York: Children's Press, 2009.

WEB SITES

"Ecological Services in the Caribbean." *US Fish and Wildlife Service.* http://www.fws.gov/ caribbean/es/Press.html (accessed on November 16, 2012).

"Economy at a Glance: Puerto Rico." *US Bureau of Labor Statistics.* http://www.bls.gov/eag/ eag.pr.htm (accessed on November 16, 2012).

Puerto Rico.com: Puerto Rico Channel. www. puertorico.com/ (accessed on November 16, 2012).

The Vieques Conservation and Historical Trust. http:// vcht.org/about/ (accessed on November 16, 2012).

Welcome to Puerto Rico! http://welcome.topuertorico. org/ (accessed on November 16, 2012).

United States Caribbean Dependencies

Navassa

Navassa is a 2-square-mile (5.4-square-kilometer) island, 90 nautical miles from Guantanamo Bay, Cuba, and about one-quarter of the way from Haiti to Jamaica in the Jamaica Channel of the Caribbean Sea. It was claimed by the United States under the Guano Act of 1856. The island, located at 18°24'10" north and 75°0'45" west, has no permanent inhabitants.

In 1999, the US Fish and Wildlife Service established a wildlife refuge on Navassa to protect the island and its coral reef. Research expeditions to the island have identified over 240 species of fish and eight reptile species (four of which are extinct as of 2012) native to the island. Several new species of fish and spiders have been documented on Navassa and in the ocean water surrounding it.

US Virgin Islands

The US Virgin Islands lie about 40 miles (64 kilometers) north of Puerto Rico and 1,000 miles (1,600 kilometers) south-southeast of Miami, between 17°40" and 18°25" north and 64°34" and 65°3" west. The island group extends 51 miles (82 kilometers) north to south

and 50 miles (80 kilometers) from east to west, with a total area of at least 136 square miles (353 square kilometers).

Only 3 of the more than 50 islands and cays are of significant size. These are St. Croix, which measures 84 square miles (218 square kilometers) in area; St. Thomas, which measures 32 square miles (83 square kilometers); and St. John, which measures 20 square miles (52 square kilometers). The territorial capital, Charlotte Amalie, is located on St. Thomas. Charlotte Amalie has one of the finest harbors in the Caribbean.

St. Croix is relatively flat, with a terrain suitable for sugarcane cultivation. St. Thomas is mountainous and little cultivated, but it has many snug harbors. St. John, also mountainous, has fine beaches and lush vegetation; about one-half of St. John's area has been declared a national park—Virgin Islands National Park.

The subtropical climate, with temperatures ranging from 70–90°F (21–32°C) and an average temperature of 77°F (25°C), is moderated by northeast trade winds. Rainfall, the main source of fresh water, varies widely, and severe droughts are frequent. The average yearly rainfall varies from around 38 inches (96.5 centimeters) on St. Thomas to around 45 inches

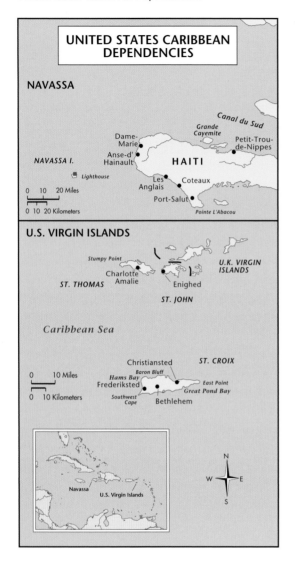

UNITED STATES CARIBBEAN DEPENDENCIES

NAVASSA

Canal du Sud

Grande
Cayemite

Dame-
Marie

Petit-Trou-
de-Nippes

Anse-d'
Hainault

NAVASSA I.

HAITI

Lighthouse

Les
Anglais

Coteaux

0 10 20 Miles

Port-Salut

0 10 20 Kilometers

Pointe L'Abacou

U.S. VIRGIN ISLANDS

Stumpy Point

U.K. VIRGIN
ISLANDS

Charlotte
Amalie

ST. THOMAS

Enighed

ST. JOHN

Caribbean Sea

Christiansted

ST. CROIX

0   10 Miles

Baron Bluff

Hams Bay

Frederiksted

East Point

0   10 Kilometers

Great Pond Bay

Southwest
Cape

Bethlehem

N

W   E

S

Navassa

U.S. Virgin Islands

The population of the US Virgin Islands was estimated at 106,405 in the 2010 US Census, down from 108,612 in 2000. The median age in 2012 was estimated at 40.9 years. The largest town in the Virgin Islands in 2010 was Charlotte Amalie, with a population of 18,481. St. Croix has two principal towns: Christiansted and Frederiksted. St. John Island was home to 4,170 people in 2010. Between 72% (St. Croix) and 81% (St. Thomas and St. John) of the population is of Afro-Caribbean descent. Most are descendants of slaves who were brought from Africa in the early days of Danish rule. English is the official and most widely spoken language, but Spanish and Creole are also spoken by around 10% of the population.

Some of the oldest religious congregations in the Western Hemisphere are located in the Virgin Islands. The Beracha Veshalom Vegmiluth Hasidim Jewish synagogue on St. Thomas, built in 1833, is the second-oldest in the United States. The Lutheran Congregation of St. Thomas, founded in 1666, is one of the three oldest congregations in the United States. Baptists make up an estimated 42% of the population, Roman Catholics 34%, and Episcopalians 17%.

In 2009, there were 1,257 kilometers (781 miles) of roads in the US Virgin Islands. Cargo shipping services operate from the US ports of Baltimore, Maryland, and Jacksonville and Miami, Florida. There are four ports in the US Virgin Islands, two on St. Croix. Both St. Croix and St. Thomas have airports. In 2008, Cyril E. King airport on St. Thomas saw 593,589 passenger enplanements, and there were 169,665 passenger enplanements at the Henry E. Rohlson airport on St. Croix. Both islands also have seaplane bases.

The US Virgin Islands has few conventional energy resources and depends on imported

(114 centimeters) on St. John, mostly during the spring and fall months.

As of September 2012, there was one hazardous waste site in the US Virgin Islands listed on the US Environmental Agency's National Priorities List. This was Tutu Wellfield in Tutu, St. Thomas, a plume of groundwater contaminated with hazardous chemicals and solvents.

A view of tropical houses on a hill overlooking the harbor on St. John. © RICHARD GOLDBERG/SHUTTERSTOCK.COM.

crude oil for electricity generation. To increase grid reliability, as of 2012, the Virgin Islands Water and Power Authority was exploring undersea cable links with Puerto Rico and the British Virgin Islands. The US Virgin Islands' largest solar project, the 451-kilowatt King Airport photovoltaic array on St. Thomas, went into operation in fall 2011 and provides 15% of the airport's electricity. In addition, solar water heaters are required for all new construction in the Virgin Islands. Net total electricity generation was 87.2 million kilowatt hours in 2009.

History Excavations at St. Croix in the 1970s uncovered evidence of a civilization dating from AD 100, although some evidence exists of an even older settlement. Christopher Columbus, who reached the islands in 1493, named them for the martyred virgin St. Ursula. At this time, St. Croix was inhabited by Carib Indians, who were eventually driven from the island by Spanish soldiers in 1555.

During the 17th century, the archipelago was divided into two territorial units, one controlled by the British, the other controlled by Denmark. Today these units are the British Virgin Islands and the US Virgin Islands.

The separate history of the US Virgin Islands began with the settlement of St. Thomas by the Danish West India Company in 1672. St. John was claimed by the company in 1683 and St. Croix was purchased from France in

Blackbeard's Castle, located on St. Thomas, is a National Historic Landmark. © ANNA M. BREMMER/SHUTTERSTOCK.COM.

1733. The holdings of the company were taken over as a Danish crown colony in 1754. Sugarcane, cultivated by slave labor, was the backbone of the islands' prosperity in the 18th and early 19th centuries.

The slaves revolted and the Danish colonizers brutally suppressed them. Finally, in 1848 Denmark abolished slavery in the colony. A long period of economic decline followed. Denmark sold the islands to the United States in 1917 for $25 million. The US Congress granted US citizenship to the Virgin Islanders in 1927.

Government In 1931, administration of the islands was transferred from the Department of the Navy to the Department of the Interior, and the first civilian governor was appointed. In the late 1970s, the US Virgin Islands government began to consider ways to expand self-rule. A UN delegation in 1977 found little interest in independence, however, and a locally drafted constitution was voted down by the electorate in 1979. Several more attempts to draft a constitution also failed. In 2008, a fifth Constitutional Convention was formed with elected representatives, to again try and draft a constitution for the territory. The constitution was submitted to the US Congress in 2010, but was returned to the island for amendment as it failed to include a number of key points, such as recognition of the United States.

The chief executive of the US Virgin Islands is the territorial governor, elected by direct popular vote. (Until 1970, territorial governors were appointed by the US president.) Governor John De Jongh Jr. assumed the office on 1 January 2007. De Jongh won a second four-year term in 2010.

Constitutionally, the US Congress has plenary authority to legislate for the territory. Enactment of the Revised Organic Act of the Virgin Islands on 22 July 1954 vested local legislative power—subject to veto by the governor—in a unicameral legislature. Since 1972, the islands have sent one nonvoting representative to the US House of Representatives. In 2010, Donna M. Christensen, a Democrat, was elected to her eighth two-year term as representative.

Courts are under the US federal judiciary; the two federal district court judges are appointed by the US president. Territorial court

An aerial view shows the island of St. Thomas with cruise ships at the dock. © IVAN CHOLAKOV/SHUTTERSTOCK.COM.

judges, who preside over misdemeanor and traffic cases, are appointed by the governor and confirmed by the legislature. The district court has appellate jurisdiction over the territorial court.

Tourism, Commerce, and Employment Tourism accounts for approximately 80% of both gross domestic product (GDP) and employment and is the islands' principal economic activity. The number of tourists has risen dramatically since the 1960s, from 448,165 in 1964 to 2.6 million in 2011.

In 2010, the majority of tourists (2 million) arrived by cruise ship. Just 589,800 stayed overnight. Total visitor expenditures that year amounted to $1 billion.

Rum remains an important manufactured product, and petroleum refining (on St. Croix) was added in the late 1960s. The Hovensa refinery on St. Croix was one of the 10 largest in the world, until it shut down in 2012. Watch manufacture was once a major industry in the territory, but only one watch manufacturer—Belair Quartz—remained in 2009. Economic development is promoted by the US-government–owned Virgin Islands Corp.

In 2012, the annual mean wage was $37,690. The unemployment rate in 2011 ranged from 7.5% on St. Thomas and St. John to 10.6% on St Croix. Exports for 2011 totaled $2.3 billion. The island's primary export in 2011 was refined petroleum products—St. Croix had one of the world's largest refineries. In 2009, the Virgin Islands' gross domestic product was $4.243 billion. That year, the per capita GDP was $39,876.

In August 2012, total nonfarm employment was 44,000, with an unemployment rate of 7.5%. Of these workers, 2,000 worked in mining or construction; 1,300 in manufacturing; 8,500 in trade, transportation, and utilities; 2,400 in financial activities; 3,600 in business or professional services; 2,400 in education and health services; 7,600 in leisure and hospitality; and 11,000 in government.

Health and Education The territorial Department of Health provides hospital and medical services, public health services, and veterinary medicine. The death rate was estimated at 7.39 deaths per 1,000 inhabitants in 2012. The infant mortality rate was 7.09 deaths per 1,000 live births. Life expectancy was nearly 80 years.

Education is compulsory. Total enrollment in public primary and secondary school was 15,768 in 2008, with per pupil expenditures of $12,358. The University of the Virgin Islands was the territory's first institution of higher learning and has around 2,600 students.

Communications, Revenue, and Taxation The Virgin Islands had 24 radio stations (5 AM, 18 FM) and 6 broadcast television stations in 2012. In 2009, 75,800 main line telephones were in use, but more people used cell phones. That same year, some 30,000 people had Internet access.

Total government revenues in 2009 were $952.7 million. Total spending was $1.428 billion. The islands received $227.5 million in federal grants. Rum production taxes amounted to around $80 million.

Individual US citizens and permanent residents of the Virgin Islands are subject to the same tax rates as are applicable to individuals under the US Internal Revenue Code, but they pay their tax on worldwide income to the US Virgin Islands Bureau of Internal Revenue rather than to the US Internal Revenue Service, and they file their return only with the US Virgin Islands. The maximum graduated income rate applicable to individuals is 39.6%. There are no additional local income taxes or surcharges.

Bibliography

BOOKS

Hoffman, Robert. *Annals of the Big Island: St. Croix, US Virgin Islands.* East Cannington, WA: Southern Cross Publications, 2008.

Philpott, Don. *US & British Virgin Islands.* Edison, NJ: Hunter, 2000.

Porter, Darwin, and Danforth Prince. *Frommer's Virgin Islands,* 11th ed. Hoboken, NJ: John Wiley & Sons, 2011.

WEB SITES

Lewin, Aldeth. "2011 Tourism Numbers Climb." *Virgin Islands Daily News,* May 21, 2012. http://virginislandsdailynews.com/news/2011-tourism-numbers-climb-1.1318197 (accessed on October 16, 2012).

"Navassa Island: A Photographic Tour." *US Geological Survey: Coastal and Marine Geology Program.* http://coastal.er.usgs.gov/navassa/index.html (accessed on October 16, 2012).

"Navassa National Wildlife Refuge." *US Fish and Wildlife Service.* http://library.fws.gov/Refuges/navassa_facts01.pdf (accessed on October 16, 2012).

"United States Virgin Islands." *United Nations Statistics Division.* http://data.un.org/CountryProfile.aspx?crName=United%20States%20Virgin%20Islands (accessed on October 16, 2012).

US Virgin Islands Department of Education. http://www.doe.vi/pages/DOEVI (accessed on October 16, 2012).

United States Pacific Dependencies

American Samoa

American Samoa is a US territory that lies in the South Pacific Ocean. It is made up of seven small islands in the Samoan archipelago (chain of islands). American Samoa lies between 14° and 15° south and 168° and 171° west. (The rest of the Samoan islands comprise the independent state of Samoa, formerly known as Western Samoa.) American Samoa has a total area (land and water) of 76 square miles (197 square kilometers). Five of the islands are volcanic, with rugged peaks rising sharply, and two are coral atolls.

The climate is warm, humid, and rainy year-round, but there is a long, wet summer season (October-May) and a slightly cooler and drier season (June-September). Normal temperatures range from 75°F (24°C) from June to September to 90°F (32°C) during December and February; mean annual rainfall is 130 inches (330 centimeters). Mean relative humidity for an average year is around 84% and ranges from 82% in July, August, and September to 87% in April. The rainy season lasts from December through March. Hurricanes are common. Native plants include tree ferns, coconut, hardwoods, and rubber trees. There are few wild animals.

As of mid-2011, the estimated population was 68,061. About 91.6% of the inhabitants, who are concentrated on the island of Tutuila, are Polynesian. Most people are bilingual: English and Samoan are the official languages, although a small portion of the population are Tongan and speak Tongan at home. Most Samoans are Christians: as of 2011 around 50% were affiliated with Christian Congregationalist churches, 20% were Roman Catholic, and 30% were Protestant.

The capital of the territory, Pago Pago, lies on Tutuila. Pago Pago has one of the finest natural harbors in the South Pacific. Many passenger cruise ships stop there on South Pacific tours. Passenger and cargo ships arrive regularly from Japan, New Zealand, Australia, and the US West Coast. There are regular air and sea services between American Samoa and Samoa, and scheduled flights between Pago Pago and Honolulu.

American Samoa was settled by Melanesian migrants around 1000 BC. The Samoan islands were visited in 1768 by the French explorer Louis-Antoine de Bougainville. He named them the Îles des Navigateurs (Islands of the Navigators) as a tribute to the skill of their native boatmen.

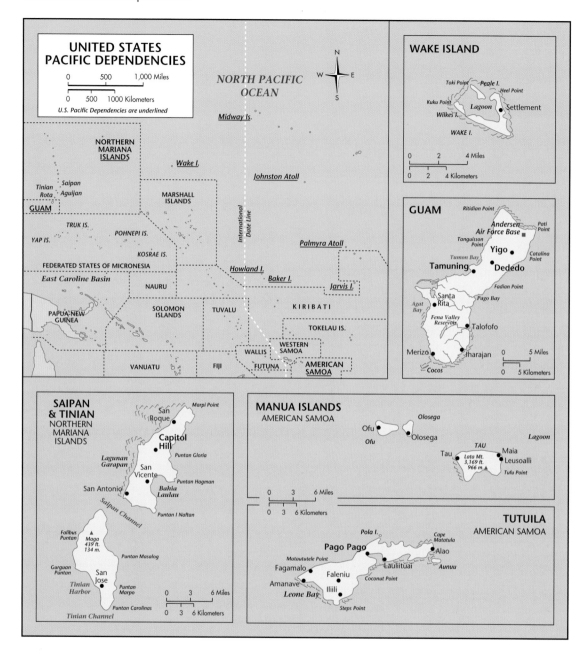

In 1889, the United States, the United Kingdom, and Germany agreed to share control of the islands, a form of governance termed a condominium. The United Kingdom later withdrew its claim. Under the 1899 Tripartite Convention of Berlin, the condominium was dissolved and the United States was acknowledged internationally as having rights over all the islands of the Samoan group lying east of 171° west. Germany was acknowledged to have similar rights to the islands west of that meridian. In exchange for surrendering its rights in Samoa, the United Kingdom was given the German colony of Tonga and additional territory in the Solomon Islands.

The islands of American Samoa were officially ceded to the United States by the various ruling chiefs in 1900 and 1904. On 20 February 1929 the US Congress formally accepted sovereignty over the entire group. From 1900 to 1951, the territory was administered by the US Department of the Navy, and thereafter by the Department of the Interior. The basic law is the constitution of 1967. Unlike residents of other US territories who are US citizens, American Samoans are US nationals. However, neither citizens nor nationals of US territories vote in federal elections or pay federal taxes. American Samoa came under federal minimum wage rules in 2007 and controls its own immigration and border matters.

The executive branch of the government is headed by a governor who, along with the lieutenant governor, is elected by popular vote. As of 2012, the governor was Togiola Tulafono, who succeeded Governor Tauese Suni following the latter's sudden death in April 2003. Tulafono was elected in 2004 and again in 2008. Before 1977, the governor and lieutenant governor were appointed by the US government. Village, county, and district councils have full authority to regulate local affairs.

The legislature (*Fono*) is composed of the house of representatives and the senate. The 15 counties elect 18 *matais* (chiefs) to four-year terms in the senate, while the 21 house members are elected for two-year terms by popular vote

within the counties. (There is one appointed member from Swains Island.)

The secretary for Samoan affairs, who heads the department of local government, is appointed by the governor. Under his administration are three district governors, the county chiefs, village mayors, and police officials.

The judiciary, an independent branch of the government, functions through the high court and five district courts. The chief justice and associate justices of the high court are appointed by the US secretary of the interior. The high court is the highest court in America Samoa; there is no US federal court there. The territory sends one nonvoting delegate to the US House of Representatives. Democrat Eni F. H. Faleomavaega has been the representative to the US Congress from American Samoa since 1989, serving 12 terms as of 2012.

The economy is primarily agricultural. Tuna fishing and tuna processing are the backbone of the economy. The islands' two tuna canneries account for around 29% of the territory's employment. The canneries are supplied with fish caught by Japanese, US, and Taiwanese fishing fleets.

Small plantations occupy about one-third of the land area; 90% of the land is communally owned. The principal crops are bananas, breadfruit, taro, papayas, pineapples, sweet potatoes, tapioca, coffee, cocoa, and yams. Hogs and poultry are the principal livestock raised; there are few dairy cattle. Canned tuna is the primary export. Most foreign trade is conducted with the United States.

In 2009, the gross domestic product (GDP) was $703 million, and the per capita GDP was $12,662. Total payroll employment was 18,862 in 2010. Of this, 12,080 people were employed in the private sector; 5,226 in government; and 1,556 by autonomous agencies. Tuna processing accounted for 1,553 workers that year.

Total government revenues in 2009 amounted to $211.2 million, and government spending was $222 million. Federal grants accounted for $134.1 million of total revenues that year.

American Samoa is nearly completely dependent on imported fossil fuels, and a significant amount of American Samoa's electricity is used to pump and treat drinking water. As of 2012, the territory is building solar facilities, including a 1.75-megawatt photovoltaic array near Pago Pago's airport, which is expected to replace 7% of electricity generation from diesel fuel. Wind power is also being explored. Net electricity generation in 2009 was 19 million megawatts. There are no reserves on the island of crude oil, coal, or natural gas.

Samoans are entitled to free medical treatment, including hospital care. Nonresidents must pay for treatment. Besides district dispensaries, the government maintains a central hospital, and there is also a small private hospital in Apia. US-trained staff physicians work with Samoan medical practitioners and nurses. The LBJ Tropical Medical Center opened in 1986. It offers dental care in additional to general medical treatment. There are no hyperbaric chambers on any of the islands for the treatment of scuba-diving-related injuries.

Education is a joint undertaking between the territorial government and the villages. School attendance is compulsory for all children from age 6 through 18. The villages furnish the elementary school buildings and living quarters for the teachers; the territorial government pays teachers' salaries and provides buildings and supplies for all but primary schools. About 98% of the population is literate. There are six high schools and 22 elementary schools in American Samoa. The American Samoa Community College is a two-year college offering associate of arts and associate of science degrees to around 1,500 students. Students wishing to attend four-year institutions must go to the United States or another country.

American Samoa was first connected to the Internet in 2009 via undersea cable. Radio-telegraph circuits connect the territory with Hawaii, Fiji, and Samoa. Every village in

An ocean landscape, as seen from American Samoa, is shown.
© CORNFORTH IMAGES / ALAMY.

American Samoa has telephone service, and cellular service is widely available.

Guam

Guam is the largest and most populous of the Mariana Islands in the Western Pacific. Guam (13° 28' north and 144° 47' east) has an area, including land and water, of 209 square miles (541 square kilometers) and is about 30 miles (48 kilometers) long and ranges from 4 to 7 miles (6 to 12 kilometers) wide. Around 80 miles (128.7 hectares) of coral reef surround the island.

The island is of volcanic origin; in the south, the terrain is mountainous, while the northern part is a plateau with shallow fertile soil. The central part of the island (where the capital, Hagatna, is located) is hilly.

Guam lies in the typhoon belt of the Western Pacific and is occasionally subject to widespread storm damage. In May 1976, typhoon Pamela, with winds of 190 miles/hour (306 kilometers/hour) struck Guam, causing an estimated $300 million in damage and leaving 80% of the island's buildings in ruins. Guam has a tropical climate with little seasonal variation. Average temperature is 79°F (26°C). Rainfall is substantial, reaching an annual average of more than 80 inches (200 centimeters). Endangered species include the giant Micronesian kingfisher and Marianas crow.

As of September 2012, there were two hazardous waste sites on Guam listed on the US Environmental Protection Agency's National Priorities List. These were Anderson Air Force Base, in Yigo, and the Ordot Landfill, in Ordot.

The population in April 2010, excluding transient US military and civilian personnel and their families, was estimated at 159,358, an increase of 2.9% over the 2000 population of 154,805. The Chamorro people comprise about half of the permanent resident population. The Chamorro descend from the intermingling of the few surviving original Chamorro (Pacific Islander) with Spanish, Filipino, and Mexican settlers and later arrivals from the United States, United Kingdom, Korea, China, and Japan. English and Chamorro are official languages. The predominant religion is Roman Catholicism.

The earliest known settlers on Guam were the original Chamorro, who migrated from the Malay Peninsula to the Pacific around 1500 BC. When Ferdinand Magellan landed on Guam in 1521, it is believed that as many as 100,000 Chamorro lived on the island; by 1741, their numbers had been reduced to 5,000—most of the population either had fled the island or been killed through disease or war with the Spanish. A Spanish fort was established in 1565, and from 1696 until 1898, Guam was under Spanish rule.

Under the Treaty of Paris that ended the Spanish-American War in 1898, the island was ceded to the United States and placed under the jurisdiction of the Department of the Navy. During World War II (1939–45), Guam was occupied by Japanese forces; the United States recaptured the island in 1944 after 54 days of fighting. In 1950, the island's administration was transferred from the Navy to the US Department of the Interior. Under the 1950 Organic Act of Guam passed by the US Congress, the island was established as an unincorporated territory of the United States. Guamanians were granted US citizenship, and internal self-government was introduced.

The governor and lieutenant governor have been elected directly since 1970. Edward

J. B. Calvo was elected governor in 2011. A 15-member unicameral legislature elected for two years is empowered to legislate on all local matters, including taxation and appropriations. The US Congress reserves the right to annul any law passed by the Guam legislature, but must do so within a year of the date it receives the text of any such law. Guam is represented in the US Congress by a nonvoting delegate. In 2011, Democrat Madeleine Mary Zeien Bordallo (1933–) was elected to her fourth term.

Judicial authority is vested in the Supreme Court of Guam. Appeals may be taken to the mainland US federal district court and ultimately to the US Supreme Court. The judge of the District Court of Guam is appointed by the US president; the judges of the other courts are appointed by the governor. Guam's laws were codified in 1953.

Guam is one of the most important US military bases in the Pacific. The island's economy has been profoundly affected by the large sums of money spent by the US defense establishment. During the late 1960s and early 1970s, when the United States was a major combatant in the Vietnam conflict, Guam served as a base for long-range US bombers. At the beginning of 2012, there were around 7,000 active-duty US military personnel stationed on the island. Following an April 2012 agreement with Japan, an additional 5,000 US military personnel will be relocated to Guam from Okinawa.

Guam has no conventional energy resources and relies on petroleum products shipped in by tanker for virtually all its needs. In 2011, the Public Utility Commission approved two Guam Power Authority contracts for the first commercial wind and solar projects, which total 35 megawatts and are due to begin operation in 2014–2015. In the early 2010s, the U.S. Navy and Air Force bases on Guam were installing solar arrays and water heaters in living quarters and linking electricity generation from solar energy to the main grid to reduce fuel use. Guam Power Authority is also pursuing the potential for seawater air-conditioning, in which cold water drawn from offshore chills seaside building air-conditioning systems. Guam's Renewable Portfolio Goal calls for 5% of net electricity sales to come from renewable energy resources by 2015 and 25% by 2035. Total net electricity generation was 1.755 billion kilowatt hours in 2009.

Prior to World War II, agriculture and animal husbandry were the primary activities. By 1947, most adults were wage earners employed by the US armed forces, although many continued to cultivate small plots to supplement their earnings. In 2007, there were 104 farms on the island, covering 1,000 acres (405 hectares). Most farms are less than 7 acres (2.8 hectares). Total farm sales in 2007 were $2.8 million, with farms averaging $26,886 in sales that year. Major crops include cassava, taro, sweet potato, betel nuts, and tropical fruits. Pigs and poultry are raised for local consumption and sale, but most food is imported. Fish catches in 2009 totaled 898,000 pounds (407,000 kilograms). In 2010, 1.78 metric tons of tuna was transshipped through Guam, almost all by Japanese shipping vessels.

Tourism became a major industry and sparked a boom in the construction industry in the mid-1980s. The number of visitors grew rapidly from 6,600 in 1967 to 1.19 million in 2010. About 75% of tourists come from Japan, and 11.3% from South Korea. Direct tourist spending reached $1 billion in 2010.

Guam's population increased 2.9% between 2000 and 2010. © TODD HACKWELDER/SHUTTERSTOCK.COM.

The Guam Rehabilitation Act of 1963 has funded the territory's capital improvement program. Further allocations in 1969 and 1977 provided over $120 million for additional capital improvements and development of the island's power installations. Total expenditures by the government of Guam were $1.08 billion in 2009; revenues were $868 million. US government grants amounted to $278.4 million that year. Guam's gross domestic product (GDP) in 2009 was $4.5 billion, while per capita GDP was $28,232.

As of 2011, total payroll employment was 60,350. Private sector employment accounted for roughly three-fourths of this number. The unemployment rate in March 2011 was 13.3%.

Private sector average weekly earnings in 2011 were $438.54, compared to average government sector earnings of $841.08.

Guam's foreign trade usually shows large deficits. The bulk of Guam's trade is with the United States, Japan, Singapore, and South Korea.

US income tax laws are applicable in Guam; all internal revenue taxes derived by the United States from Guam are paid into the territory's treasury. US customs duties, however, are not levied. Guam is a duty-free port. In its trade with the US mainland, Guam is required to use US shipping.

Typical tropical diseases are practically unknown today in Guam. The island has two hospitals, one civilian and one naval. The civilian hospital, Guam Memorial, shares some physicians with the military hospital and has a capacity of 158 beds. Village dispensaries serve both as public health units and first-aid stations. In addition, there are a number of physicians in private practice. Patients requiring specialized care often have to travel to Hawaii or the mainland. In 2010, Guam Memorial served 11,689 inpatients. There is also a specialized birthing center.

School attendance is compulsory from the age of 6 through 16. There are 27 elementary schools, 8 middle schools, 5 high schools, and an alternative school that serve more than 30,000 students. Guam is also home to 4 Department of Defense schools serving the children of military personnel, 14 Catholic schools, and several foreign language schools that serve the children of expatriates from Japan. The University of Guam offers four-year degree programs to around 3,500 students.

Howland, Baker, and Jarvis Islands

Howland Island (0° 48' north and 176° 38' west), Baker Island (0° 14' north and 176° 28' west), and Jarvis Island (0° 23' south and 160° 1' west) are three small coral islands. Each measures about 1 square mile (2.6 square kilometers) in area. They are low and nearly level sandy coral islands with fringing reefs and no natural sources of freshwater. They belong to the Line Islands group of the central Pacific Ocean. All three are administered by the US government as unincorporated territories. Public entry is by special permit and is generally restricted to scientists and educators.

Howland was first visited in 1842 by US sailors. It was claimed by the United States in 1857. It was worked for guano by US and British companies until about 1890. Howland Island was formally proclaimed a US territory in 1935. Baker Island lies 40 miles (64 kilometers) south of Howland. Jarvis Island lies 1,100 miles (1,770 kilometers) east of Howland. Both were claimed by the United States in 1857, and their guano deposits were similarly worked by US and British enterprises. The United Kingdom annexed Jarvis in 1889. In 1935, the United States sent colonists from Hawaii to all three islands, which were placed under the US Department of the Interior in 1936. Baker Island was captured by the Japanese in 1942 and recaptured by the United States in 1944.

The three islands are administered as part of the National Wildlife Refuge system and have no permanent inhabitants. They are visited annually by the US Coast Guard. A lighthouse on Howland Island is named in honor of the US pilot Amelia Earhart, who vanished en route to the island on a round-the-world flight in 1937.

Johnston Atoll

Johnston Atoll is located in the North Pacific 715 miles (1,151 kilometers) southwest of Honolulu, Hawaii. It consists of two islands—Johnston (16° 44' north and 169° 31' west) and Sand (16° 45' north and 169° 30' west)—with a total land and water area of about 1 square mile (2.6 square kilometers). The islands are enclosed by a semicircular reef.

Johnston Atoll was discovered by English sailors in 1807 and claimed by the United States in 1858. For many years, the islands were worked for guano and were declared a bird reservation in 1926. The islands were commissioned as a naval station in 1934, and the Air Force took over control in 1948. The islands remain an unincorporated US territory under the control of the US Department of the Air Force. In the 1950s and 1960s, Johnston Atoll was used for high-altitude nuclear testing. Until late 2000, it was maintained as a storage and disposal site for chemical weapons. Munitions destruction was completed in 2005, and the facilities were cleaned and closed in May of that year.

The population prior to 2001 stood at 1,100 government personnel and contractors, but decreased significantly after the September 2001 departure of the US Army Chemical Activity Pacific (USACAP). As of May 2005, all US government personnel had left the island. The atoll is equipped with an excellent satellite and radio telecommunications system.

Midway

The Midway Islands (28° 12'–17' north and 177° 19'–26' west) consist of an atoll and three small islets, Eastern Island (177° 20' west), Sand Island (177° 22'–24' west), and Spit Island, 1,300 miles (2,100 kilometers) west-northwest of Honolulu, Hawaii. Total land and water area is 2 square miles (5 square kilometers).

Midway Island was discovered and claimed by the United States in 1859 and formally annexed in 1867. It became a submarine cable station early in the 20th century and an airline station in 1935. Midway became a US naval base in 1941 (during World War II) and was attacked twice by the Japanese, in December 1941 and January 1942. In one of the great

On the Midway Atoll, albatrosses are seen on their nesting ground, the site of an old World War II anti-aircraft gun. © FRANS LANTING STUDIO / ALAMY

battles of World War II, a Japanese naval attack on 3–6 June 1942 was repelled by US warplanes.

Midway is a US unincorporated territory; there is a closed naval station, and the islands are important nesting places for seabirds. The island was designated a National Wildlife Refuge in 1988. In 2006, the islands became part of the Northwestern Hawaiian Islands Marine National Monument. As of 2010, there were no permanent residents on the islands, but the US Fish and Wildlife Service sends personnel for three to four month stints to the atoll. Visitors are allowed under the aegis of the Fish and Wildlife Service and may stay on Sand Island, where there is also an airstrip.

Northern Marianas

The Northern Marianas, a US commonwealth in the Western Pacific Ocean, comprises the Mariana Islands excluding Guam (a separate political entity). Located between 12° and 21° north and 144° and 146° east, it consists of 14 volcanic islands with a total land area of about 183.5 square miles (475 square kilometers). Only six of the islands are inhabited, and most of the people live on the three largest islands— Rota, 33 square miles (85 square kilometers); Saipan, 47 square miles (122 square kilometers); and Tinian, 39 square miles (101 square kilometers).

The climate is tropical, with relatively little seasonal change; temperatures average 70–85°F (21–29°C). Relative humidity is generally high. Rainfall averages 85 inches (216 centimeters) per year. The southern islands, which include Rota, Saipan, and Tinian, are generally lower in elevation. They are covered with moderately heavy tropical vegetation. The northern islands

A view of a park on Rota Island, which is part of the Northern Mariana Islands. © IZO/SHUTTERSTOCK.COM.

are more rugged, reaching a high point of 3,146 feet (959 meters) on Agrihan. The northern islands are generally barren due to erosion and insufficient rainfall.

Pagan and Agrihan have active volcanoes, and typhoons are common from August to November. Insects are numerous and ocean birds and ocean wildlife are abundant. The Mariana fruit bat is among the local species listed as threatened or endangered.

The Northern Marianas had an estimated population of 53,883 in 2010, down from 69,221 in 2000. Around half of the population in 2000 were of Asian origin, while around 36% were descended from the original Micronesian inhabitants, known as Chamorros. There are also many descendants of migrants from the Caroline Islands and smaller numbers of Filipino and Korean laborers and settlers from the US mainland. English and Chamorro are official languages. However, only around 14% of the population speaks English in the home. Other common languages spoken include Philippine languages (24.4%) and Chinese (23.4%). About 90% of the people are Roman Catholic.

It is believed that the Marianas were first settled by migrants from the Philippines and Indonesia. Excavations on Saipan have yielded evidence of settlement around 1500 BC. The first European to reach the Marianas, in 1521, was Ferdinand Magellan.

The islands were ruled by Spain until the Spanish defeat by the United States in the Spanish-American War (1898). Guam was then ceded to the United States and the rest of the Marianas were sold to Germany. When World War I (1914–18) broke out, Japan took over the Northern Marianas and other German-held islands in the Western Pacific. These islands (the Northern Marianas, Carolines, and Marshalls) were placed under Japanese administration as a League of Nations mandate on 17 December 1920. Upon its withdrawal from the League in 1935, Japan began to fortify the islands. During World War II the islands served as important military bases.

Several of the islands were the scene of heavy fighting during the war. In the battle for control of Saipan in June 1944, some 23,000 Japanese and 3,500 US troops lost their lives in one day's fighting. As each island was occupied by US troops, it became subject to US authority in accordance with international law. The US planes that dropped atomic bombs on Hiroshima and Nagasaki took off from Tinian.

On 18 July 1947, the Northern Mariana, Caroline, and Marshall islands formally became a United Nations Trust Territory under US administration. This Trust Territory of the Pacific Islands was administered by the US Department of the Navy until 1 July 1951, when administration was transferred to the Department of the Interior. From 1953 to 1962, the Northern Marianas, with the exception of Rota, were administered by the US Department of the Navy.

The people of the Northern Marianas voted to become a US commonwealth by a majority of 78.8% in a plebiscite (general vote) held on 17 June 1975. A covenant approved by the US Congress in March 1976 provided for the separation of the Northern Marianas from the Caroline and Marshall Islands groups, and for the Marianas' transition to a commonwealth status, similar to that of Puerto Rico.

The islands became internally self-governing in January 1978. On 3 November 1986, US president Ronald Reagan proclaimed the

Northern Marianas a self-governing commonwealth; its people became US citizens. The termination of the trusteeship was approved by the UN Trusteeship Council in May 1986 and received the required approval from the UN Security Council. On 3 November 1986, the Constitution of the Commonwealth of the Northern Marianas Islands came into force. The islands came under US federal minimum wage regulations in 2007, and federal immigration law in 2008. In 2009, the US Department of Homeland Security took over immigration and border controls.

A governor and a lieutenant governor are popularly elected for four-year terms. Governor Benigno R. Fitial was elected in 2005 and won a second term in 2009. He is up for reelection in 2013. The legislature consists of 9 senators elected for four-year terms and 18 representatives elected for two-year terms. A district court handles matters involving federal law and a commonwealth court has jurisdiction over local matters. The commonwealth is represented in the US Congress by a nonvoting delegate. As of 2012, the delegate was Democrat Gregorio Sablan (1955–), who was first elected in 2008 and reelected in 2010.

The traditional economic activities were subsistence agriculture, livestock raising, and fishing, but much agricultural land was destroyed or damaged during World War II and agriculture has never resumed its prewar importance. Following a 1986 agreement, the commonwealth garment industry was exempt from US tariffs and laws governing working conditions and wages. The garment industry consequently grew to be the largest industry on Saipan, employing around 17,000 mostly Chinese workers in 2000. Liberalization of US garment import restrictions in 2005 led to the demise of the industry by 2009 and a significant drop in population as workers returned to China.

Tourism, especially from Japan, accounts for around 50% of the remaining jobs. Tourist arrivals numbered around 340,957 in 2011. Of those, 42% were from Japan and 31.5% were from South Korea. The construction industry is also expanding, and there is some small-scale industry, chiefly handicrafts and food processing. Plans to open a casino on the island were working their way through the commonwealth legislature as of 2012. A locally owned airline, Saipan Air, began operating in 2012, bringing tourists from Japan.

The Northern Marianas is heavily dependent on funds from the US government. The United States also pays to lease property on Saipan, Tinian, and Farallon de Medinilla islands for defense purposes. US currency is the official medium of exchange.

In 2009, the gross domestic product (GDP) of the Northern Marianas was $716 million, with a per capita GDP that year of $13,288. Gross business receipts in 2010 amounted to $1.3 billion. In 2009, total government revenues were $230.2 million, while spending was $277.6 million. That year, the islands received $64.4 million in US federal grants.

The Northern Mariana Islands meets nearly all of its energy demand through the importation of petroleum products, including 22 million to 24 million gallons of diesel fuel annually to run the islands' five electricity generating plants. Nearby volcanoes make the Marianas unique in Micronesia in having abundant geothermal energy potential, and the islands also have excellent resources for both wind and solar power.

Health care is primarily the responsibility of the commonwealth government and has improved substantially since 1978. There is a hospital on Saipan and health centers on Tinian and Rota. The largest hospital in the commonwealth is a 74-bed, full-service facility.

Education is free and compulsory for children between the ages of 8 and 14, and literacy is high. There is one two-year community college on Saipan, Northern Marianas College, with an enrollment of around 1,000 students. There are two AM, eight FM, and four television stations.

Palmyra Atoll

Palmyra, an atoll in the Central Pacific Ocean, contains 50 islets with a total area of some 4 square miles (10 square kilometers). Palmyra is situated about 1,000 miles (1,600 kilometers) south-southwest of Honolulu, Hawaii, at 5° 52' north and 162° 5' west.

Palmyra was first visited in 1802 by the *USS Palmyra.* The Kingdom of Hawaii claimed the atoll in 1862, and the United States included it as a Hawaiian island when it annexed the entire archipelago in 1898. The atoll was formally annexed by the United States in 1912. It was under the jurisdiction of the city of Honolulu until 1959, when Hawaii became the 50th state of the United States. The Hawaii Statehood Act of 1959 did not include the atoll. Palmyra is now partly owned by the Nature Conservancy, with the remainder being owned by the federal government and managed by the US Fish and Wildlife Service. The Nature Conservancy and Fish and Wildlife Service jointly manage the atoll as a National Wildlife Refuge.

Palmyra, an atoll in the central Pacific Ocean, was annexed by the United States in 1912. © IMAGES & STORIES / ALAMY.

Kingman Reef, northwest of Palmyra Atoll at 6° 25' north and 162° 23' north, was discovered by the United States in 1874, annexed by the United States in 1922, and became a naval reservation in 1934. Now abandoned, it is under the control of the US Department of the Navy. The reef only has an elevation of 3 feet (1 meter) and is awash most of the time, making it hazardous for ships. In 2001, the reef was designated a National Wildlife Refuge.

Wake Island

Wake Island is actually a coral atoll and three islets (Wake, Peale, and Wilkes). Wake Island is about 5 miles (8 kilometers) long by 2.25 miles (3.6 kilometers) wide. It lies in the North Pacific 2,100 miles (3,380 kilometers) west of Honolulu, Hawaii, at 19° 17' north and 166° 35' east. The total land and water area is about 3 square miles (8 square kilometers). The atoll was possibly discovered by the Spanish in 1568, but is named for British Captain William Wake, who visited in 1796. Wake may have been settled by Marshall Islanders, but was long uninhabited.

In 1898, a US expeditionary force en route to Manila, Philippines, landed on the island. The United States formally claimed Wake in 1899. It was made a US naval reservation in 1934 and became a civil aviation station in 1935. Captured by the Japanese during World War II on 23 December 1941, Wake was subsequently the target of several US air raids. It was surrendered by the Japanese in September 1945 and has thereafter remained a US unincorporated territory under the jurisdiction, since 1972, of the Department of the Air Force. The atoll was used as a launch platform for testing military rockets and antimissile systems.

In 2009, the Wake Island National Wildlife Refuge was created on the atoll, which was also included as part of the Pacific Remote Islands Marine National Monument. At the same time, it remains a stopover and fueling station for civilian and military aircraft flying between Honolulu, Guam, and Japan. As of 2009, around 150 US military personnel and contractors inhabit the atoll. There is an ongoing legal dispute with the Marshall Islands over the sovereignty of the atoll.

Bibliography

BOOKS

Amerika Samoa Humanities Council. *History of America Samoa.* Honolulu, HI: Bess Press, 2009.

Burgan, Michael. *Puerto Rico and Outlying Territories.* Milwaukee: World Almanac Library, 2003.

Rogers, Robert F. *Destiny's Landfall: A History of Guam.* Honolulu: University of Hawaii Press, 2011.

Wukovits, John F. *Pacific Alamo: The Battle for Wake Island.* New York: New American Library, 2003.

WEB SITES

American Samoa Government. http://www.americansamoa.gov/ (accessed on November 10, 2012).

"Guam Statistical Yearbook 2010." *Bureau of Statistics and Plans.* http://www.bsp.guam.gov/index.php?option=com_content&view=article&id=128&Itemid=100002 (accessed on November 10, 2012).

"Northern Mariana Islands." *Lonely Planet.* http://www.lonelyplanet.com/northern-mariana-islands (accessed on November 10, 2012).

Official Portal for the Island of Guam. http://www.guam.gov/ (accessed on November 10, 2012).

"Pacific Islands Refuges." *US Fish and Wildlife Service.* http://www.fws.gov/pacificislandsrefuges/ (accessed on November 10, 2012).

United States

The United States of America

CAPITAL: Washington, D.C. (District of Columbia).

OFFICIAL SEAL: Obverse: An American eagle with outstretched wings bears a shield consisting of 13 alternating white and red stripes with a broad blue band across the top. The right talon clutches an olive branch, representing peace; in the left are 13 arrows, symbolizing military strength. The eagle's beak holds a banner with the motto "E pluribus unum" (From many, one); overhead is a constellation of 13 five-pointed stars in a golden glory. Reverse: Above a truncated pyramid is an all-seeing eye within a triangle; at the bottom of this triangle appear the roman numerals MDCCLXXVI (1776). The pyramid stands on a grassy ground, against a backdrop of mountains. The words "Annuit Coeptis" (He has favored our undertakings) and, on a banner, "Novus Ordo Seclorum" (A new order of the ages) surround the whole.

FLAG: The flag consists of 13 alternate stripes, 7 red and 6 white; these represent the original 13 colonies. Fifty 5-pointed white stars, representing the present number of states in the Union, are placed in 9 horizontal rows alternately of 6 and 5 against a blue field in the upper left corner of the flag.

MOTTO: In God We Trust.

SONG: The Star-Spangled Banner.

FLOWER: Rose.

TREE: Oak.

BIRD: Bald eagle.

FEDERAL LEGAL HOLIDAYS: New Year's Day, 1 January; birthday of Martin Luther King Jr., 3rd Monday in January; Presidents' Day/Washington's Birthday, 18 February; Memorial Day, last Monday in May; Independence Day, 4 July; Labor Day, 1st Monday in September; Columbus Day, 2nd Monday in October; Veterans Day, 11 November; Thanksgiving Day, 4th Thursday in November; Christmas Day, 25 December.

TIME: Eastern, 7 a.m. = noon GMT; Central, 6 a.m. = noon GMT; Mountain, 5 a.m. = noon GMT; Pacific (includes the Alaska panhandle), 4 a.m. = noon GMT; Yukon, 3 a.m. = noon GMT; Alaska and Hawaii, 2 a.m. = noon GMT; western Alaska, 1 a.m. = noon GMT.

1 Location and Size

Located in the Western Hemisphere on the southern portion of the continent of North America, the United States is the third-largest country in the world. Its total area, including Alaska and Hawaii, is 3,718,691 square miles (9,631,420 square

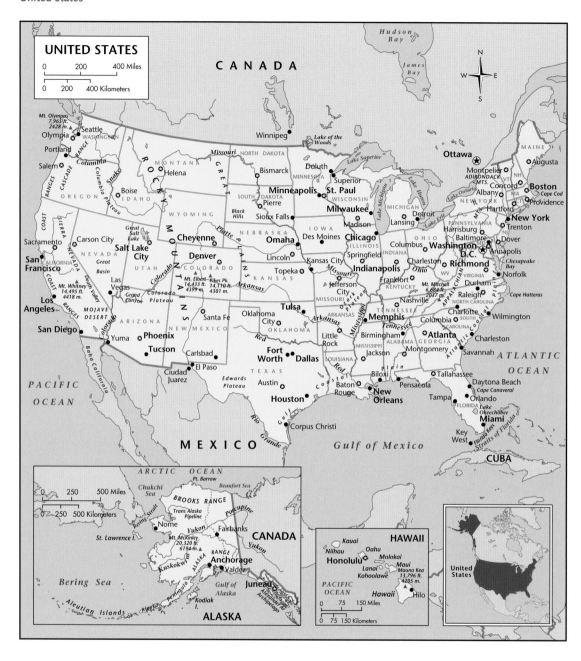

kilometers). The country shares borders with Canada and Mexico, with a total land boundary length of 7,593 miles (12,034 kilometers) and a total coastline of 12,380 miles (19,924 kilometers).

Alaska, the 49th state, is separated from the contiguous 48 states by Canada. It forms a peninsula surrounded by the Arctic Ocean and the Pacific and is separated from Russia by the

Bering Strait. The island state of Hawaii, the 50th state, is located in the Pacific Ocean. The nation's capital, Washington, D.C., is located near the mid-Atlantic coast. The United States also has dependencies in the Pacific and the Caribbean.

2 Topography

Although the northern New England coast is rocky, along the rest of the eastern seaboard the Atlantic Coastal Plain rises gradually from the shoreline. Narrow in the north, the plain widens to about 200 miles (320 kilometers) in the south and in Georgia merges with the Gulf Coastal Plain that borders the Gulf of Mexico and extends through Mexico as far as the Yucatán. West of the Atlantic Coastal Plain is the Piedmont Plateau, bounded by the Appalachian Mountains. The Appalachians, which extend from southwest Maine into central Alabama, are old mountains, largely eroded away, with rounded contours and generally forested terrain. The highest Appalachian Peak, Mount Mitchell in North Carolina, reaches 6,684 feet (2,037 meters).

Between the Appalachians and the Rocky Mountains to the west lies the vast interior plain of the United States. Running south through the center of this plain is the Mississippi River. Its major tributary, the Missouri, is the longest river in the country and the second longest in North America, with a total distance of 2,341 miles (3,767 kilometers). Its source is found in the Northern Rockies.

The eastern reaches of the great interior plain are bounded on the north by the Great Lakes, which are thought to contain about one-fifth of the world's total supply of fresh water. They include Lake Michigan, Lake Superior, Lake Huron, Lake Erie, and Lake Ontario. Lake Superior, which covers an area of 31,699 square miles (82,100 square kilometers), is the largest lake in the country and the second-largest lake by surface area in the world (after the Caspian Sea). The five lakes are accessible to oceangoing vessels from the Atlantic via the Saint Lawrence Seaway. The basins of the Great Lakes were formed by the glacial ice cap that moved down over large parts of North America some 25,000 years ago.

The great interior plain consists of two major subregions: the fertile Central Plains and the more arid Great Plains. Although they appear flat, the Great Plains rise gradually from about 1,500 feet (460 meters) to more than 5,000 feet (1,500 meters) at their western extremity.

The Continental Divide runs along the crest of the Rocky Mountains. The Rockies and the ranges to the west are part of the great system of young, rugged mountains that runs along western North, Central, and South America from Alaska to Tierra del Fuego, Chile. In the continental United States, the series of western ranges, most of them paralleling the Pacific coast, are the Sierra Nevada, the Coast Ranges, the Cascade Range, and the Tehachapi and San Bernardino Mountains. Between the Rockies and the Sierra Nevada-Cascade mountain barrier to the west lies the Great Basin, a group of vast arid plateaus containing most of the desert areas of the United States, in the south eroded by deep canyons.

The coastal plains along the Pacific are narrow. The most extensive lowland near the West Coast is the Great Valley of California, lying between the Sierra Nevada and the Coast

Ranges. There are 70 peaks in these western ranges of the continental United States that rise to an altitude of 14,000 feet (4,267 meters) or more. The greatest rivers of the Far West are the Colorado in the Southwest and the Columbia in the Pacific Northwest.

Separated from the continental United States by Canadian territory, the state of Alaska occupies the extreme northwest portion of the North American continent. The Alaskan Peninsula and the Aleutian Islands, sweeping west far out to sea, consist of a chain of volcanoes, many of which are still active. The state of Hawaii consists of a group of Pacific islands formed by volcanoes rising sharply from the ocean floor. The highest of these volcanoes, Mauna Loa, at 13,796 feet (4,205 meters), is located on the largest of the islands, Hawaii, and is still active.

The lowest point in the United States is found in Death Valley in California, 282 feet (86 meters) below sea level. At 20,320 feet (6,194 meters), Mount McKinley in Alaska is the highest peak in North America. These topographic extremes suggest the geological instability of the Pacific Coast region. The San Andreas Fault in California is one of several major fault lines that cause frequent earth tremors in the western United States.

3 Climate

The East Coast is affected mostly by masses of air moving from west to east across the continent. Its climate is basically continental, with clear contrasts between seasons. Because Florida has the Gulf of Mexico lying to its west, however, it experiences only moderate differences between summer and winter temperatures. Mean annual temperatures vary considerably

between north and south, ranging from 51°F (11°C) in Boston to 76°F (24°C) in Miami. Annual rainfall is generally more than 40 inches (100 centimeters). The Gulf and South Atlantic states are often hit by severe tropical storms in late summer and early autumn.

The number of hurricanes and their severity have measurably increased in the past few years. From 1995 to 2003, there were a total of 32 major hurricanes with sustained winds of 111 miles per hour (179 kilometers per hour) or greater. In 2005, there were 23 named Atlantic hurricanes, three of which caused severe damage to the Gulf Coast region. Hurricane Katrina, which hit Florida on 25 August 2005, eventually developed into a category 4 hurricane that made landfall in southern Louisiana. Several levees protecting the low-lying city of New Orleans broke, flooding the entire region under waters that rose over the rooftops of homes. Over 1,000 were killed by the storm. Over 500,000 people were left homeless and without jobs. Mississippi was also hit by the hurricane, which left a wave of destruction in its path.

One month later, Hurricane Rita peaked as a category 5 hurricane before making landfall as a category 3 hurricane on 24 September 2005 between Sabine Pass, Texas, and Johnson's Bayou, Louisiana. Hurricane Wilma followed on 24 October, making landfall north of Everglades City in Florida as a category 3 hurricane. In 2008, Hurricane Gustav made landfall in Louisiana as a category 2 storm, and in 2011 Hurricane Irene killed 18 people between Puerto Rico and Connecticut and caused $3 billion in damages.

In October 2012 Superstorm Sandy caused more than 100 deaths in the Caribbean and the United States. Damage estimates of up to

$60 billion were reported, with New York and New Jersey most affected.

The prairie lands in the middle of the country have more drought than heavy rainfall. The average midwinter temperature in the extreme north—Minnesota and North Dakota—is about 9°F (-13°C) or lower, while the average July temperature is 65°F (18°C). In the Texas prairie region to the south, January temperatures average 50 to 55°F (10 to 13°C) and July temperatures average 80 to 85°F (27 to 29°C). Annual rainfall in this region can be as low as 18 inches (46 centimeters).

The Great Plains are semiarid. Annual rainfall in the southern plains averages about 20 inches (50 centimeters) and in the northern plains about 10 inches (25 centimeters). The contrast between summer and winter temperatures is extreme throughout the Great Plains. Maximum summer temperatures of more than 110°F (43°C) have been recorded, while the average minimum temperature for January is -3°F (-19°C).

The higher reaches of the Rockies and the other western ranges have an alpine climate. The climate of the Western desert region varies considerably from north to south. In New Mexico, Arizona, and southeastern California, mean annual rainfall ranges from 3 inches (8 centimeters) to 30 inches (76 centimeters), while some of the mountainous areas of central Washington and Idaho receive at least 60 inches (152 centimeters) of rain per year. Phoenix, Arizona, has a mean annual temperature of 71°F (22°C).

The Pacific Coast has a maritime climate, with mild winters and moderately warm, dry summers, while climate on the southern Pacific coast is more Mediterranean. Los Angeles in the south has an average temperature of 59°F (15°C) in January and 69°F (29°C) in August; Seattle in the north has an average temperature of 39°F (4°C) in January and 72°F (22°C) in July. Precipitation ranges from an annual average of 1.78 inches (4.52 centimeters) at Death Valley in California (the lowest in the United States) to more than 140 inches (356 centimeters) in Washington's mountain regions.

Alaska has varied climatic conditions. The Aleutian Islands and the coastal panhandle strip have a moderate maritime climate. The interior is characterized by short, hot summers and long, bitterly cold winters. In the region bordering the Arctic Ocean, a polar climate prevails; the soil hundreds of feet below the surface remains frozen year round.

Northeast ocean winds give Hawaii a mild, stable climate. The mean temperature in Honolulu is 73°F (23°C) in January and 80°F (27°C) in July. Rainfall is moderate—about 28 inches (71 centimeters) per year—but it is much greater in the mountains.

The lowest temperature recorded in the United States was -79.8°F (-62°C)) in Alaska at Prospect Creek Camp on 23 January 1971; the highest, 134°F (57°C) in California at Greenland Ranch in Death Valley on 10 July 1913. The record annual rainfall is 578 inches (1,468 centimeters) on Maui in Hawaii in 1950.

4 Plants and Animals

At least 7,000 species and subspecies of indigenous plants have been categorized. The eastern forests contain a mixture of softwoods and hardwoods that includes pine, oak, maple, spruce, beech, birch, hemlock, walnut, gum, and hickory. The central hardwood forest contains oak, hickory, ash, maple, and walnut.

Pine, hickory, tupelo, pecan, gum, birch, and sycamore are found in the southern forest, which stretches along the Gulf Coast into the eastern half of Texas. The Pacific forest is the most spectacular of all because of its enormous redwoods and Douglas firs. In the southwest are saguaro (giant cactus), yucca, candlewood, and the Joshua tree.

The central grasslands lie in the interior of the continent, where the moisture is not sufficient to support the growth of large forests. The tall grassland or prairie (now almost entirely under cultivation) lies to the east of the one-hundredth meridian. To the west of this longitude, where rainfall is frequently less than 20 inches (50 centimeters) per year, is the short grassland. Mesquite grass covers parts of west Texas, southern New Mexico, and Arizona. Short grass may be found in the highlands of the latter two states, while tall grass covers large portions of the coastal regions of Texas and Louisiana and occurs in some parts of Mississippi, Alabama, and Florida. The Pacific grassland includes northern Idaho, the higher plateaus of eastern Washington and Oregon, and the mountain valleys of California.

The region of the Western Cordillera is essentially covered with desert shrubs. Sagebrush predominates in the northern part of this area, and creosote in the southern region, with saltbrush near the Great Salt Lake and in Death Valley.

The lower slopes of the mountains running up to the coastline of Alaska are covered with coniferous forests as far north as the Seward Peninsula. The central part of the Yukon Basin is also a region of softwood forests. The rest of Alaska is heath or tundra. Hawaii has extensive forests of bamboo and ferns. Sugarcane and pineapple, although not native to the islands, now cover a large portion of the cultivated land.

Small trees and shrubs common to most of the United States include hackberry, hawthorn, serviceberry, blackberry, wild cherry, dogwood, and snowberry. Wildflowers bloom in all areas, from the seldom-seen blossoms of rare desert cacti to the hardiest alpine species. Wildflowers include forget-me-not, fringed and closed gentians, jack-in-the-pulpit, black-eyed Susan, columbine, and common dandelion, along with numerous varieties of aster, orchid, lady's slipper, and wild rose.

An estimated 428 species of mammals characterize the animal life of the continental United States. Among the larger game animals are the white-tailed deer, moose, pronghorn antelope, bighorn sheep, mountain goat, black bear, and grizzly bear. Some 25 important furred species are common, including the muskrat, red and gray foxes, mink, raccoon, beaver, opossum, striped skunk, woodchuck, common cottontail, snowshoe hare, and various squirrels. The American buffalo (bison), millions of which once roamed the plains, is now found only on select reserves and farms. Other mammals, such as the elk and the gray wolf, have been restricted to much smaller ranges.

Year-round and migratory birds abound. Loons, wild ducks, and wild geese are found in lake country; terns, gulls, sandpipers, herons, and other seabirds live along the coasts. Wrens, thrushes, owls, hummingbirds, sparrows, woodpeckers, swallows, chickadees, vireos, warblers, and finches appear in profusion, along with the robin, common crow, cardinal, Baltimore oriole, eastern and western meadowlarks, and various blackbirds. Wild turkey, ruffed grouse, and ring-necked pheasant (introduced from Europe) are popular game birds.

Lakes, rivers, and streams teem with trout, bass, perch, muskellunge, carp, catfish, and pike; sea bass, cod, snapper, and flounder are abundant along the coasts, along with such shellfish as lobster, shrimp, clams, oysters, and mussels. Garter, pine, and milk snakes are found in most regions. Four poisonous snakes survive, of which the rattlesnake is the most common. Alligators appear in southern waterways, and the Gila monster makes its home in the Southwest.

As of July 2012, the US Fish and Wildlife Service listed 1,077 endangered species, including 70 mammals, 77 birds, 80 fish, 68 clams, and 644 plants. The same agency listed 317 threatened species, including 150 plants.

5 Environmental Protection

The Environmental Protection Agency (EPA), created in 1970, is an independent body with primary regulatory responsibility in the fields of air and noise pollution, water and waste management, and control of toxic substances. Other federal agencies with environmental responsibilities are the Forest Service and Soil Conservation Service within the Department of Agriculture, the Fish and Wildlife Service and the National Park Service within the Department of the Interior, the Department of Energy, and the Nuclear Regulatory Commission.

The most influential nonprofit environmental lobbies include the Sierra Club and its legal arm, the Sierra Club Legal Defense Fund. Large conservation groups include the National Wildlife Federation, the National Audubon Society, and the Nature Conservancy. Greenpeace USA has gained international attention by seeking to disrupt hunts for whales and seals.

Among the environmental movement's most notable successes have been the inauguration (and mandating in some states) of recycling programs, the banning in the United States of the insecticide dichlorodiphenyltrichloroethane (DDT), the successful fight against construction of a supersonic transport (SST), and the gradual elimination of chlorofluorocarbon (CFC) production.

Outstanding problems include inadequate facilities for solid-waste disposal; air pollution from industrial emissions; the contamination of homes by radon, a radioactive gas that is produced by the decay of underground deposits of radium and can cause cancer; cleanup of hazardous waste sites; runoffs of agricultural pesticides; continued dumping of raw or partially treated sewage from major cities into US waterways; and the decrease in arable land because of depletion, erosion, and urbanization.

As of September 2012, there were 1,314 sites listed on the US Environmental Protection Agency's National Priorities List of Superfund sites. This included sites in almost every state in the country.

6 Population

The population of the United States in 2011 was estimated at 311,591,917. The median age of the population increased from 16.7 years in 1820 to 22.9 years in 1900, and to 37.2 years in 2010. In 2010, around 26% of the population (79,284,600 people) were under 18 years old while 13% (39,178,700) were 65 years old or older. Population density varies greatly from region to region; the average is 87.4 persons per square mile (33.1 persons per square kilometer). The population is projected to reach 349,439,199 in 2025.

Approximately 80.7% of the population lived in urban areas in 2010. In 2011, the largest cities in the United States were New York City (population 8,244,910), Los Angeles (3,819,702), Chicago (2,707,120), and Houston (1,536,471).

7 Ethnic Groups

The majority of the US population is of European origin, with the largest groups having primary ancestry traceable to the United Kingdom, Germany, and Ireland. Many Americans report multiple ancestries. Major racial and national minority groups include blacks (either of US, African, or Caribbean parentage), Chinese, Filipinos, Japanese, Mexicans, and other Spanish-speaking peoples of the Americas. According to the 2010 Census, about 72.4% of the US population was white; 12.6% black and/or African American; 4.8% Asian; 0.9% Native American (including Alaskan Native); and 0.2% Native Hawaiian/Pacific Islander. Hispanics and Latinos, who can be of any race, represented 16.3% of the population. About 2.9% of the population claim a mixed ancestry of two or more races. About 12.7% of all US citizens are foreign born, with the largest numbers of people coming from Latin America (20,565,108) and Asia (10,747,229).

Groups of Native Americans are most numerous in the southwestern states of Oklahoma, Arizona, New Mexico, and California. A majority of the black population still resides in the South, the region that absorbed most of the slaves brought from Africa in the 18th and

Lewis W. Hine was a famous photographer who used film to document the human condition, whether it was child laborers or emigrants coming to America in search of a better life. This Hine's photograph shows emigrants arriving at New York's Ellis Island in 1905. © EVERETT COLLECTION INC / ALAMY

19th centuries. Many black Americans live in metropolitan areas, notably in Washington, D.C.; Atlanta; Chicago; Detroit; New Orleans; Newark; Baltimore; and New York City, which has a larger number of black residents than any other city. The Chinese population is highly urbanized and concentrated particularly in cities of more than 100,000 population, mostly on the West Coast and in New York City. Hawaii has been a popular magnet for Japanese emigration.

Hispanics in 2010 made up the largest minority group in the United States, accounting for more than 16% of the total population.

State Areas, Entry Dates, and Populations

State	Capital	Order of Entry	Date of Entry	Population at Entry	Census 2000	Census 2010
Alabama	Montgomery	22	14 December 1819	127,901	4,447,100	4,779,736
Alaska	Juneau	49	3 January 1959	226,167	626,932	710,231
Arizona	Phoenix	48	14 February 1912	204,354	5,130,632	6,392,017
Arkansas	Little Rock	25	15 June 1836	57,574	2,673,400	2,915,918
California	Sacramento	31	9 September 1850	92,597	33,871,648	37,253,956
Colorado	Denver	38	1 August 1876	39,864	4,301,261	5,029,196
Connecticut*	Hartford	5	9 January 1788	237,946	3,405,565	3,574,097
Delaware*	Dover	1	7 December 1787	59,096	783,600	897,934
Florida	Tallahassee	27	3 March 1845	87,445	15,982,378	18,801,310
Georgia*	Atlanta	4	2 January 1788	82,548	8,186,453	9,687,653
Hawaii	Honolulu	50	21 August 1959	632,772	1,211,537	1,360,301
Idaho	Boise	43	3 July 1890	88,548	1,293,953	1,567,582
Illinois	Springfield	21	3 December 1818	55,211	12,419,293	12,830,632
Indiana	Indianapolis	19	11 December 1816	147,178	6,080,485	6,483,802
Iowa	Des Moines	29	28 December 1846	192,214	2,926,324	3,046,355
Kansas	Topeka	34	29 January 1861	107,206	2,688,418	2,853,118
Kentucky	Frankfort	15	1 June 1792	73,677	4,041,769	4,339,367
Louisiana	Baton Rouge	18	30 April 1812	76,556	4,468,976	4,533,372
Maine	Augusta	23	15 March 1820	298,335	1,274,923	1,328,361
Maryland*	Annapolis	7	28 April 1788	319,728	5,296,486	5,773,552
Massachusetts*	Boston	6	6 February 1788	378,787	6,349,097	6,547,629
Michigan	Lansing	26	26 January 1837	212,267	9,938,444	9,883,640
Minnesota	St. Paul	32	11 May 1858	172,023	4,919,479	5,303,925
Mississippi	Jackson	20	10 December 1817	75,448	2,844,658	2,967,297
Missouri	Jefferson City	24	10 August 1821	66,586	5,595,211	5,988,927
Montana	Helena	41	8 November 1889	142,924	902,195	989,415
Nebraska	Lincoln	37	1 March 1867	122,993	1,711,263	1,826,341
Nevada	Carson City	36	31 October 1864	42,491	1,998,257	2,700,551
New Hampshire*	Concord	9	21 June 1788	141,885	1,235,786	1,316,470
New Jersey*	Trenton	3	18 December 1787	184,139	8,414,350	8,791,894
New Mexico	Santa Fe	47	6 January 1912	327,301	1,819,046	2,059,179
New York*	Albany	11	26 July 1788	340,120	18,976,457	19,378,102
North Carolina*	Raleigh	12	21 November 1789	393,751	8,049,313	9,535,483
North Dakota	Bismarck	39	2 November 1889	190,983	642,200	672,591
Ohio	Columbus	17	1 March 1803†	43,365	11,353,140	11,536,504
Oklahoma	Oklahoma City	46	16 November 1907	657,155	3,450,654	3,751,351
Oregon	Salem	33	14 February 1859	52,465	3,421,399	3,831,074
Pennsylvania*	Harrisburg	2	12 December 1787	434,373	12,281,054	12,702,379
Rhode Island*	Providence	13	29 May 1790	68,825	1,048,319	1,052,567
South Carolina*	Columbia	8	23 May 1788	393,751	4,012,012	4,625,364
South Dakota	Pierre	40	2 November 1889	348,600	754,844	814,180
Tennessee	Nashville	16	1 June 1796	35,691	5,689,283	6,346,105
Texas	Austin	28	29 December 1845	212,592	20,851,820	25,145,561
Utah	Salt Lake City	45	4 January 1896	276,749	2,233,169	2,763,885
Vermont	Montpelier	14	4 March 1791	85,425	608,827	625,741
Virginia*	Richmond	10	25 June 1788	747,610	7,078,515	8,001,024
Washington	Olympia	42	11 November 1889	357,232	5,894,121	6,724,540
West Virginia	Charleston	35	20 June 1863	442,014	1,808,344	1,852,994
Wisconsin	Madison	30	29 May 1848	305,391	5,363,675	5,686,986
Wyoming	Cheyenne	44	10 July 1890	62,555	493,782	563,626

*One of original 13 colonies.
†Date fixed in 1953 by congressional resolution.

Although Mexicans in the 21st century were still concentrated in the Southwest, they have settled throughout the United States; there are over 31 million Mexicans in the country, about 10% of the total population. Spanish-speaking Puerto Ricans have largely settled in the New York metropolitan area. Since 1959, many Cubans have settled in Florida and other eastern states.

8 Languages

The primary language of the United States is English, enriched by words borrowed from the languages of Indians and immigrants, predominantly European. Spanish is also spoken by a sizable number of people.

When European settlement began, Indians living north of Mexico spoke about 300 different languages now grouped into around 58 different language families. Two such families have contributed noticeably to the American vocabulary: Algonquian in the Northeast and Aztec-Tanoan in the Southwest.

Dialect studies confirm that standard English is not uniform throughout the country. Major regional variations reflect patterns of colonial settlement. Dialectologists recognize three main dialects: Northern, Midland, and Southern.

The Northern dialect is that of New England and its derivative settlements in New York; the northern parts of Ohio, Indiana, Illinois, and Iowa; and Michigan, Wisconsin, Minnesota, northeastern South Dakota, and North Dakota. Midland speech extends in a wide band across the United States with two main subdivisions, North Midland and South Midland. North Midland speech extends westward from New Jersey, Delaware, and Pennsylvania into Ohio, Illinois, southern Iowa, and northern Missouri. South Midland speech was carried by the Scotch-Irish from Pennsylvania down the Shenandoah Valley into the southern Appalachians, where it acquired many Southern speech features before it spread westward into Kentucky, Tennessee, southern Missouri, Arkansas, and northeast Texas. Southern dialect is spoken in the coastal savannah and Piedmont areas from Maryland south, in some areas of Florida, and in the lowlands and coastal areas of Georgia, Alabama, Mississippi, Louisiana, and eastern Texas.

In the western part of the United States, migration routes crossed and intermingled so much that no neat dialect boundaries can be drawn, although there are a few rather clear population pockets.

As of 2011, 79.2% of the population age five and over (230,947,071) spoke only English at home. Other languages spoken at home included Spanish (12.9%), other Indo-European languages (3.7%), and Asian and Pacific Islander languages (3.3%).

9 Religions

Religious traditions in the United States are predominantly Judeo-Christian. Most Americans identify themselves as Protestants (of various denominations), Roman Catholics, or Jews. According to the Pew Forum on Religion & Public Life, as of 2008, around 84% of Americans reported affiliation with a religious group, with 78.4% reporting affiliation with a Christian denomination, and 51% with a Protestant denomination. Catholics represented around 24%. At the same time, 26% of Americans reported being affiliated with an Evangelical Protestant tradition; 18% reported affiliation with a main-line Protestant tradition; 7% were affiliated with a historically black Protestant church; 2% were Mormon; 1% were Orthodox; 1% were Jehovah's Witnesses; 2% were Jewish; 1% were Hindu; and 1% were Muslim. All other traditions accounted for less than 0.5% of the population each.

Immigration from Ireland, Italy, Eastern Europe, French Canada, and the Caribbean accounts for the predominance of Roman Catholicism in the Northeast, Northwest, and some parts of the Great Lakes region, while Hispanic traditions and more recent immigration from Mexico and other Latin American countries account for the historical importance of Roman Catholicism in California and throughout most of the sunbelt. More than any other US religious body, the Roman Catholic Church maintains an extensive network of parochial schools.

Jewish immigrants settled first in the Northeast, where the largest Jewish population remains. Baptists predominate below the Mason-Dixon line and west to Texas. The Southern Baptist Convention is the nation's largest Protestant group, with about 16 million members. A concentration of Methodist groups extends westward in a band from Delaware to eastern Colorado. The largest of these groups, the United Methodist Church, has about 11 million adherents. Lutheran denominations, reflecting in part the patterns of German and Scandinavian settlement, are most highly concentrated in the north-central states, especially Minnesota and the Dakotas.

Two Lutheran synods, the Lutheran Church in America and the American Lutheran Church, merged in 1987 to form the Evangelical Lutheran Church in America, with around 4.2 million adherents in 2010. In June 1983, the two major Presbyterian churches, the northern-based United Presbyterian Church in the USA, and the southern-based Presbyterian Church in the United States, formally merged as the Presbyterian Church (USA), ending a division that began with the Civil War. This group claimed an estimated 2.7 million adherents in 2012.

Other Protestant denominations and their estimated adherents (as of 2008) include the Episcopal Church, 2,405,000, and the United Church of Christ, 1,921,000. One Christian group, the Church of Jesus Christ of Latter-day Saints (Mormons), with 3,158,000 million members (2008), was organized in New York in 1830 and since migrating westward has played a leading role in Utah's political, economic, and religious life.

As of 2008, there were also around 5.3 million Jews, 1.3 million Muslims, 1.2 million Buddhists, 1.2 million Unitarians, 582,000 Hindus, 342,000 Wiccans, and 340,000 Pagans; followers of various other religions also participate in US religious life. Around 16% of the population reported no religious affiliation in 2008, but only 1.6% of the population reported being atheists.

10 Transportation

The United States has well-developed systems of railroads, highways, inland waterways, oil pipelines, and domestic airways. Despite an attempt to encourage more people to travel by train through the development of a national network (Amtrak) in the 1970s, rail transport has continued to experience heavy financial losses. In 2012, there were 138,623 miles (223,092 kilometers) of mainline routes, all standard gauge.

The most widely used form of transportation is the automobile, and the extent and quality of the US road-transport system are the best in the world. More than 156 million vehicles were registered in 2010, including more than 134.9 million passenger cars, 102.2 million light trucks, and 7.9 million motorcycles. The United States has a vast network of public roads, with a total length of approximately 4.05 million miles (6.5 million kilometers) in 2010.

Major ocean ports or port areas are California, New York, Georgia, Seattle, Houston, and the San Francisco Bay area. In 2011, the top-ranking port, in terms of tonnage handled, was Los Angeles, handling 7.9 million 20-foot equivalent units (TEUs), followed by Long Beach, California, with 6 million TEUs, and New York/New Jersey ports with 5.5 million TEUs.

In 2011, the United States had an estimated 15,000 airports, with 5,202 public use airports. As of 2011, the busiest airport was Hartsfield in Atlanta, Georgia, which handled 42,155,204 passenger enplanements in 2009; followed by Chicago's O'Hare Airport, with 31,124,151 passenger enplanements; and Los Angeles International, with 27,496,850 passenger enplanements.

11 History

The first Americans, distant ancestors of the American Indians, probably crossed the Bering Strait from Asia at least 12,000 years ago. By the time Christopher Columbus came to the New World in 1492, there were probably about two million Native Americans living in the land that was to become the United States.

The Spanish established the first permanent settlement at Saint Augustine in the future state of Florida in 1565, and another in New Mexico in 1599. During the early 17th century, the English founded Jamestown in present-day Virginia (1607) and Plymouth Colony in present-day Massachusetts (1620). The Dutch and Swedish also established settlements in the 17th century, but the English eventually took over settlement of the East Coast except for Florida, where the Spanish ruled until 1821. The Southwest, California, Arizona, New Mexico, and Texas also were part of the Spanish empire until the 17th century.

Many Chinese immigrants helped build the railroads in the United States that connected the East to the West. © ARCHIVE PHOTOS/GETTY IMAGES.

Many Native American ruins are preserved in the United States. Some of the best examples are found in what is now Chaco Culture National Historical Park. Built by the Pueblo people, Chaco was an important cultural site between the years 850 and 1250. © JEFFREY M. FRANK/SHUTTERSTOCK.COM.

The American Revolution The colonies enjoyed a large measure of self-government until the end of the French and Indian War (1745–63), which resulted in the loss of French Canada to the British. To prevent further troubles with the Indians, the British government in 1763 prohibited the American colonists from settling beyond the Appalachian Mountains. The British also enacted a series of tax measures, which the colonists protested, setting off a struggle between colonial and British authority.

A series of conflicts led to the colonists' decision to separate from British rule and set up their own independent government. George Washington was appointed commander in chief of the new American army. On 4 July 1776, the 13 American colonies adopted the Declaration of Independence. The American Revolution officially began.

British and American forces met in their first organized encounter near Boston on 17 June 1775. Numerous battles up and down the East Coast followed. The entry of France into the war on the American side eventually tipped the balance. On 19 October 1781, British commander Charles Cornwallis surrendered his army at Yorktown, Virginia. American independence was acknowledged by the British

In a painting, Benjamin Franklin, John Adams, and Thomas Jefferson are shown reviewing a draft of the Declaration of Independence. © VICTORIAN TRADITIONS/SHUTTERSTOCK.COM.

in a treaty of peace signed in Paris on 3 September 1783.

The Beginnings of American Government

The first constitution uniting the 13 original states—the Articles of Confederation—denied Congress power to raise taxes or regulate commerce, and many of its authorized powers required the approval of a minimum of nine states. In 1787 Congress passed the Northwest Ordinance, providing for the establishment of new territories on the frontier. In that same year, a convention assembled in Philadelphia to revise the articles. The convention adopted an altogether new document, the present Constitution of the United States, which greatly increased the powers of the central government at the expense of the states.

This document was ratified by the states with the understanding that it would be amended to include a bill of rights guaranteeing certain fundamental freedoms. These freedoms—including the rights of free speech, a free press, and freedom of assembly, freedom from unreasonable search and seizure, and the right to a speedy and public trial by an impartial jury—are assured by the first 10 amendments to the constitution, known as the Bill of Rights, adopted on 5 December 1791. The constitution did recognize slavery, and it did not provide for universal suffrage (voting rights). On 30 April 1789, George Washington was inaugurated as the first president of the United States.

The Federalist Party, to which Washington belonged, was opposed to the French Revolution (1789), while the Democratic-Republicans (an anti-Federalist party led by Thomas Jefferson) supported it. This division of the nation's leadership was the beginning of the two-party system, which has been the dominant characteristic of the US political scene ever since.

Westward Expansion

In 1803, President Thomas Jefferson purchased the Louisiana Territory from France, including all the present territory of the United States west of the Mississippi drained by that river and its tributaries. Exploration and mapping of the new territory, particularly through the expedition of Meriwether Lewis and William Clark, began almost immediately.

To make room for the westward expansion of European American settlement, the federal government in 1817 began a policy of forcibly resettling the Native Americans. Many were moved to what later became known as Indian Territory (now Oklahoma); those Native Americans not forced to move were restricted to reservations. This "removal" of Native Americans to make way for European American settlement was a form of genocide (the deliberate destruction of a whole race, culture, or group of people).

The Missouri Compromise (1820) provided for admission of Missouri into the Union as a slave state but banned slavery in territories to the west that lay north of 36° 30'. In 1823, President James Monroe declared the Western Hemisphere closed to further colonization by European powers in a proclamation known as the Monroe Doctrine.

Development of Farming and Industry

Farming expanded with westward migration. The cotton gin, invented by Eli Whitney in 1793, greatly simplified cotton production, and the growing textile industry in New England and Great Britain needed a lot of cotton. The South remained an agricultural society based mostly on a one-crop economy. Large numbers of field hands were required for cotton farming, and black slavery became a significant part of the southern economy.

The successful completion of the Erie Canal (1825), linking the Great Lakes with the Atlantic, began a canal-building boom. Railroad building began in earnest in the 1830s, and by 1840 about 3,300 miles (5,300 kilometers) of track had been laid.

New States and the Slavery Question

In 1836, US settlers in Texas revolted against Mexican rule and established an independent republic. Texas was admitted to the Union as a state in 1845. War with Mexico over a boundary dispute led in 1848 to the addition of California and New Mexico to the growing nation. A dispute with Britain over the Oregon Territory was settled in 1846 by a treaty that established the 49th parallel as the boundary with Canada.

Westward expansion increased the conflict over slavery in the new territories. The Kansas-Nebraska Act of 1854 repealed the Missouri Compromise and left the question of slavery in the territories to be decided by the settlers themselves. Finally, the election of Abraham Lincoln to the presidency in 1860 led strong supporters of slavery to decide to secede from the United States altogether.

The Civil War

Between December 1860 and February 1861, the seven states of the Deep South—South Carolina, Mississippi, Florida, Alabama, Georgia, Louisiana, and Texas—withdrew from the Union and formed a separate government. They were known as the Confederate States of America, under the presidency of Jefferson Davis. On 12 April 1861, the Confederates opened fire on Fort Sumter in the harbor of Charleston, South Carolina, beginning the US Civil War. Arkansas, North Carolina, Virginia, and Tennessee quickly joined the Confederacy.

For the next four years, war raged between Confederate and Union forces, largely in southern territories. An estimated 360,000 men in the Union forces lost their lives, including 110,000 killed in battle. Confederate dead were estimated at 250,000, including 94,000 killed in battle. The North, with more fighters and resources, finally won. With much of the South in Union hands, Confederate General Robert

E. Lee surrendered to Union General Ulysses S. Grant at Appomattox Courthouse in Virginia on 9 April 1865.

The Post-Civil War Era President Lincoln's Emancipation Proclamation of 1863 was the first step in freeing some four million black slaves. Their liberation was completed soon after the war's end by amendments to the Constitution. Five days after General Lee's surrender, Lincoln was assassinated by John Wilkes Booth. During the Reconstruction era (1865–77), the defeated South was governed by Union Army commanders. The resulting bitterness of southerners toward northern Republican rule, which gave blacks the rights of citizens, including the right to vote, lasted for years afterward. By the end of the Reconstruction era, whites had reestablished their political domination over blacks in the southern states and had begun to enforce rules of segregation that lasted for nearly a century.

Outside the South, the age of big business dawned. Pittsburgh, Chicago, and New York emerged as the nation's great industrial centers. The American Federation of Labor, founded in 1886, established a nationwide system of organized labor that remained dominant for many decades. During this period, too, the women's rights movement began to organize to fight for the right to vote. It took women until 1920 to win their constitutional right to vote nationally.

The 1890s marked the closing of the US frontier for settlement and the beginning of US overseas expansion. (Alaska had already been acquired from Russia for $7.2 million in 1867.) In 1898, at its own request, Hawaii was annexed as a territory by the United States. In the same year, as a result of the Spanish-American War, the United States added the Philippines, Guam, and Puerto Rico to its territories. A newly independent Cuba became virtually a protectorate of the United States until the 1950s. In 1903, the United States leased the Panama Canal Zone and started construction of a 42-mile (68-kilometer) canal, completed in 1914.

World War I to World War II United States involvement in World War I (1914–18) marked the country's emergence as one of the great powers of the world. By late 1917, when US troops joined the Allied forces in the fighting on the western front, the European armies were approaching exhaustion. American intervention may well have been a key element in the eventual victory of the Allies. Fighting ended with the armistice (truce) of 11 November 1918. President Woodrow Wilson played an active role in drawing up the 1919 Versailles peace treaty.

The 1920s saw a major business boom, followed by the great stock market crash of October 1929, which ushered in the longest and most serious economic depression the country had ever known. The election of Franklin D. Roosevelt, in March 1933, began a new era in US history, in which the federal government took a much greater role in the nation's economic affairs. Relief measures were instituted, work projects established, and the federal Social Security program was set up. The National Labor Relations Act established the right of employees' organizations to bargain collectively with employers.

Following German, Italian, and Japanese aggression, World War II broke out in Europe during September 1939. In 1940, Roosevelt, ignoring a tradition dating back to Washington that no president should serve more than two terms, ran again for reelection. He easily defeated his Republican opponent, Wendell Willkie.

The United States was brought actively into the war by the Japanese attack on the Pearl Harbor naval base in Hawaii on 7 December 1941. US forces waged war across the Pacific, in Africa, in Asia, and in Europe. Germany was successfully invaded in 1944 and conquered in May 1945. After the United States dropped the world's first atomic bombs on Hiroshima and Nagasaki in Japan, the Japanese surrendered in August.

Korean War and the Civil Rights Movement The United States became an active member of the new world organization, the United Nations, during President Harry S Truman's administration. In 1949 the North Atlantic Treaty Organization (NATO) established a defensive alliance among a number of Western European nations and the United States. Following the North Korean attack on South Korea on 25 June 1950, the United Nations Security Council decided that members of the United Nations should aid South Korea. US naval, air, and ground forces were immediately sent by President Truman. An undeclared war followed, which eventually was ended by a truce signed on 27 June 1953.

During President Dwight D. Eisenhower's administration, the US Supreme Court's decision in 1954 outlawed segregation of whites and blacks in public schools. In the early 1960s, sit-ins, freedom rides, and similar expressions of nonviolent resistance by blacks and sympathizers—known collectively as the civil rights movement—led to the end of some segregationist practices.

In the early 1960s, during the administration of President Eisenhower's successor, John F. Kennedy, the Cold War heated up as Cuba, under the regime of Fidel Castro, aligned itself with the Soviet Union. In October 1962, President Kennedy successfully forced a showdown with the Soviet Union over Cuba in demanding the withdrawal of Soviet-supplied missiles from the nearby island. On 22 November 1963, President Kennedy was assassinated while riding in a motorcade through Dallas, Texas. Hours later, Vice President Lyndon B. Johnson was inaugurated president. President Johnson's ambitious "Great Society" program sought to ensure black Americans' rights in voting and public housing, to give the underprivileged job training, and to provide persons 65 and over with free hospitalization and other medical benefits.

The Vietnam War and Watergate In 1965, President Johnson sent American combat troops into South Vietnam to support anticommunist forces, and he ordered US bombing raids on communist North Vietnam. However, American military might was unable to defeat the Vietnamese guerrillas, and the American people were significantly divided over continuing the undeclared war.

Under President Richard M. Nixon (1913–1994, elected in 1968), the increasingly unpopular and costly war continued for four more years before a cease-fire was finally signed on 27 January 1973 and the last American soldiers were withdrawn. Two years later, the South Vietnamese army collapsed, and the North Vietnamese communist regime united the country. In 1972, President Nixon opened up relations with the People's Republic of China, which had been closed to Westerners since 1949. He also signed a strategic arms limitation agreement with the Soviet Union. (Earlier, in July 1969, American technology had achieved a national triumph by landing the first astronaut on the Moon.)

The Watergate scandal began on 17 June 1972 with the arrest of five men associated with Nixon's reelection campaign. They had been caught during a break-in at Democratic Party headquarters in the Watergate office building in Washington, D.C. Although Nixon was reelected in November 1972, further investigations by the press and by a Senate investigating committee revealed a pattern of political "dirty tricks," including illegal wire-tapping and other methods of spying on his opponents throughout his first term. The House voted to begin impeachment proceedings. On 9 August 1974, Nixon became the first president to resign the office. The American people's trust in their government leaders was seriously damaged.

The Reagan Era Gerald R. Ford (1913–2006) was appointed vice president in October 1973 to succeed ousted Vice President Spiro T. Agnew. Ford became president in August 1974 when Nixon resigned. Less than a month after taking office, President Ford granted a full pardon to Nixon for any crimes he may have committed as president. Ford's pardon of Nixon likely contributed to his narrow defeat by Georgia Democrat Jimmy Carter (1924–) in 1976. During 1978–79, President Carter convinced the Senate to pass treaties ending US sovereignty over the Panama Canal Zone. He also mediated a peace agreement between Israel and Egypt, which was signed at the Camp David, Maryland, retreat in September 1978. But an economic recession and an inability to force Iran to release the more than 50 US citizens taken hostage in Tehran on 4 November 1979 caused the American public to doubt his leadership. Exactly a year after the hostages were taken, former California

Governor Ronald Reagan (1911–2004) defeated Carter in the 1980 presidential election. The hostages were released on 20 January 1981, the day of Reagan's inauguration.

President Reagan used his popularity to push through significant policy changes. He made cuts in income taxes and more than doubled the military budget between 1980 and 1989, which also resulted in a doubling of the national debt. In an effort to balance the federal budget, Reagan cut welfare and Medicare benefits, reduced allocations for food stamps, and slashed the budget of the Environmental Protection Agency.

Reagan's appointment of Sandra Day O'Connor as the first woman justice of the US Supreme Court was widely praised and won unanimous confirmation from the Senate. Protests were raised, however, about his decisions to help the government of El Salvador in its war against leftist rebels, to aid groups in Nicaragua trying to overthrow the leftist Sandinista government in their country, and to send American troops to Grenada in October 1983 to overthrow a leftist government there.

Presidents Bush and Clinton Reagan was succeeded in 1988 by his vice president, George H. W. Bush (1924–). President Bush used his personal relationships with foreign leaders, forged during his tenure at the Central Intelligence Agency (CIA), to bring about peace talks between Israel and its Arab neighbors, to encourage a peaceful unification of East and West Germany, and to negotiate significant arms reductions with the Russians. Bush sent 400,000 American soldiers to lead the way in forming a multinational coalition to oppose Iraq's invasion of Kuwait in 1990. The multinational forces destroyed Iraq's main force within seven months.

One of the biggest crises that the Bush administration encountered was the collapse of the savings and loan industry in the late 1980s. The federal government was forced by law to rescue the savings and loan banks, under the Federal Savings and Loan Insurance Corporation (FSLIC), costing taxpayers more than $100 billion.

In the 1992 presidential election, Democrat Bill Clinton (1946–), governor of Arkansas, defeated Bush, winning 43% of the vote to Bush's 38% and third-party candidate Ross Perot's 18%. Clinton's major achievements as president included the passage of a budget designed to raise revenue and thereby lower the deficit, which had ballooned during the Reagan and Bush years. Clinton also persuaded Congress to approve the North American Free Trade Agreement (NAFTA), which removed or reduced tariffs on most goods moving across the borders of the United States, Canada, and Mexico.

In the 1994 midterm elections, the Republican Party gained control of both houses of Congress for the first time in more than 40 years. The elections indicated popular disappointment with the Clinton administration and the Democratic-controlled Congress.

The nation's economic recovery from the 1990–91 recession gained strength as the decade advanced, with healthy growth, falling unemployment, and moderate interest rate and inflation levels. Between 1995 and 1997, the value of the stock market increased 60%. Clinton's faltering popularity rebounded in 1996 when he was reelected, becoming the first Democratic president elected to a second term since Franklin D. Roosevelt. The Republicans retained control of both houses of Congress, however.

In 1994, Attorney General Janet Reno appointed Kenneth Starr to the position of special prosecutor. His job was to investigate allegations of financial wrongdoing by President Clinton and his wife, Hillary Rodham Clinton. In 1998, the investigation expanded to include testimony related to a previous sexual harassment lawsuit brought against Clinton for actions allegedly taken while he was governor of Arkansas. In the same year, Starr submitted a report to Congress that resulted in the House of Representatives passing four articles of impeachment against President Clinton. In the subsequent trial in the Senate, however, the articles were defeated.

In one of the closest and most controversial presidential elections in US history, Republican George W. Bush (1946–), son of the former president, was elected after defeating Democratic Vice President Al Gore in the Electoral College. (Gore won the popular vote.) Bush took office on 20 January 2001.

On 11 September 2001, 19 hijackers crashed two passenger planes into the North and South towers of the World Trade Center in New York City; one into the Pentagon in Washington, D.C.; and one into a field near Shanksville, Pennsylvania. The World Trade Center towers were destroyed. Approximately 3,000 people were confirmed or reported dead as a result of the 9/11 attacks. The terrorist organization al-Qaeda, led by Saudi Arabian-born Osama bin Laden, claimed responsibility for the attacks.

On 7 October 2001, the United States and the United Kingdom launched air strikes against Afghanistan, a country ruled by the Taliban regime that had supported the al-Qaeda organization. By December 2001, the Taliban were defeated. Remnants of al-Qaeda still remained in Afghanistan and the surrounding region, however. As of 2013, US soldiers remained in Afghanistan to suppress efforts by either the Taliban (who had re-emerged) or al-Qaeda to regroup and to support the government in Afghanistan. Osama bin Laden was tracked down and killed in Pakistan in May 2011 by a US special forces unit.

Throughout 2002, the United States stated that Saddam Hussein's regime in Iraq must disarm itself of weapons of mass destruction. In November 2002, United Nations (UN) weapons inspectors returned to Iraq (they had been expelled in 1998), but the United States and the United Kingdom expressed dissatisfaction with the inspectors' progress. They stated that military force might be necessary to remove the Iraqi regime. France, Russia, and Germany, in particular, opposed the use of military force. This disagreement caused a rift between Western democracies.

After diplomatic efforts at conflict resolution failed, war began on 19 March 2003. On 9 April, Baghdad fell to US forces and work began on restoring basic services to the Iraqi population, including providing safe drinking water, electricity, and sanitation. On 1 May, President Bush declared that major combat operations had been completed. On 13 December 2003 Saddam Hussein was found hiding in a hole near his hometown of Tikrit and captured by US forces without resisting; he was tried by an Iraqi court, found guilty, and executed in 2006.

US forces increasingly became the targets of attacks in Iraq as an insurgency against the US military presence began. By 2011, more than 4,400 US soldiers had been killed. A referendum on a new Iraqi constitution was held in October 2005 and national elections were held

in December 2005, after which a new Iraqi government was formed.

In the 2004 US presidential election, President Bush and Vice President Dick Cheney defeated Democratic challengers John Kerry and John Edwards. In 2007, the collapse of the Lehman Brothers investment bank set off a collapse of American financial institutions that were overleveraged in the rapidly shrinking housing market. As financial institutions stopped lending money, businesses faced a severe squeeze and began laying off workers, which in turn led to a recession. As the recession took hold, Democrat Barack Obama (1961–) defeated Republican John McCain to become the first African American to hold the office of US president. Obama received more than 69 million votes, the most by any candidate in US history, outpolling McCain by more than 10 million votes.

The recession lasted from 2008 to 2009, but by 2010 an economic recovery had started. However, this recovery was fairly weak, and unemployment remained relatively high, with a rate of nearly 8% by election day in November 2012. Despite the slow pace of the economic recovery, Obama won reelection with 51% of the popular vote to Republican challenger Mitt Romney's 48% (in the electoral college, Obama won 332 to Romney's 206). In that election, the Senate retained its Democratic majority and the House of Representatives its Republican majority. In both the House and the Senate, Democrats picked up additional seats.

12 State Government

The Constitution of the United States, signed in 1787, is the nation's governing document. In the first 10 amendments to the Constitution, ratified in 1791 and known as the Bill of Rights, certain individual rights are guaranteed to US citizens. In all, there have been 27 amendments to the Bill of Rights, including the 13th Amendment (1865), which banned slavery, and the 19th (1920), which gave women the right to vote. Suffrage is universal beginning at the age of 18, as set by the 26th Amendment (1971).

The United States has a federal form of government, with the distribution of powers between federal and state governments constitutionally defined. The legislative powers of the federal government rest in Congress, which consists of the House of Representatives and the Senate. There are 435 members of the House of Representatives. Each state is given a number of representatives in proportion to its population. Representatives are elected in every even-numbered year to serve two-year terms. The Senate consists of two senators from each state, elected to six-year terms. One-third of the Senate is elected in every even-numbered year.

A bill that is passed by both houses of Congress in the same form is then given to the president, who may sign it or veto (reject) it. The president must have been born in the United States, be at least 35 years old, and a resident of the United States for not less than 14 years. Under the 22nd Amendment to the Constitution, adopted in 1951, a president may not be elected more than twice.

The vice president, elected at the same time and on the same ballot as the president, serves as president pro tem of the Senate. The vice president assumes the power and duties of the presidency on the president's removal from office or as a result of the president's death, resignation, or inability to perform his duties. Both the

United States Population Profile

Total population per Census 2010:	308,745,538
Population change, 2006–10:	2.5%
Hispanic or Latino†:	16.3%
Population by race	
One race:	97.1%
White:	72.4%
Black or African American:	12.6%
American Indian/Alaska Native:	0.9%
Asian:	4.8%
Native Hawaiian/Pacific Islander:	0.2%
Some other race:	6.2%
Two or more races:	2.9%

Population by Age Group, Census 2010

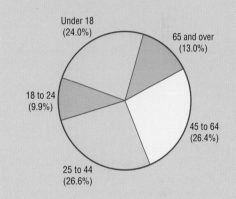

Major Cities by Population, 2011 Estimates

City	Population	% change 2005–11
New York City, NY	8,244,910	1.2
Los Angeles, CA	3,819,702	-0.7
Chicago, IL	2,707,120	-4.8
Houston, TX	2,145,146	6.4
Philadelphia, PA	1,536,471	5.0
Phoenix, AZ	1,469,471	0.5
San Antonio, TX	1,359,758	8.2
San Diego, CA	1,326,179	5.6
Dallas, TX	1,223,229	0.8
San Jose, CA	967,487	6.0

Notes: †A person of Hispanic or Latino origin may be of any race. NA indicates that data are not available. Percentages may not equal 100 due to rounding.

SOURCE: U.S. Census Bureau. Census 2010 and Population Estimates. www.census.gov/ (accessed July 2012).

United States Population by Race
CENSUS 2010

This table shows the number of people who are of one, two, or three or more races. For those claiming two races, the number of people belonging to the various categories is listed. The U.S. government conducts a census of the population every 10 years.

	Number	Percent
Total population	308,745,538	100.0
One race	299,736,465	97.1
Two races	8,265,318	2.7
White *and* Black or African American	1,834,212	0.6
White *and* American Indian/Alaska Native	1,432,309	0.5
White *and* Asian	1,623,234	0.5
White *and* Native Hawaiian/Pacific Islander	169,991	0.1
White *and* some other race	1,740,924	0.6
Black or African American *and* American Indian/Alaska Native	269,421	0.1
Black or African American *and* Asian	185,595	0.1
Black or African American *and* Native Hawaiian/Pacific Islander	50,308	—
Black or African American *and* some other race	314,571	0.1
American Indian/Alaska Native *and* Asian	58,829	—
American Indian/Alaska Native *and* Native Hawaiian/Pacific Islander	11,039	—
American Indian/Alaska Native *and* some other race	115,752	—
Asian *and* Native Hawaiian/Pacific Islander	165,690	0.1
Asian *and* some other race	234,462	0.1
Native Hawaiian/Pacific Islander *and* some other race	58,981	—
Three or more races	743,755	0.2

SOURCE: U.S. Census Bureau. Census 2010. www.census/gov/ (accessed July 2012). A dash (—) indicates that the percent is less than 0.1.

president and the vice president can be removed from office after impeachment by the House and conviction at a Senate trial for "treason, bribery, or other high crimes and misdemeanors."

The president nominates and, with the approval of the Senate, appoints ambassadors, consuls, and all federal judges, including the justices of the Supreme Court. As commander in chief, the president is ultimately responsible for the management of the land, naval, and air forces, but the power to declare war belongs to Congress. The president conducts foreign relations and makes treaties with the advice and consent of the Senate. No treaty is binding unless it wins the approval of two-thirds of the Senate, however. The president's independence also is limited by the House of Representatives, where all funding (appropriations) bills originate.

The president also appoints his cabinet, subject to Senate confirmation. The cabinet consists of the secretaries who head the departments of the executive branch. As of 2012, the executive branch included the following cabinet departments: Agriculture (created in 1862), Commerce (1913), Defense (1947), Education (1980), Energy (1977), Health and Human Services (1980), Housing and Urban Development (1965), Interior (1849), Justice (1870), Labor (1913), State (1789), Transportation (1966), Treasury (1789), Veterans' Affairs (1989), and Homeland Security (2002).

Each state is divided into counties, municipalities, and special districts such as those for water, education, sanitation, highways, parks, and recreation. There are more than 3,100 counties in the United States and more than 19,000 municipalities, including cities, villages, towns, and boroughs.

As of 2012, salaries for state legislators range from $10 per day in Alabama, to $95,290.56 per year in California.

13 Political Parties

Two major parties, Democratic and Republican, have dominated national, state, and local politics since 1860. Minority parties have been formed at various periods in American political history, but none has had any lasting national impact. The most successful minority party in recent decades was the Reform Party, founded by Texas billionaire Ross Perot in 1995. Independent candidates have been elected to state and local office, but no candidate has won the presidency without major party backing.

Traditionally, the Republican Party is more sympathetic to business interests and gets greater support from business than does the Democratic Party. A majority of blue-collar workers, by contrast, have generally supported the Democratic Party, which favors more lenient labor laws, particularly as they affect labor unions. Republicans promote private business and an increased role for state government, while Democrats generally support greater federal government participation and regulatory authority.

In 1984, Geraldine A. Ferraro, a Democrat, became the first female vice presidential nominee of a major US political party. Also in 1984, presidential candidate Jesse L. Jackson was the first black ever to win a plurality in a state primary election.

The 2008 presidential election was won by Democrat Barack Obama and his running mate Joe Biden. They defeated Republicans John McCain and Sarah Palin. Obama received 365 electoral votes and McCain received 173. Obama received 52.5% of the popular vote to McCain's 46.2%.

In 2012, President Barack Obama and Vice President Joe Biden won reelection, defeating Republican challengers Mitt Romney and Paul Ryan. Obama received 332 electoral votes; Romney received 206. Obama received 50.6% of the popular vote to Romney's 47.8%.

Following the 2012 elections, the composition of Congress was as follows: 53 Democrats, 45 Republicans, and 2 Independents in the Senate; and 234 Republicans and 201 Democrats in the House of Representatives.

In the 112th Congress (2011–12), there were 74 women, 44 African Americans, 26 Hispanics, 9 Asians or Hawaiians or other Pacific Islanders, and 1 Native American in the House of Representatives. There were 17 women, 2 Hispanics, and 2 Asians or Hawaiians or other Pacific Islanders in the Senate.

14 Local Government

Governmental units within each state comprise counties, municipalities, and such special districts as those for water, sanitation, highways, and parks and recreation. There are more than 3,100 counties in the United States; more than 19,000 municipalities, including cities, villages, towns, and boroughs; nearly 15,000 school districts; and at least 31,000 special districts. Additional townships, authorities, commissions, and boards make up the rest of the nearly 85,000 local governmental units.

The 50 states are autonomous within their own spheres of government, and their autonomy is defined in broad terms by the 10th

Presidents of the United States, 1789–2013

	Name (Birth–Death)	Other Major Offices Held	Residence at Election	Party
1	George Washington 22 February 1732–14 December 1799	Commander in Chief, Continental Army (1775-83)	Mt. Vernon, VA	Federalist
2	John Adams 30 October 1735–4 July 1826	Representative, Continental Congress (1774–77); US vice president (1797–97)	Quincy, MA	Federalist
3	Thomas Jefferson 13 April 1743–4 July 1826	Representative, Continental Congress (1775–76); governor of Virginia (1779–81); secretary of state (1790–93); US vice president (1797–1801)	Monticello, VA	Dem.–Rep.
4	James Madison 16 March 1751–28 June 1836	Representative, Continental Congress (1780–83; 1786–88); US representative (1789–97); secretary of state (1801–9)	Montpelier, VA	Dem.–Rep.
5	James Monroe 28 April 1758–4 July 1831	US senator (1790–94); governor of Virginia (1799–1802); secretary of state (1811–17); secretary of war (1814–15)	Leesburg, VA	Dem.–Rep.
6	John Quincy Adams 11 July 1767–23 February 1848	US senator (1803–8); secretary of state (1817–25); US representative (1831–48)	Quincy, MA	National Republican
7	Andrew Jackson 15 March 1767–8 June 1845	US representative (1796–97); US senator (1797–98)	The Hermitage, TN	Democrat
8	Martin Van Buren 5 December 1782–24 July 1862	US senator (1821–28); governor of New York (1829); secretary of state (1829–31); US vice president (1833–37)	New York	Democrat
9	William Henry Harrison 9 February 1773–4 April 1841	Governor of Indiana Territory (1801–13); US representative (1816–19); US senator (1825–28)	North Bend, OH	Whig
10	John Tyler 29 March 1790–18 January 1862	US representative (1816–21); governor of Virginia (1825–27); US senator (1827–36); US vice president (1841)	Richmond, VA	Whig
11	James K. Polk 2 November 1795–15 June 1849	US representative (1825–39); governor of Tennessee (1839–41)	Nashville, TN	Democrat
12	Zachary Taylor 24 November 1784–9 July 1850	—	Louisiana	Whig
13	Millard Fillmore 7 January 1800–8 March 1874	US representative (1833–35; 1837–43); US vice president (1849–50)	Buffalo, NY	Whig
14	Franklin Pierce 23 November 1804–8 October 1869	US representative, (1833–37); US senator (1837–43)	Concord, NH	Democrat
15	James Buchanan 23 April 1791–1 June 1868	US representative (1821–31); US senator (1834–45); secretary of state (1845–49)	Lancaster, PA	Democrat
16	Abraham Lincoln 12 February 1809–15 April 1865	US representative (1847–49)	Springfield, IL	Republican

Terms in Office[1]	Vice Presidents	Notable Events	
30 April 1789–4 March 1793	John Adams	Federal government organized; Bill of Rights enacted (1791); Whiskey Rebellion suppressed (1794); North Carolina, Rhode Island, Vermont, Kentucky, Tennessee enter Union.	1
4 March 1797–4 March 1801	Thomas Jefferson	Alien and Sedition Acts passed (1798); Washington, D.C., becomes US capital (1800)	2
4 March 1801–4 March 1805	Aaron Burr George Clinton	Louisiana Purchase (1803); Lewis and Clark Expedition (1803–6); Ohio enters Union.	3
4 March 1809–4 March 1813 4 March 1813–4 March 1817	George Clinton Elbridge Gerry	War of 1812 (1812–14); protective tariffs passed (1816); Louisiana, Indiana enter Union.	4
4 March 1817–4 March 1821 4 March 1821–4 March 1825	Daniel D. Tompkins Daniel D. Tompkins	Florida purchased from Spain (1819–21); Missouri Compromise (1820); Monroe Doctrine (1823); Mississippi, Illinois, Alabama, Maine, Missouri enter Union.	5
4 March 1825–4 March 1829	John C. Calhoun	Period of political antagonisms, producing little legislation; road and canal construction supported; Erie Canal opens (1825).	6
4 March 1829–4 March 1833	John C. Calhoun Martin Van Buren	Introduction of spoils system; Texas Republic established (1836); Arkansas, Michigan enter Union.	7
4 March 1837–4 March 1841	Richard M. Johnson	Financial panic (1837) and subsequent depression.	8
4 March 1841–4 April 1841	John Tyler	Died of pneumonia one month after taking office.	9
4 April 1841–4 March 1845	—	Monroe Doctrine extended to Hawaiian Islands (1842); Second Seminole War in Florida ends (1842).	10
4 March 1845–4 March 1849	George M. Dallas	Boundary between US and Canada set at 49th parallel (1846); Mexican War (1846–48), ending with Treaty of Guadalupe Hidalgo (1848); California gold rush begins (1848); Florida, Texas, Iowa, Wisconsin enter Union.	11
4 March 1849–9 July 1850	Millard Fillmore	Died after 16 months in office.	12
9 July 1850–4 March 1853	—	Fugitive Slave Law (1850); California enters Union.	13
4 March 1853–4 March 1857	William R. King	Gadsden Purchase (1853); Kansas–Nebraska Act (1854); trade opened with Japan (1854).	14
4 March 1857–4 March 1861	John C. Breckinridge	John Brown's raid at Harpers Ferry, Va. (now W. Va.; 1859); South Carolina secedes (1860); Minnesota, Oregon, Kansas enter Union.	15
4 March 1861–4 March 1865 4 March 1865–15 April 1865	Hannibal Hamlin Andrew Johnson	Confederacy established, Civil War begins (1851); Emancipation Proclamation (1863); Confederacy defeated (1865); Lincoln assassinated (1865); West Virginia, Nevada attain statehood.	16

Presidents of the United States, 1789–2013

	Name (Birth–Death)	Other Major Offices Held	Residence at Election	Party
17	Andrew Johnson 29 December 1808–31 July 1875	US representative (1843–53); governor of Tennessee (1853–57; 1862–65); US senator (1857–62); US vice president (1865)	Greeneville, TN	Republican
18	Ulysses S. Grant 27 April 1822–23 July 1885	Commander, Union Army (1864–65); secretary of war (1867–68)	Galena, IL	Republican
19	Rutherford B. Hayes 4 October 1822–17 January 1893	US representative (1865–67); governor of Ohio (1868–72; 1876–77)	Fremont, OH	Republican
20	James A. Garfield 19 November 1831–19 September 1881	US representative (1863–80)	Mentor, OH	Republican
21	Chester A. Arthur 5 October 1829–18 November 1886	US vice president (1881)	New York, NY	Republican
22	Grover Cleveland 18 March 1837–24 June 1908	Governor of New York (1882–84)	Albany, NY	Democrat
23	Benjamin Harrison 20 August 1833–13 March 1901	US senator (1881–87)	Indianapolis, IN	Republican
24	Grover Cleveland 18 March 1837–24 June 1908	Governor of New York (1882–84)	New York, NY	Democrat
25	William McKinley 29 January 1843–14 September 1901	US representative (1877–83; 1885–91); governor of Ohio (1892–96)	Canton, OH	Republican
26	Theodore Roosevelt 27 October 1858–6 January 1919	Governor of New York (1899–1900); US vice president (1901)	Oyster Bay, NY	Republican
27	William H. Taft 15 September 1857–8 March 1930	Governor of Philippines (1901–4); secretary of war (1904–8); chief justice of the US (1921–30)	Washington, DC	Republican
28	Woodrow Wilson 28 December 1856–3 February 1924	Governor of New Jersey (1911–13)	Trenton, NJ	Democrat
29	Warren G. Harding 2 November 1865–2 August 1923	US senator (1915–21)	Marion, OH	Republican
30	Calvin Coolidge 4 July 1872–5 January 1933	Governor of Massachusetts (1919–20); US vice president (1921–23)	Boston, MA	Republican
31	Herbert Hoover 10 August 1874–20 October 1964	Secretary of commerce (1921–29)	Stanford, CA	Republican
32	Franklin D. Roosevelt 30 January 1882–12 April 1945	Governor of New York (1929–1933)	Hyde Park, NY	Democrat

Terms in Office[1]	Vice Presidents	Notable Events	
15 April 1865–4 March 1869	—	Reconstruction Acts (1867); Alaska purchased from Russia (1867); Johnson impeached but acquitted (1868); Nebraska enters Union.	17
4 March 1869–4 March 1873 4 March 1873–4 March 1877	Schuyler Colfax Henry Wilson	Numerous government scandals; financial panic (1873); Colorado enters Union.	18
4 March 1877–4 March 1881	William A. Wheeler	Federal troops withdrawn from South (1877); civil service reform begun.	19
4 March 1881–19 Sept. 1881	Chester A. Arthur	Shot after 4 months in office, dead 2½ months later.	20
19 Sept. 1881–4 March 1885	—	Chinese immigration banned despite presidential veto (1882); Civil Service Commission established by Pendleton Act (1883).	21
4 March 1885–4 March 1889	Thomas A. Hendricks	Interstate Commerce Act (1887)	22
4 March 1889–4 March 1893	Levi P. Morton	Sherman Silver Purchase Act (1890); North Dakota, South Dakota, Montana, Washington, Idaho, Wyoming enter Union.	23
4 March 1893–4 March 1897	Adlai E. Stevenson	Financial panic (1893); Sherman Silver Purchase Act repealed (1893); Utah enters Union.	24
4 March 1897–4 March 1901	Garret A. Hobart Theodore Roosevelt	Spanish–American War (1898); Puerto Rico, Guam, Philippines ceded by Spain; independent Republic of Hawaii annexed; US troops sent to China to suppress Boxer Rebellion (1900); McKinley assassinated.	25
14 Sept. 1901–4 March 1905 4 March 1905–4 March 1909	Charles W. Fairbanks	Antitrust and conservation policies emphasized; Roosevelt awarded Nobel Peace Prize (1906) for mediating settlement of Russo–Japanese War; Panama Canal construction begun (1907); Oklahoma enters Union.	26
4 March 1909–4 March 1913	James S. Sherman	Federal income tax ratified (1913); New Mexico, Arizona enter Union.	27
4 March 1913–4 March 1917 4 March 1917–4 March 1921	Thomas R. Marshall Thomas R. Marshall	Clayton Antitrust Act (1914); US Virgin Islands purchased from Denmark (1917); US enters World War I (1917); Treaty of Versailles signed (1919) but not ratified by US; constitutional amendments enforce prohibition (1919), enfranchise women (1920).	28
4 March 1921–2 Aug. 1923	Calvin Coolidge	Teapot Dome scandal (1923–24).	29
3 Aug. 1923–4 March 1925 4 March 1925–4 March 1929	Charles G. Dawes	Kellogg–Briand Pact (1928).	30
4 March 1929–4 March 1933	Charles Curtis	Stock market crash (1929) inaugurates Great Depression.	31
4 March 1933–20 Jan. 1937 20 Jan. 1937–20 Jan. 1941 20 Jan. 1941–20 Jan. 1945 20 Jan. 1945–12 April 1945	John N. Garner John N. Garner Henry A. Wallace Harry S Truman	New Deal social reforms; prohibition repealed (1933); US enters World War II (1941)	32

Presidents of the United States, 1789–2013

	Name (Birth–Death)	Other Major Offices Held	Residence at Election	Party
33	Harry S Truman 8 May 1884–26 December 1972	US senator (1935–45); US vice president (1945)	Independence, MO	Democrat
34	Dwight D. Eisenhower 14 October 1890–28 March 1969	Supreme allied commander in Europe (1943–44); Army chief of staff (1945–48)	New York	Republican
35	John F. Kennedy 29 May 1917–22 November 1963	US representative (1947–52); US senator (1953–60)	Massachusetts	Democrat
36	Lyndon B. Johnson 27 August 1908–22 January 1973	US representative (1937–48); US senator (1949–60); US vice president (1961–63)	Johnson City, TX	Democrat
37	Richard M. Nixon 9 January 1913–22 April 1994	US representative (1947–51); US senator (1951–53); US vice president (1953–61)	New York, NY	Republican
38	Gerald Rudolph Ford 14 July 1913–26 December 2006	US representative (1949–73); US vice president (1973–74)	Grand Rapids, MI	Republican
39	James Earl Carter, Jr. 1 October 1924	Governor of Georgia (1951–75)	Plains, GA	Democrat
40	Ronald Wilson Reagan 6 February 1911–5 June 2004	Governor of California (1967–76)	Los Angeles, CA	Republican
41	George Herbert Walker Bush 12 June 1924	US representative (1967–71) Vice president (1981–88)	Houston, TX	Republican
42	William Jefferson Clinton 19 August 1946	Attorney general of Arkansas (1977–79) Governor of Arkansas (1979–81; 1983–92)	Little Rock, AR	Democrat
43	George Walker Bush 6 July 1946	Governor of Texas (1994–2000)	Midland, TX	Republican
44	Barack Obama 4 August 1961	US Senator (2005–2008)	Chicago, IL	Democrat

[1]In the event of a president's death or removal from office, his duties are assumed to devolve immediately upon his successor, even if he does not immediately take the oath of office.

Terms in Office[1]	Vice Presidents	Notable Events	
12 April 1945–20 Jan. 1949 20 Jan. 1949–20 Jan. 1953	 Alben W. Barkley	United Nations founded (1945); US nuclear bombs dropped on Japan (1945); World War II ends (1945); Philippines granted independence (1946); Marshall Plan (1945); Korean conflict begins (1950); era of McCarthyism.	33
20 Jan. 1953–20 Jan. 1957 20 Jan. 1957–20 Jan. 1961	Richard M. Nixon Richard M. Nixon	Korean conflict ended (1953); Supreme Court orders school desegregation (1954); Alaska, Hawaii enter Union.	34
20 Jan. 1961–22 Nov. 1963	Lyndon B. Johnson	Conflicts with Cuba (1961–62); aboveground nuclear test ban treaty (1963); Kennedy assassinated.	35
22 Nov. 1963–20 Jan. 1965 20 Jan. 1965–20 Jan. 1969	Hubert H. Humphrey	Great Society programs; Voting Rights Act (1965); escalation of US military role in Indochina; race riots, political assassinations.	36
20 Jan. 1969–20 Jan. 1973 20 Jan. 1973–9 Aug. 1974	Spiro T. Agnew Spiro T. Agnew Gerald R. Ford	First lunar landing (1969); arms limitation treaty with Soviet Union (1972); US withdraws from Vietnam (1973); Agnew resigns in tax scandal (1973); Nixon resigns at height of Watergate scandal (1974).	37
9 Aug. 1974–20 Jan. 1977	Nelson A. Rockefeller	First combination of unelected president and vice president; Nixon pardoned (1974).	38
20 Jan. 1977–20 Jan. 1981	Walter F. Mondale	Carter mediates Israel-Egypt peace accord (1978); Panama Canal treaties ratified (1979); tensions with Iran (1979–81).	39
20 Jan. 1981–20 Jan. 1985 20 Jan. 1985–20 Jan. 1989	George H. Bush George H. Bush	Defense buildup; social spending cuts; rising trade and budget deficits; tensions with Nicaragua.	40
20 Jan. 1989–20 Jan. 1993	J. Danforth Quayle	Multi-national force repelled Iraqi invaders from Kuwait; savings and loan crisis; 1991 recession.	41
20 Jan. 1993–20 Jan. 1997 20 Jan. 1997–20 Jan. 2001	Albert Gore, Jr. Albert Gore, Jr.	North American Free Trade Agreement (1993); sent troops to Haiti to restore elected president deposed by a military coup (1994); Dayton Accords (1995); Whitewater and FBI files scandals (1995–96); rapid stock market growth (1995–97); balanced federal budget plan (1997); Clinton impeached (1998).	42
20 Jan. 2001–20 Jan. 2005 20 Jan. 2005–Jan. 2009	Richard Bruce Cheney Richard Bruce Cheney	$1.35 trillion tax cut through 2010; 9/11 terrorist attack and resulting war on terror and invasion of Afghanistan and Iraq; creation of the Department of Homeland Security. housing market crashes, foreclosure rates soar; financial crisis begins; Wall Street bailouts begin.	43
20 Jan. 2009–20 Jan. 2013 20 Jan. 2013–	Joseph Biden Joseph Biden	Wall Street bailouts continue; several major US auto companies receive bailouts; American Recovery and Reinvestment Act passes in effort to stimulate the economy; Wall Street and mortgage lender reforms begin; consumer protection agency created; Patient Protection and Affordable Care Act (health insurance) passes; War in Iraq ends; Don't Ask, Don't Tell policy in military ends.	44

Amendment to the US Constitution. That amendment reserves to the states such powers as are not granted to the federal government and not denied to the states. The states may not, among other restrictions, issue paper money, conduct foreign relations, impair the obligations of contracts, or establish a government that is not republican in form. Subsequent amendments to the Constitution and many Supreme Court decisions added to the restrictions placed on the states. The 13th Amendment prohibited the states from legalizing the ownership of one person by another (slavery); the 14th Amendment deprived the states of their power to determine qualifications for citizenship; the 15th Amendment prohibited the states from denying the right to vote because of race, color, or previous condition of servitude; and the 19th, from denying the vote to women.

In 2011, there were 14,560,581 full-time and 4,852,374 part-time state and local government workers in the United States.

15 Judicial System

The Supreme Court, established by the US Constitution, is the nation's highest judicial body, consisting of the chief justice of the United States and eight associate justices. All justices are appointed for life by the president with the approval of the Senate.

The Supreme Court acts as an appeals court for federal district courts, circuit courts of appeal, and the highest courts in the states. The Supreme Court also exercises the power of judicial review, determining the constitutionality of any state laws, state constitutions, congressional statutes, and federal regulations that are specifically challenged.

The US Congress establishes all federal courts lower than the Supreme Court. On the lowest level and handling the most federal cases are the district courts, including one each in Puerto Rico, Guam, the Virgin Islands, the Northern Mariana Islands, and the District of Columbia. District courts have no appeals jurisdiction; their decisions may be carried to the courts of appeal, which are organized into 13 circuits. For most cases, this is usually the last stage of appeal, except where the court rules that a statute of a state conflicts with the Constitution of the United States, with federal law, or with a treaty. Special federal courts include the Court of Claims, Court of Customs and Patent Appeals, and Tax Court.

State courts operate independently of the federal judiciary. Most states have a court system that begins on the lowest level with a justice of the peace, and includes courts of general trial jurisdiction and appeals courts. At the highest level of the system is a state supreme court. The court of trial jurisdiction (sometimes called the county or superior court) has both original and appeals jurisdiction; all criminal cases and some civil cases are tried in this court. The state supreme court interprets the state constitution and the laws of the state.

As of 2012, there were approximately 2.2 million people in prison or jail, a 500% increase from 30 years prior. As of 2012, the death penalty was a legal sentence in 33 states. In 2011, 13 states executed 43 inmates, all by lethal injection; in 2010, 46 people were executed. Many states have a de facto moratorium on death sentences in place, due to legal uncertainties involving the method of execution. Connecticut abolished the death penalty in 2012, but the law is not retroactive.

16 Migration

According to the Census Bureau's 2010 American Community Survey (ACS), the total US immigrant population stood at just under 40 million that year. Between 2009 and 2010, approximately 1.4 million immigrants entered the United States. Of the total immigrant population in the United States, around 29% were from Mexico, 5% from China, 4% from India, and 3% from Cuba.

Under the Refugee Act of 1980, a ceiling for the number of admissible refugees is set annually, along with regional allocations. The total ceiling for refugee admissions in 2011 was 80,000, with 44% of the total reserved for refugees from the Near East/South Asia region. During 2011, the newly formed US Bureau of Citizenship and Immigration Services (USCIS—formerly the Immigration and Naturalization Service, or INS)—approved 24,988 applications for asylum. The United Nations reported that in 2011 the United States was a leading destination of refugees, accounting for around 15% of all refugee and asylum claims worldwide.

Large numbers of aliens—mainly from Latin America, especially Mexico—have illegally established residence in the United States after entering the country as tourists, students, or temporary visitors engaged in work or business. In November 1986, Congress passed a bill allowing illegal aliens who had lived and worked in the United States since 1982 the opportunity to become permanent residents. In 2001, the DREAM Act (Development, Relief, and Education for Alien Minors) was first introduced in Congress. The bill would have provided a limited amnesty for illegal immigrants who met certain conditions, such as length of residency. The bill has been reintroduced several times, but has failed to pass both houses. In 2012, President Obama announced that he would stop deporting illegal immigrants who met the conditions of the bill. That year, a deferred amnesty program was announced.

In 2010, the Department of Homeland Security estimated that there were 10.8 million undocumented immigrants living in America.

17 Economy

Industrial activity within the United States expanded southward and westward for much of the 20th century, with the most rapid expansion occurring since World War II. Louisiana, Oklahoma, and especially Texas are centers of industries based on petroleum refining; aerospace and other high-technology industries are the basis of the new wealth of Texas and California. The industrial heartland of the United States consists of Ohio, Indiana, Illinois, Michigan, Pennsylvania, and Wisconsin, with steelmaking and automobile manufacturing among the leading industries.

Regulation of inflation is an ever-present factor in the US economy, although the US inflation rate, estimated at 1.7% in June 2012, tends to be lower than that of the majority of industrialized countries. Median per capita household income stood at $51,914 in 2011, and the nation's gross domestic product (GDP) was just over $15 trillion.

Economic growth came to a standstill in the middle of 2001, largely due to the end of the long investment boom, especially in the information technology sector. The economy was in recession in the second half of 2001, affecting both the manufacturing and service sectors. The 11 September 2001 terrorist attacks on the United States worsened the poor economic situation. The US economy, which had driven global growth during the 1990s, became the cause of a worldwide recession, dragging down the rest of North America, Europe, Japan, and the developing economies of Latin America and Southeast Asia, which are strongly influenced by trends in the US economy.

The economy began to recover slowly in 2002, however, with GDP growth estimated at 2.45%. Nevertheless, domestic confidence in the economy remained low; coupled with major corporate failures (including Enron and World-Com) and additional stock market declines, the recovery remained sluggish and uneven. Growth slowed at the end of 2002 and into 2003, and the unemployment rate rose to 6.3% in July 2003.

Following the 2003 start of the war in Iraq, consumer spending rebounded, as did stock prices; the housing market remained strong; inflation was low; additional tax cuts were passed; there was an easing of oil prices; and productivity growth was strong. As a result of these factors, many analysts predicted the coming of a more favorable economic climate. Nevertheless, in 2003, the federal budget deficit soon passed $455 billion, the largest deficit on record to that point.

The American economy grew at a rate of 4.3% in the fall of 2005, despite the ravages of Hurricane Katrina, which destroyed much of the port city of New Orleans and closed down a large portion of the energy industry. But the relatively fast-growing economy had a shaky foundation. Oil prices were at their highest level since the early 1980s; the inflation rate

was at its highest level since 1991; wage growth was sluggish; and the jobs market was lagging the recovery. Consumer spending was increasingly tied to prices in the over-inflated housing market. By the end of 2007 the housing bubble, which had been propped up by a large number of unaffordable mortgage loans to consumers, had burst, and the economy entered a prolonged recession. While the economy began growing again in 2010, unemployment continued to hover around 8% into late 2012. The total GDP in 2010 was $14.66 trillion. The per capita GDP that year was $47,482. California led the way with a gross state product (GSP) in 2010 of $1.9 trillion, followed by Texas ($1.2 trillion) and New York ($1.16 trillion). The annual growth rate of GDP was estimated at 1.3% in 2011, and it was expected to rise to above 2% in 2012.

18 Income

Overall, the per capita personal income (including nonmonetary income) in the United States was $41,663 in 2011. The median annual household income in 2010 was $50,022.

19 Industry

Although the United States remains one of the world's top industrial powers, manufacturing no longer plays as dominant a role in the economy as it once did. Between 1979 and 1998, manufacturing employment fell from 20.9 million to 18.7 million, or from 21.8% to 14.8% of national employment. Throughout the 1960s, manufacturing accounted for about 29% of total national income; by 2010, the proportion was down to about 11.7%. That year, manufacturing accounted for around 17 million jobs.

Leading manufacturing industries of durable goods include nonelectrical machinery, electric and electronic equipment, motor vehicles and equipment, and other transportation equipment. The principal manufacturing industries of nondurable goods are chemicals and allied products, food, printing and publishing, and petroleum and coal products. Large corporations are dominant, especially in areas such as steel, automobiles, pharmaceuticals, aircraft, petroleum refining, computers, soaps and detergents, tires, and communications equipment.

In the 1980s and 1990s, the United States was the world leader in computer manufacturing. At the beginning of the 21st century, however, the high-tech manufacturing industry registered a decline. The high-tech industry continued to shed jobs through 2011, with only the software industry registering an increase. Employment in the high-technology sector stood at 5.75 million in 2011. Semiconductor manufacturing had been migrating out of the United States to East Asian countries, especially China, Taiwan, and Singapore.

Automobile manufacturing was an ailing industry in the 1980s, but rebounded slightly in the 1990s, only to see production fall again with the recession that began in 2008. Passenger car production fell from 12.8 million in 2000 to 7.76 million in 2010, then rose to 8.65 million in 2011. That year, America was second in passenger car production in the world, behind China.

Overall, there were 7,396,628 private nonfarm establishments in the United States in 2010, and 27,092,908 nonemployer establishments.

20 Labor

In 2010, the federal government employed some 3,007,938 civilians. About 2,583,768 of that total worked full-time.

The country's civilian labor force, including those who were unemployed, totaled 155.1 million in June 2012. That month, there were 12.7 million unemployed, for an unemployment rate of 8.1%. Of the total workforce in May 2011, farming, fishing, and forestry accounted for 0.4% of the labor force, with construction and extraction accounting for just under 4% of workers; office and administrative support at around 17%; management, business and financial operations at around 10%; and food preparation and serving at around 9%. In May 2012, national average earnings were $23.41 per hour for nonagricultural workers.

In 2011, 16,290,000 employed wage and salary workers were union members—13% of the workers. In 2010, there were 34 national labor unions that each claimed more than 100,000 members, the largest being the National Education Association, with 3.2 million members. The most important federation of organized workers in the United States is the American Federation of Labor–Congress of Industrial Organizations (AFL–CIO), whose affiliated unions had 11.6 million members as of 2011. As of 2012, however, 23 states had passed right-to-work laws, forbidding mandatory union membership as a condition of employment.

21 Agriculture

In 2011, agricultural exports were estimated at $137 billion. Less than 2% of the population lives on farms. Land used for crop production

Agricultural plays a major role in the US economy. Many picturesque barns are located throughout the United States.
© CLIMBERJAK/SHUTTERSTOCK.COM.

amounted to approximately 382 million acres in 2007, while approximately 525 million acres were used as grazing land for livestock. In 2010, there were around 2.2 million farms in the United States, with average farm acreage that year at 418 acres.

Substantial quantities of corn, the most valuable crop produced in the United States, are grown in almost every state. Annual production of selected US crops in 2011 included approximately 2.1 billion bushels of wheat, 155 million bushels of barley, 12.5 billion bushels of corn, 407 million bushels of rice, 3.06 billion bushels of soybeans, 15.7 million bales of cotton, and 173,750 tons of tobacco. The United States is the world's largest exporter of corn and a key global supplier of soybeans and wheat. The United States also produces a substantial amount of fruits and vegetables, with California leading the country in vegetable production. Leading vegetable crops include squash, valued at $2.3 billion in 2010; romaine lettuce, with a value of $1.45 billion; and tomatoes, valued at $1.4 billion in 2010.

22 Domesticated Animals

The livestock population in 2010 included an estimated 92.6 million head of cattle, 64.6 million hogs, and 5.6 million sheep and lambs. That year, there were 49.16 billion broiler chickens and 7.1 billion turkeys. Milk production totaled 192.7 million metric tons in 2010, with Wisconsin, California, and New York together accounting for much of the total. US butter production totaled 1.56 million metric tons in 2010. In that year, the United States produced 10.4 million metric tons of cheese.

23 Fishing

The 2009 commercial catch was 7.87 million pounds (3.57 million metric tons). Food fish made up 84.2% of the catch, and nonfood fish, processed for fertilizer and oil, made up the remaining 15.8%. Alaska pollock, with landings of 1,866,203 pounds (846,504 metric tons), was the most important species in quantity among the commercial fishery landings, although salmon, at a total value of $370 million in 2009, was the most valuable. Other leading species that year included Gulf menhaden, Atlantic menhaden, Pacific cod, halibut, crab, and Gulf shrimp. In 2010, exports of fish products totaled $4.13 billion (fourth after China, Thailand, and Norway).

Aquaculture production consists mostly of catfish, oysters, trout, and crayfish. In 2009, US aquaculture farms produced 773,837 pounds (351,007 metric tons) of fish and shellfish, at a value of $1.2 billion.

Pollution is a problem of increasing concern to the US fishing industry. Dumping of raw sewage, industrial wastes, spillage from oil tankers, and blowouts of offshore wells are the main threats to the fishing grounds. Overfishing is also a threat to the viability of the industry in some areas, especially Alaska. The 2010 BP *Deepwater Horizon* oil spill in the Gulf of Mexico had a negative impact on the fishing grounds there. Tuna, shrimp, crab, and oyster fishing were particularly affected by the spill.

24 Forestry

As of 2010, US forestland covered about 736.7 million acres (298 million hectares), of which approximately 249.1 million acres—33.8%—is owned by the federal government and managed as national forest. Major forest regions include the eastern, central hardwood, southern, Rocky Mountain, and Pacific coast areas. Extensive tracts of land are under ownership of private lumber companies in Alabama, Arkansas, Florida, Georgia, Maine, Oregon, and Washington.

Around 490 million acres (198 million hectares) of US forest are classified as timberlands, with federal, state, and local governments owning 131 million acres (53 million hectares) and nonindustrial private entities owning the remainder. The forest products industry owns about 70 million acres (28 million hectares) of commercial timberland.

Domestic production of roundwood during 2010 amounted to 2.4 billion cubic feet (68.5 million cubic meters), of which softwoods accounted for roughly 80%. Pine and Douglas fir are the main softwood species, while maple, oak, and yellow poplar are the predominant commercial hardwoods.

Other forest products included approximately 52 million metric tons of wood pulp produced in 2010, and 90 million metric tons of paper and paperboard (excluding newsprint) produced in 2008.

25 Mining

Rich in a variety of mineral resources, the United States is a world leader in the production of many important mineral commodities, such as aluminum, cement, copper, pig iron, lead, molybdenum, phosphates, potash, salt, sulfur, uranium, and zinc. The leading mineral-producing states are Arizona (copper, sand and gravel, portland cement, molybdenum); California (portland cement, sand and gravel, gold, boron); Nevada (gold, copper, clay, lithium compounds, molybdenite, opal); Michigan (iron ore, portland cement, sand and gravel, magnesium compounds); Georgia (clays, crushed and broken stone, portland and masonry cement, sand and gravel); Florida (phosphate rock, crushed and broken stone, portland cement, sand and gravel); Utah (copper, gold, magnesium metal, sand and gravel); Texas (portland cement, crushed and broken stone, magnesium metal, sand and gravel); and Minnesota (iron ore, construction and industrial sand and gravel, crushed and broken stone).

Oklahoma and New Mexico are important for petroleum and natural gas, and Kentucky, West Virginia, and Pennsylvania are major coal producers. Iron ore supports the nation's most basic nonagricultural industry: iron and steel manufacturing. The major domestic sources of iron ore have been in the Lake Superior area, with Minnesota and Michigan leading in iron ore yields.

In 2011, total US nonfuel mineral production amounted to more than $74 billion. Leading nonfuel mineral producing states were Nevada (accounting for $10.4 billion), Arizona ($8.2 billion), and Minnesota ($5.1 billion). Top nonfuel minerals mined included gold, copper, molybdenum ore, iron ore, and sand and gravel. In 2010, 1.2 billion metric tons of crushed stone were sold or used by producers in the United States, with a value of $11.4 billion; 820 million metric tons of sand and gravel were sold or produced, with a value of $6 billion; and 2 billion metric tons of aggregate were sold or produced, with a value of $17.5 billion.

26 Energy and Power

The United States, with about 5% of the world's population, consumes about 25% of the energy produced in the world.

Conventional thermal sources from fossil fuels provided the greatest share of energy consumed in 2010. The rest was supplied by nuclear power, hydroelectric power, and renewable energy sources including geothermal, wind, photovoltaic (solar), and wood and waste. In 2010, US coal production was an estimated 1.08 billion short tons. Natural gas production was 21.3 trillion cubic feet (603 million cubic meters), and crude oil production was 10 million barrels per day. Proven reserves of crude oil totaled an estimated 21 billion barrels in 2009. Reserves of wet natural gas were about 283.9 trillion cubic feet (8 trillion cubic meters) that

year, with an additional 60.6 trillion cubic feet (1.7 trillion cubic meters) of shale gas reserves. Recoverable coal reserves at producing mines amounted to around 17.9 billion short tons at the end of 2011, although total US coal resources were estimated at 4 trillion short tons that year. Petroleum imports stood at 8.7 million barrels per day in 2011.

As of 2012, Texas led the nation in crude oil production and accounted for about one-quarter of US total production, along with one-third of all natural gas production. Wyoming led the nation in coal production; it generally produces more coal than the next five top coal producers—West Virginia, Kentucky, Pennsylvania, Texas, and Montana—combined. Texas generated more electricity from wind energy sources than any other state, while Washington led the nation in hydroelectric power generation. Iowa led the nation in fuel ethanol production capacity.

By 2011, the nuclear portion of electricity generation represented about 19.2% of the nation's total electric power output. The number of nuclear reactors in operation peaked at 112 units in 1990, but had declined to 104 by 2012. In 2011, output by nuclear power generating plants was 790.2 billion kilowatt hours.

Total net electricity generation for the year to July 2012 was 3.95 billion megawatt hours. In 2011, the United States had 46,919 megawatts of installed wind power. That year, the United States also generated more than 2,850 megawatts of solar electricity, with around 1,700 megawatts of solar generation installed in 2011 alone.

27 Commerce

Retail sales for 2010 were $3.8 trillion, with grocery sales contributing an additional $581

Many states are actively pursuing renewable energy options. For example, solar panels are being placed in California's Mojave Desert, with its many sunny days. © ANDREI ORLOV/SHUTTERSTOCK.COM.

billion. Total e-commerce sales were estimated at $194.3 billion in 2011, an increase of 16.1% over 2010. The growth of great chains of retail stores, particularly in the form of the supermarket, was an important development in retail trade following the end of World War II. With the great suburban expansion of the 1960s emerged the planned shopping center. Between 1974 and 2000, the square footage occupied by shopping centers in the United States grew at a far greater rate than the nation's population. Since 2000, however, the growth of enclosed malls has slowed considerably, and the trend in the early 2010s was toward open-air shopping areas, often with housing units as part of the overall project mix.

In 2008, there were 429,463 wholesale trade establishments and 1,100,943 retail trade establishments in the United States. Total value of US manufactured goods in 2011 was $780 billion. Leading manufacturing products were transportation equipment ($336 billion), computer and electronic products ($334 billion), and chemicals ($325 billion). In 2011, the United States exported $1.5 trillion in goods, but imported $2.235 trillion, for a trade deficit that year of $738.4 billion.

28 Public Finance

Under the Budget and Accounting Act of 1921, the president is responsible for preparing the federal government budget. In fact, the budget is prepared by the Office of Management and Budget (established in 1970). The president submits a budget message to Congress in

January. Under the Congressional Budget Act of 1974, the Congress establishes targets for overall expenditures and broad functional categories, as well as targets for revenues, the budget deficit, and the public debt. The fiscal year runs from 1 October to 30 September. The public debt, subject to a statutory debt limit, has been raised by Congress 70 times since 1950.

The 2011 budget estimated that the US central government would take in revenues of approximately $2.3 trillion and have expenditures of $3.6 trillion. Public debt at the end of 2011 amounted to 101% of GDP. Total external public debt was limited by law in 2011 to $14 trillion, a limit reached that year. The debt ceiling was raised by Congress, but the new ceiling was reached in January 2013, when emergency debt reduction measures were scheduled to kick in.

29 Taxation

Measured as a proportion of the GDP, the total US tax burden is less than that in most industrialized countries. The greatest source of revenue for the federal government is the personal income tax, which is paid by citizens and resident aliens on their worldwide income. The main state-level taxes are sales and income taxes. The main local taxes are property and local income taxes.

The United States has a progressive personal income tax structure that as of 2012, had a top rate of 35%, payable on incomes of over $388,350. Individuals may also be subject to inheritance and gift taxes, as well as state and local income taxes, all of which vary from state-to-state and locality-to-locality. Capital gains from assets held for under a year (short term) are taxed at higher rates than gains derived from assets held for more than a year (long term). As

of 2012, long-term capital gains for individuals are taxed at a 15% rate.

Total state government tax collections totaled $757 billion in 2011. Of this, around $14 billion were state property taxes, $366 billion were sales taxes and gross receipts, and $52 billion were license fees and taxes.

30 Health

The US health care system is among the most advanced in the world, but escalating health care costs and lack of insurance leave many with inadequate care. As of 2011, some 16% of the population was without health insurance coverage. Health care legislation passed in 2010 was aimed at expanding health care coverage to the majority of the population.

In response to rising costs, the popularity of managed care grew rapidly in the 1990s. By 2011, more than 70 million Americans were insured by either an HMO (health maintenance organization) or PPO (preferred provider organization). In such organizations, medical treatment, laboratory tests, and other health services for each patient are subject to the approval of the insurer before they can be covered.

Life expectancy for someone born in 2012 was 78.49 years. Infant mortality in 2011 was 6.05 per 1,000 live births. The overall death rate in 2011 was 740.6 per 100,000 residents. The birth rate in 2011 was 63.2 per 1,000 women ages 15 to 44, the lowest birthrate ever reported in the United States.

Leading causes of death in 2011 were heart disease (173.7 deaths per 100,000 residents); cancers (168.6 deaths per 100,000 residents); chronic lower respiratory diseases (42.7 deaths per 100,000); cerebrovascular diseases such as stroke

(37.9 deaths per 100,000); accidents (38 deaths per 100,000); Alzheimer's disease (24.6 deaths per 100,000); diabetes mellitus (21.5 deaths per 100,000); pneumonia and influenza (15.7 deaths per 100,000); nephritis, nephrotic syndrome and nephrosis (13.4 deaths per 100,000); and suicide (12 deaths per 100,000).

Cigarette smoking, which has been linked to heart and lung disease, has decreased overall since the late 1980s, partly due to state laws against smoking in public places, and higher taxes on tobacco. The adult smoking rate was 19.3% in 2010. There were a cumulative total of 750,000 acquired immunodeficiency syndrome (AIDS) cases in the 1980s and 1990s, with 450,000 deaths from the disease. In the latter 1990s, both incidence and mortality decreased with the introduction of new drug combinations to combat the disease. In 2008, the number of people living with the human immunodeficiency virus (HIV)/AIDS was estimated at 871,846, with the number of deaths from AIDS estimated at 10,285. In 2011 the number of deaths had dropped to 7,638.

As of 2010, 63.8% of Americans were reported to be either overweight or obese, with around 20% categorized as obese.

Medical facilities in the United States included 4,985 hospitals in 2010, with 2.6 beds per 1,000 residents. As of 2008, there were an estimated 25.7 physicians, 87 registered nurses, 6 dentists, and 5.8 nurse practitioners per 10,000 people. National health care spending reached $2 trillion in 2010.

31 Housing

As of 2011, the housing resources of the United States included 132,316,248 housing units, of which 86.9% (114,991,725) were occupied. About 64.6% of all units (74,264,435) were owner-occupied, with about 11% of the total housing stock standing vacant in 2011. That year, 61.5% of all units (81,325,575) were single-family, detached homes; 6.5% (8,591,522) were mobile homes. The average household had 2.6 people. The median owner-occupied home value was $173,600 in 2011. The median monthly owner costs for units with a mortgage was $1,486, while median monthly rental costs were $871.

Utility gas and electricity are the most common types of heating, with around one million units not having heating. In 2011, there were 678,556 units (0.6%) lacking complete plumbing facilities and 1,170,358 (1%) lacking complete kitchen facilities.

Following World War II, new housing was constructed at a record-breaking pace; 1986 was the 38th successive year during which construction of more than one million housing units was begun. The recession that began in 2008 had a significant effect on housing construction. In 2010, there were an estimated 549,000 housing starts. By September 2012, housing starts had begun to pick up with that month's estimates at 872,000, a 34.8% increase from September 2011.

32 Education

Education is compulsory in all states, and it is considered to be a responsibility of each state and the local government. Generally, formal schooling begins at the age of 5 and continues up to age 17 or 18. Each state specifies the age and circumstances for compulsory attendance. Public schools are controlled and supported by the local authorities, as well as state or federal governmental agencies. Private schools are controlled and supported by religious or private organizations. Primary schooling is from grades one through eight. High schools (secondary) cover grades 9 through 12.

As of 2011, around 94% of the adult population had completed ninth grade, while 85.5% of students graduated high school. Around 10% of students were enrolled in private schools. That year, there were 83,131,910 children over the age of three enrolled in primary or secondary school.

Colleges include junior or community colleges, which offer two-year associate degrees; regular four-year colleges and universities; and graduate or professional schools. There are approximately 3,600 higher-education institutions. In 2011, it was estimated that about 17.9% of the population over the age of 25 had obtained a bachelor' degree, while 10.6% had obtained a postgraduate or professional degree. It was estimated that in 2010, around 20 million students were enrolled in tertiary education programs.

The adult illiteracy rate has been estimated at about 1% for both men and women.

33 Arts

The nation's arts centers are emblems of the importance of the performing arts in US life. New York City's Lincoln Center for the Performing Arts, whose first concert hall opened in 1962, is now the site of the Metropolitan Opera House, three halls for concerts and other musical performances, two theaters, the New York Public Library and Museum of the Performing Arts, and the Juilliard School. The John F. Kennedy Center for the Performing Arts in Washington,

DC, opened in 1971; it comprises two main theaters, two smaller theaters, an opera house, and a concert hall.

The New York Philharmonic, founded in 1842, and conducted by Alan Gilbert as of 2012, is the nation's oldest professional musical ensemble. Other leading orchestras include those of Boston, Chicago, Seattle, Los Angeles, Philadelphia, Pittsburgh, and Washington, D.C.'s National Symphony. Particularly renowned for artistic excellence are the Lyric Opera of Chicago, San Francisco Opera, Santa Fe Opera, New York City Opera, and Metropolitan Opera in New York.

Though still financially insecure, dance still has a wide following. The American Ballet Theater, founded in 1940, is the nation's oldest dance company still active today; the New York City Ballet is equally acclaimed. Drama remains a principal performing art, not only in New York City's renowned theater district but also in regional, university, summer, and dinner theaters throughout the United States. Television and the motion picture industry have made film the dominant modern medium. The motion picture industry had box office receipts of $31.8 billion in 2010.

34 Libraries and Museums

The American Library Association has reported that, as of 2012, there were an estimated 121,785 libraries in the country, including 9,225 public libraries (with 16,698 buildings), 3,689 academic libraries, 99,180 school libraries, 8,313 special libraries, 280 armed forces libraries, and 1,098 government libraries.

The largest library in the country and the world is the Library of Congress, with holdings of more than 151 million items, including 34.5 million books and other printed materials, 3.3 million recordings, 13.4 million photographs, 5.4 million maps, and 6.5 million pieces of sheet music. The Library of Congress serves as the national library and the site of the US Copyright Office.

The country's vast public library system is administered primarily by municipalities. The largest of these is the New York Public Library system with 132 branch locations and over 50.6 million volumes. Other major public library systems include the Boston Public Library (over 15.7 million volumes), Los Angeles County Public Library (over 7.8 million volumes),

Public Library of Cincinnati and Hamilton County (9.1 million volumes), and the Free Library of Philadelphia (6.4 million items).

There are more than 5,000 nonprofit museums in the United States. The Smithsonian Institution in Washington, D.C., sponsors 18 national museums and the National Zoo. Sixteen of the Smithsonian national museums are located in the Smithsonian complex of Washington, D.C.

Other eminent US museums include the American Museum of Natural History, the Metropolitan Museum of Art, the Museum of Modern Art, the Guggenheim Museum, the Whitney Collection of American Art, the Frick Collection,

The country's most famous museums are part of the Smithsonian Institution. The National Air and Space Museum has the most historical air and space vehicles in the world. © JORG HACKEMANN/SHUTTERSTOCK.COM.

and the Brooklyn Museum, all in New York City; the Boston Museum of Fine Arts; the Art Institute of Chicago and the Chicago Museum of Natural History; the Franklin Institute and Philadelphia Museum of Art, both in Philadelphia; and the M. H. de Young Memorial Museum in San Francisco. Also of prominence are the Cleveland Museum of Art, the St. Louis Museum of Art, and the Baltimore Museum of Art.

35 Communications

All major electronic communications systems are privately owned but regulated by the Federal Communications Commission. In 2010, broadcasting stations on the air comprised more than 14,000 radio stations (both AM and FM) and more than 1,500 television stations. Nearly 1,000 stations were affiliated with the 5 major networks. In 2012, around 84.4% of households had more than one television set and 23.6% of households had access to a satellite dish. By 2010, 91.7 million households had access to the Internet, with 68.24% having access to broadband. Around 28 million people wrote a blog in 2009, 47.3 million households watched online videos, and 22% of households listened to a podcast.

36 Press

Overall newspaper readership fell with the advent of the Internet. Total daily circulation rates were 62.3 million in 1990, but only 43.3 million in 2010. However, digital subscription rates for some major newspapers began rising significantly in 2010.

According to the Pew Research Center, the 25 US daily newspapers with the largest circulations as of 2010 were as follows: *USA Today* (national), 2,830,594; *Wall Street Journal* (national), 2,061,142; *New York Times* (NY), 876,638; *Los Angeles Times* (CA), 600,449; *Washington Post* (Washington, DC), 545,345; *New York Daily News* (NY), 512,520; *New York Post* (NY), 501,501; *San Jose Mercury News* (CA), 477,595; *Chicago Tribune* (IL), 441,506; *Houston Chronicle* (TX), 343,952; *Philadelphia Inquirer* (PA), 342,360; *Long Island/New York Newsday* (NY), 314,848; *Denver Post* (CO), 309,863; *Arizona Republic* 308,973; *Star Tribune* (MN), 297,479; *Dallas Morning News* (TX), 264,459; *Cleveland Plain Dealer* (OH), 252,608; *Seattle Times* (WA), 251,697; *Chicago Sun-Times* (IL), 250,747; *Detroit Free Press* (MI), 245,323; *St Petersburg Times* (FL), 239,684; *Oregonian* 239,684; *San Diego Union Tribune* (CA), 224,761; *San Francisco Chronicle* (CA), 223,549; and the *Star-Ledger* (NJ), 223,037.

The most popular consumer magazine in the country in 2011 was *AARP the Magazine,* published bimonthly by the AARP (American Association of Retired Persons) with a circulation of over 22.4 million. The *AARP Bulletin* had a circulation of over 22.1 million. The two general circulation magazines that appealed to the largest audiences in 2011 were *Better Homes and Gardens* (about 7.6 million) and *Game Informer Magazine* (about 7.5 million). *TIME* was the leading news magazine, with weekly circulations in 2010 of about 3,298,390.

The US book-publishing industry consists of the major book companies (mainly located in the New York metro area), nonprofit university presses distributed throughout the United States, and numerous small publishing firms.

There were 328,259 print book titles published in the United States in 2010, up from 135,000 titles in 2001. Also, several hundred thousand books were published in digital format.

The US Constitution provides for freedom of speech and of the press in its Bill of Rights, and the government supports these rights. Citizens express a wide range of opinions in all media, where debate, editorial opinion, and government opposition viewpoints are represented in some form or another. Nearly all media are privately owned.

37 Tourism, Travel, and Recreation

Foreign visitors to the United States numbered 62.7 million in 2011. Of these visitors, 21.3 million came from Canada and 13.5 million from Mexico. With a few exceptions, such as Canadians entering from the Western Hemisphere, all visitors to the United States are required to have passports and visas. Canadians must have a passport or an approved travel document. Visitors from Mexico may apply for visas that remain valid for 10 years.

The United States has a total of 398 areas in its National Park system. Among the most striking scenic attractions in the United States are the Grand Canyon in Arizona; Carlsbad Caverns in New Mexico; Yosemite National Park in California; Yellowstone National Park in Idaho, Montana, and Wyoming; Niagara Falls, partly in New York and partly in Canada; and the Everglades in Florida.

Historical attractions include the Liberty Bell and Constitution Hall in Philadelphia; the Statue of Liberty in New York City; the White House, the Capitol, and the monuments to Washington, Jefferson, and Lincoln in

The United States is home to numerous scenic wonders, such as the Yellowstone River Lower Falls that cut through the Grand Canyon of the Yellowstone in Wyoming. © WARREN PRICE PHOTOGRAPHY/SHUTTERSTOCK.COM.

Washington, D.C.; Colonial Williamsburg in Virginia; the Alamo in San Antonio, Texas; and Mount Rushmore in South Dakota.

Among many other popular tourist attractions are the movie and television studios in Los Angeles; the cable cars and the Golden Gate Bridge in San Francisco; casino gambling in Las Vegas, Nevada, and in Atlantic City, New Jersey; the Grand Ole Opry in Nashville, Tennessee; and such amusement parks as Disneyland (Anaheim, California) and Walt Disney World (near

Among the country's most iconic bridges is San Francisco's Golden Gate Bridge, seen here from Marshall Beach. © CAN BALCIOGLU/ SHUTTERSTOCK.COM.

Orlando, Florida). For amount and variety of entertainment—theater, movies, music, dance, and sports—New York City has few rivals.

Americans' recreational activities range from home gardening to the major spectator sports, such as professional baseball, football, basketball, ice hockey, soccer, horse racing, and college football and basketball. Participant sports are a favorite form of recreation, including running, biking, swimming, aerobics, tennis, and golf. Skiing is a popular recreation in New England and the western mountain ranges. Sailing, power boating, and rafting are popular water sports. In 1994, the United States hosted the World Cup Soccer Championship. The United States hosted the Summer Olympics in 1904, 1932, 1984, and 1996. The Winter Olympics were held in the United States in 1960, 1980, and 2002. There are state fairs in most states, and numerous other annual events, such as music festivals, film festivals, and local celebrations.

38 Sports

Baseball has long been honored as the national pastime. During the 2011 regular season, around 75 million fans attended Major League Baseball games. In addition, there is an extensive network of minor league baseball teams, each related to a major league franchise.

The National Basketball Association, created in 1946, included 30 teams in 2012. The 2011 NBA season was marred by a 161-day lockout imposed by owners after a failure to agree to a new collective bargaining agreement. The season was shortened from 82 games to 60 games as a result. The Women's National Basketball Association (WNBA), founded in 1997, included 12 teams as of 2012. During the WNBA's third season (1999), 1,959,733 fans attended regular season games, establishing an attendance record for women's professional sports. In 2011, WNBA season attendance was 1,622,685.

In 2011, the National Football League included 32 teams, and the season-ending Super Bowl is often the most-watched television event in the country.

The National Hockey League (NHL), formally organized in 1917, consists of 30 clubs located throughout the United States and Canada. While all of the league's franchises are located in North America, the league is truly a global league, employing players from over 20 countries around the world.

As of 2012, Major League Soccer fielded 19 teams in two divisions.

Several other professional sports are popular nationwide. Thoroughbred racing is among the nation's most popular spectator sports, with an estimated 12 million fans visiting horse-racing tracks annually. Annual highlights of thoroughbred racing are the three jewels of the Triple Crown—the Kentucky Derby, the Preakness, and the Belmont Stakes. In 2000, jockey Julie Krone became the first woman jockey to be inducted into the Horse Racing Hall of Fame.

The prize money that Henry Ford won on a 1901 auto race helped him start his now-famous car company two years later; since then, automobile manufacturers have backed sports car, stock car, and motorcycle racing at tracks throughout the United States.

From John L. Sullivan to Muhammad Ali, the personality and power of the great boxing champions have drawn millions of spectators ringside, although mixed martial arts (MMA) has gained in popularity over boxing during the 21st century.

Football has been part of US college life since the game was born on 6 November 1869 with a New Jersey match between Rutgers and Princeton. The National Collegiate Athletic Association (NCAA) and National Association of Intercollegiate Athletics (NAIA) coordinate collegiate football and basketball. Colleges recruit top athletes with sports scholarships in order to win media attention, and to keep the loyalty of the alumni, thereby boosting fundraising. Baseball, hockey, swimming, gymnastics, crew, lacrosse, track and field, and a variety of other sports also fill the intercollegiate competitive program.

The Amateur Athletic Union (AAU), a national nonprofit organization founded in 1888, conducts the AAU/USA Junior Olympics, offering competition in 41 sports in order to help identify candidates for international Olympic competition. St. Louis hosted the 1904 summer Olympics; Los Angeles was home to the games in 1932 and 1984. The winter Olympic Games were held in Squaw Valley, California, in 1960, and at Lake Placid, New York, in 1932 and 1980. Atlanta hosted the summer

Olympic Games in 1996. Salt Lake City, Utah, was the site of the 2002 winter Olympic Games.

39 Famous Americans

Political and Military Figures Printer, inventor, scientist, and statesman Benjamin Franklin (1706–1790) was one of America's outstanding figures of the colonial period. George Washington (1732–1799), military leader in the American Revolution and first president of the United States, is known as the father of his country. The chief author of the Declaration of Independence and the country's third president was Thomas Jefferson (1743–1826). His leading political opponents were John Adams (1735–1826), the nation's second president, and Alexander Hamilton (b. West Indies, 1755–1804), the first secretary of the Treasury. James Madison (1751–1836), a leading figure in drawing up the US Constitution, served as the fourth president.

Abraham Lincoln (1809–1865) led the United States through its most difficult period, the Civil War, during the course of which he issued the Emancipation Proclamation. Jefferson Davis (1808–1889) served as the only president of the short-lived Confederacy. Among the foremost presidents of the 20th century were Nobel Peace Prize winner Theodore Roosevelt (1858–1919); Woodrow Wilson (1856–1924), who led the nation during World War I; and Franklin Delano Roosevelt (1882–1945), who was elected to four terms spanning the Great Depression and World War II. Presidents during the 1961–2012 period have been John Fitzgerald Kennedy (1917–1963), Lyndon Baines Johnson (1908–1973), Richard Milhous Nixon (1913–1994), Gerald Rudolph Ford (1913–2006), Jimmy Carter (James Earl

Washington, DC, features many monuments honoring US leaders. The statue of Abraham Lincoln, who freed the slaves, is found inside the Lincoln Memorial. © SHU-HUNG LIU/ SHUTTERSTOCK.COM.

Carter Jr., 1924–), Ronald Wilson Reagan (1911–2004), George Herbert Walker Bush (1924–), Bill Clinton (William Jefferson Blythe III, 1946–), George Walker Bush (1946–), and Barack Hussein Obama (1961–).

Outstanding military leaders of the Civil War included Union General Ulysses Simpson Grant (1822–1885), who later served as the 18th president; and Confederate General Robert Edward Lee (1807–1870). Douglas MacArthur (1880–1964) commanded the United States forces in Asia during World War II, oversaw the postwar occupation and reorganization of Japan, and directed United Nations forces in the first year of the Korean conflict. Dwight D. Eisenhower (1890–1969) served as supreme Allied commander during World War II, later becoming the 34th president. General Colin Luther Powell (1937–), former secretary of state (2001–05), became the highest-ranking African American government official in the history of the United States (a position assumed by African American Condoleezza Rice in 2005). Powell was a general in the army who also served as national security adviser (1987–89) and chairman of the Joint Chiefs of Staff (1989–93).

John Marshall (1755–1835), chief justice of the United States from 1801 to 1835, established the power of the Supreme Court through the principle of judicial review. Earl Warren (1891–1974), who was chief justice from 1953 to 1969, saw important decisions on desegregation, reapportionment, and civil liberties. William O. Douglas (1898–1980), who served from 1939 to 1975, had the longest tenure on the court. Sandra Day O'Connor (1930–) was the first woman to serve on the court.

Native American guide Sacagawea (c. 1788–1812) helped Lewis and Clark explore the West. She is acknowledged in states such as Idaho, Oregon, Washington, and others with statues and parks named in her honor. Native American chiefs renowned for their resistance to white invasion were Tecumseh (1768–1813), Geronimo (1829?–1909), Sitting Bull (1831?–1890), and Crazy Horse (1849?–1877). Historical figures who have become part of American folklore include pioneer Daniel Boone (1734–1820); silversmith, engraver, and patriot Paul Revere (1735–1818); frontiersman David "Davy" Crockett (1786–1836); scout and Indian agent Christopher "Kit" Carson (1809–1868); William Frederick "Buffalo Bill" Cody (1846–1917); and the outlaws Jesse Woodson James (1847–1882) and Billy the Kid (William H. Bonney, 1859–1881).

Inventors and Scientists Outstanding inventors have included Robert Fulton (1765–1815), who developed the steamboat; Samuel Finley Breese Morse (1791–1872), who invented the telegraph; and Elias Howe (1819–1867), who invented the sewing machine. Alexander Graham Bell (b. Scotland, 1847–1922) invented the telephone. Thomas Alva Edison (1847–1931) was responsible for hundreds of inventions, among them the incandescent electric lamp, the phonograph, and a motion picture camera and projector. Two brothers, Wilbur Wright (1867–1912) and

Astronaut Sunita Williams was one of the first women of Indian ancestry to travel in space. She holds several spacewalk records. © UNIVERSAL IMAGES GROUP LIMITED / ALAMY.

Orville Wright (1871–1948), designed, built, and flew the first successful motor-powered airplane. Amelia Earhart (1898–1937) and Charles Lindbergh (1902–1974) were aviation pioneers. Space program pioneers include John Glenn (1921–1999), the first American astronaut to orbit Earth, and Neil Armstrong (1930–2012), the first man to set foot on the Moon.

Outstanding botanists and naturalists include George Washington Carver (1864–1943), known especially for his work on industrial applications for peanuts, and John James Audubon (1785–1851), who won fame as an ornithologist and artist.

Albert Abraham Michelson (b. Germany, 1852–1931) measured the speed of light and became the first of a long line of US Nobel Prize winners. The theory of relativity was conceived by Albert Einstein (b. Germany, 1879–1955), generally considered one of the greatest minds in the physical sciences. Enrico Fermi (b. Italy, 1901–1954) created the first nuclear chain reaction and contributed to the development of the atomic and hydrogen bombs. Also prominent in the splitting of the atom were J. Robert Oppenheimer (1904–1967) and Edward Teller (b. Hungary, 1908–2003). Jonas Edward Salk (1914–1995) developed an effective vaccine for polio, and Albert Bruce Sabin (1906–1993) contributed oral, attenuated live-virus polio vaccines. Physicist Richard Feynman (1918–1988) won the Nobel Prize for his work in developing quantum physics. James D. Watson (1928–) shared the 1962 Nobel Prize in Physiology or Medicine with Francis Crick and Maurice Wilkins for determining the structure of DNA. Watson later went on to direct the Human Genome Project (mapping every human gene).

Social Reformers Social reformers of note include Frederick Douglass (Frederick Augustus Washington Bailey, 1817–1895), a prominent abolitionist; Elizabeth Cady Stanton (1815–1902) and Susan Brownell Anthony (1820–1906), leaders in the women's suffrage movement; Clara Barton (1821–1912), founder of the American Red Cross; Eugene Victor Debs (1855–1926), labor leader and an organizer of the Socialist movement in the United States; Jane Addams (1860–1935), who started the Hull House in Chicago to help the poor; and Martin Luther King Jr. (1929–1968), a central figure in the civil rights movement and winner of the Nobel Peace Prize in 1964.

One of America's most famous activists was Susan B. Anthony who devoted her life to the cause of women's rights and suffrage. COURTESY OF THE LIBRARY OF CONGRESS.

Religious leaders include Roger Williams (1603–1683), an early advocate of religious tolerance in the United States; Jonathan Edwards (1703–1758), New England preacher and theologian; Joseph Smith (1805–1844), founder of the Church of Jesus Christ of Latter-day Saints (Mormons), and his chief associate, Brigham Young (1801–1877); and Mary Baker Eddy (1821–1910), founder of the Church of Christ, Scientist (Christian Science). Pat Robertson (1930–), televangelist and leader of the Christian Coalition organization, and Jerry Falwell (1933–2007), a fundamentalist Baptist pastor, televangelist, and founder of the Moral Majority movement and Liberty University, were contemporary leaders of the Christian religious right.

Literary Figures The first American author to be widely read outside the United States was Washington Irving (1783–1859). James Fenimore Cooper (1789–1851) was the first popular American novelist. The writings of two men from Concord, Massachusetts—Ralph Waldo Emerson (1803–1882) and Henry David Thoreau (1817–1862)—influenced philosophers, political leaders, and ordinary men and women in many parts of the world. The novels and short stories of Nathaniel Hawthorne (1804–1864) explore New England's Puritan heritage. Herman Melville (1819–1891) wrote the novel *Moby-Dick,* a symbolic work about a whale hunt that has become an American classic. Louisa May Alcott (1832–1888) is most famous for her novel *Little Women.* Mark Twain (Samuel Langhorne Clemens, 1835–1910) is the best-known American humorist.

Other leading novelists of the late 19th and early 20th centuries were Henry James (1843–1916), Edith Wharton (1862–1937),

Stephen Crane (1871–1900), Willa Cather (1873–1947), and Sinclair Lewis (1885–1951), first American winner of the Nobel Prize for literature (1930). Later Nobel Prize-winning US novelists include Pearl S. Buck (1892–1973) in 1938; William Faulkner (1897–1962) in 1949; Ernest Hemingway (1899–1961) in 1954; John Steinbeck (1902–1968) in 1962; Saul Bellow (b. Canada, 1915–2005) in 1976; Isaac Bashevis Singer (b. Poland, 1904–1991) in 1978, and Toni Morrison (1931–) in 1993. Among other noteworthy writers are James Thurber (1894–1961), Francis Scott Key Fitzgerald (1896–1940), Elwyn Brooks (E. B.) White (1899–1985), Richard Wright (1908–1960), Eudora Welty (1909–2001), James Baldwin (1924–1987), John Updike (1932–2009), John Cheever (1912–1982), Norman Mailer (1923–2007), and J. D. Salinger (1919–2010).

Notable 19th-century American poets include Henry Wadsworth Longfellow (1807–1882), Edgar Allan Poe (1809–1849), Walt Whitman (1819–1892), and Emily Dickinson (1830–1886). Poets who came to prominence in the 20th century include Robert Frost (1874–1963), Ezra Pound (1885–1972), Marianne Moore (1887–1972), and Wallace Stevens (1879–1955). Carl Sandburg (1878–1967) was a noted poet, historian, novelist, and folklorist. Robert Lowell (1917–1977), John Ashbery (1927–), James Merrill (1926–1995), Allen Ginsberg (1926–1997), Maya Angelou (1928–), Adrienne Rich (1929–2012), and Sylvia Plath (1932–1963) are among the best-known poets since World War II. The foremost US playwrights include Eugene (Gladstone) O'Neill (1888–1953), who won the Nobel Prize for literature in 1936; Tennessee Williams (Thomas Lanier Williams, 1911–1983); and Arthur

Miller (1915–2005). Neil Simon (1927–) is one of the nation's most popular playwrights and screenwriters.

Artists Two renowned painters of the early American period were John Singleton Copley (1738–1815) and Gilbert Stuart (1755–1828). Outstanding 19th-century painters included James Abbott McNeill Whistler (1834–1903) and John Singer Sargent (b. Italy, 1856–1925). In the 20th century, Edward Hopper (1882–1967), Georgia O'Keeffe (1887–1986), Norman Rockwell (1894–1978), and Andrew Wyeth (1917–2009) achieved wide recognition, as did their more recent colleagues, abstract expressionists Jackson Pollack (1912–1956) and Mark Rothko (1903–1970) and "pop" artists Andy Warhol (1928–1987) and Jasper Johns (1930–).

Famous American photographers include Edward S. Curtis (1868–1952); Ansel Adams (1902–1984); Dorothea Lange (1895–1965); Margaret Bourke-White (1904–1971); and Annie Leibovitz (1949–).

Entertainment Figures The first great American "showman" was Phineas Taylor "P. T." Barnum (1810–1891). Outstanding figures in the motion picture industry include producers Samuel Goldwyn (1882–1974), Irving Thalberg (1899–1936), and Louis B. Mayer (1885–1957); animation pioneer and entertainment entrepreneur Walter Elias "Walt" Disney (1906–1966); and legendary directors John Ford (1895–1973), Frank Capra (1897–1991), Sir Charles Spencer "Charlie" Chaplin (b. England, 1889–1978), Sir Alfred Hitchcock (b. England, 1899–1980), and George Orson Welles (1915–1985). More recent American directors who have achieved renown include Steven Spielberg (1947–), Martin Scorsese (1942–), Woody

Allen (Allen Konigsberg, 1935–), Kathryn Bigelow (1951–), and Spike Lee (1957–).

World-famous American actors and actresses include Humphrey Bogart (1899–1957); Clark Gable (1901–1960); Cary Grant (Alexander Archibald Leach, b. England, 1904–1986); John Wayne (Marion Michael Morrison, 1907–79); Katharine Hepburn (1907–2003); Lucille Ball (1911–1989); Judy Garland (Frances Gumm, 1922–1969); Marlon Brando (1924–2004); Marilyn Monroe (Norma Jean Mortenson, 1926–1962); Elizabeth Taylor (b. England, 1932–2011); Dustin Hoffman (1937–); Jack Nicholson (1937–); Meryl Streep (1949–); Denzel Washington (1954–); Angelina Jolie (1975–); Julia Roberts (1967–); Ben Affleck (1972–); and Tom Hanks (1956–). Other well-known American entertainers are W. C. Fields (William Claude Dukenfield, 1880–1946); Jack Benny (Benjamin Kubelsky, 1894–1974); Fred Astaire (Fred Austerlitz, 1899–1987); Bob (Leslie Townes) Hope (b. England, 1903–2003); Whoopi Goldberg (1955–); Frank (Francis Albert) Sinatra (1915–1998); Elvis Aaron Presley (1935–1977); Barbra (Barbara Joan) Streisand (1942–); Bruce Springsteen (1949–); Madonna (Madonna Louise Ciccone, 1958–); Michael Jackson (1958–2009); and Jennifer Lopez (1969–).

American-born television journalists and personalities include Edward R. Murrow (1908–1965); Walter Cronkite (1916–2009); Tom Brokaw (1940–); David Letterman (1947–); Jay Leno (1950–); Barbara Walters (1929–); and Oprah Winfrey (1954–).

Composers and Musicians The songs of Stephen Collins Foster (1826–1864) have achieved folk-song status, as have those of Woodrow Wilson "Woody" Guthrie (1912–1967), whose work heavily influenced the folk-rock singers of the 1960s. Among the foremost composers are Edward MacDowell (1861–1908), Aaron Copland (1900–1990), and Leonard Bernstein (1918–1990). Leading composers of music included John Philip Sousa (1854–1932) and George Gershwin (1898–1937). Prominent in the blues tradition are Leadbelly (Huddie Ledbetter, 1888–1949), Bessie Smith (1898?–1937), and Muddy Waters (McKinley Morganfield, 1915–1983). Leading jazz figures include the composers Scott Joplin (1868–1917), Edward Kennedy "Duke" Ellington (1899–1974), William "Count" Basie (1904–1984), and performers Louis Armstrong (1900–1971), Ella Fitzgerald (1917–1996), Billie Holiday (Eleanora Fagan, 1915–1959), John Birks "Dizzy" Gillespie (1917–1993), Charlie "Bird" Parker (1920–1955), John Coltrane (1926–1967), and Miles Davis (1926–1991).

Sports Figures Among the many noteworthy sports stars are baseball's Tyrus Raymond "Ty" Cobb (1886–1961) and George Herman "Babe" Ruth (1895–1948); football's Jim Brown (1936–); and golf's Mildred "Babe" Didrikson Zaharias (1914–1956), Jack Nicholaus (1940–), Arnold Palmer (1929–), and Eldrick Tont "Tiger" Woods (1975–). Billie Jean (Moffitt) King (1943–) and sisters Venus (1980–) and Serena (1981–) Williams have starred in tennis; Joe Louis (Joseph Louis Barrow, 1914–1981) and Muhammad Ali (Cassius Marcellus Clay, 1942–) in boxing; Wilton Norman "Wilt" Chamberlain (1936–1999) and Michael Jordan (1963–) in basketball; Mark Spitz (1950–) and Michael Phelps (1985–) in swimming; Eric Heiden (1958–) and Apolo Anton Ohno (1982–) in speed skating; and Jesse Owens (1913–1980) and Wilma Rudolph (1940–1994) in track and field.

40 Bibliography

BOOKS

Bausum, Ann. *Our Country's First Ladies.* Washington, DC: National Geographic Children's Books, 2007.

Bausum, Ann. *Our Country's Presidents: From George Washington to Barack Obama.* Washington, DC: National Geographic Children's Books, 2009.

Bollinger, Michele. *101 Changemakers: Rebels and Radicals Who Changed U.S. History.* Chicago: Haymarket Books, 2012.

Burns, Ken, and Dayton Duncan. *The National Parks: America's Best Idea.* New York: Knopf, 2011.

Marsico, Katie. *It's Cool to Learn about Countries: United States of America.* Ann Arbor, MI: Cherry Lake Publishing, 2011.

Meltzer, Milton. *Lincoln: In His Own Words,* reprinted edition. Orlando, FL: Sandpiper, 2009.

Reader's Digest, eds. *Off the Beaten Path: A Travel Guide to More Than 1,000 Scenic and Interesting Places Still Uncrowded and Inviting.* Pleasantville, NY: The Reader's Digest Association, Inc., 2009.

Rozett, Louise. *Fast Facts about the 50 States, Plus Puerto Rico and Washington, D.C.* New York: Children's Press, 2009.

Takaki, Ronald; adapted by Rebecca Stefoff. *A Different Mirror for Young People: A History of Multicultural America.* New York: Seven Stories Press, 2012.

Uschan, Michael V. *The Civil Rights Movement.* Detroit: Lucent Books, 2010.

Zinn, Howard, and Rebecca Stefoff. *A Young People's History of the United States: Columbus to the War on Terror.* New York: Seven Stories Press, 2009.

WEB SITES

American Historical Association. http://www.historians.org/ (accessed on November 27, 2012).

American Library Association. http://www.ala.org (accessed on November 27, 2012).

Centers for Disease Control and Prevention. http://www.cdc.gov/ (accessed on November 27, 2012).

"Crime in the United States." *Federal Bureau of Investigation.* http://www.fbi.gov/about-us/cjis/ucr/crime-in-the-u.s/2010/crime-in-the-u.s.-2010/violent-crime/violent-crime (accessed on November 27, 2012).

"Economy at a Glance: United States." *US Bureau of Labor Statistics.* http://www.bls.gov/eag/eag.us.htm (accessed on November 27, 2012).

"Endangered Species Program." *US Fish & Wildlife Service.* http://www.fws.gov/endangered/ (accessed on November 27, 2012).

"Fisheries of the United States." *National Marine Fisheries Service.* http://www.st.nmfs.noaa.gov/st1/publications.html (accessed on November 27, 2012).

"State & County QuickFacts: United States." *US Bureau of the Census.* http://quickfacts.census.gov/qfd/states/00000.html (accessed on November 27, 2012).

"United States: Country Analysis Brief." *US Energy Information Administration.* http://www.eia.gov/countries/country-data.cfm?fips=US&trk=p1 (accessed on November 27, 2012).

US Department of Agriculture. http://www.usda.gov/wps/portal/usda/usdahome (accessed on November 27, 2012).

US Department of Energy. http://energy.gov/ (accessed on November 27, 2012).

US Environmental Protection Agency. http://www.epa.gov/ (accessed on November 27, 2012).

US Travel Association. http://www.ustravel.org/ (accessed on November 27, 2012).

USA.gov: Government Made Easy. http://www.usa.gov/ (accessed on November 27, 2012).

The White House. http://www.whitehouse.gov/ (accessed on November 27, 2012).

Abbreviations & Acronyms

Various abbreviations and acronyms are found within these pages. Here is a handy guide showing various abbreviations/acronyms and their meanings.

AD—Anno Domini
AFL–CIO—American Federation of Labor–Congress of Industrial Organizations
AI—American Independent
a.m.—before noon
AM—amplitude modulation
American Ind.—American Independent Party
Amtrak—National Railroad Passenger Corp.
b.—born
BC—Before Christ
Btu—British thermal unit(s)
bu—bushel(s)
c.—circa (about)
C—Celsius (Centigrade)
CIA—Central Intelligence Agency
cm—centimeter(s)
Co.—company
comp.—compiler
Conrail—Consolidated Rail Corp.
Corp.—corporation
CST—Central Standard Time
cu—cubic
cwt—hundredweight(s)
d.—died
D—Democrat
E—east
ed.—edition, editor
e.g.—exempli gratia (for example)
EPA—Environmental Protection Agency
est.—estimated
EST—Eastern Standard Time
et al.—and others (Latin)
etc.—et cetera (and so on)
F—Fahrenheit

FBI—Federal Bureau of Investigation
FCC—Federal Communications Commission
FM—frequency modulation
Ft.—fort
ft—foot, feet
GDP—gross domestic product
gm—gram
GMT—Greenwich Mean Time
GNP—gross national product
GRT—gross registered tons
GSP—gross state product
Hist.—Historic
I—interstate (highway)
i.e.—that is (Latin)
in—inch(es)
Inc.—incorporated
Jct.—junction
K—kindergarten
kg—kilogram(s)
km—kilometer(s)
km/h—kilometers per hour
kw—kilowatt(s)
kWh—kilowatt-hour(s)
lb—pound(s)
m—meter(s); morning
mi—mile(s)
Mon.—monument
mph—miles per hour
MST—Mountain Standard Time
Mt.—mount
Mtn.—mountain
MW—megawatt(s)
MWh—megawatt-hour(s)
N—north

NA—not available
Natl.—National
NATO—North Atlantic Treaty Organization
NCAA—National Collegiate Athletic Association
n.d.—no date
NEA—National Education Association or National
    Endowment for the Arts
NF—National Forest
NWR—National Wildlife Refuge
oz—ounce(s)
p.m.—after noon
PST—Pacific Standard Time
r.—reigned

R—Republican
Res.—reservoir, reservation
rev. ed.—revised edition
s—south
S—Sunday
sq—square
SRD—States' Rights Democrat
St.—saint
TANF—Temporary Assistance for Needy Families
UN—United Nations
US—United States
USIA—United States Information Agency
w—west

Names & Abbreviations of States and Other Select Areas

Alabama
- Standard: Ala.
- Postal: AL

Alaska
- Postal: AK

American Samoa
- Postal: AS

Arizona
- Standard: Ariz.
- Postal: AZ

Arkansas
- Standard: Ark.
- Postal: AR

California
- Standard: Calif.
- Postal: CA

Colorado
- Standard: Colo.
- Postal: CO

Connecticut
- Standard: Conn.
- Postal: CT

Delaware
- Standard: Del.
- Postal: DE

District of Columbia
- Standard: D.C.
- Postal: DC

Federated States of Micronesia
- Postal: FM

Florida
- Standard: Fla.
- Postal: FL

Georgia
- Standard: Ga.
- Postal: GA

Guam
- Postal: GU

Hawaii
- Postal: HI

Idaho
- Postal: ID

Illinois
- Standard: Ill.
- Postal: IL

Indiana
- Standard: Ind.
- Postal: IN

Iowa
- Postal: IA

Kansas
- Standard: Kans. or Kan.
- Postal: KS

Kentucky
- Standard: Ky.
- Postal: KY

Louisiana
- Standard: La.
- Postal: LA

Maine
- Standard: Me.
- Postal: ME

Marshall Islands
- Postal: MH

Maryland
- Standard: Md.
- Postal: MD

Massachusetts
- Standard: Mass.
- Postal: MA

Michigan
- Standard: Mich.
- Postal: MI

Minnesota
- Standard: Minn.
- Postal: MN

Mississippi
- Standard: Miss.
- Postal: MS

Missouri
- Standard: Mo.
- Postal: MO

Montana
- Standard: Mont.
- Postal: MT

Nebraska
- Standard: Neb. or Nebr.
- Postal: NE

Nevada
- Standard: Nev.
- Postal: NV

New Hampshire
- Standard: N.H.
- Postal: NH

New Jersey
- Standard: N.J.
- Postal: NJ

New Mexico
- Standard: N.Mex. or N.M.
- Postal: NM

New York
- Standard: N.Y.
- Postal: NY

North Carolina
- Standard: N.C.
- Postal: NC

North Dakota
- Standard: N.Dak. or N.D.
- Postal: ND

Northern Mariana Islands
- Postal: MP

Ohio
- Postal: OH

Oklahoma
- Standard: Okla.
- Postal: OK

Oregon
- Standard: Ore.
- Postal: OR

Pennsylvania
- Standard: Pa.
- Postal: PA

Puerto Rico
- Standard: P.R.
- Postal: PR

Rhode Island
- Standard: R.I.
- Postal: RI

South Carolina
- Standard: S.C.
- Postal: SC

South Dakota
- Standard: S.Dak. or S.D.
- Postal: SD

Tennessee
- Standard: Tenn.
- Postal: TN

Texas
- Standard: Tex.
- Postal: TX

Utah
- Postal: UT

Vermont
- Standard: Vt.
- Postal: VT

Virgin Islands
- Standard: V.I.
- Postal: VI

Virginia
- Standard: Va.
- Postal: VA

Washington
- Standard: Wash.
- Postal: WA

West Virginia
- Standard: W.Va.
- Postal: WV

Wisconsin
- Standard: Wis.
- Postal: WI

Wyoming
- Standard: Wyo.
- Postal: WY

Appendix of State Data Tables

Population and Rank, Median Age, and Sex Ratio
2011 Estimates

	Population rank among the 50 states	Total population	Median age (years)	Sex ratio (males per 100 females)
Alabama	23	4,802,740	38.1	93.8
Alaska	47	722,718	33.9	106.6
Arizona	16	6,482,505	36.2	99.2
Arkansas	32	2,937,979	37.5	97.2
California	1	37,691,912	35.4	99.0
Colorado	22	5,116,796	36.2	100.8
Connecticut	29	3,580,709	40.3	94.9
Delaware	45	907,135	39.1	94.2
District of Columbia	NA	617,996	33.4	89.7
Florida	4	19,057,542	41.1	95.7
Georgia	9	9,815,210	35.5	96.1
Hawaii	40	1,374,810	38.5	100.3
Idaho	39	1,584,985	35.0	100.6
Illinois	5	12,869,259	36.8	96.2
Indiana	15	6,516,922	37.1	96.9
Iowa	30	3,062,309	38.1	97.6
Kansas	33	2,871,238	36.3	98.3
Kentucky	26	4,369,356	38.2	96.3
Louisiana	25	4,574,836	35.9	95.6
Maine	41	1,328,188	43.2	96.2
Maryland	19	5,828,289	38.0	93.8
Massachusetts	14	6,587,536	39.3	93.8
Michigan	8	9,876,187	39.2	96.4
Minnesota	21	5,344,861	37.6	98.8
Mississippi	31	2,978,512	36.1	94.4
Missouri	18	6,010,688	38.0	96.1
Montana	44	998,199	39.7	100.5
Nebraska	38	1,842,641	36.3	98.1
Nevada	35	2,723,322	36.7	101.6
New Hampshire	42	1,318,194	41.5	97.6
New Jersey	11	8,821,155	39.2	95.0
New Mexico	36	2,082,224	36.6	99.1
New York	3	19,465,197	38.1	94.1
North Carolina	10	9,656,401	37.7	94.4
North Dakota	48	683,932	36.6	101.2
Ohio	7	11,544,951	39.1	95.6
Oklahoma	28	3,791,508	36.3	98.1
Oregon	27	3,871,859	38.7	97.8
Pennsylvania	6	12,742,886	40.3	95.3
Rhode Island	43	1,051,302	39.5	93.6
South Carolina	24	4,679,230	38.0	94.6
South Dakota	46	824,082	37.1	99.3
Tennessee	17	6,403,353	38.3	95.0
Texas	2	25,674,681	33.7	98.5
Utah	34	2,817,222	29.6	101.3
Vermont	49	626,431	42.0	97.0
Virginia	12	8,096,604	37.6	96.6
Washington	13	6,830,038	37.3	99.6
West Virginia	37	1,855,364	41.4	97.2
Wisconsin	20	5,711,767	38.7	98.6
Wyoming	50	568,158	36.8	103.8
Puerto Rico	NA	3,706,690	37.5	91.4

Notes: Data are based on a sample and are subject to sampling variability. NA (not applicable) is used to indicate that the District of Columbia and Puerto Rico are not included in the state rankings.

SOURCE: U.S. Census Bureau, 2011 American Community Survey.

Educational Attainment among 18 to 24 Year Olds
2011 Estimates

	Population 18 to 24 years	Less than high school graduate	High School graduate (includes equivalency)	Some college or associate's degree	Bachelor's degree or higher
Alabama	485,274	17.7%	29.1%	46.3%	6.9%
Alaska	77,633	18.5%	35.9%	40.2%	5.4%
Arizona	647,258	19.0%	30.5%	44.1%	6.4%
Arkansas	283,366	15.5%	32.7%	45.5%	6.3%
California	3,980,604	15.8%	28.8%	47.2%	8.2%
Colorado	500,909	15.9%	28.4%	45.1%	10.5%
Connecticut	332,686	14.5%	28.3%	44.6%	12.7%
Delaware	91,390	16.2%	27.4%	46.2%	10.3%
District of Columbia	84,255	11.0%	20.5%	45.4%	23.1%
Florida	1,795,011	17.7%	30.2%	44.4%	7.7%
Georgia	1,018,180	20.5%	31.2%	40.9%	7.3%
Hawaii	130,941	10.1%	38.1%	44.3%	7.5%
Idaho	158,872	14.1%	32.5%	47.8%	5.6%
Illinois	1,251,025	14.9%	28.3%	44.6%	12.2%
Indiana	664,206	18.4%	30.9%	42.7%	8.0%
Iowa	311,252	12.2%	25.4%	52.4%	9.9%
Kansas	296,731	13.7%	25.5%	51.8%	9.1%
Kentucky	422,007	15.8%	31.9%	45.8%	6.5%
Louisiana	482,851	20.5%	30.7%	42.2%	6.6%
Maine	115,329	11.5%	31.1%	46.4%	10.9%
Maryland	566,000	13.0%	29.2%	45.8%	12.0%
Massachusetts	680,381	11.4%	26.6%	47.6%	14.5%
Michigan	994,778	15.1%	28.1%	48.0%	8.7%
Minnesota	506,399	12.9%	25.8%	50.2%	11.2%
Mississippi	313,863	19.1%	29.9%	45.0%	6.0%
Missouri	588,439	15.2%	29.4%	46.3%	9.1%
Montana	98,335	12.3%	34.0%	44.6%	9.1%
Nebraska	185,903	12.6%	25.8%	52.0%	9.6%
Nevada	249,259	21.1%	32.6%	41.1%	5.2%
New Hampshire	124,318	11.0%	30.9%	47.5%	10.5%
New Jersey	774,117	13.0%	28.9%	45.3%	12.9%
New Mexico	210,285	21.5%	27.5%	46.0%	5.0%
New York	1,987,871	14.8%	25.6%	45.8%	13.9%
North Carolina	967,902	17.0%	29.8%	45.3%	7.8%
North Dakota	84,509	9.3%	27.8%	54.4%	8.5%
Ohio	1,103,343	15.7%	30.5%	45.4%	8.4%
Oklahoma	386,679	18.7%	33.3%	41.2%	6.9%
Oregon	365,085	15.5%	30.1%	46.7%	7.7%
Pennsylvania	1,267,737	13.5%	30.7%	44.7%	11.0%
Rhode Island	119,962	11.6%	25.9%	49.7%	12.8%
South Carolina	486,685	18.2%	31.6%	43.4%	6.8%
South Dakota	84,645	16.6%	27.8%	49.8%	5.8%
Tennessee	618,507	13.8%	36.8%	41.8%	7.5%
Texas	2,642,608	19.3%	29.5%	44.1%	7.1%
Utah	327,475	12.1%	28.6%	53.6%	5.7%
Vermont	65,858	8.4%	25.4%	54.8%	11.4%
Virginia	824,667	12.3%	29.4%	46.1%	12.1%
Washington	666,370	16.5%	29.5%	45.1%	8.9%
West Virginia	174,335	15.9%	34.6%	40.9%	8.7%
Wisconsin	555,994	13.3%	31.4%	46.5%	8.9%
Wyoming	57,459	12.8%	30.1%	50.4%	6.7%
Puerto Rico	386,680	15.0%	28.6%	50.5%	5.9%

Note: Data are based on a sample and are subject to sampling variability.

SOURCE: U.S. Census Bureau, 2011 American Community Survey.

Health Insurance Coverage among 19 to 25 Year Olds 2009 vs 2011*

Area	Any health insurance coverage			Private health insurance		
	2009 Percent	2011 Percent	Difference**	2009 Percent	2011 Percent	Difference**
United States	**68.3**	**71.8**	**3.6**	**58.1**	**60.8**	**2.7**
Alabama	68.0	71.8	3.8	58.6	63.2	4.6
Alaska	61.4	64.7	3.3	55.5	53.2	−2.3
Arizona	66.1	70.1	4.0	50.6	51.6	1.0
Arkansas	60.6	63.1	2.5	50.2	54.4	4.1
California	63.7	67.0	3.3	53.3	55.1	1.8
Colorado	68.2	73.9	5.7	61.6	65.4	3.8
Connecticut	79.3	83.2	3.8	68.6	69.4	0.8
Delaware	75.8	82.4	6.6	58.9	66.4	7.5
District of Columbia	87.5	91.6	4.1	66.8	74.6	7.8
Florida	59.3	61.2	1.8	51.2	52.0	0.8
Georgia	60.6	63.9	3.3	53.5	55.8	2.3
Hawaii	82.7	86.1	3.4	70.5	71.8	1.3
Idaho	67.6	70.3	2.7	61.3	62.7	1.4
Illinois	69.9	74.6	4.7	59.6	64.1	4.5
Indiana	69.7	73.1	3.4	60.6	64.3	3.7
Iowa	80.1	83.2	3.1	71.2	74.6	3.4
Kansas	73.2	77.1	3.9	67.5	71.5	4.0
Kentucky	65.8	69.3	3.5	55.9	60.0	4.1
Louisiana	64.6	68.0	3.3	54.0	55.5	1.6
Maine	74.1	81.4	7.3	56.3	61.1	4.8
Maryland	75.0	81.7	6.7	66.8	70.7	3.8
Massachusetts	90.3	92.1	1.7	73.0	75.0	2.0
Michigan	71.2	76.3	5.1	56.6	61.5	4.9
Minnesota	78.8	82.6	3.8	66.5	69.3	2.9
Mississippi	62.8	64.3	1.5	50.0	52.7	2.7
Missouri	71.4	74.2	2.8	62.7	65.5	2.7
Montana	66.1	66.4	0.3	59.7	59.1	−0.7
Nebraska	72.4	76.9	4.5	66.9	71.1	4.2
Nevada	55.2	61.7	6.5	51.6	55.2	3.6
New Hampshire	77.2	80.3	3.1	71.1	75.8	4.7
New Jersey	69.9	74.6	4.7	63.0	65.9	2.9
New Mexico	61.4	60.6	−0.8	47.1	45.7	−1.4
New York	74.5	79.7	5.2	58.4	61.1	2.7
North Carolina	66.9	69.6	2.7	55.8	58.7	2.9
North Dakota	81.6	82.5	0.9	74.9	74.9	–
Ohio	72.4	77.9	5.6	59.8	65.0	5.2
Oklahoma	61.7	64.9	3.2	54.2	56.5	2.4
Oregon	64.6	70.2	5.6	57.5	59.9	2.4
Pennsylvania	75.9	80.9	5.0	64.8	68.6	3.8
Rhode Island	74.5	77.7	3.2	66.2	69.1	2.9
South Carolina	63.9	70.1	6.3	53.4	58.9	5.5
South Dakota	72.1	75.6	3.5	64.0	68.2	4.1
Tennessee	69.4	72.7	3.3	55.1	58.3	3.2
Texas	56.5	59.3	2.7	50.4	52.1	1.8
Utah	75.1	77.0	1.9	71.0	72.3	1.3
Vermont	75.2	89.1	13.9	59.2	69.7	10.5
Virginia	73.5	75.5	1.9	67.8	69.6	1.8
Washington	69.4	70.8	1.4	60.7	62.8	2.1
West Virginia	65.1	69.5	4.4	54.5	59.9	5.4
Wisconsin	77.3	79.4	2.1	65.6	68.1	2.5
Wyoming	70.2	74.6	4.4	63.1	67.7	4.6
Puerto Rico	85.6	87.2	1.7	38.4	35.8	−2.6

*Civilian noninstitutionalized population. ** Figures were rounded when the difference between the years was calculated.
Note: Data are based on a sample and are subject to sampling variability.

SOURCE: U.S. Census Bureau, 2009 and 2011 American Community Surveys, and 2009 and 2011 Puerto Rico Community Surveys.

Median Household Income in the Past 12 Months 2010 and 2011

Area	2010 ACS* median household income (dollars)	2011 ACS* median household income (dollars)	Change in median income (percent)	Area	2010 ACS* median household income (dollars)	2011 ACS* median household income (dollars)	Change in median income (percent)
United States	**51,144**	**50,502**	**−1.3**	Montana	44,145	44,222	0.2
Alabama	41,459	41,415	−0.1	Nebraska	49,770	50,296	1.1
Alaska	66,311	67,825	2.3	Nevada	52,045	48,927	−6.0
Arizona	48,108	46,709	−2.9	New Hampshire	62,770	62,647	−0.2
Arkansas	39,375	38,758	−1.6	New Jersey	69,829	67,458	−3.4
California	59,540	57,287	−3.8	New Mexico	43,326	41,963	−3.1
Colorado	55,580	55,387	−0.3	New York	55,712	55,246	−0.8
Connecticut	65,883	65,753	−0.2	North Carolina	44,726	43,916	−1.8
Delaware	57,289	58,814	2.7	North Dakota	50,026	51,704	3.4
District of Columbia	62,009	63,124	1.8	Ohio	46,275	45,749	−1.1
Florida	45,609	44,299	−2.9	Oklahoma	43,239	43,225	—
Georgia	47,659	46,007	−3.5	Oregon	47,989	46,816	−2.4
Hawaii	65,191	61,821	−5.2	Pennsylvania	50,548	50,228	−0.6
Idaho	44,867	43,341	−3.4	Rhode Island	53,879	53,636	−0.5
Illinois	54,644	53,234	−2.6	South Carolina	43,311	42,367	−2.2
Indiana	45,898	46,438	1.2	South Dakota	46,993	48,321	2.8
Iowa	49,401	49,427	0.1	Tennessee	42,453	41,693	−1.8
Kansas	49,687	48,964	−1.5	Texas	50,010	49,392	−1.2
Kentucky	40,948	41,141	0.5	Utah	56,227	55,869	−0.6
Louisiana	43,804	41,734	−4.7	Vermont	50,707	52,776	4.0
Maine	47,069	46,033	−2.2	Virginia	62,173	61,882	−0.5
Maryland	70,976	70,004	−1.4	Washington	57,201	56,835	−0.6
Massachusetts	63,967	62,859	−1.7	West Virginia	39,444	38,482	−2.4
Michigan	46,692	45,981	−1.5	Wisconsin	50,293	50,395	0.2
Minnesota	56,936	56,954	—	Wyoming	55,213	56,322	2.0
Mississippi	37,838	36,919	−2.4	Puerto Rico	19,370	18,660	−3.7
Missouri	45,600	45,247	−0.8				

*ACS is the American Community Survey conducted annually by the US Census Bureau.
– Represents or rounds to zero.

Notes: Amounts are shown in 2011 inflation-adjusted dollars. Data are limited to the household population and exclude the population living in institutions, college dormitories, and other group quarters. Data are based on a sample and are subject to sampling variability.

SOURCE: U.S. Census Bureau, 2010 and 2011 American Community Surveys, 2010 and 2011 Puerto Rico Community Surveys.

Number and Percenage of People in Poverty* in the Past 12 Months 2010 and 2011

State	Below poverty in 2010		Below poverty in 2011		Change in poverty (2011 less 2010)	
	Number	Percentage	Number	Percentage	Number	Percentage[1]
United States	46,215,956	15.3	48,452,035	15.9	2,236,079	0.6
Alabama	888,290	19.0	892,483	19.0	4,193	–
Alaska	69,279	9.9	73,905	10.5	4,626	0.5
Arizona	1,094,249	17.4	1,203,501	19.0	109,252	1.5
Arkansas	534,898	18.8	555,876	19.5	20,978	0.6
California	5,783,043	15.8	6,118,803	16.6	335,760	0.8
Colorado	659,786	13.4	674,195	13.5	14,409	0.1
Connecticut	350,145	10.1	377,856	10.9	27,711	0.8
Delaware	103,427	11.8	104,831	11.9	1,404	0.1
District of Columbia	109,423	19.2	109,363	18.7	−60	−0.5
Florida	3,047,343	16.5	3,173,456	17.0	126,113	0.5
Georgia	1,688,932	17.9	1,827,743	19.1	138,811	1.3
Hawaii	142,185	10.7	161,290	12.0	19,105	1.3
Idaho	242,272	15.7	255,027	16.5	12,755	0.7
Illinois	1,731,711	13.8	1,879,965	15.0	148,254	1.2
Indiana	962,775	15.3	1,011,017	16.0	48,242	0.7
Iowa	370,507	12.6	378,864	12.8	8,357	0.2
Kansas	377,530	13.6	383,467	13.8	5,937	0.2
Kentucky	800,226	19.0	811,277	19.1	11,051	0.2
Louisiana	825,144	18.7	908,375	20.4	83,231	1.7
Maine	167,242	12.9	182,448	14.1	15,206	1.2
Maryland	557,140	9.9	571,887	10.1	14,747	0.2
Massachusetts	725,143	11.4	738,514	11.6	13,371	0.1
Michigan	1,618,257	16.8	1,693,294	17.5	75,037	0.8
Minnesota	599,516	11.6	621,970	11.9	22,454	0.4
Mississippi	643,883	22.4	650,524	22.6	6,641	0.2
Missouri	888,570	15.3	920,118	15.8	31,548	0.5
Montana	140,969	14.6	144,054	14.8	3,085	0.2
Nebraska	229,923	12.9	234,710	13.1	4,787	0.2
Nevada	398,027	14.9	426,741	15.9	28,714	1.0
New Hampshire	105,786	8.3	112,715	8.8	6,929	0.5
New Jersey	884,789	10.3	897,376	10.4	12,587	0.1
New Mexico	413,851	20.4	439,914	21.5	26,063	1.1
New York	2,821,470	14.9	3,027,342	16.0	205,872	1.0
North Carolina	1,627,602	17.5	1,680,963	17.9	53,361	0.4
North Dakota	84,895	13.0	80,882	12.2	−4,013	−0.8
Ohio	1,779,032	15.8	1,845,800	16.4	66,768	0.6
Oklahoma	616,610	16.9	633,298	17.2	16,688	0.3
Oregon	596,408	15.8	662,283	17.5	65,875	1.6
Pennsylvania	1,648,184	13.4	1,695,996	13.8	47,812	0.4
Rhode Island	142,188	14.0	148,819	14.7	6,631	0.7
South Carolina	815,755	18.2	856,938	18.9	41,183	0.7
South Dakota	113,760	14.4	110,681	13.9	−3,079	−0.5
Tennessee	1,095,466	17.7	1,142,299	18.3	46,833	0.6
Texas	4,414,481	17.9	4,628,758	18.5	214,277	0.6
Utah	359,242	13.2	374,859	13.5	15,617	0.4
Vermont	76,352	12.7	69,075	11.5	−7,277	−1.2
Virginia	861,969	11.1	905,914	11.5	43,945	0.5
Washington	888,718	13.4	929,258	13.9	40,540	0.5
West Virginia	326,507	18.1	334,885	18.6	8,378	0.4
Wisconsin	731,479	13.2	725,797	13.1	−5,682	−0.1
Wyoming	61,577	11.2	62,629	11.3	1,052	0.1
Puerto Rico	1,659,792	45.0	1,673,610	45.6	13,818	0.5

– Represents or rounds to zero.

[1]Figures were rounded when the difference between the years was calculated.

*Poverty status is determined for individuals in housing units and noninstitutional group quarters. The poverty universe excludes children under age 15 who are not related to the householder, people living in institutional group quarters, and people living in college dormitories or military barracks.

Notes: Data are based on a sample and are subject to sampling variability. The United States figures do not include Puerto Rico.

SOURCE: U.S. Census Bureau, 2010 and 2011 American Community Survey and 2010 and 2011 Puerto Rico Community Survey.

Race
2011 Estimates

	Total Population	White alone	Black or African American alone	American Indian and Alaska Native alone	Asian alone	Native Hawaiian and Other Pacific Islander alone	Some other race alone	Two or more races
Alabama	4,802,740	3,318,110	1,281,095	24,408	54,259	1,919	58,499	64,450
Alaska	722,718	482,698	23,143	102,293	37,971	7,785	8,599	60,229
Arizona	6,482,505	5,141,027	265,940	289,812	177,297	11,941	402,195	194,293
Arkansas	2,937,979	2,296,248	463,364	16,772	34,342	7,279	62,745	57,229
California	37,691,912	23,698,393	2,253,905	289,597	4,970,627	146,894	4,738,489	1,594,007
Colorado	5,116,796	4,318,187	203,243	51,677	143,760	5,949	221,207	172,773
Connecticut	3,580,709	2,787,171	359,683	7,481	141,081	1,416	195,293	88,584
Delaware	907,135	636,680	193,899	2,794	29,930	22	19,682	24,128
District of Columbia	617,996	246,505	309,845	1,956	22,510	0	24,420	12,760
Florida	19,057,542	14,535,897	3,046,628	63,416	463,164	12,545	512,411	423,481
Georgia	9,815,210	5,961,961	3,021,927	24,980	322,841	5,659	287,608	190,234
Hawaii	1,374,810	343,352	26,281	3,942	523,824	128,087	17,772	331,552
Idaho	1,584,985	1,465,484	8,392	20,511	20,913	1,287	28,938	39,460
Illinois	12,869,259	9,328,438	1,867,304	25,818	599,115	1,378	783,647	263,559
Indiana	6,516,922	5,512,023	589,109	12,817	102,695	786	157,123	142,369
Iowa	3,062,309	2,800,812	88,258	12,009	56,040	1,010	43,292	60,888
Kansas	2,871,238	2,442,531	167,669	23,830	67,235	1,642	71,792	96,539
Kentucky	4,369,356	3,837,605	348,778	9,662	50,424	729	41,911	80,247
Louisiana	4,574,836	2,874,839	1,469,876	28,830	72,484	3,126	48,020	77,661
Maine	1,328,188	1,264,494	13,598	8,148	13,498	134	3,249	25,067
Maryland	5,828,289	3,414,300	1,725,923	14,530	329,770	1,924	189,897	151,945
Massachusetts	6,587,536	5,305,948	451,127	13,160	365,968	858	282,417	168,058
Michigan	9,876,187	7,830,903	1,388,139	54,719	242,232	2,118	105,245	252,831
Minnesota	5,344,861	4,577,875	279,142	60,842	216,270	763	74,998	134,971
Mississippi	2,978,512	1,770,546	1,115,359	11,815	27,077	108	19,265	34,342
Missouri	6,010,688	4,991,510	688,379	22,326	96,187	5,692	61,460	145,134
Montana	998,199	891,294	4,305	66,644	5,714	968	5,149	24,125
Nebraska	1,842,641	1,624,885	83,693	17,985	34,517	693	40,493	40,375
Nevada	2,723,322	1,948,463	222,551	32,805	194,695	16,360	202,603	105,845
New Hampshire	1,318,194	1,240,868	14,655	2,154	29,002	117	8,756	22,642
New Jersey	8,821,155	6,104,543	1,182,905	21,103	747,620	3,365	544,803	216,816
New Mexico	2,082,224	1,492,790	44,365	190,825	25,637	1,171	263,221	64,215
New York	19,465,197	12,710,382	3,036,099	67,731	1,447,760	5,562	1,670,880	526,783
North Carolina	9,656,401	6,768,523	2,091,558	111,633	211,328	4,132	264,372	204,855
North Dakota	683,932	614,327	6,857	38,515	7,070	147	4,362	12,654
Ohio	11,544,951	9,566,847	1,396,483	19,589	194,814	1,981	99,138	266,099
Oklahoma	3,791,508	2,792,094	275,392	260,733	65,513	5,393	90,736	301,647

[CONTINUED]

Race
2011 Estimates (CONTINUED)

	Total Population	White alone	Black or African American alone	American Indian and Alaska Native alone	Asian alone	Native Hawaiian and Other Pacific Islander alone	Some other race alone	Two or more races
Oregon	3,871,859	3,279,357	70,067	52,026	152,909	15,100	167,719	134,681
Pennsylvania	12,742,886	10,485,910	1,372,685	17,315	358,168	2,009	259,538	247,261
Rhode Island	1,051,302	859,000	63,397	4,370	33,235	188	62,356	28,756
South Carolina	4,679,230	3,135,216	1,305,093	13,244	63,356	2,042	75,888	84,391
South Dakota	824,082	707,944	9,517	71,532	7,855	63	7,031	20,140
Tennessee	6,403,353	4,990,068	1,071,463	18,732	92,286	2,299	107,031	121,474
Texas	25,674,681	19,149,157	3,011,795	128,773	999,118	18,726	1,770,210	596,902
Utah	2,817,222	2,486,869	32,524	31,795	56,679	27,209	112,788	69,358
Vermont	626,431	596,253	5,194	2,140	7,733	245	1,227	13,639
Virginia	8,096,604	5,615,742	1,581,452	24,374	455,242	5,084	173,964	240,746
Washington	6,830,038	5,357,161	239,665	91,703	501,712	40,300	278,678	320,819
West Virginia	1,855,364	1,741,915	56,178	2,834	11,492	126	4,452	38,367
Wisconsin	5,711,767	4,980,495	356,550	48,065	130,617	1,485	77,758	116,797
Wyoming	568,158	515,335	5,079	12,241	4,833	201	14,829	15,640
Puerto Rico	3,706,690	2,539,680	290,083	8,254	9,489	0	361,521	497,663

Note: Data are based on a sample and are subject to sampling variability.
SOURCE: U.S. Census Bureau, 2011 American Community Survey.

Death Penalty in the United States
(as of February 15, 2013)

States with the Death Penalty	
State	**Last Execution**
Alabama	2011
Arizona	2012
Arkansas	2005
California	2006
Colorado	1997
Delaware	2012
Florida	2012
Georgia	2011
Idaho	2012
Indiana	2009
Kansas	1965
Kentucky	2008
Louisiana	2010
Maryland	2005
Mississippi	2012
Missouri	2011
Montana	2006
Nebraska	1997
Nevada	2006
New Hampshire	1939
North Carolina	2006
Ohio	2012
Oklahoma	2012
Oregon	1997
Pennsylvania	1999
South Carolina	2011
South Dakota	2012
Tennessee	2009
Texas	2012
Utah	2010
Virginia	2013
Washington	2010
Wyoming	1992

States/Dependencies without Death Penalty	
State	**Year Abolished**
Alaska*	1957
Connecticut**	2012
District of Columbia	1981
Hawaii*	1957
Illinois	2011
Iowa	1965
Maine	1887
Massachusetts	1984
Michigan	1846
Minnesota	1911
New Jersey	2007
New Mexico**	2009
New York	2007
North Dakota	1973
Puerto Rico	1929
Rhode Island	1984
Vermont	1964
West Virginia	1965
Wisconsin	1853

* The death penalty was abolished in Alaska and in Hawaii two years prior to each becoming a state in 1959.

** When Connecticut and New Mexico repealed their death penalty statutes, the repeal was not retroactive. Anyone on death row at the time of the repeal can still be executed.

Crime in the United States by State, 2010
(Rates per 100,000 inhabitants)

	Population	Violent crime	Murder and nonnegligent manslaughter	Forcible rape	Robbery	Aggravated assault	Property crime	Burglary	Larceny-theft	Motor vehicle theft
Alabama	4,779,736	377.8	5.7	28.2	99.6	244.2	3,516.8	879.4	2,415.6	221.8
Alaska	710,231	638.8	4.4	75.0	83.6	475.8	2,852.5	437.2	2,187.3	228.0
Arizona	6,392,017	408.1	6.4	33.9	108.5	259.3	3,534.0	794.3	2,403.2	336.5
Arkansas	2,915,918	505.3	4.7	45.0	81.3	374.3	3,558.9	1,114.9	2,253.8	190.1
Califorina	37,253,956	440.6	4.9	22.4	156.0	257.4	2,635.8	614.3	1,612.1	409.4
Colorado	5,029,196	320.8	2.4	43.7	62.3	212.4	2,684.2	520.0	1,940.5	223.6
Connecticut	3,574,097	281.4	3.6	16.3	99.4	162.0	2,193.2	424.5	1,581.0	187.7
Delaware	897,934	620.9	5.3	34.7	203.7	377.1	3,448.2	836.9	2,396.5	214.8
District of Columbia[1]	601,723	1,330.2	21.9	31.1	718.8	558.4	4,778.9	703.1	3,238.9	836.9
Florida	18,801,310	542.4	5.2	28.6	138.7	369.8	3,558.4	899.5	2,438.4	220.5
Georgia	9,687,653	403.3	5.8	21.6	127.7	248.2	3,640.5	998.4	2,329.3	312.8
Hawaii	1,360,301	262.7	1.8	26.8	77.5	156.7	3,314.2	636.8	2,302.4	374.9
Idaho	1,567,582	221.0	1.3	33.5	13.7	172.6	1,995.8	414.8	1,496.7	84.3
Illinois	12,830,632	435.2	5.5	23.6	156.3	249.7	2,681.0	587.6	1,868.9	224.4
Indiana	6,483,802	314.5	4.5	27.2	95.9	186.9	3,042.4	726.7	2,113.4	202.3
Iowa	3,046,355	273.5	1.3	27.4	33.2	211.6	2,242.5	546.8	1,571.8	124.0
Kansas	2,853,118	369.1	3.5	38.8	54.1	272.7	3,119.9	680.1	2,229.2	210.6
Kentucky	4,339,367	242.6	4.3	31.8	86.4	120.1	2,551.3	698.5	1,709.7	143.1
Louisiana	4,533,372	549.0	11.2	27.2	114.9	395.6	3,647.5	1,002.2	2,427.1	218.2
Maine	1,328,361	122.0	1.8	29.3	31.2	59.8	2,479.3	554.0	1,850.8	74.5
Maryland	5,773,552	547.7	7.4	21.3	191.5	327.5	2,997.3	632.9	2,051.7	312.6
Massachusetts	6,547,629	466.6	3.2	26.7	105.0	331.8	2,350.5	576.8	1,598.8	174.9
Michigan	9,883,640	490.3	5.7	47.3	116.3	321.0	2,713.6	747.4	1,689.5	276.8
Minnesota[2]	5,303,925	236.0	1.8	33.9	63.9	136.4	2,572.3	460.3	1,950.0	161.9
Mississippi	2,967,297	269.7	7.0	31.2	93.7	137.8	2,985.0	1,026.0	1,778.4	180.6
Missouri	5,988,927	455.0	7.0	23.9	102.4	321.7	3,346.4	735.4	2,343.0	268.0
Montana	989,415	272.2	2.6	32.4	15.9	221.2	2,543.8	369.3	2,020.3	154.2
Nebraska	1,826,341	279.5	3.0	36.8	56.1	183.6	2,673.2	455.9	2,019.4	197.9
Nevada	2,700,551	660.6	5.9	35.7	196.2	422.9	2,774.7	823.0	1,574.5	377.1
New Hampshire	1,316,470	167.0	1.0	31.3	34.3	100.4	2,186.3	413.3	1,699.5	73.5
New Jersey	8,791,894	307.7	4.2	11.2	134.4	157.9	2,081.9	440.5	1,464.5	176.9
New Mexico	2,059,179	588.9	6.9	46.5	78.4	457.1	3,435.4	1,020.5	2,160.1	254.8
New York	19,378,102	392.1	4.5	14.3	146.9	226.4	1,941.2	335.3	1,500.4	105.4
North Carolina	9,535,483	363.4	5.0	21.1	100.8	236.5	3,447.3	1,076.9	2,178.4	192.0
North Dakota	672,591	225.0	1.5	35.2	13.4	174.8	1,768.5	292.3	1,348.5	127.7
Oklahoma	3,751,351	479.5	5.2	38.7	89.0	346.7	3,415.5	999.0	2,144.8	271.6
Oregon	3,831,074	252.0	2.4	31.7	62.4	155.6	3,012.9	512.6	2,267.7	232.6
Pennsylvania	12,702,379	366.2	5.2	26.9	128.8	205.3	2,173.0	434.3	1,607.4	131.2
Rhode Island	1,052,567	256.6	2.8	28.1	74.1	151.6	2,556.6	581.5	1,747.2	227.9
South Carolina	4,625,364	597.7	6.1	31.7	107.7	452.3	3,900.4	997.9	2,617.2	285.3
South Dakota	814,180	268.5	2.8	47.9	18.9	198.9	1,852.4	390.7	1,364.1	97.6
Tennessee	6,346,105	613.3	5.6	33.7	131.8	442.2	3,657.9	1,012.2	2,411.9	233.8
Texas	25,145,561	450.3	5.0	30.3	130.6	284.4	3,783.0	909.1	2,603.3	270.5
Utah	2,763,885	212.7	1.9	34.3	45.9	130.6	3,179.6	543.3	2,421.0	215.2
Vermont	625,741	130.2	1.1	21.1	11.8	96.2	2,282.3	537.9	1,673.9	70.5
Virginia	8,001,024	213.6	4.6	19.1	70.7	119.1	2,327.2	382.8	1,812.5	131.8
Washington	6,724,540	313.8	2.3	38.1	88.2	185.3	3,706.6	820.3	2,503.7	382.6
West Virginia	1,852,994	314.6	3.3	19.1	44.7	247.5	2,239.6	580.5	1,531.7	127.4
Wisconsin	5,686,986	248.7	2.7	20.9	79.2	145.9	2,507.7	467.1	1,897.5	143.1
Wyoming	563,626	195.9	1.4	29.1	13.5	151.9	2,461.6	381.3	1,975.4	104.9

[1] Includes offenses reported by the Zoological Police and the Metro Transit Police.
[2] The data collection methodology for the offense of forcible rape used by the Minnesota state Uniform Crime.

SOURCE: Uniform Crime Reports, Federal Bureau of Investigation.

Unemployment Rates for States
December 2012 and Historical Highs/Lows

	Dec. 2012 Rate[P]	Historical High		Historical Low	
		Date	Rate	Date	Rate
Alabama	7.1	Dec. 1982	14.3	Apr. 2007	3.2
Alaska	6.6	June 1986	11.5	Apr. 2007	5.9
Arizona	7.9	Jan. 1983	11.6	July 2007	3.5
Arkansas	7.1	July 1983	10.1	Nov. 2000	4.0
California	9.8	Oct. 2010	12.4	Jan. 2001	4.7
Colorado	7.6	Nov. 2010	9.0	Jan. 2001	2.6
Connecticut	8.6	Dec. 2010	9.4	Oct. 2000	2.1
Delaware	6.9	Dec. 1976	9.3	Feb. 1989	2.8
District of Columbia	8.5	Feb. 1983	11.6	May 1989	4.8
Florida	8.0	Feb. 2010	11.4	Aug. 2006	3.3
Georgia	8.6	Jan. 2010	10.5	Dec. 2000	3.3
Hawaii	5.2	Jan. 1976	9.9	Dec. 2006	2.3
Idaho	6.6	Feb. 1983	9.6	Mar. 2007	2.7
Illinois	8.7	Feb. 1983	12.9	Feb. 1999	4.2
Indiana	8.2	Jan. 1983	12.7	Apr. 1999	2.6
Iowa	4.9	Mar. 1983	8.6	Oct. 1999	2.5
Kansas	5.4	Aug. 2009	7.6	Apr. 1979	3.0
Kentucky	8.1	Jan. 1983	12.0	June 2000	4.1
Louisiana	5.5	Nov. 1986	12.8	July 2006	3.6
Maine	7.3	Jan. 1977	9.0	Jan. 2001	3.1
Maryland	6.6	Nov. 1982	8.4	Feb. 2008	3.3
Massachusetts	6.7	Jan. 1976	11.1	Oct. 2000	2.6
Michigan	8.9	Dec. 1982	16.8	Mar. 2000	3.3
Minnesota	5.5	Dec. 1982	9.1	Mar. 1999	2.5
Mississippi	8.6	Apr. 1983	13.5	Apr. 2001	4.9
Missouri	6.7	Feb. 1983	10.6	Jan. 2000	2.8
Montana	5.7	Mar. 1983	8.8	Dec. 2006	3.1
Nebraska	3.7	Feb. 1983	6.7	Feb. 1998	2.2
Nevada	10.2	Oct. 2010	14.0	Apr. 2000	3.8
New Hampshire	5.7	Sept. 1992	7.6	May 1987	2.1
New Jersey	9.6	Dec. 1976	10.7	July 2000	3.6
New Mexico	6.4	Mar. 1983	10.0	June 2007	3.4
New York	8.2	Nov. 1976	10.3	Apr. 1988	4.0
North Carolina	9.2	Feb. 2010	11.4	Mar. 1999	3.1
North Dakota	3.2	Feb. 1983	6.8	July 2001	2.6
Ohio	6.7	Jan. 1983	13.9	Jan. 2001	3.8
Oklahoma	5.1	June 1983	9.2	Dec. 2000	2.8
Oregon	8.4	Jan. 1983	12.1	Feb. 1995	4.7
Pennsylvania	7.9	Mar. 1983	12.9	Mar. 2000	4.0
Rhode Island	10.2	Jan. 2010	11.9	July 1988	2.9
South Carolina	8.4	Dec. 2009	12.0	Mar. 1998	3.2
South Dakota	4.4	Feb. 1983	6.0	Mar. 2000	2.5
Tennessee	7.6	Jan. 1983	12.8	May 2000	3.9
Texas	6.1	Nov. 1986	9.3	Jan. 2001	4.2
Utah	5.2	Mar. 1983	10.0	Mar. 2007	2.4
Vermont	5.1	Jan. 1976	8.8	Apr. 2000	2.4
Virginia	5.5	Jan. 1983	7.8	Dec. 2000	2.2
Washington	7.6	Nov. 1982	12.2	May 2007	4.4
West Virginia	7.5	Mar. 1983	18.1	Apr. 2008	3.9
Wisconsin	6.6	Jan. 1983	11.5	Feb. 2000	3.0
Wyoming	4.9	Jan. 1987	9.1	Apr. 1979	2.3

P = preliminary.

Note: Rates shown are a percentage of the labor force. Data refer to place of residence. Series began in January 1976. Estimates for at least the latest five years are subject to revision early in the following calendar year.

SOURCE: U.S. Bureau of Labor Statistics, U.S. Department of Labor.

Language Spoken at Home
2011 Estimates

State	Total population 5 years and over	Those who speak only English	Those who speak a language other than English	Spanish or Spanish Creole	Other Indo-European languages	Asian and Pacific Island languages	Other languages
Alabama	4,504,275	94.8%	5.2%	3.4%	0.8%	0.8%	0.2%
Alaska	668,687	83.4%	16.6%	3.8%	2.7%	5.2%	5.0%
Arizona	6,034,541	73.0%	27.0%	20.6%	2.0%	1.9%	2.5%
Arkansas	2,740,313	92.5%	7.5%	5.4%	0.8%	1.1%	0.1%
California	35,158,257	56.2%	43.8%	28.8%	4.5%	9.6%	0.9%
Colorado	4,775,755	83.3%	16.7%	11.7%	2.3%	2.0%	0.7%
Connecticut	3,384,503	78.6%	21.4%	10.9%	7.5%	2.2%	0.8%
Delaware	851,887	86.4%	13.6%	7.1%	3.6%	1.9%	1.0%
District of Columbia	581,764	85.0%	15.0%	7.2%	4.5%	1.6%	1.8%
Florida	17,983,218	72.4%	27.6%	20.3%	5.3%	1.5%	0.6%
Georgia	9,141,183	86.7%	13.3%	7.8%	2.4%	2.2%	0.8%
Hawaii	1,286,790	74.8%	25.2%	2.1%	1.4%	21.6%	0.1%
Idaho	1,466,499	89.6%	10.4%	7.8%	1.3%	0.9%	0.4%
Illinois	12,042,289	77.3%	22.7%	13.4%	5.5%	2.7%	1.0%
Indiana	6,088,598	91.8%	8.2%	4.6%	2.2%	1.0%	0.4%
Iowa	2,864,107	92.7%	7.3%	4.0%	1.7%	1.1%	0.4%
Kansas	2,669,198	88.6%	11.4%	7.4%	1.6%	1.7%	0.7%
Kentucky	4,090,258	95.2%	4.8%	2.4%	1.3%	0.7%	0.4%
Louisiana	4,261,861	91.3%	8.7%	3.7%	3.6%	1.3%	0.2%
Maine	1,261,967	93.4%	6.6%	1.0%	4.5%	0.7%	0.4%
Maryland	5,465,168	83.3%	16.7%	6.9%	4.5%	3.6%	1.7%
Massachusetts	6,224,979	78.0%	22.0%	8.0%	9.0%	3.9%	1.1%
Michigan	9,292,794	90.9%	9.1%	2.9%	3.0%	1.4%	1.8%
Minnesota	4,992,262	89.2%	10.8%	3.9%	2.2%	3.0%	1.7%
Mississippi	2,773,115	96.2%	3.8%	2.2%	0.5%	0.7%	0.3%
Missouri	5,629,071	93.6%	6.4%	2.7%	2.0%	1.2%	0.5%
Montana	937,750	95.3%	4.7%	1.6%	1.3%	0.4%	1.3%
Nebraska	1,711,659	89.7%	10.3%	6.8%	1.5%	1.4%	0.6%
Nevada	2,538,136	70.3%	29.7%	20.9%	2.5%	5.5%	0.9%
New Hampshire	1,250,588	92.2%	7.8%	2.1%	3.8%	1.2%	0.6%
New Jersey	8,285,611	69.6%	30.4%	15.5%	8.7%	4.8%	1.4%
New Mexico	1,937,824	63.5%	36.5%	28.9%	1.4%	0.8%	5.4%
New York	18,307,740	69.9%	30.1%	14.7%	9.1%	4.7%	1.6%
North Carolina	9,029,678	89.3%	10.7%	7.3%	1.6%	1.3%	0.5%
North Dakota	637,666	94.9%	5.1%	1.5%	2.0%	0.7%	0.9%
Ohio	10,836,508	93.3%	6.7%	2.2%	2.6%	1.1%	0.8%
Oklahoma	3,527,312	90.7%	9.3%	6.3%	0.9%	1.4%	0.7%
Oregon	3,633,190	85.1%	14.9%	8.9%	2.5%	2.8%	0.7%
Pennsylvania	12,021,912	89.7%	10.3%	4.3%	3.6%	1.9%	0.5%
Rhode Island	995,856	78.8%	21.2%	10.7%	7.4%	2.3%	0.8%
South Carolina	4,376,509	93.4%	6.6%	4.3%	1.3%	0.9%	0.2%
South Dakota	765,534	93.4%	6.6%	2.3%	1.7%	0.8%	1.9%
Tennessee	6,003,565	93.1%	6.9%	4.1%	1.3%	1.0%	0.5%
Texas	23,721,334	65.3%	34.7%	29.5%	2.0%	2.5%	0.6%
Utah	2,554,924	85.1%	14.9%	10.1%	2.0%	2.1%	0.7%
Vermont	595,658	95.1%	4.9%	1.0%	3.1%	0.7%	0.2%
Virginia	7,588,188	85.1%	14.9%	6.7%	3.5%	3.4%	1.2%
Washington	6,390,691	81.4%	18.6%	8.1%	3.8%	5.6%	1.0%
West Virginia	1,751,216	97.7%	2.3%	0.9%	0.9%	0.4%	0.1%
Wisconsin	5,362,567	91.3%	8.7%	4.4%	2.3%	1.6%	0.4%
Wyoming	529,136	93.6%	6.4%	4.8%	0.6%	0.6%	0.3%
Puerto Rico	3,489,898	4.8%	95.2%	95.1%	0.1%	0.0%	0.0%

Note: Data are based on a sample and are subject to sampling variability.

SOURCE: U.S. Census Bureau, 2011 American Community Survey.

Index

This index contains terms from all four volumes of this encyclopedia. *Italic type* indicates volume numbers; **boldface** indicates main entries. Illustrations are marked by (ill.); tables and charts are marked with a *t* notation.

B

E

G

H

J

N

T

Tennessee

Texas

Utah

Vermont

Virginia

Washington

West Virginia

Wisconsin